本书为2022年度吉林省教育科学规划重点项目（ZD22167）"麦克拉伦批判教育学思想研究"的研究成果

本书获长春师范大学学术专著出版计划项目资助

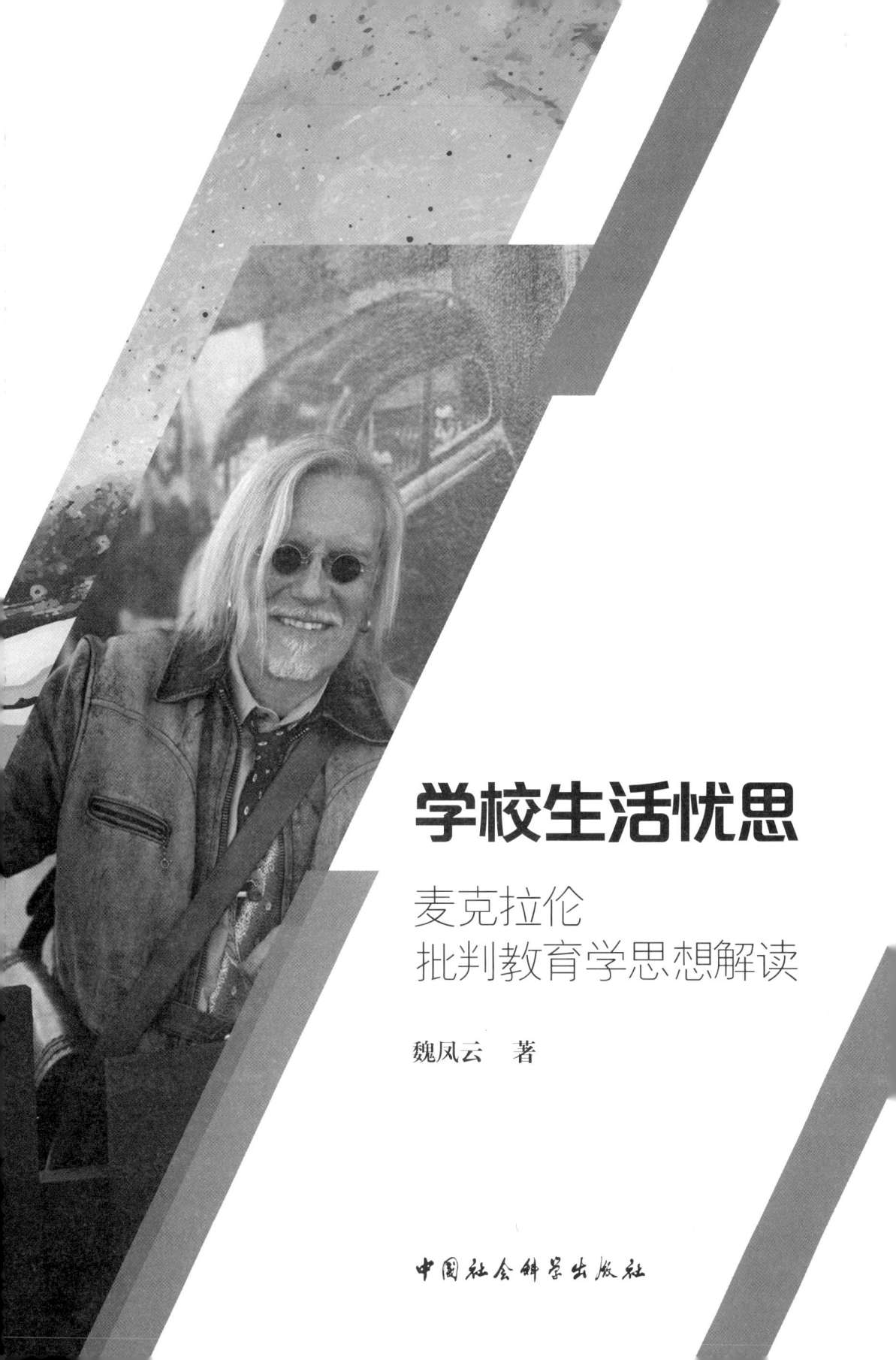

学校生活忧思

麦克拉伦
批判教育学思想解读

魏凤云 著

中国社会科学出版社

图书在版编目（CIP）数据

学校生活忧思：麦克拉伦批判教育学思想解读 / 魏风云著 . —北京：中国社会科学出版社，2023.9
ISBN 978 – 7 – 5227 – 1306 – 9

Ⅰ.①学… Ⅱ.①魏… Ⅲ.①麦克拉伦(McLaren, Peter Lawrence 1948 –)—教育学—思想评论 Ⅳ.①G40

中国国家版本馆 CIP 数据核字(2023)第 031165 号

出 版 人	赵剑英
责任编辑	范晨星
责任校对	周　昊
责任印制	王　超

出　　版	中国社会科学出版社
社　　址	北京鼓楼西大街甲 158 号
邮　　编	100720
网　　址	http://www.csspw.cn
发 行 部	010 – 84083685
门 市 部	010 – 84029450
经　　销	新华书店及其他书店
印　　刷	北京明恒达印务有限公司
装　　订	廊坊市广阳区广增装订厂
版　　次	2023 年 9 月第 1 版
印　　次	2023 年 9 月第 1 次印刷
开　　本	710×1000　1/16
印　　张	23.5
插　　页	2
字　　数	362 千字
定　　价	128.00 元

凡购买中国社会科学出版社图书，如有质量问题请与本社营销中心联系调换
电话：010 – 84083683
版权所有　侵权必究

序 一

彼得·麦克拉伦（Peter McLaren，1948-）是批判教育学的重要代表人物。麦克拉伦教授多年来致力于探索教育、政治和文化之间的关系等问题，基于经典马克思主义、西方马克思主义、法兰克福学派、后现代主义等思想，形成了关于资本主义、学校、教育本质的独创性见解，对批判教育理论的发展做出了历史性的贡献，其教育哲学思想成为推动批判教育理论发展的重要话语和研究基础。近年来，他的思想在教育理论界得到越来越多的关注。

在过去的40年里，麦克拉伦一直是一个敏锐的政治观察家，是一位有献身精神的知识分子，试图揭开资产阶级意识形态的神秘面纱，从而清晰地揭露资本主义文化的利益和运作，为社会主义替代资本主义而努力。在致力于改造世界的过程中，他不惧生命危险，勇于口诛笔伐，揭露黑暗真相，不仅体现了他对革命性的批判教育学的深刻信仰，也为革命性的批判教育的实践树立了一个真实的榜样。

该书是魏凤云博士在批判教育学领域深耕近十年完成的一本学术专著，是在其博士学位论文的基础上修改加工而成的重要成果。作为指导教师及该书的最早读者，在我看来，魏凤云博士的这本专著在研究资料、研究方法方面均有所突破，具有一定的学术价值。目前国内外已有的对麦克拉伦的研究整体地把握其思想的较少；基于文本、访谈、未刊稿等独家材料的研究还不多见。作者近十年来一直关注和思考批判教育学问题，主持相关课题。本书的内容是她长期研究的积累和集中的表达。作者基于对麦克拉伦教授本人及其亲友、同事进行访谈及查阅大量一手文献资料及未刊手稿的基础上，以麦克拉伦的成名作代表作——《学校生活》(Life in School) 为线索，从麦克拉伦批判教育学的产生及发展历程、理论渊源与核心理论武器、主旨、立场与特色等方面对麦克拉伦的批判教育学理论和实践进行了阐释、分析与评价，麦克拉伦批判教育学的形成因素、影响与局限性以及本书的研究局限与展望，为学界同仁进一步了解麦克拉伦教授的学术思想、了解批判教育学发展的最新动态提供了重要参考。

2014年，魏凤云读博士一年级的时候，作为东北师范大学批判教育学研究中心特聘教授的麦克拉伦教授在东北师范大学给全校的硕士研究生讲授批判教育学专题课程，魏凤云的英语不错，担任了麦克拉伦教授的助教兼翻译，在此期间开始接触麦克拉伦教授的批判教育学思想，并对批判教育学产生了研究兴趣。之后我建议她研究麦克拉伦的批判教育学思想，她表示很感兴趣。2017年，魏凤云成功申请了国家留学基金委的访学项目，赴麦克拉伦教授的工作地——美国查普曼大学访学。一年的访学，魏凤云旁听了麦克拉伦教授当年所有的硕士、博士课程，对麦克拉伦教授及其同事亲友做了大量的访谈，收集了大量有价值的第一手研究资料。作者由于与被研究者多年来建立了密切的联系，不但占有大量的独家文献资料，而且在研究过程中一直有被研究者的直接参与。麦克拉伦教授也多次当面向我表扬了魏凤云博士在研究过程中所表现出来的勤奋和严谨，称赞她是一位有潜力的青年学者。麦克拉伦教授的学术著作颇丰，要想把握这样一位国外著名学者的思想脉络和学术精髓是很不容易的。2018年9月，魏凤云带着沉甸甸的纸质资料和大量的电子资料回国，开始了为期一整年的毕业论文写作，在此期间，麦克拉伦教授也一直与魏凤云分享他的最新思想动态与研究重点以及对以往研究问题的反思。

该书从麦克拉伦教授的思想发展来动态地、整体地把握他的批判教育学理念，系统地梳理出了他的批判教育学思想与实现社会拯救之间的关系。作者认为：对资本主义的痛恨伴随着麦克拉伦批判教育学思想的产生及发展的全部历程；社会批判理论、马克思主义、后现代主义、弗莱雷和吉鲁的批判教育学等为麦克拉伦批判教育学思想的理论来源；寻找资本主义社会的替代形式是麦克拉伦革命性的批判教育学思想的主旨；麦克拉伦对合理化剥削与压迫的资本主义全球化、新自由主义导致的教育私有化与市场化、加剧人的物化与异化和阶级复制的标准化考试进行了无情的、深刻的批判和揭露；麦克拉伦认为他所倡导的革命性的批判教育学是一种致力于实现资本主义社会替代形式的实践哲学，因为革命性的批判教育学的目标就是废除阶级，建立新社会。

麦克拉伦教授有广泛的世界影响，与中国教育学界建立起了密切的联系。他本人多次来中国讲学，是很多大学的特聘教授和外国专家。多年来，国内陆续有多位青年教师和博士生到麦克拉伦身边访学，他对这些教师和学生都非常友好，有问必答。麦克拉伦教授对中国社会和教育的发展也非常感兴趣，多次在《中国日报》英文版上发文，如 2020 年 4 月 13 日麦克拉伦教授与王雁博士在《中国日报》网发文《美国需要脱离谴责中国的轨道》（*US needs to move away from its blame-China trajectory*）。

当然，麦克拉伦教授思想宏阔多元，作者的学养及精力所限，著作中难免挂一漏万、顾此失彼，希海内外专家斧正。期待望魏凤云的这本著作，能够唤起大家对批判教育学理论与实践的兴趣，用批判教育理论的眼光，透视教育问题，寻找改进策略，积极参与，为更美好、高质量、更公平的教育未来而努力。

于 伟
2022 年 8 月 30 日于长春

序　二[*]

很高兴能为魏博士的优秀著作书写序言。作为一位教育学者，魏博士已经研究我以及其他西方教育理论家和活动家的作品很多年了，并且特别擅长把这些作品与当前教育学术研究联系起来进行研究。可以说她汲取、掌握了我这三十多年的所有成就的精髓，这本书是目前在中国对于我的思想及研究动态的最完整的解读和诠释。三十多年来，从我在加拿大担任小学教师到成为美国的一所大学的教授再到成为国际批判教育学的倡导者，在此期间，我曾经到访过印度和中国以及南美洲、欧洲、东南亚的许多国家。魏博士洞察到批判教育学在国际合作与和平斗争中的潜力，当然也认识到其局限性。因此，她给所有的教育工作者，无论他们的地缘政治位置如何，提出了以下重要挑战：教育如何服务于所有学生的利益？在一个充满全球冲突和人类福祉持续受到威胁的世界里，教育如何促进人类有尊严地生存？为了避免人类灭绝于战争、饥荒和气候灾难，世界范围内的社区教育应如何促进民族国家之间的全球合作？为了共同解决地方、地区和全球冲突，大学应该如何被重组从而使其课程能够跨国进行合作建设？

面对人为的气候变化、核战争的威胁，以及争夺土地和水资源等基础资源的暴力冲突，作为人类，我们正处于生存的危险边缘。然而，历史之箭会朝着避免毁灭的方向前进。我们仍然有办法为人类的生存创造可能的条件，比如，可再生能源系统和粮食主权。但是，这在很大程度

---

[*] 本篇序原文是英语（见英文版序），此中文版是魏凤云根据英语原文翻译而成。

上取决于我们的教育系统是否愿意以激光般的强度和切割宝石的精度来创建一个学校系统，这个系统以不同学生的独特经验为基石，尊重以多元方法解决同一问题，促进国际合作，而不是引发战争，不是导致自相残杀的激烈内部竞争。为了在21世纪生存下去，我们必须超越已有的观念，站在政治角度，重新思考我们的教育体系，以追求世界和平。资本主义生产模式是建立在武力的基础之上的：某些个人甚至国家对土地的盗窃、对被剥削的人民和奴隶的压迫、殖民主义的横行。随着时间的推移，一方面，资本主义的生产能力养活了世界大量人口，也在各个历史时期经历了重大变革；另一方面，资本主义仍继续在世界各地进行血腥大扫荡。资本再生产衍生出的阶级与企业关系的专制暴政和工人阶级（即使是那些未就业或失业的人），对资本的生产能力至关重要。事实上，马克思把所有在资本主义制度下受压迫和被剥削的人都包括在无产阶级中，阐明了反殖民主义和社会主义革命事业之间的关系。

资本积累的普遍趋势是追求剩余价值，而绝对的普遍趋势是生产失业，或者马克思所说的创造相对过剩人口或劳动力储备部队。马克思深知在资本主义社会，工人的实际工资只能勉强维持生计；失业者将会变得越来越穷。自马克思生活的时代以来，资本主义历经了多次转变（凯恩斯资本主义、新自由主义资本主义、交际资本主义或认知资本主义），但马克思的劳动价值理论在今天仍然提供了强大的解释力，一场重大的经济崩溃迫在眉睫。21世纪已经见证了三次经济崩溃（2000年、2008年和2020年），每一次都比前一次更糟糕，这凸显了美国人口面临的核心突出问题，比如美国政府、企业和家庭的极端债务水平，这些债务都达到了历史最高水平，而且还在不断上升。伴随着贫困和社会分层的加剧而产生的极端不平等已经成为美国生活的一个核心显著特征，新冠疫情大流行突出并加剧了这种经济不平等。世界对美国如此富裕的全球超级大国（人口占全球人口的4.25%，但其死于新冠疫情的人数大约占全球死亡人数的20%）却未能很好地应对大流行而感到震惊。随着新自由主义资本主义进一步退化为拥有巨型银行和大公司的新封建—紧缩—黑帮资本主义，我们期待教育能够带来创造社会共同体的机会，在这个共同体中，价值生产（即货币化财富）不再成为日常生活的基础。换句话说，我们着眼于社会主义。为了实现社会主义，我们寻求革命性的批判教育学，即发起一场以社会主义替代资本主义为核心，以和平、合作和团结的价值观为前提的社会运动。

批判教育学的运作是基于这样一种理解：教育的基础是政治性的，需要创造空间，在这个空间内，学生可以想象资本主义价值法则（即劳动的社会形式）之外的不同世界，在这个空间内可以讨论和辩论资本主义和资本主义制度的替代方案——比如，工人合作社的建立——以及在这个空间内可以展开生产性对话，并对人类繁荣产生实际影响。这不仅仅是关于马克思对所有存在的事物的犀利批判，而是通过经验认识到人类不仅仅是资本所需要的技能的集合、不仅仅是劳动力的商品，意识到人类是不可交换的。革命性的批判教育学是一种教学项目，可以发生在不同的空间（教室、街道、办公室、农村和城市社区中心）和时间（午间休息、上课、早晨和晚上），它是理论的和实践的、偶然的和必然的。它不满足于请求或呼吁统治阶级的馈赠或怜悯来使资本主义社会更宜居；相反，它旨在为学习者创造条件，以检验从学习者经验中产生的存在情境的局限性和可能性——这些经验有时对学习者造成创伤，有时候也是对学习者生命的不尊重。批判性意识要求拒绝被动，并鼓励实践性对话，其中学习者能够辨别他们生活经历中的矛盾，并能对成为世界中的一个"客体"形成新的认知水平，在这个世界中只有"主体"有办法决定他们的生活方向；在这个世界中你能够选择创造历史，而不是成为历史的牺牲品。如果教育不能引导人们创造一个更加美好的世界，那么它很可能注定会以不同的形式重现当前的野蛮、暴力和混乱。从某种意义上讲，这就是巴西教育家保罗·弗莱雷所描述的"被压迫者的教育学"，因为它旨在通过支持那些被排除在正式生产系统之外的人、被歧视的种族和被边缘化的文化以及经常受到虐待和被剥夺与男子同等权利和地位的妇女，创造一个更公正、更自由和更人道的社会制度。

在我看来，"社会主义"是通往更美好世界的必由之路。但是在美国，"社会主义"是一个被污名化的词，在公共场合谈论会被强烈嘲讽。由于批判教育学与社会主义以及种族正义的正相关关系，使其在美国还没有成为一种合法的教育备选方案。批判教育学的实践派认为，每一种教育学都需要进行及时的自我批判，否则，它就会退化为自命不凡的虚伪，并且他们还认为，用更具创造性的方法来克服人类在这个关键的历史节点面临的无数障碍是有必要的。魏博士犀利的分析强调了这一挑战的内在可能性。

虽然教育活动对于创造社会主义是必要的，但它们本身并不足以实现社会主义。沿着社会变革的漫长而曲折的道路，社会主义的不同变体和实例确实会显现出来，当教育活动将社会主义的各个方面转向资本主义目标时，就会带来冲突。争取新世界的斗争并不会以"现在我们有社会主义"这一宣告而终结。这仅仅标志着人类走向繁荣与和平的漫长道路的一个新的开始。我希望魏博士的研究能进一步推进这一进程。

彼得·麦克拉伦（Peter McLaren）
2022年7月

Foreword*

It gives me great pleasure to write the preface to this excellent work by Dr. Joy Wei, an educational scholar who has studied my works and those of other Western educational theorists and activists for many years and is exceptionally adept in evaluating them in relationship to current educational scholarship. She has captured the essence of my efforts over three decades—from my work as an elementary school teacher in Canada to my work as a university professor in the U. S. and as an international advocate of revolutionary critical pedagogy that has taken me to numerous countries in South America, Europe, Southeast Asia, India and China. Dr. Wei recognizes both the potential of critical pedagogy in the struggle for international cooperation and peace and, of course, its limitations, and in doing so she poses these important challenges for all educators regardless of their geopolitical location: How can education serve the interests of all students? How can education foster dignified survival in a world rife with global conflict and constant threats to human well being? How can educational communities worldwide foster global cooperation among nation states such that the extermination of the human race through war, famine and climate disaster need not be inevitable? How can universities be restructured so that their curricula can be transnationally co-constructed with the purpose of co-operatively solving local, regional and global conflicts?

---

* 本篇序是麦克拉伦教授为本书撰写的序的英文原文。

In the face of man-made climate change, the threat of nuclear war, and violent conflicts over essential resources such as land and water, we are living on a knife's edge of survivability as a human species. There is no singular arrow of history that arcs towards the inevitability of destruction. We still have the means to create conditions of possibility for the survival of the human race, such as renewable energy systems and food sovereignty, but this depends greatly on the willingness of our educational system to focus with laser-like intensity and lapidary precision on creating school systems that build upon the unique experiences of each and every student, that respects diverse approaches to common problems, and that fosters international cooperation rather than the ruthless competition and internal rivalry that leads to war and mutually assured destruction. We must move beyond our own truncated notions of what is politically tenable for survival in the 21st century and dramatically rethink our educational systems in the pursuit of world peace. The capitalist mode of production was founded on force: the individual and state-sanctioned thefts of land, the repression of dispossessed peoples, slavery, and colonialism. And while its forces of production have, over time, created the possibility of feeding and housing and caring for all human beings across the globe, and have gone through major transformations over various historical epochs, capitalism still continues to wreak bloody havoc throughout the world. The reproduction of capital reproduces the tyranny of the class-corporate relationship and the working class—even those underemployed or unemployed—are still essential to capital's viability. In fact, Marx includes everyone oppressed and exploited under capitalism as part of the proletarian class, an exposition that clarifies the relationship between anti-colonial and socialist revolutionary projects.

The general tendency of capitalist accumulation is the pursuit of surplus-value and the absolute general tendency is the production of unemployment, or what Marx called the creation of a relative surplus population or reserve army of labor. Marx understood that under capitalism real wages of the worker will remain at a subsistence level; and that the unemployed will become poorer and poorer. The composition of capitalism has gone through many transformations since Marx's time (Keynesian capitalism, neoliberal capitalism, communicative or cognitive capitalism) but Marx's labor theory of value still offers much explanatory power today, as we acknowledge that a major economic crash looms large at this time. This new century has already witnessed three economic crashes (2000, 2008, and 2020), each worse than the one before, underlining the core salient issues facing the U. S. population such as the extreme levels of debt in the U. S. —government, corporate and household—which are all at historical records and rising. Extreme inequality has become a central distinguishing feature of life in the United States and the Covid-19 pandemic has highlighted and exacerbated this economic inequality, often along racial lines, as rising poverty and social divisions escalate. The world was shocked at how a rich global superpower like the United States (that has 4.25 percent of the world's population yet accounts for about 20 percent of global deaths from COVID-19) could have failed so miserably to cope with a viral pandemic. As neoliberal capitalism degenerates further into a neo-feudal-austerity-gangster-capitalism with its megabanks and megafirms, we look to education to bring about opportunities to create a social universe in which value production (i. e., monetized wealth) no longer becomes the basis of everyday life. We look, in other words, towards socialism. And to bring about socialism, we look to revolutionary critical pedagogy— that is, to creating a social movement focused on a socialist alternative to capitalism premised on the values of peace, cooperation and solidarity among the peoples of this planet. Revolutionary critical pedagogy operates from an understanding that the basis of education is political and that spaces need to be created where students can imagine a different world outside of capitalism's law of value (i. e., the social form of labor), where alternatives to capitalism and capitalist institutions can be discussed and debated—such as the creation of worker cooperatives—and where productive dialogue can occur and have practical consequences for human flourishing. It's not just about Marx's "ruthless criticism of all that exists" but about imagination and recognizing through experience that human beings are more than the collection of skills that capital demands, more than the commodity of labor-power. It's about realizing that humanity is not exchangeable. Revolutionary critical pedagogy is a pedagogical project that can happen in different spaces (classrooms, streets, offices, rural and urban community centers) and times (lunch breaks, classes, mornings and evenings). It is theoretical and practical, contingent and necessary. It does not remain content to make capitalist society more inhabitable by lyrical demands and appeals to the ruling class for more social harmony; rather, it is designed to create the conditions for learners to examine the limits and possibilities of the existential situations that emerge from learners' experiences—experiences that are sometimes traumatic for the learners as well as life-denying. Critical consciousness demands a rejection of passivity and encourages the practice of dialogue wherein learners are able to identify contradictions in their lived experiences and are able to reach new levels of awareness of being an "object" in a world where only "subjects" have the means to determine the direction of their lives; where you are able to make a choice to create history rather than being a casualty of history. If education cannotlead to creating a better world then it is likely destined to recreate in different forms the barbarism, violence and chaos of the present. It is a "pedagogy of the oppressed" in the sense described by Brazilian educator Paulo Freire, as it is designed to create a social system that is more just, more free and more humane by supporting those excluded from the formal productive system, despised races and marginalized cultures and women who are often abused and denied the same rights and status as men.

I take the idea of 'socialism' as the path to that better world. In the United States, socialism is a dirty word that cannot be uttered in public without a backlash of derision. Because of its positive relationship to socialism and racial justice, critical pedagogy has not been rendered a legitimate alternative approach to schooling in the United States. Practitioners of critical pedagogy believe that every pedagogy needs to be self-critical, otherwise, in time it will degenerate into a self-righteous hypocrisy, and that more creative ways to fight against the myriad obstacles that face humanity at this crucial historical juncture are necessary. Dr. Wei's trenchant analysis underscores the possibilities inherent in such a challenge.

While educational efforts are necessary to the creation of socialism, they are not in themselves sufficient to bring about socialism. And along the long and winding path to social change, different variations and instantiations of socialism will indeed manifest themselves, bringing about conflicts when efforts are made to repurpose aspects of socialism towards capitalist ends. The struggle for a new world does not end with the pronouncement, "now we have socialism." That will only mark a new beginning in humanity's long road to prosperity and peace. It is my hope that this work by Joy Wei will further this process.

摘　　要

彼得·劳伦斯·麦克拉伦（Peter Lawrence McLaren，1948－）是西方马克思主义教育理论代表人物之一、美国批判教育学的主要奠基者之一，也是世界范围内批判教育学的主要倡导者之一。他在批判教育理论与实践方面成绩卓著，在通过教育寻找资本主义社会替代形式方面的创见值得深入研究和探讨。本书基于对麦克拉伦教授本人及其亲友、同事进行大量访谈及查阅大量一手文献资料及未刊手稿的基础上，以麦克拉伦的成名作也是代表作——《学校生活》（*Life in School*）为线索从麦克拉伦批判教育学的产生及发展历程、理论渊源与核心理论武器、主旨、立场与特色四个方面对麦克拉伦的批判教育学理论和实践进行阐释、分析与评价，最后总结麦克拉伦批判教育学的形成因素、影响与局限性以及本书的研究局限与展望。本书具体内容主要包括以下方面。

第一，对资本主义的痛恨伴随着麦克拉伦批判教育学思想的产生及发展的全部历程。写作《学校生活》之前的童年、少年及青年时期的生活、学习、社会体验与工作经历是麦克拉伦的叛逆与批判思想萌芽时期。作为对小学教师工作经历与第一部作品《来自走廊地区的呐喊》（*Cries from the Corridor*）的反思与申辩，《学校生活》第一版于1989年问世。这个时期麦克拉伦成为马克思主义的后现代主义者，在看待后现代主义思想的功效时也总是坚持与马克思主义的分析形式保持紧密的联系。1994年和1998年出版了《学校生活》第二版和第三版，这个时期麦克拉伦的作品经历了一个方向的变化。他厌倦了后现代左派的温和与改革主义政治，开始把马克思主义人道主义、阶级斗争和政治带回教育的核心。

2003—2014 年出版了《学校生活》第四版到第六版，麦克拉伦的思想更加激进，发展聚焦了革命性的批判教育学，明确倡导彻底改造批判教育学。2013 年的后《学校生活》阶段，解放神学成为麦克拉伦的研究重点，他认为科学和宗教应该联合起来反对它们的共同敌人——资本主义。

第二，麦克拉伦的批判教育学思想的理论渊源和核心理论。麦克拉伦的批判教育学思想批判借鉴了多家理论作为他的理论渊源，如：马克思主义——运用历史唯物论、辩证法、阶级冲突论、劳动论、物化和异化等思想以追求人类的自由与解放为中心；美国进步主义和社会重建主义思想——寻找资本主义体制的替代方案，进行社会重建，实现真正的民主；法兰克福学派批判理论——要让没有权力的人，变得更有能力、有权力，以改变社会不平等和不公义的现象；后现代主义——后现代的反本质主义可以剥离有关性别角色、人性本质、种族偏见等传统思想中所根深蒂固的意识形态，而后现代的反实证主义可以挑战学校教育中信奉客观真理的科学主义迷思；保罗·弗莱雷的解放教育学思想——建立教育学和政治学之间的关系，突出教育学的政治方面，对教育赋予积极性的解放意义；亨利·吉鲁的批判教育学思想——批判教育学要能够有效批判宰制的霸权，也能够达成自我反省、自我解放和社会解放的目的，并且必须同时具备批判的语言和可能性的语言。马克思主义人道主义旨在为世界上的居民（人类和非人类）创造更好的生活，最终实现某种社会主义的社会形式替代资本主义的理想。麦克拉伦以马克思主义人道主义作为其批判教育学的理想，并以马克思人道主义的概念作为武器去批判全球资本主义下的剥削关系。

第三，寻找资本主义社会的替代形式是麦克拉伦批判教育学思想的主旨。麦克拉伦对合理化剥削与压迫的资本主义全球化、新自由主义导致的教育私有化与市场化、加剧人的物化与异化和阶级复制的标准化考试进行了无情的、深刻的批判和揭露。麦克拉伦认为他所倡导的革命性的批判教育学是实现资本主义社会替代形式的实践哲学。因为革命性的批判教育学的目标就是废除阶级，建立新社会；革命性的批判教育学是一种哲学，一种敏锐性，一种理解我们所在世界的方式；是在对社会主义的想象中进行的，是帮助我们实现社会、文化、性别公平的教学实践的哲学方向。麦克拉伦的革命性的批判教育学指出抵制与替代资本主义的实践方式：在抗争与行动中养成批判意识——不是透过自我意识达到批判性的抗争，而是通过抗争才具有批判性的意识；质疑与揭露——能够为革命思想的发展创造必要的教育条件及一整套能够使人们自觉地反对这一压迫性制度的做法；集体行动——批判教育学应该扩展到教室之外，成为一种国际性和区域性的新的社会运动；阶级斗争——使劳动阶级团体发现其劳动力的使用价值如何被资本所剥削，劳动阶级的倡议与权力如何被这种决定力量的形态所诋毁，进而在多重面向上挑战资本主义；宣扬示范性的革命偶像人物——麦克拉伦将切·格瓦拉、保罗·弗莱雷等视为马克思主义人道主义立场的典范，是对偶像的象征价值、激励示范作用的重视，而不是任何形式的盲目崇拜，不意味着任何教义或宗教。

第四，麦克拉伦批判教育学的立场、特色与各方评价。与亨利·吉鲁、迈克尔·阿普尔等北美的主要批判教育家的思想相比，麦克拉伦批判教育学思想有着本质的不同。其马克思主义人道主义的立场倡导通过教育实现某种资本主义社会形式的替代，而亨利·吉鲁、迈克尔·阿普尔等人倡导通过教育改革资本主义。麦克拉伦的批判教育学思想体现出坚守质疑与希望、兼顾理论与实践的特色。学界对麦克拉伦在学术成就与贡献、其学者与教师身份及革命激情与行动等方面进行了充分肯定，而且世界各地、社会各界授予了麦克拉伦数量相当可观的奖项。当然麦克拉伦也受到了各种批判与攻击。无论如何，麦克拉伦知行合一、做有献身精神的知识分子、拒绝故步自封等品质可作为世界各地教育者的表率。

最后是结语部分。麦克拉伦的批判教育学的形成是由内部因素，包括自身的经历的与他人的影响、勤奋及对教育事业的忠诚与热爱，以及外部因素，包括资本主义全球化导致的严重负面后果、以往批判教育学的被驯化等因素共同促成的。以《学校生活》为代表的麦克拉伦批判教育学思想对当下的教育理论与实践都产生了重要的影响与启示，但是也存在其自身的局限性。麦克拉伦基于马克思主义人道主义的革命性批判教育学思想与我国所坚持的马克思历史唯物主义教育思想是不尽相同的，需要批判地审视其作用，取其精华，弃其糟粕。

尽管本书尝试对麦克拉伦的批判教育学思想进行系统的梳理，但相对于麦克拉伦思想的丰富性和深刻性来说，在分析的深度和广度上都有待加强。未来还需进一步对相关问题进行更深入研究。

关键词：麦克拉伦；批判教育学；《学校生活》；资本主义

Abstract

Peter Lawrence McLaren (1948 –) is one of the representatives of western Marxist education theory, one of the main founders of critical pedagogy in the United States, and one of the main advocates of critical pedagogy worldwide. His achievements in critical education theory and practice are outstanding, and his ideas on pursuing alternative forms of capitalist society through education are worth studying and discussing in depth. This book taking McLaren's most famous and representative work—*Life in School* as the clue, explains, analyzes and evaluates McLaren's critical pedagogy theory and practice from four aspects: the emergence and development, the theoretical origin and core theoretical weapons, the themes, the positions and characteristics of McLaren's critical pedagogy thoughts. Finally, it summarizes the formation mechanism, influence, enlightenment and limitations of McLaren's critical pedagogy thoughts, as well as the research limitations and prospects of this paper. Specific research contents mainly include the following aspects:

First, the hatred of capitalism is accompanied by the whole process of the emergence and development of McLaren's critical pedagogy thought. The life, study, social experience and work experience in his childhood, adolescence and youth before writing*Life in School* are the embryonic period of McLaren's rebellious and critical thought. The first edition of *Life in School* was published in 1989 as a reflection and defense of the primary school teaching experience and his first work—*Cries from the Corridor*. In this period, McLaren became a postmodernist of Marxism and always insisted on keeping close contact with the analytical form of Marxism when he looked at the efficacy of post-modernist thought. The second and third editions of *Life in School* were published in 1994 and 1998, a period in which McLaren's work underwent a change of direction. Tired of the moderate and reformist politics of postmodernism, he began to bring Marxist Humanism, class struggle and politics back to the core of education study. From 2003 to 2014, the fourth edition to the sixth edition of *Life in School* were published, and McLaren's thoughts were more radical. His focused on the revolutionary critical pedagogy, and he clearly advocated the thorough reform of critical pedagogy. From the post- *Life in School* years of 2013, liberation theology became a focus for McLaren, who argued that science and religion should unite against their common enemy-capitalism.

Secondly, the theoretical origin and core theory of McLaren's critical pedagogy thought. McLaren's critical pedagogy theory is based on several theories, such as Marxist thought—the use of historical materialism, dialectics, class conflict theory, labor theory, materialization and alienation and other ideas to pursue human freedom and liberation as the center; American progressivism and social reconstruction thought—seeking alternative to capitalist system, carrying out social reconstruction and realizing true democracy; the critical theory of Frankfurt School—to make the powerless more capable and empowered to change social inequalities and injustices; Postmodernism—postmodern anti-essentialism can strip away the deep-rooted ideology in traditional thoughts such as gender role, nature of human nature and racial prejudice, while post-modern anti-positivism can challenge the myth of scientism that believes in objective truth in school education; Paulo Freire's thought of emancipated pedagogy—establishing the relationship between pedagogy and political science, highlighting the political aspects of pedagogy, and giving positive emancipating significance to education; Henry Giroux's critical pedagogy thought—critical pedagogy must be able to effectively criticize the dominated hegemony and achieve the goals of self-reflection, self-liberation and social liberation, and must have both language of critique and language of possibility. Marxist humanism aiming to create a better life for the inhabitants of the world (human and non-human), and finally to realize the ideal of a socialist social form replacing capitalism. McLaren took Marxist humanism as his ideal of critical pedagogy and the concept of Marxist as a weapon to criticize the exploitative relations under global capitalism.

Third, the pursuing for alternative forms of capitalist society is the main idea of McLaren's critical pedagogy. McLaren made a merciless and profound criticism and expose of the capitalist globalization that rationalized exploitation and oppression, the privatization and marketization of education caused by neoliberalism, the standardized test that aggravated the objectification and alienation of human beings and class duplication. McLaren believed that the revolutionary critical pedagogy he advocated was a practical philosophy to realize alternative forms of capitalist society. Because the goal of revolutionary critical pedagogy is to abolish classes and establish a new society; The revolutionary critical pedagogy is a philosophy, a sensitivity, a way of understanding the world we live in. The revolutionary critical pedagogy is carried out in the imagination of socialism, and it is the philosophical direction that helps us realize the teaching practice of social, cultural and gender equality. McLaren's revolutionary critical pedagogy argues that the practices of resisting and substituting capitalism include: developing critical consciousness in the struggle and action—not through self-consciousness to achieve critical struggle, but through the struggle to have critical consciousness; questioning and exposing—can create necessary educational conditions for the development of revolutionary ideas and a set of practices that can make people consciously oppose this oppressive system; collective action—critical pedagogy should be extended beyond the classroom and become a new international and regional social movement; class struggle—to make the working class groups discover how the use value of their labor force is exploited by the capital, and how the initiative and power of the working class are denigrated by this form of determining power, so as to challenge capitalism in multiple aspects; exemplary revolutionary ICONS—Mr. McLaren sees Che Guevara,

Paulo Freire and others as examples of Marxist humanitarian positions—as an emphasis on the symbolic value and exemplary role of ICONS, not idolatry of any kind, not doctrine or religion.

Fourth, the standpoint, characteristics and evaluation of McLaren's critical pedagogy thoughts. Compared with the thoughts of Henry Giroux, Michael W. Apple and other major critical educators in North America, Marxist humanitarian position advocated the certain replacement of capitalist social forms through education, while Henry Giroux, Michael W. Apple and others advocated the reform of capitalism through education. McLaren's thought of critical pedagogy embodies the characteristics of persistent questioning and hope, and giving consideration to both theory and practice. The academic circle has fully recognized McLaren's academic achievements and contributions, his status as a scholar and teacher, revolutionary passion and action, etc. Moreover, he has received a considerable number of awards from all walks of life around the world. Of course, McLaren has also got a lot of criticism and attack. In any case, McLaren's combination of knowledge and action, being a dedicated intellectual and refusing to stand still can set an example for educators all over the world.

The final part is the conclusion. The formation of McLaren's critical pedagogy thought is jointly facilitated by internal and external factors. The internal factors include his personal experience and the influence of others, diligence, and loyalty and love for education. The external factors include the serious negative consequences caused by capitalist globalization and the domestication of previous critical pedagogies. McLaren's critical pedagogy thought represented by *Life in School* has exerted an important influence and enlightenment on current educational theory and practice. But it has its own limitations. Maclaren's revolutionary critical pedagogy thought based on marxist humanism is not the same as the marxist historical materialism educational thought in China, so we need to critically examine its function, select its essence and discard its dregs. Although this book attempts to make a systematic review of McLaren's thought of critical pedagogy, compared with the richness and depth of McLaren's thought, the depth and breadth of analysis need to be strengthened. Further research on relevant issues is needed in the future.

Key words: McLaren; Critical Pedagogy; *Life in School*; Capitalism

目 录

引言 ·· (1)
  第一节 研究缘起 ··· (1)
    一 基于麦克拉伦的学术地位与贡献 ······································· (1)
    二 基于《学校生活》的独特价值 ··· (5)
    三 基于研究者的个人兴趣与条件 ··· (7)
  第二节 相关文献综述 ·· (8)
    一 国内对麦克拉伦的研究概况 ·· (8)
    二 关于麦克拉伦的国外研究状况 ··· (13)
    三 国内外对《学校生活》的研究概况 ······································ (28)
    四 已有研究成果评价 ··· (39)
  第三节 研究方法 ·· (39)
    一 文献法 ··· (39)
    二 访谈法 ··· (40)

第一章 产生及发展历程 ·· (42)
  第一节 《学校生活》前的思想萌芽 ·· (42)
    一 从事教师工作前 ·· (42)
    二 从事教师工作后 ·· (49)
  第二节 《学校生活》后的思想发展 ·· (58)
    一 《学校生活》第一版——反思与申辩 ·································· (58)
    二 《学校生活》第二版到第三版——马克思主义的回归 ·········· (66)

三　《学校生活》第四版到第六版——革命性的批判
　　　　教育学 ………………………………………………（71）
　　四　后《学校生活》阶段的研究重点——解放神学…………（76）

第二章　理论渊源与核心理论武器 ………………………………（79）
　第一节　批判借鉴多家理论——麦克拉伦批判教育学的
　　　　　理论渊源 ………………………………………………（79）
　　一　马克思主义 ……………………………………………（79）
　　二　美国进步思想、法兰克福学派批判理论与后现代主义 ……（88）
　　三　保罗·弗莱雷与亨利·吉鲁的教育思想 ………………（91）
　第二节　马克思主义人道主义——麦克拉伦批判教育学的
　　　　　核心理论武器 …………………………………………（97）
　　一　马克思主义人道主义作为麦克拉伦批判教育学的理想 ……（97）
　　二　时代呼唤马克思主义人道主义作为麦克拉伦批判资本
　　　　主义的武器 …………………………………………（103）

第三章　主旨 ……………………………………………………（115）
　第一节　资本主义体制——麦克拉伦批判教育学批判的主要
　　　　　对象 ……………………………………………………（115）
　　一　合理化剥削与压迫的资本主义全球化 ………………（115）
　　二　新自由主义导致的教育私有化与市场化 ……………（121）
　　三　加剧人的物化与异化和阶级复制的标准化考试 ……（129）
　第二节　革命性的批判教育学——实现资本主义社会
　　　　　替代形式的实践哲学 …………………………………（134）
　　一　革命性的批判教育学——一种实践哲学 ……………（134）
　　二　革命性的批判教育学——抵制与替代资本主义的实践
　　　　方式 ……………………………………………………（144）

第四章　立场、特色与评价 ……………………………………（170）
　第一节　麦克拉伦批判教育学的立场与特色 ……………………（170）

一　麦克拉伦批判教育学的马克思主义人道主义立场 ……… (170)
　　二　麦克拉伦批判教育学的特色 ………………………… (176)
第二节　学界对麦克拉伦及其思想的肯定与批判 …………… (179)
　　一　对麦克拉伦的肯定与赞誉 ………………………… (179)
　　二　对麦克拉伦的批判与攻击 ………………………… (189)
第三节　麦克拉伦对世界各地教育者的影响 ………………… (192)
　　一　知行合一 …………………………………………… (192)
　　二　做有献身精神的知识分子 ………………………… (196)
　　三　拒绝故步自封 ……………………………………… (200)

结　语 …………………………………………………………… (205)
第一节　麦克拉伦批判教育学的形成因素 …………………… (205)
　　一　内在因素 …………………………………………… (205)
　　二　外在因素 …………………………………………… (207)
第二节　《学校生活》为代表的麦克拉伦批判教育学的影响与
　　　　局限性 …………………………………………………… (209)
　　一　影响 ………………………………………………… (209)
　　二　局限性 ……………………………………………… (211)

参考文献 ………………………………………………………… (213)

附　录 …………………………………………………………… (231)
附录一　访谈麦克拉伦提纲 …………………………………… (231)
附录二　麦克拉伦世界各地讲学年表（1987—2022） ………… (239)
附录三　麦克拉伦学术作品列表（1979—2022） ……………… (262)

后　记 …………………………………………………………… (339)

Contents

Introduction ·· (1)

1. Research Reasons ·· (1)

    1.1   Based on McLaren's Academic Standing and
           Contributions ··· (1)

    1.2   Based on the Unique Value of *Life in School* ················· (5)

    1.3   Based on the Researcher's Personal Interest and Research
           Conditions ·· (7)

2. Literature Review ··· (8)

    2.1   Overview of Research on McLaren at Home and
           Abroad ··· (8)

    2.2   Overview of Research on *Life in School* at Home and
           Abroad ·· (13)

    2.3   Evaluation of Existing Research Results ·························· (28)

3. Research Methods ·· (39)

    3.1   Literature Research Method ··· (39)

    3.2   Interviewing Method ·· (40)

**Chapter 1   The Emergence and Development of McLaren's
                    Thought of Critical Pedagogy** ······························· (42)

1. The Germ of Thought Before *Life in School* ···························· (42)

    1.1   BeforeWorking as a Elementary School Teacher ············· (42)

1.2　After Working as a Elementary School ················ (49)
　2. The Development of Thought After *Life in School* ············ (58)
　　2.1　The First Edition of *Life in School*-Reflection and Justification ··· (58)
　　2.2　The Second to Third Edition of *Life in School*-The Return of Marxism ·· (66)
　　2.3　The fourth to Sixth Edition of *Life in School*-Revolutionary Critical Pedagogy ··· (71)
　　2.4　The Research Focus of Post-*Life in School*-Liberation Theology ··· (76)

Chapter2　The Theoretical Origins and Core Theoretical Weapons of McLaren's Thought of Critical Pedagogy ·· (79)

　1. Criticize and Draw on Many Theories-Theoretical Origins of McLaren's Thought of Critical Pedagogy ·················· (79)
　　1.1　Marxism ··· (79)
　　1.2　American Progressive Thought, Frankfurt School Critical Theory and Postmodernism ·· (88)
　　1.3　The Critical Pedagogy Thought of Paul Freire and Henry Giroux ··· (91)
　2. Marxist Humanism-The Core Theoretical Weapons of McLaren's Thought of Critical Pedagogy ································· (97)
　　2.1　Marxist Humanism- The Ideal of McLaren's Critical Pedagogy ··· (97)
　　2.2　The Times Call for Marxist Humanism as McLaren's Weapon to Criticize Capitalism ·· (103)

Chapter 3　TheGist of McLaren's Thought of Critical Pedagogy (115)

1. Capitalist System—The Main Object of McLaren's Critical Pedagogy (115)

    1.1　Capitalist Globalization Rationalizes Exploitation and Oppression (115)

    1.2　The Privatization and Marketization of Education Caused by Neoliberalism (121)

    1.3　Standardized Tests that Intensifies Human Objectification and Alienation and Class Duplication (129)

2. Revolutionary Critical Pedagogy—Practical Philosophy to Realize an Alternative Form of Capitalist Society (134)

    2.1　Revolutionary Critical Pedagogy—A Practical Philosophy (134)

    2.2　Revolutionary Critical Pedagogy—The Practice of Resisting and Replacing Capitalism (144)

Chapter4　Stance, Characteristics and Evaluation of McLaren's Thought of Critical Pedagogy (170)

1. The Stance and Characteristics of McLaren's Critical Pedagogy (170)

    1.1　Mc Laren's Marxist Humanitarian Stance on Critical Pedagogy (170)

    1.2　The Characteristics of McLaren's Critical Pedagogy (176)

2. The Academic Affirmation and Criticism to McLaren and His Thought (179)

    2.1　Affirmation and Praise to McLaren (179)

    2.2　Criticism and attacks on McLaren (189)

3. McLaren's Influence on Educators around the World (192)

    3.1　Walk the Talk (192)

3.2　Be a Dedicated Intellectual ·············· (196)
　　3.3　Refuse to Stand Still ·············· (200)

Conclusion ·············· (205)
　1. The Formative Factors of McLaren's Thought of Critical
　　　Pedagogy ·············· (205)
　　1.1　Intrinsic Factor ·············· (205)
　　1.2　Extrinsic Factors ·············· (207)
　2. The Influence and Limitation of McLaren's Thought of Critical
　　　Pedagogy Represented by *Life in School* ·············· (209)
　　2.1　Influence ·············· (209)
　　2.2　Limitation ·············· (211)

References ·············· (213)

Appendixes ·············· (231)
　Appendix Ⅰ: Outline of the Interviews with McLaren ·············· (231)
　Appendix Ⅱ: Chronology of McLaren Lectures around the
　　　World (1987–2022) ·············· (239)
　Appendix Ⅲ: List of McLaren's Scholarly Works
　　　(1979–2022) ·············· (262)

Afterword ·············· (339)

引　言

第一节　研究缘起

一　基于麦克拉伦的学术地位与贡献

彼得·劳伦斯·麦克拉伦（Peter Lawrence McLaren，以下简称麦克拉伦[①]）是马克思主义教育理论代表人物之一、美国批判教育学的主要奠基者之一、美国批判教育学的主要实践者之一，也是世界范围内批判教育学的主要倡导者之一。他是马克思主义者、社会活动者、教师。迄今为止，麦克拉伦致力于教育理论研究与实践已达近40年，著作等身，获奖无数。2017年麦克拉伦在美国教育研究联合会[②]中成为唯一的一位终身成就奖的获得者。近年来，他的思想在教育理论界得到越来越多的关注。

对于任何对当代批判教育感兴趣的人来说，麦克拉伦几乎不需要介

[①] 对于彼得·劳伦斯·麦克拉伦（Peter Lawrence McLaren）的名字除了本书以及国内多数译者所惯用的"彼得·麦克拉伦"这一译名之外，也有学者将其翻译为"皮特·麦克劳伦"（王占魁：《阿普尔批判教育研究的批判逻辑》，《教育研究》2012年第4期）、"麦克莱伦"（李宝庆，樊亚峤：《麦克莱伦的多元文化教育观及其启》，《比较教育研究》2012年第5期；李宝庆，靳玉乐：《麦克莱伦的批判课程理论及其启示》，《西南大学学报》2014年第6期；张聪：《为了儿童的解放和自由——麦克莱伦（Peter McLaren）〈反抗教育学〉（*Pedagogy of insurrection*）的价值意蕴》，《外国教育研究》2017年第2期）。

[②] 美国教育研究联合会（American Education Research Association，以下简称AERA）是世界上重要的教育研究组织，每年该联合会均举办为期一周的年会，年会通过各种方式进行学术交流，包含的学科方向广泛，几乎涵盖教育学科的各个方向。参会者不限于美国本土的教育工作者和研究者，每年该年会参与人数均保持在20000人左右，是国际上重要的教育学科交流平台。

绍。他被称为"批判教育学的主要缔造者之一"①，以及"所有教师的老师"②。正如保罗·罗宾逊（Paul Robinson）在《纽约时报书评》（*New York Times Book Review*）上对诺姆·乔姆斯基（Noam Chomsky）所写的那样："从他的思想的力量、范围、新奇性和影响力来判断，乔姆斯基可以说是当今最重要的知识分子。"同样，毫无疑问，"从他思想的力量、范围、新奇性和影响力来判断"，麦克拉伦可以说是当今最重要的教育理论家（无论是批判性的还是其他的）。③ 正如艾丽西亚·德·阿尔巴（Alicia de Alba）和马塞拉·冈萨雷斯·阿里纳斯（Marcela Gonzalez Arenas）所言："今天的教育者可以站在麦克拉伦一边，也可以与他站在对立的一边，但不能没有他。"④ 他被公认为是教育左派的"桂冠诗人"⑤。亨利·吉鲁（Henry Giroux）写道："作为一名作家，他（麦克拉伦）将稀有的精明的理论家天赋与著名的瓦尔特·本雅明（Walter Benjamin）的讲故事方式结合起来。"⑥ 在《批判教育学和掠夺性文化》（*Critical Pedagogy and Predatory Culture*）的封底，威廉·F. 派纳（William F. Pinar）（1995）写道："麦克拉伦能够准确地感知什么是重要的，他的杰出的学术成就使他成为当今这个领域的核心政治理论家。"⑦ 保拉·奥尔曼（Paula Allman）（2000）描述了麦克拉伦的作品：麦克拉伦的作品是激情、承诺和批判性

---

① Wikipedia (2014) Peter McLaren, http：//en. wikipedia. org/wiki/Peter_McLaren（accessed 14 April 2018）.

② Steinberg, R. S. （2005）Foreword, in M. Pruyn & L. M. Herta – Charles, eds., *Teaching Peter McLaren*：*Paths of Dissent*, New York：Peter Lang, p. xxiii.

③ David Gabbard, Karen Anijar, Fearless Speech in Fearful Times：An Essay Review of Capitalists and Conquerors, Teaching against Global Capitalism and the New Imperialism, and Teaching Peter McLaren, https：//mronline. org/2005/10/30/fearless – speech – in – fearful – timesan – essay – review – of – capitalists – and – conquerors – teaching – against – global – capitalism – and – the – new – imperialism – and – teaching – peter – mclaren/, 2019 – 05 – 22.

④ Marc Pruyn and Luis Huerta – Charles（editors）, *Teaching Peter McLaren*：*Path of Dissent*, New York：Peter Lang Publications, 2005, p. 55.

⑤ Kincheloe, J., "Peter McLaren：the poet of the educational left", in *P. McLaren CheGuevara, Paulo Freire, and the pedagogy of revolution*, Boulder, CO：Rowman & Littlefield, 2000, p. ix.

⑥ Giroux, H., "Preface", in *P. McLaren Schooling as a Ritual Performance*：*towards a political economy of educational symbols and gestures*, 3rd edn. Lanham, MD：Rowman & Littlefield, 1999.

⑦ Pinar, W. F., "Back Cover", in *P. McLaren Critical Pedagogy and Predatory Culture*, London：Routledge, 1995.

分析和洞察力的绝妙结合。他的作品像是一种跳着亲密舞蹈的诗歌和散文，能够立刻触及读者的心灵和思想。麦克拉伦的朋友保罗·弗莱雷（Paulo Freire）写道："彼得·麦克拉伦是我在诸多杰出的'知识分子'中发现的，反过来我又被他发现。在我认识彼得·麦克拉伦之前，我读过他的书……当我读完了麦克拉伦的第一篇文章，我就几乎可以肯定，我们属于一个完全相同的'知识分子家族'（'intellectual family'）。"[①] 麦克拉伦是一位敬业的学者，他的教学生涯致力于唤醒学生认识到彻底社会变革的潜力。他从来没有停止倾听他人批判的声音，重新建构自己的思路或者公开承认自己的错误。他是一个具有非凡天赋的人，尽管遇到各种障碍和困难，却已经设法浮出水面并闪耀着光芒。他是一个谦逊但坚持不懈、逐渐成长的学者。他拥有艺术灵魂且对社会科学的论述有着重要的贡献。一个非凡的人做了一些非凡的事情，但仍然保持谦虚、温暖并向各界人士开放。长长的银发、文身、土著服饰和珠宝、不可缺少的皮包，以及众所周知的约翰·列侬（John Lennon）式的眼镜，麦克拉伦一直忠于自己的反主流文化出身，并与这个造就他的世界保持着联系。麦克拉伦总是强调并且一直以身示范"与穷人一起"（speak with）而不是"为穷人"（speak for）。"speak with"和"speak for"的不同在于，后者的意涵是我站在"我"的位置上，研究你们（穷人）的情况，然后为你们的利益说话；而前者的意蕴是，我跟你们站在一起，与你们一起与不公正和不平等做斗争。前者是后者的一个更加深入的层次，我不再是一个武断的观察者和报告员，而是跟穷人站在一个战壕的战友。麦克拉伦以其独特的方式说出被我们大多数人所忽视的我们大部分人都无能力言说的事情。他命名了人类无法立刻感知的推动社会、政治、经济、文化和教育事件的极其复杂、隐形及阴险的势力因素。这种天才般的命名向我们展示了这些隐藏的模糊的因素是如何型塑我们在学校及其他地方的日常生活的。随着经年累月的积累麦克拉伦的这种能力和智慧变得越来越强大。乔·金奇洛（Joe L. Kincheloe）这样评价麦克拉伦："简单地

---

① Freire, P., "Preface", in *P. McLaren, Critical Pedagogy and Predatory Culture*, London: Routledge, x, 1995, pp. ix – xi.

曝光不为人所见的东西，说出不可言说的事件是一回事，作为批判理论家他把这种行动还推向了实践领域，他将他的思想表达与社会和教育行动结合起来。拥有如此行动能力的头脑在本质上是十分重要的，也是难能可贵的，因为它点燃了黑暗岁月的希望之光，在阴暗的学校地狱里点燃了可能之光。"[1] 麦克拉伦的学术贡献和个人特点使他成为当代左翼的偶像和当代批判教育学的活纪念碑——虽然他从未寻求过这个地位，并且总是保持着谦逊的态度。麦克拉伦建立了他自己的英雄类型：一个智慧的英雄，一个谦虚并尊重每一个人的英雄，他激励并温和地推动他遇到的每一个人尽他们的能力为人类造福。麦克拉伦对自己的工作非常挑剔，从不满足于自己目前的成绩，总是在寻求进一步的提高。麦克拉伦不邀请人们复制他的作品，而是用他的作品与世界共存。他的工作体现了对人类福祉的承诺，对真理的追求，对其他观点的尊重，以及保护弱者和穷人的义务。"他不仅是一位激进的教育哲学家，也是一位国际活动家和有远见的梦想家。"[2] 当今，任何想研究教育左派的思想、政治、哲学、意识形态或研究的人都必须读麦克拉伦的作品，很多人都是从读他的作品开始的。[3] 在过去的30多年里，麦克拉伦在批判教育学这个领域做出了重要的贡献，他一直是反资本主义教育的导游，举着一面反映资产阶级社会的狂欢节杂耍镜。保罗·弗莱雷使批判教育学永垂不朽，麦克拉伦将其重新发扬光大。随着新自由主义经济将大学转变为公司，将教育降低到一种可转让商品的地位，麦克拉伦在极权主义、法西斯主义和恐怖主义的新黑暗时代成为社会良知和左翼政治激进主义的罕见灯塔。到目前为止，他是当今学术界最多产的作家之一。他在世界范围内发表期刊文章350多篇，其书籍和文章被翻译成20多种语言，在这个跨国经

---

[1] Peter McLaren, *Life in Schools: An Introduction to Critical Pedagogy in the Foundations of Education* (Fifth Edition), Pearson Publishers, 2007, p. xi.

[2] Eryaman, Mustafa Yunus, *Editorial Statement (English): Understanding Critical Pedagogy and Peter McLaren in the Age of Global Capitalism*, International Journal of Progressive Education, Vol. 3, No. 2, 2006, p. 6.

[3] Marc Pruyn and Luis Huerta-Charles (editors), *Teaching Peter McLaren: Path of Dissent*, New York: Peter Lang Publications, 2005, Foreword, p. xviii.

济残酷剥削无权无势的穷人的时代,他以其社会主义导向的革命性的批判教育学大大地扩展了我们的批判视野。①在某种程度上,由于麦克拉伦多产,他现在可以说是学术界最有影响力的马克思主义教育家。他是马克思主义思潮的坚定支持者。在社会主义在美国受敌视的时候,他为马克思主义教育注入了新的生命。②对于麦克拉伦批判教育学的研究,有助于马克思主义教育哲学及时运用相关领域的新成果、新理论充实自身,以形成本学科的新范畴、表达的新形式,充分体现马克思主义教育哲学作为一个开放性系统存在的本质特征。本研究期望为中国学者进一步了解这位教育家提供参考信息。

二 基于《学校生活》的独特价值

麦克拉伦开创性的代表作《学校生活——批判教育学导论》(*Life in Schools—An Introduction to Critical Pedagogy in the Foundations of Education*,以下简称《学校生活》)作为一部批判教育学名著,近 30 年来无疑是一部教育学经典之作;"是一本最早的,将教师教育引向与批判理论,批判的社会科学对话的导读性教科书"③。该书在清晰而具启发性的教室叙事的基础上,论述叙事所反映出的政治、经济和社会因素,而这些因素往往在当今很多教育类教材中没有得到足够的重视。麦克拉伦描述《学校生活》是一个他作为教育者由一个聚焦社会、教育改革的自由人道主义者彻底改造成一个主张革命实践、通过批判教育学进行社会革命的马克思主义人道主义者的故事。虽然"本书没有对开国先父的甜美赞歌,没有慷慨陈词给出如何培养企业精神和缩小数字鸿沟的建议,也没有关于教师如何提高学生标准化测试成绩的妙招"④,但是书中提出的对教育问

---

① Marc Pruyn and Luis Huerta‐Charles (editors), *Teaching Peter McLaren: Path of Dissent*, New York: Peter Lang Publications, 2005, Foreword, p. xvi.
② Kincheloe, J., "Peter McLaren: The poet of the educational left", In P. McLaren, *Che Guevara, Paulo Freire, and the pedagogy of revolution*, Boulder, CO: Rowman & Littlefield, 2000, p. ix.
③ 王雁:《美国批判教育学者麦克拉伦的学术生命研究》,硕士学位论文,东北师范大学,2013 年,第 18 页。
④ Peter McLaren, *Life in Schools: An Introduction to Critical Pedagogy in the Foundations of Education* (Sixth Edition), Boulder, CO: Paradigm, 2014, p. 131.

题的这种分析通常涉及教育学的根本。而这种从批判角度来写的教育学教材基本从20世纪80年代起就没有了。《学校生活》的诞生是为了在北美这块资本主义占支配地位的土地上挑战种族、阶级和性别特权，这正是《学校生活》强有力的被关注点和卖点。1989年《学校生活》第一版问世，2014年7月在美国出版第6版。25年间一共5次再版，在全美多所大学被选为批判教育学经典教材。保罗·弗莱雷作为20世纪批判教育理论和实践方面最重要和最有影响的作家之一对《学校生活》的评价是"对所有未能促进人类解放的教育形式的有力挑战……值得所有人去阅读"[1]。拉明·法拉曼德普尔（Ramin Farahmandpur）在为这本书的第四版作序时给予的评价是"毫无疑问，麦克拉伦的《学校生活》对于成千上万在公共学校奋战的教育者带来了希望和鼓舞"[2]。近30年间，该书赢得很多著作奖，如首次出版便获得"1989年美国教育研究协会评论家推荐奖"，第四版被莫斯科社会经济科学学院召集的国际专家组评为在教育理论、政策、实践领域中12部最有影响力的作品之一，包括《学校生活》在内的他的5部书都获得了美国教育研究协会的"评论家推荐奖"。该书也被译为20多种语言在多个国家和地区流传（如加拿大、美国、墨西哥、巴西、委内瑞拉等，还包括我国台湾地区的繁体中文版，第六版于2020年在中国大陆翻译出版[3]）。一本讨论教育问题的书有如此深远和持久的反响，这本身就是一个值得注意的文化现象。《学校生活》作为他的成名作和代表作，是他所有的专著中知名度和影响力最大的，麦克拉伦成为批判教育学领域一位世界闻名的人物的部分原因是这本书的巨大成功。[4]然而，这本书不仅仅是一本基础课程的教科书，它还见证了麦克

---

[1] Peter McLaren, *Life in Schools: An Introduction to Critical Pedagogy in the Foundations of Education* (Second Edition), New York: Longman, 1994, p. back cover.

[2] Peter McLaren, *Life in Schools: An Introduction to Critical Pedagogy in the Foundations of Education* (Fourth Edition), Pearson Publishers, 2003, pp. xxi, xx.

[3] 本文作者自从2014年开始翻译《学校生活》第六版，预计2023年出版。

[4] Peter McLaren, *Life in Schools: An Introduction to Critical Pedagogy in the Foundations of Education* (Fifth Edition), Pearson Publishers, 2007, p. xi.

拉伦在过去 40 年里作为思想家和教育家的发展历程。[①] 在六个版本中，尽管内容发生了显著的变化和扩展，该书的基本结构保持相对一致。麦克拉伦思想的激进进步可以追溯到这本书的每一个版本，每一版都随着他的思考视角、思想变化、时事变化而有所变化和不同。《学校生活》作为麦克拉伦的成名作，与他的成长背景、工作经历及学术道路有着密不可分的关系，所以研究者认为以这本书为线索研究麦克拉伦的批判教育学思想是合理而具有说服力的。

三 基于研究者的个人兴趣与条件

研究者自 2014 年开始在东北师范大学攻读教育学原理专业博士学位，在导师的帮助下，研究者有幸结识了麦克拉伦夫妇，开始接触批判教育学理论并承担《学校生活》第六版的翻译工作，由此对麦克拉伦的批判教育学理论及其成名作《学校生活》产生了浓厚的研究兴趣。自 2014 年开始每年麦克拉伦教授都会在东北师范大学履行客座教授的职责并且于吉林省几所高校如长春师范大学、吉林师范大学等进行巡回讲座，研究者在此期间担任麦克拉伦教授的助教兼翻译，不但工作上合作愉快，而且建立了较深的友情。研究者所就读的东北师范大学是国内首家批判教育学研究中心，能为研究者提供最好的研究指导、环境和机会。研究者于 2017 年 8 月至 2018 年 9 月得到中国国家留学基金委的全额资助在麦克拉伦工作的查普曼大学访学一年，访学期间与他本人及他的家人、朋友、同事、学生进行了深入交流，获得了大量的一手资料。在准备这部书稿的过程中，麦克拉伦慷慨地提供了各种各样的资料和帮助。最重要的是，麦克拉伦在与本书作者的直接接触中提供了大量的信息，这些独家信息在任何其他来源中都找不到，因此为本书的写作创造了得天独厚的条件。研究者初听他的课、翻译他的书，一开始并不完全同意他的观点，认为他对资本主义的美国社会作了过于激进的批判，只是看到了坏的一面，

[①] Derek R. Ford, Book review: *Life in Schools: An Introduction to Critical Pedagogy in the Foundations of Education* (6th edition), *Peter McLaren*, Boulder and London: Paradigm Publishers, 2014 Educational Studies, Vol. 51, No. 5, 2015, p.440.

完全看不到好的一面。通过读他更多的书以及与他更多的接触，参与更多的学术活动，想法慢慢转变，他看到了资本主义的本质，而我们看到的大多是繁荣的表象，其实繁荣的表象是以牺牲大多数人和整个世界环境为代价的，便越来越认同他的观点和理论。研究者对麦克拉伦的认识的转变，更激发了对麦克拉伦的思想作进一步分析与研究的兴趣：他在过去30多年里的学术轨迹是什么？他的思想来源于哪里？他的思想核心是什么？他的思想立场和特色是什么？学界是如何评价他的？这些问题都是作者所关心的和感兴趣的，本研究将带着这些疑问展开。

第二节　相关文献综述

迄今为止，麦克拉伦致力于教育理论与实践的研究已达30余年，著作等身，讨论的主题庞杂而分散。他本人的著作已经被翻译成20多种文字在世界各地传播。这些著作为国内外学者全面了解麦克拉伦及其思想提供了全面而集中的素材。本书意图是以《学校生活》为线索，从整体上把握麦克拉伦的批判教育学思想。所以本研究综述所聚焦者有二：其一是关于麦克拉伦的；其二是关于《学校生活》的。国外学界关于他思想的研究早于国内学界的开展，通过对一系列国内外文献的研读，下面将国内外学者关于麦克拉伦的各方面思想的研究作文献梳理。

一　国内对麦克拉伦的研究概况

相对于麦克拉伦卷帙浩繁的著作来说，目前翻译到国内的著作并不多。大陆方面，东北师范大学正在组织学者翻译麦克拉伦的部分著作，预期2020年年底出版一部分。2013年麦克拉伦受邀成为东北师范大学批判教育学研究中心荣誉主任，并于2015年10月以主要参加者的身份参加了东北师范大学举办的第一届批判教育学国际研讨会。大陆方面在各种学术搜索系统里能搜到的与麦克拉伦有关的文章不超过20篇，其中硕士论文1篇，无博士论文。在中国大陆范围内，麦克拉伦的作品并未如保罗·弗莱雷那样被引介并引发学界的高度关注。台湾地区方面对批判教育学的引介比大陆更多一些，一些台湾学者也在试图建立本地批判教育学,但也仍在起步阶段。2003 年台湾巨流图书公司出版了由萧昭君、陈巨擘翻译的《校园生活——批判教育学导论》(第四版)一书。在《批判教育学——台湾的探索》[①] 一书中台湾学者对他的零星研究停留在 2010 年。在"台湾博硕士论文知识加值系统"里搜索到关于麦克拉伦的有 3 篇论文,其中有两篇硕士论文,一篇博士论文。而到目前为止国内已经出现对于保罗·弗莱雷、亨利·吉鲁和迈克尔·阿普尔(Michael W. Apple)等批判教育家的大量研究,不仅有他们的译著而且分别有针对他们所做的博士论文。由此可以看出,国内对于麦克拉伦批判教育学思想的研究相对非常薄弱(见表1)。

表1　　　　　　　中国研究麦克拉伦的硕博论文一览表

	论文级别	毕业年份	作者及所在地	题　目	主要研究内容
1	博士论文	2010	蔡幸芬 中国台湾	Peter McLaren 批判教育学之转向——重回马克思主义	探讨了麦克拉伦的革命性的批判教育学和多元文化主义,以马克思主义转向作为麦克拉伦的理论独特性
2	硕士论文	1995	黄彦文 中国台湾	Peter McLaren 革命性的批判教育学思想及其对课程理论的启示	研究麦克拉伦从革命性的批判教育学出发,批判资本主义全球化,反思后现代思潮,然后思考革命性的批判教育学对台湾课程理论的启示
3	硕士论文	1996	钱克玮 中国台湾	Peter McLaren 革命性多元文化主义及其对台湾多元文化教育的启示	从革命的多元文化主义的产生背景、思想渊源、内涵、限制出发,得出对台湾多元文化教育的启示

---

① 李锦旭、王慧澜:《批判教育学——台湾的探索》,台北:心理出版社 2006 年版。

续表

论文级别	毕业年份	作者及所在地	题　目	主要研究内容
4　硕士论文	2013	王雁 中国大陆	美国批判教育学者麦克拉伦的学术生命研究	研究了麦克拉伦的整个学术生命发展图谱，在描述麦克拉伦这一条线索的同时，介绍每一时期的批判教育学发展的大趋向和大环境，包括每一时期的代表作品分析，以及众多作品背后的逻辑与联系

1. 对麦克拉伦学术思想发展的研究

蔡幸芬（2010）探讨了麦克拉伦批判教育学之转向，从最初的马克思主义到后现代主义，最终还是回到了马克思思想的主要思想变化历程及理论观点。蔡幸芬和杨忠斌（2011）[1]指出了麦克拉伦从赞同后现代主义到批判后现代主义而后提出抗拒的后现代主义的思想发展与转变过程。他们认为麦克拉伦的批判教育学思想和后现代主义有密切的关系。在后现代思潮下，他亦受到影响，并融入他的批判教育学论点当中。他赞同后现代主义所提及的消弭二元划分与对立、强调与尊重差异（diversity）、破除种族、性别的歧视，但是在后现代的尊重多元下，他注意到不是所有的差异都要肯定，阶级的差异是要排除的。而且要先排除阶级差异，其他的差异才能得到肯定。也就是具有各种不同特质的人要先能生存下去，各种差异也才能存在。在赞同后，其中对多元文化主义的质疑、被资本主义利用的后现代主义以及忽视差异的重要性则是麦克拉伦对于后现代主义所进行的批判，忧心虚无的后现代主义与嬉戏的后现代主义（ludic postmodernism），而提出抗拒的后现代主义（resistance postmodern-

---

[1] 蔡幸芬，"Peter McLaren 的批判教育学后现代主义观点"，*Intelligent Information Technology Application Association. Proceedings of the 2011 Second International Conference on Education and sports Education*（ESE 2011 V3），Intelligent Information Technology Application Association：智能信息技术应用学会，2011，p.4.

ism）则是他所提出的改革之道。王雁（2013）将麦克拉伦的学术轨迹分为两个主要阶段：第一阶段是从 1984 年到 1994 年，第二阶段是从 1994 年至今。她总结第一阶段麦克拉伦的主要研究倾向于四个方向，包括批判的民族志、批判教育学、课程研究和批判的多元文化主义。第二阶段的作品与前一阶段的作品相比并没有巨大的转变，而是一种修正与延伸，研究重点转移到对政治经济学的批判，主要关心生产的社会关系，关注批判教育学与更大的社会脉络的关联性，重回马克思主义。于伟[①]对麦克拉伦进行了访谈，访谈内容包括麦克拉伦的民族志研究、后现代主义、马克思人道主义、教育研究中的立场问题，以及巴西教育家保罗·弗莱雷的思想及其影响。该访谈体现出麦克拉伦教授投身教育界 30 余年对北美批判教育学的创始和发展所做出的努力。张聪[②]指出麦克拉伦在"回归马克思"、力主"社会正义"、澄清"价值观与文化资本"的基础上构建了反抗教育学，以期从理论上促进儿童发展。

2. 对麦克拉伦批判课程理论的研究

黄彦文（1995）从麦克拉伦的革命性的批判教育学角度出发，分别就"多元文化课程观""全球化课程观""后现代课程观""课程理论与实务结合"等面向进行探讨，探析了麦克拉伦革命性的批判教育学思想对于中国台湾课程理论的启示。李宝庆和靳玉乐（2014）[③]认为麦克拉伦的批判课程理论注重学生批判意识与能力的养成，并以学生的自由与解放为根本旨归。他以社会批判理论、马克思主义、后现代主义、保罗·弗莱雷和亨利·吉鲁的批判教育学等为理论来源，对课程价值、课程决策、课程内容、课程实施、课程研究方法作了深刻的阐释，从而丰富了当代的课程研究话语，同时也为我国的课程改革提供了诸多启示。

---

① 彼得·麦克拉伦，于伟：《学者对于正义的追寻——彼得·麦克拉伦（Peter McLaren）访谈录》，《外国教育研究》2015 年第 42 卷第 6 期，第 3—13 页。

② 张聪：《为了儿童的解放和自由——麦克莱伦（Peter McLaren）〈反抗教育学〉（Pedagogy of Insurrection）的价值意蕴》，《外国教育研究》2017 年第 44 卷第 2 期，第 36—46 页。

③ 李宝庆、靳玉乐：《麦克莱伦的批判课程理论及其启示》，《西南大学学报》（社会科学版）2014 年第 40 卷第 6 期，第 57 - 64 + 182 页。

3. 对麦克拉伦批判多元文化思想的研究

由于麦克拉伦积极致力于美国以及拉美地区的多元文化教育运动，并与诸多学者和社会人士合作，郑蕾[①]对麦克拉伦教授进行了访谈，与其主要就美国多元文化教育的历史发展过程以及批判的多元文化主义的核心内容进行了探讨和交流。李宝庆和樊亚峤[②]指出麦克拉伦的多元文化教育观强调培养学生的批判意识与实践能力，并以学生的自由与解放为根本旨归；他以社会批判理论、后现代主义、马克思主义、保罗·弗莱雷和亨利·吉鲁的文化研究等为理论来源，对多元文化教育的教育目标、教育内容、教育方法、教师角色作了深刻阐释。钱克玮（1996）追溯了麦克拉伦革命性多元文化主义的产生背景与思想渊源，阐述了麦克拉伦革命性多元文化主义的内涵，评论了麦克拉伦革命性多元文化主义的限制，诠释了麦克拉伦革命性多元文化主义对台湾地区多元文化教育的启示。

4. 对麦克拉伦革命性的批判教育学思想的研究

麦克拉伦和周霖[③]简要地回顾其批判教育学的发展，指出教育学是完全关乎政治的，而政治也包含着一个教育学的向度。当前，批判教育学作为教师教育主流的保守教育学一个重要的对立面，其最具政治性的特征已被磨掉和清除。他们认为，对改革与变革的关系必须辩证地看待，而批判教育学可以担当其间人为的媒介因素。旨在改进 21 世纪社会主义原理和实践的革命性的批判教育学是教师教育的重要方向。蔡幸芬（2010）指出麦克拉伦提出了革命性的批判教育学的目的就是对抗资本主义，革命性的批判教育学不再仅是纸上谈兵的理论文字，它已经成为对抗资本主义，唤起人民批判意识、重视人性尊严的、改变社会阶层的学

[①] 郑蕾：《批判教育学视野下的美国多元文化教育——访美国加州大学洛杉矶分校 Peter Mclaren 教授》，《全球教育展望》2012 年第 41 卷第 3 期，第 7 – 11 + 18 页。

[②] 李宝庆、樊亚峤：《麦克莱伦的多元文化教育观及其启示》，《比较教育研究》2012 年第 34 卷第 5 期，第 62—67 页。

[③] 彼得·麦克拉伦、周霖：《革命的批判教育学：教师教育项目的解毒剂》，《东北师大学报》（哲学社会科学版）2009 年第 2 期，第 142—147 页。

说。周勇[①]认为在麦克拉伦的教育社会学实践中，可以清楚看到马克思主义者对于"资本主义"及"帝国主义"体制的强烈愤怒。

作为一位在国际批判教育研究领域已经活跃了近40年的大师级人物，麦克拉伦极大地增进了我们对民主、权力、政治和教育学之间关系的理解。作为批判教育学的先驱，他的贡献是杰出和独特的。然而，从以上国内已有麦克拉伦研究的情况来看，这些研究纵然能够对麦克拉伦理论的某个方面进行探讨，然而，截至2019年8月，国内尚没有学者对其思想形成和发展的深层原因及其思想的整体脉络进行揭示。从整体上讲，国内现有的麦克拉伦研究与麦克拉伦对中国及其国际影响相比显得有些不太相称。更为根本地讲，迄今为止，国内所作的麦克拉伦研究，还不足以让我们通过一个问题抓住麦克拉伦思想的灵魂，对麦克拉伦近40年的研究成果有一个整体的把握。

二 关于麦克拉伦的国外研究状况

（一）以麦克拉伦为专题的学术专著

目前，关于麦克拉伦的不同语言的学术著作和读本有六本（见表2）：(1)《讲授彼得·麦克拉伦：异见之路》(*Teaching Peter McLaren: Paths of Dissent*)（2005年彼得·朗出版社出版，已经被翻译成西班牙语）由马克·普鲁恩（Marc Pruyn）和路易斯·M.韦尔塔·查尔斯（Luis M. Huerta-Charles）编写；(2)《彼得·麦克拉伦，教育与解放斗争》(*Peter McLaren, Education, and the Struggle for Liberation*) 由穆斯塔法·埃尔亚曼（Eryaman, M.）编写（2009年汉普顿出版社出版）；(3)《联邦危机：马尔库塞、马克思、麦克拉伦》(*Crisis of Commonwealth: Marcuse, Marx, McLaren*) 由查尔斯·赖茨（Charles Reitz）编写（2013年列克星敦出版社出版）；(4)《这拳头呼唤我的心：彼得·麦克拉伦读本（第一卷）》(*This Fist Called My Heart: The Peter McLaren Reader*) 由马克·普鲁恩和路易斯·M.韦尔塔·查尔斯编写（2015信息时代出版社出版）；(5)《挣

---

① 周勇：《忧伤与愤怒：教育社会学的情感动力——以涂尔干、麦克拉伦为例》，《教育学术月刊》2014年第9期，第3—10页。

脱束缚：激进的教育家彼得·麦克拉伦的生活和时代》（*Breaking Free：The Life and Times of Peter McLaren，Radical Educator*）由麦克拉伦撰写、麦尔斯·威尔逊（Miles Wilson）插图阐释（2019年迈尔斯教育出版社出版）；(6)《通往无尽之径：彼得·麦克拉伦读本（第二卷）》（*Tracks to Infinity：The Peter McLaren Reader*）由马克·普鲁恩和路易斯·M.韦尔塔·查尔斯编写（预计于2020年由信息时代出版社出版）。

表2　　　　　　　关于麦克拉伦的主要著作

1. 《讲授彼得·麦克拉伦：异见之路》（2005）、（2007）.
西班牙语版：Pruy, M., & Charles, L. M. H. (Eds.). (2005). De la pedagogía crítica a la pedagogía de la revolución. Ensayos para comprender a Peter McLaren. New York, NY: Peter Lang Publications.
英语版：Pruyn, M., & Charles, L. M. H. (Eds.). (2007). Teaching Peter McLaren: Paths of dissent. New York, NY: Peter Lang Publications.

2. 《彼得·麦克拉伦，教育与解放斗争》（2009）.
Eryaman, M. (Ed.). (2009). *Peter McLaren, Education, and the Struggle for Liberation*. New York, NY: Hampton Press.

3. 《联邦危机：马尔库塞、马克思、麦克拉伦》（2013）.
Reitz, C. (Ed.). (2013). *Crisis of Commonwealth: Marcuse, Marx, McLaren*. Lanham, MD: Lexington Books, Rowman & Littlefield.

4. 《这拳头呼唤我的心：彼得·麦克拉伦读本（第一卷）》（2015）.
Pruyn, M. & Huerta-Charles, L. (Eds.). (2015). *This Fist Called My Heart: The Peter McLaren Reader*. Charlotte, NC: Information Age Publishers.

5. 《挣脱束缚：激进的教育家彼得·麦克拉伦的生活和时代》（2019）
Peter McLaren & Miles Wilson. (2019). Breaking Free: The Life and Times of Peter McLaren, Radical Educator. Gorham, Maine: Myers Education Press.

6. 《通往无尽之径：彼得·麦克拉伦读本（第二卷）》（预计于2020年出版）
Pruyn, M., Huerta-Charles, L. & Malott, C. (Eds.). *Tracks to Infinity: The Peter McLaren Reader*. (will be published Fall, 2020). Collected Essays by Peter McLaren. Charlotte, North Carolina: Information Age Publishers.

《讲授彼得·麦克拉伦：异见之路》由若干篇对麦克拉伦的评论性文章编辑而成的，是系统评价麦克拉伦的一本书，这些作者对麦克拉伦的生平、工作、思想和影响作了相应的论述。从该书的整体内容结构上来讲，除了雪莉·斯坦伯格（Shirlay R. Steinberg）和安东尼娅·达尔德（Antonia Darder）的序言、编者的导论，它既像是由 10 位不同学者所撰写的有关麦克拉伦著作的 10 篇"读后感"，又像是 10 名学者有关麦克拉伦 30 多年来通过其著作和实践留给国际教育学界印象的总体性评论集。它们分别统领在"麦克拉伦作品的影响""跨越不同背景的麦克拉伦""麦克拉伦与马克思主义"三个主题之下，每个主题下面分别有 4 位学者从不同角度对麦克拉伦的理论展开分析（见表3）。从 10 位学者各自不同的主题名称来看，我们就能初步感受到麦克拉伦学术思想的多元性和综合性特征，以及他对于马克思主义与革命性的批判教育学的聚焦。

表3　　《讲述彼得·麦克拉伦：异见之路》一书的内容结构

	作者	题目
第一部分：介绍与背景	Shirlay R. Steinberg	序言
	Antonia Darder	序言 阅读彼得·麦克拉伦
	Marc Pruyn & LiusHuerta-Charles	导论 讲述彼得·麦克拉伦：这位学者以及这本书
第二部分：麦克拉伦作品的影响	Roberto Bahruth	彼得·麦克拉伦：学者中的学者
	Alipio Casali & Ana Maria Araujo Freire	彼得·麦克拉伦：创造性的异见
	Zeus Leonardo	彼得·麦克拉伦团结的政治与伦理：批判教育学与激进教育笔记
第三部分：跨越不同背景的麦克拉伦	Alicia de Alba & Marcela Gonzalez Arenas	麦克拉伦：一个矛盾而杰出的知识分子
	Pepi Leistyna	革命的可能性：公立学校多元文化专业发展
	Marcia Moraes	彼得·麦克拉伦：两个现实中的一个知识分子

续表

	作者	题目
第四部分： 麦克拉伦与马克思主义	Mike Cole	"全球化资本的必然性"与"不能决定者的苦难"：马克思主义的批判
	Ramin Farahmandpur	彼得·麦克拉伦的革命性的批判教育学
	Dave Hill	为了经济与社会公平的批判教育：一种马克思主义的分析与宣言
	Curry Malott	卡尔·马克思（Karl Marx），激进教育和彼得·麦克拉伦

《彼得·麦克拉伦，教育与解放斗争》呈现了彼得·麦克拉伦的教学和行动主义[①]。它是在麦克拉伦快 60 岁的时候出版的，像是为这位具有强大影响力的学者在这个职业生涯阶段举办的庆功宴。是继《讲述彼得·麦克拉伦：异见之路》之后的第二本由麦克拉伦的朋友、学生、同事等对其进行各方面评价的学术专著。学者们对麦克拉伦最新的关于革命与教育之间的关系、他在委内瑞拉（及其他地方）的国际主义活动以及登顶加州大学洛杉矶分校"肮脏三十"教授榜单的事件的关注和评论。本书的许多文章都反映"肮脏三十"教授榜单事件，这些文章共同表明，从麦克拉伦的角度来看，这种学术压制既需要道德上的愤怒，也需要反霸权的回应。

《联邦危机：马尔库塞、马克思、麦克拉伦》将马尔库塞（Herbert Marcuse）、卡尔·马克思和麦克拉伦的批判理论扩展到分析当前美国日益加剧的不平等现象。它为其替代的联邦范式制定了可行的政治经济战略。该丛书旨在吸引当代大学生和教师对社会学、社会问题、经济学、伦理学、商业伦理学、劳动教育、历史学、政治哲学、多元文化教育和批判教育学等相关学科的兴趣。目的是为变革的政治行动提供信息，以

[①] http：//www.devriesboeken.nl/boeken/onderwijs－algemeen/onderwijskunde/gb/peter－mclaren%2C－education%2C－and－the－struggle－for－liberation－eryaman－mustafa－yunus－edt－9781572737563/，2019－07－26.

及批判的、多元文化的教育学实践，支持麦克拉伦为激进教育者撰写的宣言。

《这拳头呼唤我的心：彼得·麦克拉伦读本（第一卷）》是一部重要的历史和当代文献，记录了麦克拉伦从批判理论到批判后现代主义，再到马克思主义，以及他创立革命性的批判教育学的激烈、丰富而曲折的历程。麦克拉伦极大地增进了我们对民主、权力、政治和教育学之间关系的理解。这本书展示了他的重要工作和贡献，是他学术成就的宝贵档案。这是一本真正令人惊叹的书——充满力量、激情、目标明确，将情感、愤怒和希望巧妙地交织在一起，对正义和平等的要求进行了极具分析性的爆炸性阐述。这本书的预期读者是那些对人类进步抱有希望的人，是那些对提高生活质量的教育抱有希望的人，而不是那些对资本运作缺乏思考和行动能力的人。

《挣脱束缚：激进的教育家彼得·麦克拉伦的生活和时代》是麦克拉伦所著的一本自传体漫画书。在书中插画家迈尔斯·威尔逊和麦克拉伦的创作碰撞出了一幅黑色幽默和励志的自传体素描，描绘了麦克拉伦从出生到革命理论家、学者和活动家的人生演变。这本浓缩的自传艺术地讲述了麦克拉伦的人生故事，同时提供了一个让人们了解批判教育学背后的这个人和思想的路线图。这本漫画书将麦克拉伦的人生历程分为八个阶段，从"少年时代"（"Early Life"）到"愤怒的日子"（"Days of Rage"）。前两个部分，"少年时代"（"Early Life"）和"嬉皮士的日子"（"Hippie Days"）描述了麦克拉伦从唱诗班男孩到一个叛逆、好奇、质疑的年轻人的转变。第三、第四和第五部分，"大学时代"（"College Days"）、"教学时光"（"Teaching Days"）、"与走廊的孩子在一起"（"Working with the Corridor Kids"）描述了麦克拉伦不断质疑一切的本性，并进入行动主义的世界。在很大程度上，威尔逊避免把麦克拉伦放在教室里，巧妙地展示了麦克拉伦的信念，即教育不仅来自阅读，而且来自生活经验。麦克拉伦在走廊里的教学经历，使他认识到通过教师培训和牧师指导方针所宣称的教育学是有缺陷的教育学。在第六部分"研究生学习"（"Graduate Study"）中，威尔逊描述了麦克拉伦在研究生院的经历，对众多学者和理论家作品的阅读和个人参与，记录了麦克拉伦的理论发展。在第七部分"教授时期"（"Professor Days"）中，威尔逊巧妙地描绘了麦克拉伦从一个天真的老师到一个有影响力的教育家的旅程，把麦克拉伦定位为永远的学习者。在第八部分"愤怒的日子"（"Days of Rage"）中麦克拉伦描述了他在安卡拉街头抗议时的可怕经历、他搬到查普曼大学的经历以及在中美洲和南美洲解放神学家被暗杀的经历。这本书以艺术的方式讲述了激进教育家麦克拉伦的一生，同时，也引发了读者对教育的反思，不再把它看作是一套课堂实践，而是把教学看作是一生的旅程，看作是一种生存和发展的方式，看作是为我们自己、我们的学生和我们的未来构建一个社会主义替代方案的政治项目。

《通往无尽之径：彼得·麦克拉伦读本（第二卷）》系马克思主义、社会主义和共产主义教育研究丛书。是继《这拳头呼唤我的心：彼得·麦克拉伦读本（第一卷）》后的关于麦克拉伦的第二卷读本。自20世纪80年代早期以来，麦克拉伦出版了几十本书，发表了数百篇文章，在美洲及其他大陆发表了数千次演讲和讲座（见附录二），并在批判教育学、批判多元文化主义、革命教育学和人文主义马克思主义的不断发展和应用中走在前列。本卷寻求探索在麦克拉伦30多年的学术生涯中所涉猎的这些主题，囊括他最重要的和最有代表性的文章。

（二）以麦克拉伦为专题的书评、期刊论文

对新近出版的著作及时地发表回应性的学术评论，这似乎不是中国教育学界的学术传统。然而，通过对麦克拉伦近40年来学术著作的系统整理，令笔者惊讶的是，自1980年出版《来自走廊地区的呐喊》（*Cries from the Corridor*）至今，麦克拉伦的几乎每一本书都或多或少得到国际诸多领域的学者的回应性评论。不论是从其作者的国别及其所在的学术领域来讲，还是从这些评论所登载的学术刊物的学科门类及其国际影响力来看，它们都构成了一幅壮观的学术图景。为了便于读者一览其详，研究者将其以表格的形式整理如下（见表4）。

表 4　麦克拉伦部分著作所引发的主要学术评论明细列表

麦克拉伦的著作名称（中英文）（首次出版年代）	所引发的学术评论		
	评论人	评论来源	评论时间
《来自走廊地区的呐喊》（Cries from the Corridor）（1980）	Gordon West	Canadian Journal of Education	1981 年第 6 卷第 1 期
《学校教育作为一种仪式表演：迈向教育符号和姿态的政治经济》（Schooling as A Ritual Performance: Toward A Political Economy of Educational Symbols and Gestures）（1986）	DavideE. Purpel	Educational Theory	1988 年第 38 卷第 1 期
	Mary Ann Doyle	Educational Researcher	1996 年第 25 卷第 4 期
	John H. Simpson	Sociological Analysis	1988 年
《学校生活——批判教育学导论》（Life in Schools-An Introduction to Critical Pedagogy in the Foundations of Education）（1989）	Walter Werner	Pedagogy and Phenomenology	1989 年第 7 期
	John M. Novak	The Journal of Education	1989 年第 171 卷第 2 期
	John Smyth	Educational Theory	1990 年第 40 卷第 2 期
	Douglas E. Foley	The SAGE Social ScienceCollections	1990 年
	Ursula A. Kelly	Journal of Education	1991 年第 173 卷第 3 期
	John P. Portelli	Journal of Education	1991 年第 173 卷第 3 期
	Tan Karp	The Radical Teacher	1991 年第 39 期
	Mary Ann Doyle	Educational Researcher	1996 年第 25 卷第 4 期
	蔡幸芬	General Education and Trandisciplinary Research	2009 年第 6 期
	Samuel Day Fassbinder	Journal for Critical Education Policy Studies	2016 年第 14 卷第 1 期
	Derek R. Ford.	Educational Studies	2015 年第 51 卷第 5 期
	E Wayne Ross	Popular Educational Classics	2016 年
	Paul Street Truthout	Institute for Critical Education Studies https://blogs.ubc.ca/ices/2015/02/08/	2015 年 1 月 25 日

续表

麦克拉伦的著作名称（中英文）（首次出版年代）	所引发的学术评论		
	评论人	评论来源	评论时间
《批判教育学和掠夺性文化》（*Critical Pedagogy and Predatory Culture*）（1995）	Mary Ann Doyle	Educational Researcher	1996 年第 25 卷第 4 期
《切·格瓦拉（Che Guevara）、保罗·弗莱雷与革命教育学》（*Che Guevara, Paulo Freire, and the Pedagogy of Revolution*）（2000）	Kenneth Zeichner	Journal of Educational Change	2001 年第 2 期
	John D. Holst	Adult Education Quarterly	2001 年第 51 卷第 2 期
《马克思主义反对教育理论中的后现代主义》（*Marxism Against Postmodernism in Educational Theory*）（2002）	Gabrielle Ivinson	Gender & Education	2009 年第 21 卷第 3 期
	Dan Butin	Teachers College Record	2004 年第 106 卷第 2 期
	Emery Hyslop Margison	Interchange	2005 年第 36 卷第 3 期
	Richard Richard Brosio	Journal ofFish Biology	2014 年第 58 卷第 1 期
《反对全球资本主义和新帝国主义的教学：一种批判教育学》（*Teaching Against Global Capitalism and the New Imperialism: A Critical Pedagogy*）（2005）	David Gabbard & Karen Anijar	https：//mronline.org/2005/10/30/	2005 年 10 月 30 日
	Junrui Chang & Changyong Yang	International Journal of Progressive Education	2006 年第 2 卷第 3 期
	Tyson Edward Lewis	Historical Materialism	2009 年第 17 期
《资本家与征服者：反对帝国的批判教育学》（*Capitalists and Conquerors: A Critical Pedagogy Against Empire*）（2005）	David Gabbard & Karen Anijar	https：//mronline.org/2005/10/30/	2005 年 10 月 30 日
	Eduardo Duarte	Journal of Philosophy of Education	2006 年第 40 卷第 1 期
	John D. Holst	Adult Education Quarterly	2007 年 5 月
	Tyson Edward Lewis	Historical Materialism	2009 年第 17 期

续表

麦克拉伦的著作名称（中英文）（首次出版年代）	所引发的学术评论		
	评论人	评论来源	评论时间
《愤怒与希望：对彼得·麦克拉伦关于战争、帝国主义与批判教育学的访谈》(Rage and Hope: Interviews with Peter McLaren on War, Imperialism, and Critical Pedagogy) (2006)	Tyson Edward Lewis	Historical Materialism	2009年第17期
	David Geoffrey Smith	Interchange	2009年第40卷第1期
《帝国时代的教育学与实践：走向新人道主义》(Pedagogy and Praxis in the Age of Empire: Toward a New Humanism) (2007)	Richard Kahn	Journal of Educational Controversy https://paperity.org/p/84799695/pedagogy-and-praxis-in-the-age-of-empire-toward-a-new-humanism-by-peter-mclaren-and	2008年12月
	Mark Abendroth	Radical Teacher	2008年第82卷
	Goodman, G. S.	Educational Philosophy and Theory	2008年第40卷
《批判消费教育学："末日启示录"阴影下的生活与学习》(Critical Pedagogies of Consumption: Living and Learning in the Shadow of the "Shopocalypse") (2010)	Nicholas D. Hartlep	Educational Studies	2013年第49卷第6期
《反抗的教育学：从复活到革命》(Pedagogy of Insurrection: From Resurrection to Revolution) (2015)	Zane C. Wubbena	http://www.hamptoninstitution.org/pedagogy-of-insurrection-review.html#.XT6g6y2B3FQ	2015年10月8日
	Macris Vicki	Educational Studies	2016年第52卷第4期

续表

麦克拉伦的著作名称（中英文）（首次出版年代）	所引发的学术评论		
	评论人	评论来源	评论时间
《反抗的教育学：从复活到革命》(Pedagogy of Insurrection: From Resurrection to Revolution)（2015）	Lazaroiu George	Review of Contemporary Philosophy https://www.questia.com/read/1P3-4171447271/pedagogy-of-insurrection-from-resurrection-to-revolution	2016年1月1日
	Kevin Russel Magill	Journal for critical education policy studies	2016第14卷第1期
	Emile Bojesen	Policy Futures in Education	2017年第15卷第5期
	Anonymous	Policy Futures in Education	2017年第15卷第5期
	Curry Malott	Policy Futures in Education	2017年第15卷第5期
	Mike Neary	Policy Futures in Education	2017年第15卷第5期
	John Baldacchino	Policy Futures in Education	2017年第15卷第5期
	James D Kirylo	Education Review http://dx.doi.org/10.14507/er.v23.2104	2016年11月16日
	Darko Štrajn.	International Review of Education	2017年第63卷第3期
	Geraldine Mooney Simmie	Journal for Critical Education Policy Studies	2015第13卷第3期
《挣脱束缚：激进的教育家彼得·麦克拉伦的生活和时代》(Breaking Free: The Life and Times of Peter McLaren, Radical Educator)（2019）	Aroline G. Whitcomb	Post-digital Science and Education, https://doi.org/10.1007/s42438-019-00061-y	2019年5月

从这些评论文章所在刊物的出版地来看，其中，既有来自美国本土的教育类的许多知名杂志如《教育杂志》（Journal of Education），也有来自加拿大的《加拿大教育杂志》（Canadian Journal of Education）。从这些刊物所在的学术领域来看，既包括跟教育密切相关的教育测量、教育史、高等教育、教育社会学、教育评价、教育哲学、教育政治学、教育经济学、比较教育和教育政策等诸多交叉学科，也包括许多来自其他学科和其他研究领域的社会专门杂志，由此也足见麦克拉伦著作在西方世界诸多教育领域中的广泛影响。在美国教育研究领域，撰写书评已然成为不少学者进行学术训练的必修课，但许多学者同时针对一本著作反复评论的现象却并不多见。在某种程度上，我们也可以将其视为麦克拉伦著作影响力的一种体现。

在上面表4当中，有五位作者的评论文章都是源于美国学术期刊《教育政策未来》（Policy Futures in Education）的同期作品。究其原因，在2017年该期刊专门为麦克拉伦的《反抗的教育学：从复活到革命》（Pedagogy of Insurrection: From Resurrection to Revolution）开辟了专题论坛。相关期刊为麦克拉伦开辟专题论坛已经不是第一次。2001年麦克拉伦的作品第一次成为专门出版物的主题，例如《国际教育改革杂志》（International Journal of Educational Reform）的特刊《彼得·麦克拉伦的革命性教育学》（The Revolutionary Pedagogy of Peter McLaren）（2001）。2006年《国际进步教育杂志》（International Journal of Progressive Education）在第二卷第三期专门为研究麦克拉伦开辟了专题论坛。包括主编声明这期论坛由10篇文章组成：主编穆斯塔法·尤努斯·厄利曼（Mustafa Yunus Eryaman）的《理解全球资本主义时代的批判教育学和彼得·麦克拉伦》（Understanding Critical Pedagogy and Peter McLaren in the Age of Global Capitalism）、塞缪尔（Fassbinder Samuel Day）的《干扰资本主义魔咒：彼得·麦克拉伦的革命性阈限》（Interfering with Capitalism's Spell: Peter McLaren's Revolutionary Liminality）、瓦莱丽（Valerie）的《想象不可能：反对21世纪美国帝国主义的革命性批判教育学》（Imagining the Impossible: Revolutionary Critical Pedagogy Against the 21st Century American Imperium）、索然塔·胡（Suoranta Juha）和毛索·奥利·派卡（Moisio

Olli-Pekka）的《批判教育学作为高等教育的集体社会专业知识》（Critical Pedagogy as Collective Social Expertise in Higher Education）、马丁·格雷戈里（Martin Gregory）的《重建批判教育学：彼得·麦克拉伦对集体工作的贡献》（Remaking Critical Pedagogy: Peter McLaren's Contribution to a Collective Work）、普菲里欧·布拉德·J.（Porfilio Brad J.）的《转变的可能性：批判性研究和彼得·麦克拉伦》（The Possibilities of Transformation: Critical Research and Peter McLaren）、盖博·大卫（Gabbard David）的《彼得麦克拉伦与3R：反思，抵抗和革命》、丹真·诺曼·K.（Denzin Norman K.）的《唐宁街的秘密备忘录与真相政治：一段表演文本》（The Secret Downing Street Memo and The Politics of Truth: A Performance Text）、肖尼西·迈克尔·F.（Shaughnessy Michael F.）的《对彼得·麦克拉伦的采访：对世界现状的评论——2005》（An Interview with Peter McLaren: Comments on the State of the World – 2005）、常君睿（Junrui Chang）和杨昌勇（Changyong Yang）的《反对全球资本主义和新帝国主义的教学：一种批判教育学》（Review on Teaching against Global Capitalism and the New Imperialism: A Critical Pedagogy）书评。主编穆斯塔法·尤努斯·厄利曼写道："作为执行主编，我很高兴能将这期特刊奉献给彼得·麦克拉伦的作品和批判教育学的未来，批判教育学已经并将被麦克拉伦的革命性愿景所塑造。"[1]

（三）以麦克拉伦为专题的访谈文集

无论是国内学者还是国外学者都倾向于对于某个学术领域做出突出成就、发挥突出影响的学者以采访或对话的形式增进对他的了解。几十年来，麦克拉伦接受过数百次广播、电视、网络采访。报纸、杂志的访谈更是不计其数，除了很多散布在各种期刊、报纸、网络上的访谈之外，为了让他的作品更容易被人理解、更有助于传播，以下是对于麦克拉伦访谈所编辑而成的访谈集（见表5）。

---

[1] Mustafa Yunus Eryaman, "Understanding Critical Pedagogy and Peter McLaren in the Age of Global Capitalism", *International Journal of Progressive Education*, Vol. 2, No. 3, 2006, p. 7.

表5　　　　　　　　麦克拉伦访谈集访谈主题列表

所属访谈集	访谈者	访谈主题
《红色研讨会：教育理论、文化政治和教育学的激进探索》（2005 年）(Red Seminars: Radical Excursions Into Educational Theory, Cultural Politics, and Pedagogy)	Angela Calabrese Barton	资本主义、批判教育学和城市科学教育
	Glenn Rikowski	反对资本教育的革命教育学：当今关于资本主义教育的电子对话
	Marcia Moraes	异见之路：对彼得·麦克拉伦的采访
	Mitija Sardoc	愤怒与希望：彼得·麦克拉伦的革命性教育学
《愤怒与希望：对彼得·麦克拉伦关于战争、帝国主义与批判教育学的访谈》（2006 年）(Rage and Hope: Interviews with Peter McLaren on War, Imperialism, and Critical Pedagogy)	Michael Pozo	走向批判的革命教育学
	Mitija Sardoc	愤怒与希望：彼得·麦克拉伦的革命性教育学
	Lucia Coral Aguirre Munoz	资本的全球化、批判教育学和"9·11"之后的余波
	Marcia Moraes	异见之路：对彼得·麦克拉伦的采访
	Shirley Steinberg	批判多元文化主义和民主教育：与彼得·麦克拉伦和乔·金切罗的对话
	Gustavo Fischman	挑战与希望：多元文化主义作为革命实践
	Kris Gutierrex	持不同意见与变革的教育学：关于后现代性、社会背景以及文学政治的对话
	Mashhood Rizvi	一个激进的教育家对媒体的看法
	Mashhood Rizvi	社会正义与解放教育
	Dianne Smith	大众文化与教育学
	Angela Calabrese Barton	资本主义、批判教育学和城市科学教育
	Glenn Rikowski	反对资本教育的革命教育学：当今关于资本主义教育的电子对话
	Glenn Rikowski	当今的反资本主义教育学
	Kenneth McClelland	行走在阻力最大的道路上：彼得·麦克拉伦异议教育学
	Michael Shaughnessy	彼得·麦克拉伦与辩证法的自由
	Glenn Rikowski	重新审视批判教育学

续表

所属访谈集	访谈者	访谈主题
《这拳头呼唤我的心：彼得·麦克拉伦读本》（2015年）（*This Fist Called My Heart: The Peter McLaren Reader*）	Kris Gutierrez	一场关于后现代性、社会语境与政治的对话
	Shirley Steinberg	批判多元文化主义和民主教育
	Gustavo Fischman	挑战与希望：多元文化主义作为革命实践
	Curry Malott, Pierre Orelus	打破阶级斗争的枷锁
	Luis Charles-Huerta, Marc Pruyn	作为革命实践的批判教育学
	Glenn Rikowski	后现代主义，虚无主义和尼采，人力资本和劳动力，资本主义中劳动力的社会生产，马克思主义，社会运动与批判教育学，个人历史、知识生活和教育
《后数字时代通信：对批判教育学、解放神学以及信息科技的跨界反思》（2019年）（*Post-Digital Correspondences: Cross Border Reflections on Critical Pedagogy, Liberation Theology and Information Technology*）	Petar Jandrić	革命性的批判教育学是脚踏实地走出来的：在一个许多世界共存的世界里
	Petar Jandrić	网络学习的批判性挑战：利用信息技术为人类服务
	Petar Jandrić	从解放到救赎：革命性的批判教育学与解放神学相遇
	Petar Jandrić	马克思与解放神学：辩证唯物主义与基督教精神
	Petar Jandrić	保罗·弗莱雷与解放神学：批判教育学的基督教意识
	Petar Jandrić	我们必须拯救自己：处于并反对全球新自由主义法西斯主义的革命性的批判教育学
	Petar Jandrić	我们想要别人想要的东西：安·兰德（Ayn Rand）、勒内·吉拉德（Rene Girard）和贪婪的模仿
	Petar Jandrić	席特哈尔塔（Siddhartha）在《真实的甜点》中遇见了耶稣：《人类世与基督教生态教育学》
	Petar Jandrić	后数字时代的科学与教育

麦克拉伦于2005年和2006年分别编辑出版了被广泛引用的采访合集《红色研讨会：教育理论、文化政治和教育学的激进探索》（Red Seminars: Radical Excursions into Educational Theory, Cultural Politics, and Pedagogy）（以下简称《红色研讨会》）①和《愤怒与希望：对彼得·麦克拉伦关于战争、帝国主义与批判教育学的访谈》（Rage and Hope: Interviews with Peter McLaren on War, Imperialism, and Critical Pedagogy）（以下简称《愤怒与希望》）②。此外，由马克·普鲁恩和路易斯·M. 韦尔塔·查尔斯于2015年编辑出版的《这拳头呼唤我的心：彼得·麦克拉伦读本》（This Fist Called My Heart: The Peter McLaren Reader）（以下简称《这拳头呼唤我的心》）③有三分之一的篇幅是两位学者对麦克拉伦的访谈和对话。2019年由麦克拉伦和佩塔·詹德里克（Petar Jandrić）④编辑出版了《后数字时代通信：对批判教育学、解放神学以及信息科技的跨界反思》（Post-Digital Correspondences: Cross Border Reflections on Critical Pedagogy, Liberation Theology and Information Technology）（以下简称《后数字时代通信》），这本书是基于2011—2019年麦克拉伦和佩塔·詹德里克（Petar Jandrić）之间关于批判教育学、解放神学、信息科技等有关问题的访谈而形成的通信往来。

这些访谈为我们提供了一扇洞见世界上最具影响力的批判教育家之一的麦克拉伦的思想和人性的窗户。成为研究批判教育学、教育社会学、批判理论、文化研究、政治学、多元文化主义、后殖民主义和教育的社会基础等不可或缺的资源，对于读者了解麦克拉伦在全球资本主义、帝国主义、社会正义的多元文化教育、流行文化和城市教育、哲学、马

---

① McLaren P., *Red seminars: Radical excursions into educational theory, cultural politics, and pedagogy*, Cresskill, New York NY: Hampton Press, 2005.

② McLaren, P. ed., *Rage + hope: interviews with Peter McLaren on war, imperialism, + critical pedagogy*, New York, NY: Peter Lang Publishing, 2006.

③ Luis Charles-Huerta and Marc Pruyn, *This Fist Called My Heart: The Peter McLaren Reader*, Information Age Publishing Inc, 2015.

④ 佩塔·詹德里克（Petar Jandrić），就职于克罗地亚萨格勒布应用科学大学研究及知识进步研究所（Institute for Research and Knowledge Advancement, Zagreb University of Applied Sciences, Zagreb, Croatia），近年来持续关注麦克拉伦的理论研究进展。

思主义、后数字时代的教育、解放神学等问题的认识上提供了清晰的答案。为本书的写作提供了重要的信息资料。

综上所述，国外所作的麦克拉伦研究，大多还只是根据麦克拉伦的一两本书所做的书评，或者根据麦克拉伦某个时期的思想做的评价，它们充其量只能呈现麦克拉伦批判教育学思想中的一些"亮点"，然而，这些亮点以这种读本的方式凑在一起还显得有些散乱。为此，要想真正理解这些亮点，我们就需要找到隐藏在麦克拉伦批判教育思想之中的那条"主线"，用它来将这些亮点贯串起来，这样，我们才能看清这些亮点的来龙去脉。要想抓住麦克拉伦批判教育学思想的灵魂，找到隐藏在麦克拉伦批判教育学思想之中的那条主线，就需要对麦克拉伦做一种更为整体的把握和更为系统的研究。

三 国内外对《学校生活》的研究概况

《学校生活——批判教育学导论》（*Life in Schools—An Introduction to Critical Pedagogy in the Foundations of Education*）作为一部批判教育学名著，从 1989 年的第一版到 2014 年的第六版，25 年间一共 5 次再版，被翻译成 20 多种文字在全世界流传。自初版后，它很快受到了各方学者的重视，通过谷歌学术检索发现，1989 年当年的被引次数即达到了 784 次之多，到 2019 年 6 月止，被引用次数达近 4000 次，不仅获得广泛的关注、赞誉和肯定，也迎来不断的批评和质疑。作者麦克拉伦也不断地在后续的新版本中及其他的学术研究中充实、扩展其批判教育学思想并对相关的批判与质疑进行相应的回应。

（一）对不同版本变化的关注

《学校生活》这本书是一段永无止境的旅程，因为它的每个新版本都更具深度和广度。诸多学者对于这本书的六个版本的变化进行了关注。

第一，对于思想动态变化的关注。王雁指出："1989 年面世的《校园生活》第一版便是他对自己，对社会和对 10 年前掀起轩然大波的著作的解读的开始，也许我们可以说从《来自走廊地区的呐喊》到 5 次陆续再版的《校园生活》就是一个从爬行到走路的转变。"① 《来自走廊地区的呐喊》提供的是一种原始的、未经解读的、偏向于感性的有关学生、教师、学校的叙述，更多的是一种呈现，而非背后的探索，而《校园生活》是利用理论武器对这些宝贵经验体验的分析和挖掘，每一个新的版本的略微增减，从中读者可以看到麦克拉伦学术轨迹的走向以及思想的变迁。《学校生活》从第一版到第六版，虽然内容产生了显著的变化和扩展，其基本结构相对未变。读者可以通过每一个版本追踪麦克拉伦激进思想的不断进步。在第五版里，麦克拉伦介绍了革命性的批判教育学思想，出版商培生集团（Pearson）最终因此放弃了对此书的出版，不久标登集团（Paradigm）以其极大的包容性拿到了这本书的版权予以出版。② 在第五版中，他试着向我们解释说明残酷的资本主义的持续的全球化及美国地理军事及经济帝国的不断扩张。乔·金奇洛提道："麦克拉伦成为批判教育学领域一位世界闻名的人物的部分原因是这本书的巨大成功。在他游历北美、拉丁美洲、欧洲和亚洲时，他向过去几十年未受美国对外政策侵害的人学习了很多经验教训。他近距离地倾听他们的故事，仔细地研究他们的情况。读者可以很容易地在每个新版本中发现这些研究成果。我对每一个新版本都很着迷，因为更新的文本能让我捕捉到麦克拉伦最新的知识和批判方面的发展动态。"③《学校生活》一直表达解放政治学的思想，批判资本主义、种族主义、文化帝国主义以及不对称的权力关系等弊端，但是早期版本中左倾的后现代主义和政治改革已经被删除了。塞缪尔（2014）认为麦克拉伦对《学校生活》从第一版到目前第六版所作的修订中最重要的，也在持续不断作的是对革命内容文本的完善。④ 在

---

① 王雁：《美国批判教育学者麦克拉伦的学术生命研究》，硕士学位论文，东北师范大学，2013年，第7页。

② McLaren, *Life in Schools: An Introduction to Critical Pedagogy in the Foundations of Education* (SixthEdition), Boulder, CO: Paradigm, 2014, p. 4.

③ Peter McLaren, *Life in Schools: An Introduction to Critical Pedagogy in the Foundations of Education* (Fifth Edition), Pearson Publishers, 2007, p. xi.

④ Samuel Day Fassbinder, "Book Review: Life in Schools: An Introduction to Critical Pedagogy in the Foundations of Education by Peter McLaren", Boulder, CO: Paradigm, 2014, *Journal for Critical Education Policy Studies*, 2014, pp. 228–233.

第一版中,"可能性的语言"没有"批判的语言"论述得那么到位。在后续的版本中尤其是最近的两版中,麦克拉伦更有深度地论述了"可能性的语言",强调革命性的批判教育学。然而很多读者会抵制以破坏资本主义为前提的"可能性的语言",不可否认的是革命性的批判教育学将批判性分析与乌托邦的想法相结合,比任何时候都有更多的可能性。

第二,对于内容变化的关注。麦克拉伦的这本书的每一个新版本都在持续不断地关注最新存在的压迫、社会、政治、经济和教育状况。内容上每个版本都与时俱进。如在这本书第六版中麦克拉伦对世界上最具挑战性的问题如军国主义、新自由主义、资本主义、金融化、技术、环境恶化等给予了最新的评价。汤姆·威尔森(Tom Wilson)和苏珊娜·苏霍(Suzanne SooHoo)(2014)指出第六版语言基础丰富,对政治和经济方面提出了新鲜的、毫无保留的批判:比如,在第五版中他热切地关注了布什(George W. Bush)的阴谋。追随保罗的传统,他对右翼地狱般的复杂生活提出的质疑比他提供的答案多。以经典的保罗·弗莱雷式风格,他针对以下问题提出了诸多质疑:由贪婪的公司企业所创造的新世界、好战的帝国建设者的震慑战术、"不让一个孩子掉队"(No Child Left Behind)的荒谬、标准化教育政策的欺人之谈。麦克拉伦在第五版里记录的这个时代最悲剧的面向之一是"9·11"事件被可笑地利用来创造21世纪的社会、政治和教育的地狱。[①] 在第六版中他的关注点转向了奥巴马(Barack Obama)[②]。在塞缪尔(2016)看来,第六版是目前最易懂的一版。他认为"目前所有的版本中,第六版的个人手法及其整合的导论性主题更适合那些将其作为入门教科书的目标受众。例如,第三版(1998)第一部分的标题是'在落败时代教育的妄想',这样的标题对于那些已经了解美国教育商品化过程的读者是没有问题的,但是对于其他的读者来

---

① Peter McLaren, *Life in Schools: An Introduction to Critical Pedagogy in the Foundations of Education* (Fifth Edition), Pearson Publishers, 2007, p. xii.

② Peter McLaren, *Life in Schools: An Introduction to Critical Pedagogy in the Foundations of Education* (Sixth Edition), Boulder, CO: Paradigm, 2014, p. xiv.

说就可能一头雾水,不知所云"①。

(二)肯定与赞扬

麦克拉伦的这部作品一经问世就引起极大关注,得到了无数的肯定和赞誉。瓦特·维尔纳(Walter Werner)(1989)虽然提出了一些质疑,但是非常支持麦克拉伦的目标并写了一篇极具肯定与赞扬的评论,并总结道:"只有通过《学校生活》这样的书,教师们才能恢复他们的教学效能感,形成集体性的反社会和经济不平等。"②

约翰·史密斯(John Smyth)(1990)年在《教育理论》(Educational Theory)上发表了一篇很长的对《学校生活》的评论,认为《学校生活》是一种批判的民族志,并且与20世纪80年代如潮的对于学校教育的研究和报告作对比,认为麦克拉伦的这本书"既对学校教育展开了理性的论证又具有很强的实证基础。"约翰·史密斯把麦克拉伦的日志与科尔(Kohl)(1961),考泽尔(Kozol)(1967),威利斯(Willis)(1977),赫恩登(Herndon)(1985)的作品以及其他杰出的教学记叙文与民族志相比较,认为麦克拉伦的日志可视为尖刻地激发读者兴趣的真实个人记录,是作者本人作为教师的生命抗争,也是为他的学校的学生的抗争。约翰·史密斯坦言在《学校生活》里,麦克拉伦达到了批判民族志所必须具备所有条件,成为批判民族志的典范。他认为麦克拉伦的这些未删改的日志体叙述让无数的读者体验到了教室经验,让他们间接感受到不断演变的教学思想。③

莱昂纳多·博夫(Leonardo Boff)在为《学校生活》作序时指出,很多巴西人正致力于在学校、社区及整个社会的教育过程中培养具有批判

---

① Samuel Day Fassbinder, "Book Review: Life in Schools: An Introduction to Critical Pedagogy in the Foundations of Education by Peter McLaren", Boulder, CO: Paradigm, 2014, *Journal for Critical Education Policy Studies*, 2014, pp. 228 – 233.

② Walter Werner, "Book Review: Life in Schools: An Introduction to Critical Pedagogy in the Foundations of Education by Peter McLaren", New York: Longman, 1989, *Pedagogy + Phenomenology*, No. 7, 1989, pp. 271 – 277.

③ John Smyth, "Book Review: Life in Schools: An Introduction to Critical Pedagogy in the Foundations of Education by Peter McLaren", New York: Longman, 1989, *Educational Theory*, Vol. 40, No. 2, 1990, pp. 267 – 280.

性的、积极参与社会改造的、有创造性的公民。这本书对于这些巴西人提供了非常肯定的支持。这本书对于巴西教育学的发展可以起到促进作用。[1]

乔·金奇洛认为在右翼取得胜利的状态下,当今的学校生活越来越像地狱生活,他"感谢麦克拉伦为我们提供了观察、思考并帮助我们逃离越来越地狱化的学校的一种方式。对于所有的对这种'大逃亡'感兴趣的人,《学校生活》这本书提供了找寻逃亡之门的路径"[2]。

塞缪尔指出:"有关批判教育学、批判理论、批判媒体分析、批判种族理论和马克思主义批判资本主义领域有很多著作,但是实在是没有这样一部书,这就是为什么《学校生活》是值得一读的。我相当怀疑还会有哪位教育领域的作家敢做麦克拉伦在《学校生活》中所做的。在学术写作中大多数的学者已经把他们作品的潜在读者限定在已经上大学的人群,同时寻求与这一小部分预期的读者建立共鸣的路径。但是这本书却既是面向教师的、也是面向教授的、面向学生的,甚至是面向世界的。"[3]

(三) 批判与质疑

任何一本书历经25年由不同的出版商进行六次再版一定是拥有广泛的喜欢这本书的读者。但是《学校生活》像任何一部与大众持相反立场的作品一样当然会得到很多批判。以下列举一些学者不同视角的批判。

第一,对于日志部分的批判与质疑。瓦特·维尔纳(1989)指出:"他书写的故事确实是学校生活的一部分。但是每天的教室生活不只是一系列的暴力事件,还有日复一日、年复一年每天在一起共处的五六个小时的(正常)时光。我不明白在他的教室里教学对孩子意味着什么,他的教学计划及基本原理是什么。这些片段对于普通孩子的教学几乎没有

---

[1] Peter McLaren, *Life in Schools: An Introduction to Critical Pedagogy in the Foundations of Education* (Sixth Edition), Boulder, CO: Paradigm, 2014, p. xx.

[2] Peter McLaren, *Life in Schools: An Introduction to Critical Pedagogy in the Foundations of Education* (Fifth Edition), Pearson Publishers, 2007, p. xi.

[3] Samuel Day Fassbinder, "Book Review: Life in Schools: An Introduction to Critical Pedagogy in the Foundations of Education by Peter McLaren", Boulder, CO: Paradigm, 2014, *Journal for Critical Education Policy Studies*, 2014, pp. 228–233.

任何启发";"当我阅读这些故事的时候我越发感觉到,这些是以一个记者而非教师的视角写出来的,更适合作为新闻出版物而非教科书。这些情节不断重复,当我读到100多页的时候也没有发现教室生活的其他方面和其他的认识。如此看来,这些日志相对于这本书的长度来说是不合适的。这些故事可以通过精心的筛选节选掉三分之二,然后再详细阐释批判教育学的思想"。[①] 1996年玛丽·安·道尔(Mary Ann Doyle)在《教育研究者》(Educational Researcher)上发表一篇论文,评论包括《学校生活》两个版本在内的麦克拉伦的四部书。玛丽·安·道尔批判道:"一篇篇日志残酷地坦白并揭露细节,麦克拉伦并没有删除粗俗的语言、暴力和咒骂,甚至也没有删去他自己在保证学生平等上的失败尝试。"没有认可麦克拉伦在自身教学上的自我批评,也没有强调麦克拉伦战略性地运用教学日志作为批判和解构的材料来源,玛丽·安·道尔在她的评价中不乏指责的论调:"麦克拉伦努力地与那些最活跃最有反抗性的学生建立团结一致的关系,经常使他陷入矛盾的行为中,即在支持一些学生时却以牺牲另一些学生的情感,有时是以身体安全为代价。"[②] 还有一些学者对于用加拿大的教学状况来分析美国的教育状况是否合适提出质疑。

第二,其他方面的质疑。玛丽·安·道尔(1996)与瓦特·维尔纳(1989)等其他一些读者一样对这本书关于性别问题的薄弱阐述提出了抗议。她们认为麦克拉伦的自我反思看起来更夸张而不够真实。由于他的参考文献和建议阅读的书目大部分是男性批判理论家所作的,因此引起了一些女权主义者如凯莉(Kelly)(1989)[③] 波特利(Portelli)(1989)的强烈不满。[④] 还有很多读者认为这本书的语言过于艰涩难懂,如瓦特·

[①] Walter Werner, "Book Review: Life in Schools: An Introduction to Critical Pedagogy in the Foundations of Education by Peter McLaren", New York: Longman, 1989, *Pedagogy + Phenomenology*, No. 7, 1989, pp. 271-277.

[②] Mary Ann Doyle, "Peter McLaren and the Field of Critical Pedagogy", *Educational Researcher*, Vol. 25, No. 4, 1996, pp. 28-32.

[③] Ursula A. Kelly, "From Text to Textuality: 'Reading' McLaren's Life in Schools", *Journal of Education*, Vol. 173, No. 3, 1991, pp. 8-14.

[④] John P. Portelli, "From Text to Textuality: 'Reading' McLaren's Life in Schools" *Journal of Education*, Vol. 173, No. 3, 1991, pp. 15-27.

维尔纳(1989)指出:"这本书经常让读者承担太多,在书写语言上应该更简单一些,让读者更容易理解那些理论化的东西。"① 还有相当一部分学者和读者认为麦克拉伦的这本书只是提出了若干关于资本主义社会、关于教育学等一系列问题,但是并没有给出答案。一部分学者疑问为什么麦克拉伦作为官方认定的白人却如此批判白人?为什么麦克拉伦信奉革命社会主义政治?为什么麦克拉伦由后现代主义转向马克思主义?包华士(Bowers, C. A.)(1991)在批判麦克拉伦的文章里写道:"把期刊上的文章拼凑在一起,即使是经过最仔细的编辑,也很少会产生一幅关于问题的重叠和不均匀展开的讨论的马赛克。以亨利·吉鲁的《老师作为知识分子》(Teachers as Intellectuals)和彼得·麦克拉伦《学校生活》为例,这是令人失望的马赛克,而不是对一本书的综合和逐步发展的分析。"②

(四) 麦克拉伦对批判与质疑的回应

对于上述的批判和质疑,麦克拉伦在后续版本的书中及一些文章中都给予了相应的回应,有接受、有改进、有解释也有反驳。针对"残酷"地呈现一篇篇日志的质疑,麦克拉伦解释道:"我向读者呈现这份早年的教学日志,就是要告诉各位我的初任经验。我也邀请各位读者以日志后面提供的观点,一起来分析这些教学经验,在各位读者有机会深入阅读随后的章节之前,我不希望读者完全不假思索地称赞我的经验,或者是批判我的作为。我希望在教学日志后面的理论篇章,可以帮助各位了解及进一步分析我的教学作为。"他"相信《学校生活》中的分析能够至少初步并清晰地解释:身处一个选择不多且自身的历史不是为自己所写甚至干脆被历史遗忘的世界中,为什么个体在面临抉择时会做出相应的行为"。③

---

① Walter Werner, "Book Review: Life in Schools: An Introduction to Critical Pedagogy in the Foundations of Education by Peter McLaren", New York: Longman, 1989, *Pedagogy + Phenomenology*, No. 7, 1989, pp. 271-277.

② Bowers, C. A., "Review: Some Questions about the Anachronistic Elements in the Giroux - McLaren Theory of a Critical Pedagogy" *Curriculum Inquiry*, Vol. 2, No. 21, 1991, p. 239.

③ Peter McLaren, *Life in Schools: An Introduction to Critical Pedagogy in the Foundations of Education* (Sixth Edition), Boulder, CO: Paradigm, 2014, p. 32.

针对有些读者对于用加拿大的教学状况来分析美国的教育状况是否合适提出的质疑,麦克拉伦的解释是:"我努力要唤起大家去关注的那些弱势学童,以及那些跟弱势学童在一起挣扎奋斗的老师,他们每天在学校、教室所面对的困境,其实是没有国界的差别的,不管是在加拿大还是在美国,都一样得受其苦。"① "把我的加拿大教学经验整合进来这本书,其实是非常合适的安排,因为我从全美各地收到许多非常正面积极的反应,这些反馈包括来自内城学校的老师、研究生(他们中有许多人是在内城学校任教的全职老师)、教育学院的同人,以及各种不同种族背景的家长。加拿大和美国的教学现状当然有很多差异之处,但是,两个国家的相似性却远远要超过其差异性。最令人感到震撼的反应是,我的教学日志中所反映的经验和处境,确确实实就是美国内城学校的老师共同的感受。这两个国家的老师要共同面对的处境包括:过度拥挤的教室;大量的移民人口涌入;过时落后的教育理论;令人窒息的官僚需求;由上而下的集中控制;基于行为目标以及标准化测试的管理模式;对老师的能力以及在课堂上的判断力缺乏信任,因此这严重降低了老师的教学能力;经费与资源的不足;追踪评价体系;以及基于种族、阶级、性别、残疾等情况设立的专门迎合某一类群体的隐性课程——这样的清单还会源源不断地增加。北美洲大陆上的所有贫民窟学校,跟我所描述的加拿大教学经历非常相似。"②

针对《学校生活》中性别问题论述的薄弱及女权主义者对于忽略女性学者声音的批判,麦克拉伦态度诚恳,并做了一些补救行动。麦克拉伦同意凯莉和她的学生以及波特利等学者关于他在《学校生活》中关于性别问题(与其他的问题相比)缺乏理论深度这一判断。因此,他很关注这个问题。他承认:"虽然我在书中总结了例如安吉拉·麦克罗比(Angela McRobbie)等女性研究者的主要观点,但是我过度概括了她们的论点,几乎没有尝试使用女性理论去批判我作为教师的实践。"他坦言:

---

① Peter McLaren, *Life in Schools: An Introduction to Critical Pedagogy in the Foundations of Education* (Sixth Edition), Boulder, CO: Paradigm, 2014, pp. 31 – 32.

② Peter McLaren, *Life in Schools: An Introduction to Critical Pedagogy in the Foundations of Education* (Sixth Edition), Boulder, CO: Paradigm, 2014, pp. 31 – 32.

"在我对女性学生的描述中,我明显没有成功地避开很多男性教师在主流的制度、文化、社会话语及实践中所形成的性别歧视。我自身的男性立场未能免受性别歧视者社会和文化习惯的影响,这些习惯仍然在教师教育项目以及大多数的公开和私人领域被再制着。我本应该对学生之间的性骚扰进行干预,现在想来我很痛苦。"不仅态度诚恳,麦克拉伦还在后续的写作研究过程中加大了对性别问题的关注,以弥补在《学校生活》中论述的欠缺,他认为:"显然,凯莉对批判教育学是赞同的,对于近期男性理论家的作品也非常了解,因此她在努力地纠正批判教育学有史以来的男性偏见。因此,她和她的学生可能对我最近的尤其关于性别议题的其他作品感兴趣,这些议题我在《学校生活》中论述得并不充分。这些作品主要针对研究生阶段的读者,讨论关于女性殖民化、两性的身体结构、欲望的政治形成、男权观点的滥用等问题。"①麦克拉伦在第二版的附录中介绍了一些有代表性的教育家,如保罗·弗莱雷、亨利·吉鲁、迈克尔·阿普尔、杜威(John Dewey),但是最先介绍的是两位女性学者贝尔·胡克思(bell hooks)和玛克辛·格林(Maxine Greene)的主要思想和代表作品,可见其已经意识到忽略女性学者的错误,并极力在后续的版本及写作中进行弥补。

针对很多读者认为这本书的语言过于艰涩难懂,作为本科英语文学专业出身的麦克拉伦,他在本书的后记中解释道:"我一直有着不同的写作风格,与其他作品比起来《学校生活》并没有呈现那么多,我深受一些被认为过于'文学的'教育书籍和文章的作者所影响。这导致一些读者认为我的写作方法过于华丽及描述手法过多,而其他的读者则欣赏我所选择的用来阐释教育生活的某些维度的语言,这些东西是更多的科学文献很难表达出来的。"②

针对一部分学者和读者认为麦克拉伦的这本书只是提出了若干关于资本主义社会、关于教育学等一系列问题,但是并没有给出答案,麦克

---

① Peter McLaren, *Life in Schools: An Introduction to Critical Pedagogy in the Foundations of Education* (Second Edition), New York: Longman, 1994, p. 270.
② Peter McLaren, *Life in Schools: An Introduction to Critical Pedagogy in the Foundations of Education* (Sixth Edition), Boulder, CO: Paradigm, 2014, p. 256.

拉伦指出:"我知道这本教育学导论提出的问题比回答的问题更多。保罗·弗莱雷常说批判教育学就是提出问题,而不是提供落俗套的答案。找到正确的答案是基于提出正确的问题。我相信新版《校园生活》里我提出的问题正是对于此时此刻我们政治历史的提问。这些问题的提出会加深读者对批判教育学以及创建无剥削社会的政治议程的理解。"①

针对麦克拉伦作为官方认定的白人却如此批判白人,麦克拉伦的解释是:"我对于反种族主义教育学的支持与作为白人的自我厌恶几乎没有什么关系,更多的是因为我认识到忘却白人特权是一个正在进行的、永远不能放弃的工程。我同意新废除主义者废除白人特权的号召,我明确表示白人特权必须废除。马克思人道主义者反对恐怖主义和暴力。废除白人特权意味着忘记白人的特权、停止认同17世纪殖民地——弗吉尼亚所虚构的白种人。"将"作为白人"这种隐形的现象视为有关权力和特权的一组种族化了的社会和文化实践也是笔者要增加第五篇章篇幅的重要原因。笔者想要让"作为白人"的概念更明显可见,以便揭露它的论述,它潜在的文本、它的社会运作以及它的历史和物质状态,这些都在掩饰"作为白人"概念持续、强迫性的宰制现实。我们必须揭开白人的面具,以便让"作为白人"这个论述关系、叙述空间、符号密度和社会与经济关系的切身经历的组合可以被解构、被挑战,而且,简而言之,可以被消灭。"白人概念"必须被废除,因为它就是促使白人主义以及种族化偏见的主要力量。当然,当我说要废除"作为白人"的概念时,并不表示说那些被认为是白人的人都必须要被消灭。他提醒读者:"避免在不假思索的情况下用种族(race)的概念进行任何分析,因为种族并没有任何的生物学上的根基或哲学上的合法性。我同意种族不应当被视为决定智力或人格特质的特定现象。我们不应该赞同或合法化下述的观点:人类的存在就是可以在遗传上将种族团体界定区分的存在,区分的标准就是一种在生物学上的特性或想象的显性外表特性以及特别的文化活动的组合。"②

---

① Peter McLaren, *Life in Schools*: *An Introduction to Critical Pedagogy in the Foundations of Education* (Sixth Edition), Boulder, CO: Paradigm, 2014, p. 28.

② Peter McLaren, *Life in Schools*: *An Introduction to Critical Pedagogy in the Foundations of Education* (Sixth Edition), Boulder, CO: Paradigm, 2014, pp. 193 – 195.

针对为什么麦克拉伦信奉社会主义政治的疑问,麦克拉伦认为:"资本主义显然在结构上已经不符合民主的定义,即使在最低限度上也不符合了,因为它,再也不能包容,更不用说吸收,不符合经济正义与平等的原则。不断的阶级斗争是资本主义社会所固有的,资本主义生产方式在一定程度上是一种令人吃惊的结构性暴力";"挑战资本主义剥削的社会制度一直是一个值得追求的目标。把这错认为是反美主义是不明智的。真实存在的资本主义民主与我们听到的民主党和共和党政治家口中的民主之间的差距在成倍增长。诸如诺姆·乔姆斯基、霍华德·津恩(Howard Zinn)和亨利·吉鲁等一些杰出的政治名人已经针对此问题争论了几十年";"一些读者显然是要否认我的主张,即用民主社会主义取代资本主义的必要性。这是可以预料到的,特别是在美国社会。当我第一次开始把我的想法放在第一版的《学校生活》时,我就应该已经开始反对这种专制了。它在很大程度上已经是我与那些在权力上受侵害的群体之间的国际合作,这让我相信,民主与资本主义是不相容的,只有社会主义才是我们拯救地球的必要条件"。①

针对为什么由"批判教育学"更名为"革命性的批判教育学"、由后现代主义转向马克思主义的疑问,麦克拉伦认为,革命性的批判教育学是要帮助学生了解劳动力如何被资本主义的统治阶级所剥削,劳动阶级具有破坏与改组阶级关系的能力与潜力,而不是只能顺从于资产阶级。因而理解与进行阶级斗争也是教育中重要的一环,当然此种斗争是以爱为基础的,而不是暴力革命。阶级斗争着重在打破阶级再制的不平等现象,反对不公平的竞争。②麦克拉伦对保罗·弗莱雷和切·格瓦拉"将理论化为实践"的抗争行动情有独钟,可以说麦克拉伦在批判教育学这个词中加上"革命"两个字,用意就是在于强调"实践"。强调阶级的存在,是对后现代主义的质疑,是向马克思主义的回归,但同时不是简单地企图用阶级解释一切,只是反对在没有阶级在场的情况下谈论种族、

---

① Peter McLaren, *Life in Schools: An Introduction to Critical Pedagogy in the Foundations of Education* (Sixth Edition), Boulder, CO: Paradigm, 2014, pp. 256–257.

② Peter McLaren, *Life in Schools: An Introduction to Critical Pedagogy in the Foundations of Education* (Sixth Edition), Boulder, CO: Paradigm, 2014, pp. 256–257.

性别等社会议题。因此，麦克拉伦呼吁"革命性的批判教育学"的研究必须重回马克思早期的文本以及马克思主义人道主义的传统，务求将理论与实践联系起来。

四 已有研究成果评价

综上所述，麦克拉伦身为美国批判教育学的奠基性人物，国外对他的研究显然不少，而且褒贬不一。但是洋洋大观的研究并不意味着对麦克拉伦及其思想的透彻理解。究其原因，一方面是因为麦克拉伦独特的诗化而又满是激情的论述方式，在很大程度上掩盖了对其思想的洞察；另一方面，也更为根本的，乃是思想的本质所必然导致的对思想之解读的永不停息。国内对麦克拉伦的研究远不如国外的广泛和精深，不过我们仍能够从上述国内的研究倾向中明显感觉出中国教育界所关注的问题。国内外已有的对麦克拉伦的研究大多是从他的思想体系中抽取一两点来谈，而未能整体地去把握麦克拉伦的思想。对于《学校生活》这本在批判教育领域举足轻重的一本名著的研究也仅限于对每一个版本孤立的不成系统的研究，尚未出现将六个版本对比整合并与麦克拉伦的整个批判教育学思想发展结合起来的研究。本书以《学校生活》为线索，在收集了大量的文献与独家资料之后试图去把握麦克拉伦的思想脉络，从他的思想发展来动态地整体地把握他的批判教育学理念，系统地梳理出麦克拉伦的批判教育学思想与实现社会拯救之间的关系，而不是抽取他的某些个别的思想观点来进行论述。这也是本书较为突出的一个创新之处。但是国内外既往研究对于麦克拉伦的理论定位、学术认识和研究的重点以及对《学校生活》的分析与评价，将为本书研究命题的寻找和研究重点的确立提供重要参考，它同时也将使得本书的研究找到自己的研究内容，并为构思与之相适应的研究设计提供重要理论依据。

第三节 研究方法

一 文献法

文献法是以往人们研究教育学人物时所普遍采用的研究方法。本书的研究也建立在这种文献研究的基础之上：首先，通过系统阅读麦克拉伦主要的一些英文原著，捕捉麦克拉伦作品中的关键词汇和经典命题，了解麦克拉伦开展批判教育学研究的提问方式和核心思想。其次，通过研读和梳理介绍、评价与研究麦克拉伦的相关著作与文章，将麦克拉伦的批判教育学思想放置在一定的学术传统之中审视其学术地位和理论价值，凸显麦克拉伦与同时代人物相比在思想上所具有的共性特征与个性品质。最后，结合以上两个方面，归纳麦克拉伦批判教育学思想的核心问题和主导思想。在这个过程中一共阅读400多万字的外文原版文献资料，翻译整理其中较有价值的文献近90万字。此外，本书所采用的文献研究的独特性在于：在国内除了台湾版的《学校生活》一本译著之外，没有麦克拉伦著作的其他中文译本，因此，本书是在阅读麦克拉伦英文原著的基础上展开的，而不是像大多数研究人物思想的研究者那样可以直接阅读中文译本进行参考。

但是仅仅从文献的角度研究一个人的思想未免有失偏颇，在条件允许的情况下，将来自被研究者本人的叙说、故事、观点与文献资料结合在一起会使研究更客观、更全面。因此，需要访谈法来支撑。

二 访谈法

本书采取将文献法与访谈法相结合的方式来开展研究，而对在世教育家的研究也使得这种必要性具有了现实的可能性。研究者从2014年开始至今每年都有机会与麦克拉伦夫妇在中国接触一个多月的时间，其间还有13个月的时间在美国麦克拉伦所任教的查普曼大学做访问学者。研究者从2014年一共对麦克拉伦教授做了60次正式访谈，累计访谈时长约150小时，整理访谈资料约30万字（访谈提纲见附录一），获取了麦克拉伦思想动态和对作品诠释的最新的第一手资料。除了这些正式访谈，随着研究者与麦克拉伦的关系从陌生到熟悉到成为好朋友的逐步密切，在日常接触中还生产了许多非正式的访谈。很多时候已经不仅仅是简单的对事先设计好的问题的一问一答，而是在研究者与麦克拉伦的日常接触交流中，麦克拉伦给研究者讲的故事、人生经历、对某些问题的观点、分享的视频影视资料等都对研究者认识这位教育家提供了切实的帮助。除此之外，研究者与麦克拉伦教授也通过邮件往来访谈一些问题，研究期间一共收到麦克拉伦教授152封邮件回复。如此，对人物作品的解读就不至于完全受到文本本身的控制。

第一章

产生及发展历程

当研究者越来越深入地研究麦克拉伦的作品和思想时，就越来越觉得把他的作品和他的人生故事与生活经历联系起来是非常重要的。因为对于麦克拉伦人生中的重大事件及主要影响人物进行了解和分析，能够有效地探求他人生中的重大事件或主要影响人物与其思想之间形成的关联性。于是研究者把了解到的麦克拉伦的人生故事、经历与他每一个时期思想的变化进行串联，以形成麦克拉伦批判教育学思想的产生及发展历程的全面图景。麦克拉伦的作品跨越了他丰富的一生，呈现了一条复杂的发展曲线。有时它近似于一条直线，但有时它会做出明显的曲线和转向。无论是好是坏，麦克拉伦唯一真正武断或自以为是的思想和价值观是他对人类的爱和关怀。

第一节 《学校生活》前的思想萌芽

一 从事教师工作前

（一）青春期的家庭变故带来的愤怒

麦克拉伦1948年8月2日出身在多伦多一个保守的工人阶级家庭。麦克拉伦是家里唯一的孩子。然而，在他众多堂、表兄弟姐妹的簇拥下，他从不感到孤独。这些兄弟姐妹分别是他父亲的姐姐和母亲的四个姐姐和两个哥哥的孩子。麦克拉伦的母亲弗朗西斯·特蕾莎·伯纳黛特·麦克拉伦（Frances Teresa Bernadette McLaren）先是做家庭主妇，后来又当了电话接线员。他的父亲劳伦斯·奥姆德·麦克拉伦（Lawrence Omand

McLaren）是一名第二次世界大战老兵，从一名电视销售人员晋升为加拿大东部飞利浦电子（Phillips Electronics）的总经理，让他们暂时步入到了中产阶级。他们从安大略省的农场搬到汉密尔顿、多伦多和其他大都市。"我父亲生病之前，我们的房子有一个老式的普通的日光浴室，晚上电视上演侦探故事和西部片、曲棍球游戏、喜剧节目；简而言之：一种电视里呈现的未知生活的快乐和幸福。"麦克拉伦的母亲是天主教徒，他的父亲是长老会教徒，麦克拉伦的童年在圣公会的保守传统中度过，平顺无奇。

1965 年，麦克拉伦 16 岁，他就排除了在大公司工作的可能性。那时他的父亲刚满 50 岁，他担任总经理的那家电子公司的新老板决定解雇所有 45 岁以上的主管人员，在此经营策略下，他的父亲被解雇。作为独生子女，在麦克拉伦步入青春期的时候他眼看着他的父亲，一位"二战"老兵、加拿大皇家工程师，被飞利浦解雇后成为劳动后备军，被迫从事一系列低薪工作；他的母亲，一个家庭妇女，当他父亲的肺气肿使得他不可能继续电子商店的兼职工作时，为了贴补家用不得不出去做电话接线员的工作。他父亲的被迫提早退休并提早去世使得他开始对资本主义不仅失望而且愤怒，他发誓永远远离商业世界，不会把他的一生交给一个公司或者所谓的一身"西装"。

（二）高中生活的迷茫与批判思想的萌芽

从十几岁时，麦克拉伦就对文学、诗歌、文艺批评、哲学和社会科学很感兴趣。中学时，麦克拉伦因创作科幻小说而获得写作奖；高中时，他拍了 35 毫米的电影，想成为一名电影导演。但是麦克拉伦回忆："像许多在 50 年代和 60 年代在加拿大长大的年轻人一样，我觉得自己越来越像被某些迟钝的令人头脑麻木的大众惯例所吞噬，特别是我的上学经历，因为我喜欢区分上学（being schooled）和受教育的经历（experiencing an education）。"[①] 高中时期的麦克拉伦已经意识到，"教育需要培养批判性

[①] Peter McLaren, *Life in Schools: An Introduction to Critical Pedagogy in the Foundations of Education* (Sixth Edition), Boulder, CO: Paradigm, 2014, p.267.

或批判意识"①，一直困扰他的是"拥有智慧或能够把概念应用到分析中并不能赢得同龄人的很多关注"②，他经常思索的问题是"为什么我在学校的生活看起来是如此败坏的空洞的，为什么我会如此漫无止境地痛苦，为什么创新行为、创造力和智慧似乎是禁止的并被许多教师认为是不明智的，是一种不明智的认识论"③。但在他高中的最后一年确实有两位极好的、例外的老师哈罗德·伯克（Harold Burke）和丹尼斯·哈钦（Dennis Hutcheon）。"在我高中时代的后期有两位了不起的老师使我对教育产生了兴趣。直到我上高中的最后一年我才开始不讨厌学校。"④伯克先生会在课堂上阅读戏剧。他大声地朗读莎士比亚和当代戏剧中的部分段落，他认为这是良好的教育中不可或缺的一部分。在他的课上学生们认真地试图理解民意和悖论、日常生活中的刻板印象和创新。从伯克先生那里麦克拉伦学会了欣赏修辞的力量，并经常以大胆的言语参与辩论。麦克拉伦进入大学学习莎士比亚文学及日后的写作风格与伯克的影响不无关系。哈钦开发了沟通和媒体课程，研究马歇尔·麦克卢汉（Marshall McLuhan）的理论和思想。他也是一个天主教教徒，很大程度上是由于他的影响麦克拉伦开始对神学感兴趣，他想加入神职，却没有太多的宗教信仰，于是他放弃了这个想法，"注定让自己生活在当时被认为是正常的世界的世俗的边缘——在那样的世界里男人不再被要求戴帽，但在一些冰冷的石头建筑里无菌办公室隔间成为了很多我的同龄人的惨淡命运"⑤。那时的麦克拉伦经常让自己沉浸在一个阅读世界里——尼采（Nietzsche）、加缪（Camus）、萨特（Sartre）、汉森（Hesse）、杰内特

---

① Peter McLaren, *Life in Schools: An Introduction to Critical Pedagogy in the Foundations of Education* (Sixth Edition), Boulder, CO: Paradigm, 2014, p. 267.

② Peter McLaren, *Life in Schools: An Introduction to Critical Pedagogy in the Foundations of Education* (Sixth Edition), Boulder, CO: Paradigm, 2014, p. 267.

③ Peter McLaren, *Life in Schools: An Introduction to Critical Pedagogy in the Foundations of Education* (Sixth Edition), Boulder, CO: Paradigm, 2014, p. 267.

④ Peter McLaren, *Life in Schools: An Introduction to Critical Pedagogy in the Foundations of Education* (Sixth Edition), Boulder, CO: Paradigm, 2014, p. 267.

⑤ Peter McLaren, *Life in Schools: An Introduction to Critical Pedagogy in the Foundations of Education* (Sixth Edition), Boulder, CO: Paradigm, 2014, p. 267.

(Genet)、普鲁斯特（Proust）、诺思洛普·弗莱（Northrop Frye）、马歇尔·麦克卢汉（Marshall McLuhan）、哈罗德·英尼斯（Harold Innis）、格雷戈里·鲍姆（Gregory Baum）——在这个阅读的世界，麦克拉伦回忆道："我徒劳地试图将自己从多伦多郊区威洛代尔（Willowdale）的日常生活中解脱，那里对我来说是一片悲观和绝望的土地。迪伦·托马斯（Dylan Thomas）、林赛（Vachel Lindsay）、莱昂纳德·科恩（Leonard Cohen）、欧文·莱顿（Irving Layton）的作品，当然，还有垮掉的诗人（Beat Poets）的作品，帮助我暂时从我的不适中脱离，但青春的酷烈的绝望还是不可避免地压倒我。"[1]在高中的最后一年，麦克拉伦对那些似乎枯燥无味、毫无意义的课程不再抱有幻想。尽管如此，他还是在学业上取得了很好的成绩。他会想象自己站在一节课前，尽可能地教授最具影响力的一课。凭着天真烂漫的自负，他确信他能成为一名完美的老师。此时，批判思想的种子和成为一名教育工作者的种子悄悄地埋入麦克拉伦的心灵而逐渐萌芽。

（三）叛逆齐克的影响

超凡叛逆的齐克（Zeke）把生活在循规蹈矩世界里的麦克拉伦带进多元的叛逆世界。麦克拉伦回忆[2]说："对于一个在郊区梦想的保护下长大的刻板的孩子来说，我很少冒险去超越被认为是'正常'的范围。我的 T 恤白得可以和汰渍的广告媲美。我的网球鞋吱吱作响。绑在我的奥斯汀迷你车（Austin Mini）上的是一个放冲浪板的行李架，我一直在谈论要买冲浪板，但从未买过。""私下里，我觉得自己被困在了一个循规蹈矩的世界里，为自己的想法比米色斜纹棉布裤更黑暗而感到内疚。我的生活在横向漂移，等待着一些事情的发生。在我遇见齐克的那一天之前，我的未来看起来是可以预测的，也是残酷的。"1966 年，也就是麦克拉伦 17 岁那年，对他而言独特的是他遇到了齐克。他回忆道："那是 1966 年的夏天，在那之后，我生命里那令人安慰的虚饰永远被刮掉了。齐克坐

---

[1] Peter McLaren, *Life in Schools: An Introduction to Critical Pedagogy in the Foundations of Education* (Sixth Edition), Boulder, CO: Paradigm, 2014, p. 267.

[2] 本段所有的回忆内容均来自本文作者对麦克拉伦的访谈及日常对话交流。

在柳树下的路边，读着杰克·凯鲁亚克（Jack Kerouac）的小说。"在学校里，每个人都知道齐克。齐克是他认识并走近的："第一个不墨守成规的人，一半是恶棍，一半是圣人。"齐克重视交谈的艺术。"即使是和齐克简短的讨论，也有可能让你的大脑被扭断。他很少和你说话——更多的是在嘲笑你，试图用新的方式重新安排你的思维模式。这可能是一种痛苦或兴奋的经历。""齐克属于另一个世界，教育了我的感官，使我摆脱了日常生活的无聊，使我从舒适的情感麻醉中苏醒过来。"齐克借给他几十本书，里面充满了奇怪的滑稽动作和反英雄人物——《第二十二条军规》（Catch 22）、《姜人》（The Ginger Man）、《在路上》（On the Road）、《飞越杜鹃巢》（One Flew over the Cuckoos'Nest）和弗朗索瓦·维隆（Francois Villon）的诗歌。麦克拉伦开始把家庭作业放在一边。"我很快就发现我不可能跟上我的学习进度。为了齐克的陪伴，或者为了进入齐克让我进入的那个叛逆的世界，我很容易放下一本书或推迟一项学习任务。相比之下，学校似乎常常是一个无关紧要的干扰，阻碍而不是促进我的教育。"他从未见过像齐克这样的人。作为一个成长于电子时代的郊区年轻人，麦克拉伦觉得他的身体和精神已经被工业时代的道德所束缚。而齐克超凡的才华和拉伯雷式的世界观帮助他减轻了他生命中的混乱与不安，在工业社会道德的枷锁中得以从麻醉的情绪中进一步苏醒。

（四）反战行动与约克维尔的反主流叛逆生活

高中毕业后，1968年麦克拉伦在大学入学前搭便车去了美国加利福尼亚州（State of California）的旧金山（San Francisco）和洛杉矶（Los Angeles），加入了萌芽中的反主流文化。他参加了反越南战争的抗议活动，会见了黑豹党（Black Panthers）、蒂莫西·利里（Timothy Leary）和艾伦·金斯伯格（Allen Ginsburg）。他还认识了一些非裔美国人，开始了解马丁·路德·金（Martin Luther King），了解黑人在美国所受到的不公平待遇。他回忆[①]说："在20世纪60年代，尤其是在1968年搭便车到旧金山（San Francisco）和洛杉矶（Los Angeles）抗议越南战争之后我开始

---

① 本段的回忆内容均来自本书作者对麦克拉伦的访谈及日常对话交流。

关注政治。"他和其他嬉皮士住在破旧的房子里，几乎每天晚上，他和他的旅伴们都要接受联邦调查局的审问，因为他们想要逮捕那些反对征兵的人。他回忆道："在那个时期，我开始写短篇小说和诗歌。在艾伦·金斯伯格（Allen Ginsburg）的诗歌指导和帮助下，我开始探索内心世界，将自己的创作潜力置于身体享受之上：当蒂莫西·利里（Timothy Leary）和我一起服用迷幻药，陷入了 LSD① 的错误中时，艾伦·金斯伯格（Allen Ginsburg）劝我停止服用迷幻药，专心写作。"1968 年麦克拉伦从美国加利福尼亚州（State of California）回到加拿大多伦多（Toronto）后，加拿大爆发种族冲突，麦克拉伦身体力行参与抗争行动，被警方逮捕关进监狱，并被用探照灯夜训及毒打，他后来回忆说，在那里，他"得到了一个重要的政治教训。开始意识到新一代的人正在出生，生活将变得不容易，特别是如果你的生活与主流社会背道而驰的话"。更让麦克拉伦体会到公权力沦为欺压群众的工具的悲哀。也让他体会到实践的重要性，"我在多伦多（Toronto）反主流文化的日子里学到的一件事是，你得通过行走来开创自己的道路，在你走这条路之前，你必须先成为这条路。这就是实践的本质。"

1968 年从美国回到加拿大的麦克拉伦进入多伦多大学（University of Toronto）学习杰弗里·乔叟（Geoffrey Chaucer）②、贝奥武夫《Beowulf》③、中世纪英语和古英语。他还和著名雕塑家罗伯特·唐宁（Robert Downing）一起上过一门课，讨论了那座城市的各种雕塑。唐宁曾开着麦克拉伦的跑车在多伦多兜风，他们在那里抽大麻。麦克拉伦意识到他没有雕刻家的真正天分。大学一年级的时候，麦克拉伦加入了约克维尔村（Yorkville Village）的嬉皮士社区，成为一个兼职人员，叫作"周末行者"（weekender）。他花了相当多的时间和各种丰富多彩的、有创造力的人在一起，他们的生活在富有表现力的解放仪式和病态的自我毁灭仪式之间矛盾地跳跃。毒品成为许多人生活的一部分。对许多人来说，毒品

---

① LSD：麦角酰二乙胺，是一种迷幻药。
② 杰弗里·乔叟（Geoffrey Chaucer）（1343—1400 年），被誉为英国文学之父，被广泛认为是中世纪最伟大的英国诗人。
③ 贝奥武夫《Beowulf》：有记载的最早的一部英国文学作品。

似乎是一种象征性的媒介,可以穿透自由与限制之间的矛盾。麦克拉伦告诉研究者:"约克维尔在我的记忆里更多的是一种心态、是一条我们经常在那里闲逛的街道,我们尝试每种我们能想到的毒品……约克维尔是一个你有可能发展出一种更敏锐的眼光的地方,在这里你可能理解文化的生产,有时能够识别出大众文化生产与寻求自我的人如车手、润滑工、嬉皮士、少女流行音乐迷、有时聚集在咖啡馆和廉价旅馆里的政治组织者等之间的巧合,或者有时只是在街上闲逛,假装我们都在创建一个脱离传统道德规范和生活方式束缚的自由的新社会,但从根本上说,我们是正在寻找毒品、性、摇滚以及我们的 20 分钟热度……约克维尔对我们来说更多的是一种生活方式和反主流文化。"在那里,他被邀请参加多伦多地下艺术社区的派对和聚会——麦克拉伦还清楚地记得在一个派对上,一位年轻女子表演了《七面面纱》(The Dance of the Seven Veils)的舞蹈——并对嬉皮(反)文化生产的双重话语的动态有了第一手的了解:"所有人都在假装我们正在创造一个新社会,摆脱传统道德和生活方式的束缚,但基本上我们是在寻找毒品、性、摇滚和我们 20 分钟的名气。"①为了测试自己的意志力,麦克拉伦整晚都在普莱森特山公墓(Mount Pleasant Cemetery)吸食迷幻药,一边背诵他最喜欢的迪伦·托马斯的诗《挽歌》(Lament),一边试图在墓碑周围跳希腊佐尔巴舞(Zorba),墓碑似乎也跟着他起舞。给他印象最深的是真人大小的石头天使的舞蹈动作。经过反思,麦克拉伦认为,这段插曲与他无法将自己与 20 世纪 60 年代毒品文化中自我毁灭的方面保持距离有关。但是麦克拉伦回忆在那时"可以自信地说,我觉得我已经吸收了垮掉派诗人(Beat Poets)的精神,我可以在一个脑壳里装下尽可能多的地下文化,而又不至于发疯——诗歌,哲学,东方宗教,迷幻药,各种各样的新思想——格式塔理论(gestalt theory),理性情绪疗法(rational emotive therapy),欧文·莱顿,莱昂纳德·科恩(Leonard Cohen),乔妮·米切尔(Joni Mitchell),巴菲·圣·

---

① Peter McLaren, "Self and Social Formation and the Political Project of Teaching: Some Reflections", in B. J. Porfilio, D. Ford, Leaders in Critical Pedagogy: Narratives for Understanding and Solidarity, Rotterdam: Sense, 2015, p. 132.

玛丽（Buffy Saint-Marie），格雷戈里·贝特森（Gregory Bateson），R. D. 莱恩（R. D. Laing），一般语义（general semantics），精神分析（psychoanalysis），无政府主义（anarchism），约翰·C. 莉莉（John C. Lilly），神秘（the occult），金字塔能量（pyramid energy），神学（theosophy），达尔文（Darwin），禅宗（Zen Buddhism），布鲁姆斯伯里集团之迹（the Bloomsbury group），达达主义（Dadaism），麦克卢汉（McLuhan），戈登快脚（Gordon Lightfoot），路加福音与使徒（Luke and the Apostles）"。或许，是在这段日子里，由于麦克拉伦开始接受大量的反主流文化的思想、事物与情境，对其日后能在大学时期彻底地研究多元文化与包容差异的思想起到了奠基的作用。

而后麦克拉伦从多伦多大学辍学，因为他的一些好朋友如齐克染上了海洛因毒瘾，他想逃离他们的影响，搬到安大略（Ontario）的基钦纳（Kitchener），在那里他决定在滑铁卢大学（University of Waterloo）完成他的英语学位。1973年，麦克拉伦在滑铁卢大学获得英国文学学士学位，专攻伊丽莎白时期的戏剧。一些越南战争的抵抗者在加拿大旅行，帮助麦克拉伦进一步了解了战争和美国帝国主义政治的历史。1974年麦克拉伦搬回多伦多，结婚生子，出于养家的需求，他选择考取教师资格证，开始准备工作。所以他进入当时被称为多伦多师范学院（Toronto Teachers College）的学校，这个学院是在1953年由师范学校（Normal School）演变而来。麦克拉伦得到教从幼儿园到八年级的资格认证。[①] 那之后他变得政治化了，主要是受那些由于越南战争而离开美国的美国人以及最终他在滑铁卢大学和多伦多大学的教授们所影响。

二 从事教师工作后
（一）初为人师的使命感及校长吉姆·蒙哥梅力的影响

1974年取得教师资格证后，作为一名新晋教师，麦克拉伦花了一年

---

① 因为麦克拉伦获得的是证书而不是大学学位，所以他在博士课程期间选修了额外的课程，所以在他获得博士学位的同一年，他还获得了教育学学士学位（B. Ed. Degree）。在多伦多大学安大略教育研究所（Ontario Institute for Studies in Education）攻读博士学位之前，他已经在布鲁克大学（Brock University）获得了教育学硕士学位（M. Ed Degree）。

时间在多伦多郊外的一个富裕的社区教书。虽然他喜欢学生，喜欢教学，但他觉得自己是多余的。他认为这些学生本来就享有财富和社会权力，即使他们的老师不在，他们也可能在社会上过得不错。他们的富裕背景几乎保证了他们在体制内的成功。他想拯救工薪阶层的孩子，他想在最需要他的地方服务，所以他搬到了贫困的、多元文化的、多种族的、高密度的多伦多近郊贫民区，这里被称为"简·芬奇走廊"（Jane-Finch Corridor）。简·芬奇走廊是一个多民族、多语言的工人阶级聚居的郊区，那里的公共住宅区功利主义色彩严重，没有任何生态合理性可言。这种高密度的景观展示了资本主义如何集中不平衡的经济和城市发展。在简·芬奇走廊，麦克拉伦学习了由他的老师同伴们发展起来的教学方法和教学策略，他觉得这些策略在很大程度上只是当一天和尚撞一天钟的策略。然而，他想要在这个充满挑战的环境超越"生存"的需求，为了学生的利益，他开始了一系列的教学实验。作为一名年轻的教师，麦克拉伦学到了一个重要的教训，那就是教学不是一份工作，而是一种使命——在他的职业生涯的剩余时间里，他会珍惜与学生之间温暖的个人关系。

麦克拉伦在简·芬奇走廊教学时吉姆·蒙哥梅力（Jim Montgomerie, 1930—1985）在简·芬奇走廊的浮木公立学校（Driftwood Public School）当校长。吉姆担任过加拿大智障协会的副执行长、安大略智障协会执行长以及负责"为生命付现"彩券运动的募捐工作召集人等工作，虽然已经有许多报道称赞他在人道关怀方面的努力，但是，麦克拉伦认为真正让吉姆成为他那个时代的传奇人物的原因，其实是他在担任内城学校校长那种开拓、创新的领导风格。吉姆的哲学理念是"喜爱每一个和所有的孩子"。麦克拉伦常常记得吉姆成功地让每一个老师养成对所有学生的尊重。他是一位"喜爱拥抱人的校长"，在解放人类的精神和想象力以及拯救儿童命运的战斗中，他一直坚定，无人能及。他大部分的时间，都在努力地尝试用各种方法，鼓励教育行政界的同人和老师放弃古老的教学方法，面对迅速变迁的社会，让学校可以重新改造为自由的实验场。麦克拉伦评价道："吉姆是一位才华横溢的老师，他以爱融入实务技能或抽象概念的教学，对他而言，教学基本上是一种道德的工作，他的教学方式是完美教学行动最有力的比喻。他终其一生都在实践和赋予爱更真实的意义。他一直是一个不轻言放弃、勇往直前的人。他那充满活力的个性、无人可比的智慧，以及锐敏、智慧的洞察力，让吉姆成为一个足以让全国人尊敬的教育领袖。"[1]对许多从事教育工作和社会改革的人而言，吉姆的教育理念一直是策动人们前进的力量。吉姆用自己的示范，遗留给老师们一个崭新的教学和领导模式，他的传奇人生始终激励着麦克拉伦要不断前进。他用他的一生体现给麦克拉伦的启示是，实现人道目标有很多的可能性。因此，即使麦克拉伦最终离开贫民区的教学阵地，他的一生也都在为教育公平的人道目标而战斗。

（二）《学校生活》前身——《来自走廊地区的呐喊》的成功带来理论缺乏的挫败感

麦克拉伦在简·芬奇走廊目睹的贫困对他产生了深刻的情感影响，他对学校缺乏能够帮助学生解决贫困、种族主义、当地社区暴力及其他问题的教育感到遗憾。麦克拉伦并没有私下抱怨，作为回应，麦克拉伦诚实而残酷地描述了简·芬奇走廊社区所面临的挑战，对加拿大学校体系内的"野蛮的不平等"进行了猛烈的揭露，而这些"不平等"对于那些因特权和发展不平衡而与这个世界隔绝的人来说是"看不见的"。1980年麦克拉伦基于他在简·芬奇走廊的教学经历出版他的第一本日记体专著——《来自走廊地区的呐喊》（Cries from the Corridor）。这本书相当详细地描述了他在"黑板丛林"（Blackboard Jungle）[2]里的真实学校经历，你会惊叹于这位年轻教师生动的描述、敏锐的洞察力和对中小学校园生活的真实写照。它不仅揭露了加拿大内城郊区的阴暗面，还打破了困扰各地教育部门的自满情绪。这是一本完全真实、极其诚实的小书，吸引了大量的流行媒体评论，随即这本书成为加拿大的畅销书，被《麦克林》（Maclean）杂志和《多伦多太阳报》（Toronto Sun）列入年度瞩目好书的名单，成为意外的畅销书。麦克拉伦说过："就我对学校和社会的看法而

---

[1] Peter McLaren, *Life in Schools: An Introduction to Critical Pedagogy in the Foundations of Education* (Sixth Edition), Boulder, CO: Paradigm, 2014, p. 118.

[2] "黑板丛林"（Blackboard Jungle），指城市学生经常打架、秩序混乱的顽童学校。在那些日子里，北约克的简·芬奇走廊地区的学校被贴上了这样的标签。

言，有《一本关于学校的杂志》（This Magazine is About Schools）是我在60年代末到70年代读到的，由乔治·马泰尔（George Martell）和萨图·里普（Satu Repo）编辑。这个杂志社位于罗奇代尔学院（Rochdale College），我经常和朋友们在那里闲逛、聚会。我想它是在70年代的某个时候改名变成《这本杂志》（This Magazine）的。我从那本杂志中学到了很多，但我从不订阅，而是断断续续地阅读。我从未被左翼组织招募，也从未真正尝试加入政治团体，甚至是学校的活动人士。这也许可以解释为什么我在1979年开始职业写作时，没有一个连贯的理论轨迹。"①然而，麦克拉伦和其他人一样心跳加速惊讶它成为全国畅销书，甚至引发全国性的关于加拿大贫民区学校状态的辩论。《加拿大教育学刊》（the Canadian Journal of Education）这样描述《来自走廊地区的呐喊》日常的、日记风格的陈述，按年月顺序记载的短小的教室情节，偶有穿插一些教育学上的担忧思考，比如麦克拉伦意识到标准化方法或课程作用甚微，而需要更多相关的"自由的""开放的"或者"进步的"风格的话题……但是几乎整本书所包含的都是对赤裸的真实的原生态报告，几乎记录了每一场可想象的教室恐怖秀。②像戈登·韦斯特（Gordon West）这样经验丰富的教育学院教师们都认为这本书"学术效用有限"，因为它描绘了"个性化和孤立的学生"，没有分析"工人阶级生活"的整体背景。③戈登·韦斯特评论这本书"理论性、学术性有限"，但是"它提出了一些重要的问题，呈现了教室生活的阴暗面，不是很好的民族志（研究）"，"几乎缺乏任何分析"，但是他发表的对这本书的评论的关键部分认为这本书指出了困扰整个（教育）领域的（教育）不足的症状："问题个体地存在于被孤立的学生中，甚至当整个班级或学校全是这样的学生……分析随意地止于家庭、糟糕的居住环境或者邻居，并未分析这背后的原因，甚至也没有追问他们是怎么变成那样的……假如，这些显而

---

① 本段内容来自本书作者对麦克拉伦的访谈及日常对话交流。
② West, G., "Book Review: Cries from the Corridor: The Suburban Ghettoes", *Canadian Journal of Education*, No. 6, 1981, pp. 81, 82.
③ West, G., "Book Review: Cries from the Corridor: The Suburban Ghettoes", *Canadian Journal of Education*, No. 6, 1981, pp. 81, 82.

易见的问题和残酷的状况是工人阶级生活不可否认的部分,那么人们可能会问,谁会在他们的这种持续状态中获得利益?他们发挥了何种功能?由于在加拿大工人阶级组织和意识的缺乏,在何种程度上这种阶级分析在加拿大的教育工作者当中是不受欢迎的?这样的组织如何能够为教育进步做出贡献?《来自走廊地区的呐喊》是一部典型的未对这些问题提供答案的加拿大教育作品,尽管如此,值得赞扬的是它确实成功地呈现了这些问题的原始资料。"[1]麦克拉伦的这本日志体专著比任何一本加拿大教育书籍都更能引起公众对内城学校困境的关注。然而,作为一个有抱负的学者,麦克拉伦困扰于大肆渲染的媒体将这些儿童和社区贴上"失败者"的标签,被理论家和学术界的吹毛求疵所刺痛。

麦克拉伦表示写作这本书的最初目的仅仅是想让他那些处于备受压迫境况的学生受到关注,这些学生住在附近的公共住房里(政府为低收入者所建的住房);想让那些在过度拥挤的、经费不足的教室里感到无助的教师得到关注。他希望权力部门能够提供城市学校更多的资源来缩减班额,根据学生的需求发展一些项目,落实一些文化回应的课程和教育学。但是麦克拉伦认识到这本书的问题只是对他的教学经历的一种新闻式描述,几乎没有分析,以至于一直被解读为他是在指责学生和他们的家庭在学校内外的生活中充斥的暴力。当许多评论家和同事都质疑麦克拉伦在《来自走廊地区的呐喊》一书中的真实性时,吉姆·蒙哥梅力站出来支持麦克拉伦,对多伦多星报(Toronto Star)说:"那本书里面的每件事都是真的。"[2] 他跟记者大卫·维雅诺(David Vienneau)说:"我保证所有的事情都发生过……我们应当把它看作是弱势学童在呐喊,只是它是经由一个有这种见地、视野的人,把他们看到的故事说出来而已。"[3] 吉姆·蒙哥梅力比大多数的人都清楚,学校教育根本不是一种价值中立

---

[1] West, G., "Book Review: Cries from the Corridor: The Suburban Ghettoes", *Canadian Journal of Education*, No. 6, 1981, pp. 81, 82.

[2] Peter McLaren, *Life in Schools: An Introduction to Critical Pedagogy in the Foundations of Education* (Sixth Edition), Boulder, CO: Paradigm, 2014, p. 118.

[3] Peter McLaren, *Life in Schools: An Introduction to Critical Pedagogy in the Foundations of Education* (Sixth Edition), Boulder, CO: Paradigm, 2014, p. 118.

的机构,而且往往与民主的真义和目的为敌,通过阶级、资本和权力、特权的关系,学校剥夺了弱势学生的能力,让学生学习到的是他们无能改造自己。但是当时的麦克拉伦对学校与社会关系的认识还处在很浅的层面,缺乏这种有深度的理论认识。最终他开始讨厌这本书——也许"厌恶"是一个更好的词——但他觉得在美国出版这本书是有用的,前提是它要附有一种延伸的自我批评。于是他决定辞去简·芬奇走廊地区的教职,重新回到大学学习相关理论。他接下来的在批判教育学上的学术研究可以看作是对戈登·韦斯特所提出的那些未解问题的直接回应。批判教育学追问谁会在维系贫困和不平等的状态中获益。更广泛地说,批判教育学超越了表面的意思,获取了理解以下问题的智慧:根本原因、社会环境以及行动过程、实践及话语对个人的影响。

(三) 研究生学习阶段的理论增长与反思

《来自走廊地区的呐喊》出版的同年,麦克拉伦辞去贫民区的教职工作,被多伦多大学安大略教育研究所(Ontario Institute for Studies in Education)录取为博士生。研究生学习阶段是麦克拉伦在贫民区教学经历之后理论大幅增长及开始对教育前线反思的时期。他花大量的时间阅读批判理论领域的书籍,如马克思主义革命理论、文化研究、女权主义研究;学习到有关的批判理论之后,麦克拉伦发觉当时他对于贫民区教学时的观点,是如同帝国主义职员的身份,遵循着"自由与民主"口号的资本主义论述的指导,进行的是一种服务于主流文化、官方知识课程的教学。麦克拉伦也发觉到他以前的教学方法,是脱离了弱势学生的背景情况并去责备他们弱势的自身文化的。他开始意识到,教师可以受益于理论上和政治上的脚踏实地——他们通过实际的、非正式的、隐性的知识和正式的理论结构折射自己的经历——这意味着发展一个连贯的实践哲学的艰难工作。《来自走廊地区的呐喊》的写作和研究生阶段的学习让麦克拉伦变得激进起来,他逐渐摆脱了"有经验的"老资格贫民区教师的名声,逐渐弥补他在批判性理论、马克思主义理论、文化研究和女权主义研究方面的不足。

他与他的博士导师理查德·考特尼(Richard Courtney)建立了密切的关系。理查德·考特尼是世界上最重要的儿童戏剧权威之一。他也是一名职业演员。理查德·考特尼教授凭借他的著作和声誉获得了学术职位以及在英国皇家艺术学会（Royal Society of Arts）的会员资格。但是他只有一个学位——利兹大学（Leeds）的学士学位。因此，那些成果较少、影响力较小的教授瞧不起理查德·考特尼教授，因为他们拥有博士学位。当麦克拉伦在理查德·考特尼的指导下攻读博士学位时，他被梅西学院（Massey College）理事会选为初级研究员。

在梅西学院，麦克拉伦参加了著名学者的晚宴和讲座。初级研究员被要求穿一件黑色长袍，偶尔要尝试用拉丁语、德语或法语交谈（麦克拉伦在第二语言方面完全失败了）。这激起了他对仪式的兴趣。同年，他从圣公会（Anglican Church）改信罗马天主教（Roman Catholic Church）。那一年，他成功完成了自己的论文——《教育是一种仪式表演》（Schooling as a Ritual Performance）的答辩，麦克拉伦被选为英国皇家艺术、制造和商业学会（Royal Society of Arts, Manufactures and Commerce）会员[1]。1984年获得加拿大多伦多大学（University of Toronto）渥太华教育研究所（Ottawa Institute of Education）的博士学位。尽管麦克拉伦在毕业时作为一名学者获得了广泛的认可，麦克拉伦认为自己很幸运能被任命为布鲁克大学教育学院的特别讲师——作为为期一年的代课教师。麦克拉伦在与教师和教育工作者的合作中开始发展保罗·弗莱雷的思想，他的学生对他的评价褒贬不一。尽管院长答应延长他的合同一年，但因为他们在政治和教育方面产生矛盾，麦克拉伦在合同期满后被解雇了。

他申请了加拿大各地的工作，但由于他直言不讳的政治观点，以及他对保罗·弗莱雷的作品和亨利·吉鲁作品的赞赏，许多大学的招聘委员会认为麦克拉伦可能会成为他们眼中的刺。亨利·吉鲁因发展批判教育学而被波士顿大学（Boston University）的校长开除，他的终身教职之争在1983年引起了美国全国的关注。最终亨利·吉鲁获得了俄亥俄（Ohio）迈阿密大学（Miami University）的教职。

---

[1] 本杰明·富兰克林（Benjamin Franklin）、亚当·斯密（Adam Smith）、查尔斯·狄更斯（Charles Dickens）、威廉·霍加斯（William Hogarth）和古格里莫·马可尼（Guglielmo Marconi）等著名历史人物也都曾是英国皇家艺术、制造和商业学会的会员。

(四) 与亨利·吉鲁一起合作为北美批判教育学奠基

1985 年,麦克拉伦在亨利·吉鲁的邀请下离开他的出生地加拿大去美国迈阿密大学(Miami University)的教育学院任教,并担任助理教授一职。在此期间,他和亨利·吉鲁一起工作长达八年之久,两人共同致力于多元文化主义与文化研究方面的探索,并见证了批判教育学在北美的诞生和成长。他曾告诉本书作者:

> 从我还是博士生的时候算起,最开始对我产生较大影响的是亨利·吉鲁,然后亨利·吉鲁帮我引见了保罗·弗莱雷。……在这群从美国来的学者当中,我对亨利·吉鲁最为钦佩。亨利·吉鲁的异于常人的魅力,他的独特的演讲方式,他的飞速旋转的大脑会让你不由得心生钦佩。……所以从 1985 年,我们的合作就开始了,之后他为我做的第一件事就是在芝加哥举办的全美教育年会(American Educational Research Association,AERA)上将我介绍给保罗·弗莱雷。(来自本书作者对麦克拉伦的访谈)

此时的麦克拉伦也在教育与文化研究中心兼职,并由于杰出的表现获得知名学者的荣称。在他到达迈阿密大学后,麦克拉伦继续他博士期间对仪式的教育价值的研究,出版《学校教育作为一种仪式表演:迈向教育符号和姿态的政治经济》(Schooling As A Ritual Performance: Toward A Political Economy of Educational Symbols And Gestures)(1986)一书并获奖,后来再版了几个版本并以多种语言再版。麦克拉伦在这段时期的研究兴趣反映了他在(伊丽莎白时代)戏剧、电影、艺术方面的本科学习,以及他在课程、民族志和人类学方面的研究生学习。他对学校环境中的种族、性别、性、政治和宗教认同的形成以及揭示了学校教育的意识形态基础的对立的文化政治特别感兴趣。他回忆说:"我的作品不再那么直接针对课堂本身,而是更多地关注诸如政治、文化和种族认同、反种族主义、多元文化教育、白人至上的政治、抵抗和流行文化、学校作为抵抗和顺从的工具的仪式等问题;主体性与解放神学的形成。我开始关注批判教育学更大的关联性。换句话说,我觉得批判教育学在实践解决方案方面通常是难以捉摸的,但在解决生活中长期存在的剥削情况方面却非常重要。我意识到,有些老师可以写关于课堂的文章,这样做可以提供比我更多的实际见解,但我可以为重新思考教育文献中批判性教育学的概念和政治领域做出贡献。"[1]

麦克拉伦和亨利·吉鲁将批判教育家保罗·弗莱雷的作品和思想带到了北美,而麦克拉伦为英国劳特利奇出版社(Routledge)编辑的两本书则将保罗·弗莱雷的作品重新介绍给了英国的教育工作者和社会工作者。他们的合作者和朋友多纳尔多·马塞多(Donaldo Macedo)翻译了保罗·弗莱雷的主要作品;麦克拉伦和亨利·吉鲁写了介绍、后记和解释。但他们不仅普及了保罗·弗莱雷;相反,他们积极地在保罗·弗莱雷作品的基础上,为我们今天所知的北美批判教育学的传统奠定了基础。麦克拉伦在这一时期的主要著作包括《批判教育学、国家与文化斗争》(Critical Pedagogy, The State, And Cultural Struggle)[2]、《保罗·弗莱雷:批判遭遇》(Paulo Freire: A Critical Encounter)[3]、《批判素养:政治、实践和后现代主义》(Critical Literacy: Politics, Praxis, And The Postmodern)[4]、《解放的政治:保罗·弗莱雷之路》(Politics of Liberation: Paths from Freire)[5]、《跨越国界:教育学与文化研究的政治学》(Between Borders: Pedagogy And The Politics of Cultural Studies)[6]。从1983年到1986年麦克拉伦把主要研究重心放在了城市教育场域的民族志研究,这一时间

---

[1] Pozo M., "Toward a Critical Revolutionary Pedagogy: An Interview with Peter McLaren", (2003) [EB/OL]. http://facpub.stjohns.edu/~ganterg/sjureview/vol21/mclaren.html, 2018-04-02.

[2] Giroux H. A., McLaren P., eds., *Critical pedagogy, the state, and cultural struggle*, Albany: ny Suny Press, 1989.

[3] Leonard P., McLaren P., eds., *Paulo Freire: A critical encounter*, New York: ny Routledge, 1993.

[4] Lankshear C., McLaren P., eds., *Critical literacy: Politics, praxis, and the postmodern*, Albany: ny Suny Press, 1993.

[5] McLaren P. L., Lanshear C., eds., *Politics of liberation: Paths from Freire*, NewYork: ny Routledge, 1994.

[6] Giroux H. A., McLaren P., eds., *Between borders: Pedagogy and the politics of cultural studies*, New York: ny Routledge, 1994.

跨度包含了他在加拿大布鲁克大学（Brock University）和一年的俄亥俄迈阿密大学（Miami University）的教育经历。①

第二节 《学校生活》后的思想发展

一 《学校生活》第一版——反思与申辩

麦克拉伦与亨利·吉鲁合作，深入进行文化研究，以及哲学和批判理论的语言学转向，后来被称为后现代主义。在他30岁晚期和40岁早期，麦克拉伦成为一位年轻有为的学者，肩负着一项激动人心的使命。麦克拉伦与亨利·吉鲁、保罗·弗莱雷、多纳尔多·马塞多、乔·金奇洛等伟大人物并肩合作，在北美开创了我们今天所知的批判教育学运动。1989年，当他还是一名教育学副教授的时候，他被迈阿密大学教育学院和相关专业授予著名的"驻校学者"（Scholar-in-Residence）称号，成为历史上拥有这一称号的最年轻的人。在迈阿密教书的时候，麦克拉伦建立了几十年来一直等待主流认可的概念和理念。

随着他的作品离教室越来越远，他的思维变得越来越复杂，他可能成为了对自己畅销书《来自走廊地区的呐喊》最严厉的批评者："从批判理论家的角度来阅读它，使我面临着自己思想和教学上的不足；它让我直面自己作为一名年轻教师的处境，在不知不觉中违背了我的解放意图。读到这些日志对我来说是痛苦的，因为我意识到，我并没有对许多批评免疫，这些批评现在都指向不公正的教育实践，以及种族主义、性别歧视和文化帝国主义社会形态的运作。"②

于是，1989年他以一种创新的、细致入微的理论评论把他的畅销书《来自走廊地区的呐喊》一书加入左派的分析观点，以及一些政治理论观点，改写成极度受到赞扬的《学校生活》一书。在这本书中他甚至自我反省"以前的他"也是"资本主义的帮凶"。在《学校生活》的序言中，

---

① 王雁：《美国批判教育学者麦克拉伦的学术生命研究》，硕士学位论文，东北师范大学，2013年，第10页。

② Peter McLaren, *Life in Schools: An Introduction to Critical Pedagogy in the Foundations of Education* (Sixth Edition), Boulder, CO: Paradigm, 2014, p.32.

麦克拉伦承认戈登·韦斯特的批评："我的日志主要是描述，没有理论框架来帮助读者更好地理解我力图描写的状况……由于没有把我的教学日志置于一个批判的理论情境中，我不能充分地揭示权力和知识在资产阶级利益对抗工人阶级时是如何运作的。结果，我冒险让读者强化了对'黑板丛林'中学校的样态及处于经济不利地位的学生在行为构成方面的刻板印象。我也处于把贫困社区描述为暴力、仇恨、毫无人道和尊严的熔炉的危险中。"[1]麦克拉伦认为在没有提供对型塑他的学生及家庭的社会、经济状况的批判性分析就出版日志，是一个"极其严重的错误"[2]，他已经将这个错误转变成一个引人注目的教育学契机。这本书邀请读者去阅读、批判、解析他早期的教学实践。这本书见证了他作为教育者由一个聚焦社会、教育改革的自由人文主义者彻底变成一个主张革命实践、通过批判教育学进行社会革命的马克思主义人道主义者的转变。

这本书应该被看作是三部曲的第三部分，也是麦克拉伦前两部作品《来自走廊地区的呐喊》（1982）和《学校作为一种仪式表演》（*Schooling as a Ritual Performance*）（1986）的辩证结果。前者是关于他在多伦多市区一所"郊区贫民窟"学校教书四年的日志体作品；后者是他博士论文的学术成果，是对多伦多市内一所天主教学校的葡萄牙和意大利裔学生进行的一项理论丰富的人种学研究。据他自己承认，如果他的第一本书缺乏理论，那么他的第二本书在学术上就很有价值。[3] 然而，这两种方法都广受好评，并引发了积极的反响。在这本书中他试图结合和扩展这些早期书籍的能量和洞察力，"开发一种语言，通过这种语言，教育者和其他人可以解开和理解学校教育之间的关系，更广泛的社会关系以及历史上学生为学校带来的需求和竞争力"[4]。完成这个项目是一个巨大的工程，

---

[1] Peter McLaren, *Life in Schools: An Introduction to Critical Pedagogy in the Foundations of Education* (Sixth Edition), Boulder, CO: Paradigm, 2014, p. xxv.

[2] Peter McLaren, *Life in Schools: An Introduction to Critical Pedagogy in the Foundations of Education* (Sixth Edition), Boulder, CO: Paradigm, 2014, p. xxv.

[3] Purpel, D., "Review article – Schooling as a Ritual Performance" *Educational Theory*, Vol. 38, No. 1, 1988, pp. 155–163.

[4] McL Peter McLaren, *Life in Schools: An Introduction to Critical Pedagogy in the Foundations of Education* (First Edition), New York: Longman, 1989, p. vii.

对于介绍性的文本来说实在是太多了。然而，本书在指出"我们在课堂上所做的事情与我们为建设一个更美好的社会所做的努力之间的关系"①这一更为温和的任务上做得更好。它以一种新颖而富有创造性的方式来完成这项更容易完成的任务。截至2016年，该书已是第六版。韦恩·罗斯（Wayne Ross）说："在六个版本中，该书的基本结构保持相对一致，尽管内容发生了显著的变化和扩展。麦克拉伦思想的激进进步可以追溯到这本书的每一个版本。《学校生活》总是反映出一种解放的政治，批判资本主义的滥用、种族主义、性别歧视、同性恋恐惧症、文化帝国主义和不对称的权力关系，但早期版本中所体现的左倾后现代主义和改革政治已经被一扫而光。"②

麦克拉伦以一种让大多数初入校门的教师难以安心的方式，将《学校生活》划分为四部分。他明确地想要激怒读者，并很快就成功了。他热情洋溢的介绍试图解构这样一个神话：对许多人来说，甚至对所有人来说，学校正在使世界变得更美好。相反，他认为，在一个衰落的时代，富人变得更富，穷人却得到孩子；反过来，获得更差的生活可能性，不仅不受学校教育的影响，反而会因为学校教育而恶化。在当前绝望的乐观论调的表面之下，他混合使用了定量数据和文化批判的数据，来攻击那种想当然的消费主义和鼓励这种轻率过程的个人主义心态。"贪吃的小脑袋埋在沙子下面"的社会生活态度巧妙地暴露了它对我们集体生活可能性的质量的影响。

第二部分约占全书的一半，是对《来自走廊地区的呐喊》的一个略加编辑的版本。如果书的第一部分是有意错开天真，那么这一部分将会让那些对贫民窟学校日常生活的绝望一无所知的人感到震惊。麦克拉伦在学校的四年不仅让读者走进像 T. J.、杜克、肌肉小姐（Muscle Lady）这样的学生的课堂，而且也让读者看到了作者的内心，他哭着要把他们

---

① Peter McLaren, *Life in Schools: An Introduction to Critical Pedagogy in the Foundations of Education* (First Edition), New York: Longman, 1989, p. x.

② Ross E. W., "Peter McLaren, Life in Schools: An Introduction to Critical Pedagogy in the Foundations of Education (1988)", in J. L. De Vitis, ed., *Popular educational classics: A reader*, New York: Peter Lang, 2016.

的兴趣和精力与教育联系起来。这里有大量的信息指出了在压倒性的情况下成为一个"反思实践者"的困难。麦克拉伦在本节的最后提供了他的反思分析。在书的后面，他评论了这些经历和反思。第二部分结尾的后记不仅包括文体上的修改，也包括实质性的修改。这篇后记最初写于1981年的《来自走廊地区的呐喊》上，是麦克拉伦在第一波对他的书的反应之后的反思。公平地说，当时他还处在一个被他自己描述为"资产阶级民粹主义与自由主义人文主义相结合"的阶段[1]。原文很好地说明了这一点。然后，他认为学校是"学生可以自豪地学习的地方"[2]，"学生需要按照自己的方式学习"[3] 并需要"以平等和进步教育的名义……面对压迫的结构"[4]。在《学校生活》中，这些相同的术语解读起来不一样。他认为学校是"学生可以被增能赋权的地方"[5]，"学生首先需要按照他们自己的方式来学习，然后学习如何批判性地超越这些方式，以增强自己和他人的能力"[6]，并需要以平等和民主的名义面对压迫的结构"[7]。从自豪到权力，从学生到批判超越，从进步教育到民主，这些概念和政治运动是麦克拉伦重新构建的反思、研究和写作发展的一部分。

在本书的第三部分，麦克拉伦试图将前一部分的具体经验与批判教育学的一些抽象理论概念联系起来。他综合了传统中几个重要思想家的观点。他在承认批判性信念的不同之处的同时，认为它们"在赋予无权

---

[1] Peter McLaren, *Life in Schools: An Introduction to Critical Pedagogy in the Foundations of Education* (First Edition), New York: Longman, 1989, p. 232.

[2] Peter McLaren, *Cries from the corridor: The new suburban ghettos* (revised with new Afterword), Ontario: Methuen, 1982, p. 209.

[3] Peter McLaren, *Cries from the corridor: The new suburban ghettos* (revised with new Afterword), Ontario: Methuen, 1982, p. 209.

[4] Peter McLaren, *Cries from the corridor: The new suburban ghettos* (revised with new Afterword), Ontario: Methuen, 1982, p. 210.

[5] Peter McLaren, *Life in Schools: An Introduction to Critical Pedagogy in the Foundations of Education* (First Edition), New York: Longman, 1989, p. 152.

[6] Peter McLaren, *Life in Schools: An Introduction to Critical Pedagogy in the Foundations of Education* (First Edition), New York: Longman, 1989, p. 153.

[7] Peter McLaren, *Life in Schools: An Introduction to Critical Pedagogy in the Foundations of Education* (First Edition), New York: Longman, 1989, p. 153.

者权力和改变现有不平等的目标方面是一致的"①。这种统一的变革主义视角的基本原则随后被应用于政治、文化和经济，变熟悉的为陌生的。虽然没有以系统或详尽的方式处理，但本节提供和分析的主要概念和原则所做的正是它们所宣称的：它们激发并提供了一种超越社会学想当然的方式。在最后一节中，麦克拉伦使用了上一节中提出的观点，以批判的眼光回顾了他自己的教学。例如，他"谴责他没有能力更早地指出种族主义，并将其与社会结构的根源联系起来"②。他引用了亨利·吉鲁著作中的一些概念，认为学校需要被视为民主的公共领域，教师应该成为具有变革性的知识分子（transformative intellectuals）。然而，这一道德和意志观点的含义仅仅是粗略的。

　　研究产生弱势群体的原因是一回事，制定切实可行的教育策略是另一回事。最后一章的语言，出现了一些关于佩德罗·阿尔贝祖·坎波斯（Pedro Albezu Campos）波多黎各高中和可能性的语言的问题。这所学校作为一个民主领域是如何运作的？教师作为变革的知识分子，采取了什么具体行动来阐明解放的可能性？为什么有洞察力的批判和乌托邦式的推测比构建甚至描述具体的可能性要容易得多？如何用可能性的语言更好地为教育工作者为维护、保护和加强这一激进项目而进行的长期斗争做好准备？批判者的批评空间在哪里？有先见之明的教授所宣扬的乌托邦计划的局限性和危险性是什么？我们该如何开始呢？我们将何去何从？

　　在《学校生活》中的问题既不容易提出也不容易回答。没有人，包括麦克拉伦，会说追求激进的教育学将是容易的，只是它是非常值得的。它以一种新颖而精辟的方式提供了许多东西。现状受到挑战；我们被带到教室里，面对着许多人不愿讨论的情况；提出了追求解放可能性的展望；以授权增能的语言作为传播思想的方法。它应该是激发思想和对话的丰富来源。麦克拉伦让我们把这场辩论的焦点放在社会的不良结构以

---

① Peter McLaren, *Life in Schools: An Introduction to Critical Pedagogy in the Foundations of Education* (First Edition), New York: Longman, 1989, p.160.

② Peter McLaren, *Life in Schools: An Introduction to Critical Pedagogy in the Foundations of Education* (First Edition), New York: Longman, 1989, p.212.

及它们与学校生活的关系上。参与这场辩论是激进教育传统的一个重要组成部分。这本书对这一传统作了有力而又发人深省的介绍。

最早对这本书的评论是1989年由瓦特·维尔纳撰写的发表在《教育学+现象学》(Pedagogy + Phenomenology)上。瓦特·维尔纳的评论聚焦在他的学生们的需求和问题上,这些学生当时在做实习教师,学习一门批判教育学的课程。瓦特·维尔纳非常支持麦克拉伦的目标并写了一篇极具肯定与赞扬的评论,并总结道:"只有通过《学校生活》这样的书,教师们才能恢复他们的教学效能感,形成集体性的反社会和经济不平等。"[1]但是瓦特·维尔纳对于这本导读性教科书也提出了三点批评与质疑:第一,"这本书经常让读者承担太多,在书写语言上应该更简单一些,让读者更容易理解那些理论化的东西。"[2]根据瓦特·维尔纳的观点:"这本书清晰地提出知识是根植于历史和社会的,知识是生活在特定时空中的一群人不间断地建构的,一些形式的知识总比其他的知识更具有合法性和地位。这些主张与那些没有社会学知识的人沟通也是很容易的,但是让教师们感到困惑的是知识的边界是不明晰的。在知识、信念、风格、日常的'现实建构'、常识甚至是意识本身之间几乎是没有什么区分的。"[3]节选列举了书中的一些阐释性论述之后,瓦特·维尔纳说:"这些更包罗万象更广义的论述比书中更多的概念和细致的分析更有利于读者理解。暂且不谈很多的对于知识、意识形态和客观性的合理性怀疑。如果所有的描述、意义、思想和知识都是意识形态的,那么麦克拉伦的书里的分类就是空洞的、是无用的分析,使读者困惑不解。如果权利是决定真理和思想价值的主要标准,那么任何严肃的批判都几乎是无意义

---

[1] Walter Werner, "Book Review: Life in Schools: An Introduction to Critical Pedagogy in the Foundations of Education by Peter McLaren", New York: Longman, 1989, *Pedagogy + Phenomenology*, No. 7, 1989, pp. 274 – 275.

[2] Walter Werner, "Book Review: Life in Schools: An Introduction to Critical Pedagogy in the Foundations of Education by Peter McLaren", New York: Longman, 1989, *Pedagogy + Phenomenology*, No. 7, 1989, pp. 274 – 275.

[3] Walter Werner, "Book Review: Life in Schools: An Introduction to Critical Pedagogy in the Foundations of Education by Peter McLaren", New York: Longman, 1989, *Pedagogy + Phenomenology*, No. 7, 1989, pp. 274 – 275.

的。"①瓦特·维尔纳对此书提出的第二个质疑是："在批判教育学领域可不可以不使用自身的术语？"瓦特·维尔纳叹息，这种特定的语言让"外行"很难理解。是的，任何一个领域的学生面对这些新术语的时候通常都很苦恼，但是在研究者看来，这种批评是一种悖论。我们如何能够在不介绍"新"的概念的时候开发一种新的语言？（例如，霸权、意识形态、辩证等）。最后，瓦特·维尔纳提出了教师对于批判教育学的中心即解构学校教学和教育的迷思的反应："他们一开始被学校如何被社会所型塑的不平等完全存在于学校里这一问题压得透不过气来。他们无法做出任何有意义的影响或改变，这种看似无望的状态让他们沮丧。他们发现批判教育学所阐明的问题是根植于每一个独特的教室之外的世界，这经常使他们感到极其的悲观。"②

约翰·史密斯1990年在《教育理论》（Educational Theory）上发表了一篇很长的对《学校生活》的评论，认为《学校生活》是一种批判的民族志，并且与20世纪80年代如潮的对于学校教育的研究和报告作对比，认为麦克拉伦的这本书"既对学校教育展开了理性的论证又具有很强的实证基础"③。约翰·史密斯把麦克拉伦的日志与科尔（1961）、考泽尔（1967）、威利斯（1977）、赫恩登（1985）的作品以及其他杰出的教学记叙文与民族志相比较，认为麦克拉伦的日志可视为尖刻地激发读者兴趣的真实个人记录，是作者本人作为教师的生命抗争，也是为他的学校的学生的抗争。④麦克拉伦的批判教育学不是一幅学校发展路径的清晰蓝

---

① Walter Werner, "Book Review: Life in Schools: An Introduction to Critical Pedagogy in the Foundations of Education by Peter McLaren", New York: Longman, 1989, *Pedagogy + Phenomenology*, No. 7, 1989, p. 276.

② Walter Werner, "Book Review: Life in Schools: An Introduction to Critical Pedagogy in the Foundations of Education by Peter McLaren", New York: Longman, 1989, *Pedagogy + Phenomenology*, No. 7, 1989, p. 277.

③ John Smyth, "Book Review: Life in Schools: An Introduction to Critical Pedagogy in the Foundations of Education by Peter McLaren", New York: Longman, 1989, *Educational Theory*, Vol. 40, No. 2, 1990, p. 267.

④ John Smyth, "Book Review: Life in Schools: An Introduction to Critical Pedagogy in the Foundations of Education by Peter McLaren", New York: Longman, 1989, *Educational Theory*, Vol. 40, No. 2, 1990, p. 268.

图，也不是权宜之计，而是一种消解所有的批判理论家们常有的但缺乏实证的论断的漫长路途。麦克拉伦的作品充满了实践，但并非以实践本身为目的；他以其深刻的哲学、道德和人道主义视角认为学校实践应该以朝向平等主义为目的。①约翰·史密斯认为麦克拉伦的这些未删改的日志体叙述让无数的读者体验到了教室经验，让他们间接感受到不断演变的教学思想。他赞扬了麦克拉伦在政治上的诚恳："在描述他作为教师的实践以及他的学生们的经历时，麦克拉伦费尽心思地既描述了'真实的、现存的状况，也有他为之奋斗的尚未到来的条件。'他在这部批判民族志中最关注的是为人们草拟出一条路径，通过这条路径，人们得以控制和改变他们共同生活和工作的条件和境况，以及如何定义对他们自身及其他人来说什么是可能的、需要的。"②约翰·史密斯在评论的最后一段引用布洛基（Brodkey）（1987）和西蒙（Simon）、迪普（Dippo）（1986）的论述来说明批判民族志必须具备的基本条件：（1）研究必须设置有组织的问题情境，从而可以促使资料和分析程序与它的研究计划保持一致；（2）研究工作在一定范围内必须从公共领域的范畴寻求出发点来批判及改革压迫的、不公平的道德与社会状况；（3）研究工作必须思考并承认自身的局限，作为社会现实的一种形式，它是如何被建构并受制于历史权力关系与现有的物质条件的。③然后，约翰·史密斯坦言在《学校生活》里，麦克拉伦做到了所有的这些要求，成为批判民族志的典范。

　　受亨利·吉鲁的影响，第一版的《学校生活》主要基于后现代主义，但是他回忆道："我那时（在迈阿密大学工作期间）一直被一种意识所困扰，那就是我没有充分参与马克思和马克思主义思想家的工作。1980 年

---

① John Smyth, "Book Review: Life in Schools: An Introduction to Critical Pedagogy in the Foundations of Education by Peter McLaren", New York: Longman, 1989, *Educational Theory*, Vol. 40, No. 2, 1990, p. 272.

② John Smyth, "Book Review: Life in Schools: An Introduction to Critical Pedagogy in the Foundations of Education by Peter McLaren", New York: Longman, 1989, *Educational Theory*, Vol. 40, No. 2, 1990, p. 279.

③ John Smyth, "Book Review: Life in Schools: An Introduction to Critical Pedagogy in the Foundations of Education by Peter McLaren", New York: Longman, 1989, *Educational Theory*, Vol. 40, No. 2, 1990, p. 278.

《来自走廊地区的呐喊》成为了加拿大畅销书之后,我修习了米歇尔·福柯(Michel Foucault)和翁贝托·艾柯(Umberto Eco)、埃内斯托·拉克劳(Ernesto Laclau)和其他批判理论家的课程。然后我在 1985 年遇见了我真正的导师,保罗·弗莱雷,我的生活发生了改变。保罗·弗莱雷的思想后来一直是我作品的核心。"[1] 麦克拉伦的第一个国际演讲的正式邀请就是来自保罗·弗莱雷,1987 年保罗·弗莱雷邀请他去古巴哈瓦那参加一个学术会议,在那里,他与古巴的学者和活动人士以及来自巴西和墨西哥的参会者成为了朋友。他开始花时间在拉丁美洲,对马克思主义对政治经济学的批判越来越感兴趣。后来,他开始意识到后现代主义理论如果不能用时代所要求的气魄和持久的努力去挑战资本主义生产和再生产的社会关系,那么它可能是相当反动的。当他还在用批判后现代主义或抵抗后现代主义的词汇来描述他的作品时,他意识到他没有充分参与到马克思和马克思主义思想家的工作中。随着他越来越多地参与到马克思主义的工作中来,并且在美洲各地会见了由马克思主义反帝国主义计划所驱动的社会活动家,他不再觉得后现代主义的"激进民主"的工作有力地证明了它优于马克思主义的问题。在他看来,后现代主义大体上已绝望地屈服于资本规则和商品制度的必然性。他认为马克思主义的批判更充分地论述了当代社会的分化总体及其在全球资本主义世界体系中的历史意义。麦克拉伦马克思主义的回归始于这个时期前后思想的转变。

二 《学校生活》第二版到第三版——马克思主义的回归

1994 年和 1998 年出版了《学校生活》第二版和第三版,这个时期麦克拉伦的作品经历了一个方向的变化。他厌倦了后现代左派的温和的改革主义政治,对马克思主义和教育学之间关系的兴趣复苏对他产生了很大的影响。他与大学内外的马克思主义学者和活动人士建立了新的关系,开始把马克思主义、阶级斗争和政治带回教育的核心。在俄亥俄州迈阿密大学(Miami University)工作 8 年后,麦克拉伦于 1993 年至 2013 年在

---

[1] 本段的回忆内容来自本书作者对麦克拉伦的访谈及日常对话交流。

加州大学洛杉矶分校（University of California, Los Angeles, UCLA）教育与信息研究所（Graduate School of Education and Information Studies）担任教育学教授。在美国加州大学洛杉矶分校（UCLA）任职后，麦克拉伦和流亡到美国的保罗·弗莱雷再次相遇，除了早先对保罗·弗莱雷著作和事迹的涉猎，麦克拉伦还和他一起发展解放的剧场，通过剧场表现的方法使得弱势者从中得以发声。之后，麦克拉伦写了许多宣传保罗·弗莱雷的文章。在一篇纪念保罗·弗莱雷的文章中，他推崇保罗·弗莱雷是"最具有重要意义的解放哲学家之一，也是批判素养和批判教育的先驱之一，他的作品持续为那些在教育主流之外工作的教育者所采用"。如果说亨利·吉鲁是他的引路人，那么巴西激进学者保罗·弗莱雷就是他的北极星。受保罗·弗莱雷和美洲"马克思主义反殖民工程"（Marxist anti-colonial projects）的影响越来越大，麦克拉伦的马克思主义思想不断深化，他认为"马克思主义批判"是应对"当代社会的分化总体及其对全球资本主义世界体系的历史影响"的关键。

在 UCLA 任职之初，他继续在文化研究和后现代主义的调和传统中与亨利·吉鲁合作。这些作品的例子包括《批判教育学和掠夺性文化：后现代时代的对立政治》（Critical Pedagogy and Predatory Culture: Oppositional Politics in a Postmodern Era）[1] 和《反思媒体素养：一种批判的表征教育学》（Rethinking Media Literacy: A Critical Pedagogy of Representation）[2]。值得一提的是保罗·弗莱雷在《批判教育学与掠夺性文化》的序言中写道："彼得·麦克拉伦（Peter McLaren）是我在诸多杰出的'知识分子'中发现的，反过来我又被他发现。在我认识彼得·麦克拉伦之前，我读过他的书……当我读完了麦克拉伦的第一篇文章，我就几乎可以肯定，我们属于一个完全相同的'知识分子家族'（intellectual family）。"[3]

---

[1] Peter McLaren, *Critical pedagogy and predatory culture: Oppositional politics in a postmodern era*, New York: Routledge, 1995.

[2] McLaren P., Hammer R., Sholle D., Reilly S., *Rethinking media literacy: A critical pedagogy of representation*, New York: ny Peter Lang Publishing, 1995.

[3] Freire P., Preface, in P. McLaren, *Critical Pedagogy and Predatory Culture*, London: Routledge, 1995, p. x.

然而，随着麦克拉伦逐渐认识到调和传统在理论和实践上的局限性，他的思想也越来越倾向于马克思主义。多年后，他给佩塔·詹德里克（Petar Jandrić）发的邮件中写道："我认为，阻碍学生获得批判性看待世界所需资源的一个基本社会关系是阶级剥削。剥削，即掠夺社区，剥夺工人的人性。……早在20世纪80年代，我就在问自己：我们如何回应今天年轻人的呼救声？我认为必须倡导他们仔细阅读马克思和马克思主义理论家的著作，并最终参与马克思主义教育家的工作。"[1]

麦克拉伦逐渐从批判后现代主义的信徒转变为马克思主义的革命教育学的世俗先知。他放弃了最初的尝试，在《来自走廊地区的呐喊》中他说"越来越不喜欢这本书"，甚至说这本书现在让他"反感"，因为它完全缺乏"连贯的实践哲学"（a coherent philosophy of praxis）。在接下来的30年里，他对《学校生活》一书进行了6次重写，成功地删去了书中不好的部分，使之成为了一本激进的教科书，为教师们抵制全球资本主义及其伴随的问题做准备。

1996年玛丽·安·道尔在《教育研究者》（Educational Researcher）上发表一篇论文，评论《学校生活》。与瓦特·维尔纳和约翰·史密斯不同，在她的评论里《学校生活》是完全不同的一本书。书评一开始就称麦克拉伦是一个"尖锐而多产的"批判理论家。说来也奇怪，麦克拉伦对教学日志的真诚呈现，是约翰·史密斯及其他评论者大加赞赏的地方，却遭到了道尔的批判："一篇篇日志残酷地坦白并揭露细节，麦克拉伦并没有删除粗俗的语言、暴力和咒骂，甚至也没有删去他自己在保证学生平等上的失败尝试。"[2]

没有认可麦克拉伦在自身教学上的自我批评也没有强调麦克拉伦战略性地运用教学日志作为批判和解构的材料来源，道尔在她的评价中不乏指责的论调："麦克拉伦努力地与那些最活跃、最有反抗性的学生建立团结一致的关系，经常使他陷入矛盾的行为中，即在支持一些学生时却以

---

[1] Peter McLaren, Petar Jandrić, "Critical revolutionary pedagogy is made by walking-in a world where many worlds coexist" *Policy Futures in Education*, Vol. 12, No. 6, 2014, pp. 806 – 807.

[2] Mary Ann Doyle, "Peter McLaren and the Field of Critical Pedagogy" *Educational Researcher*, Vol. 25, No. 4, 1996, p. 28.

牺牲另一些学生的情感，有时是身体安全为代价。"①

没有详细的阐述或分析，道尔假设麦克拉伦对学校课程及教师教育项目的批判减少了教师成为"帝国的职员"，而且"充满艰辛"；她认为批判教育理论可成为一种"真理政权"（regime of truth）。道尔与其他一些读者一样对这本书关于性别问题的薄弱阐述提出了抗议。她认为麦克拉伦的自我反思看起来更夸张而不够真实，他的参考文献和建议阅读的书目大部分是男性批判理论家所作的。当然，所有的这些都是合理的批判。值得注意的是，道尔大部分的参考文献都是这本书第二版中所翻印的书评。书中列有凯莉和波特利对第一版的书评并配有麦克拉伦的回应。道尔为此为其贴上一个"错过的机会"的标签，因为这是麦克拉伦对评论者所提出的特定挑战进行的"自我辩护"。

然而，道尔确实也承认这本书第二版在重点上的转换："麦克拉伦对于其文章评论所做的回应算是他完成《学校生活》第一版后在论述重点上转换的重新表述。他认识到了这些领域：身份与种族、性别与性倾向、语言与愿望的生产（production of desire），流行文化政治与流行娱乐政治。他阐释了特蕾莎·艾伯特（Teresa Ebert）在'反抗的后现代领域的作品，让自己远离嬉戏的后现代主义，是一种认识论的相对主义。"②

其他读者对《学校生活》第二版中麦克拉伦展示的对于批评的高度的坦率及自我反思给予了高度的评价，但道尔不以为然，只是勉强地肯定："虽然麦克拉伦在第二版《学校生活》认识到了他写作上更宽泛的学术影响，但是我相信他会继续缺少对于宣扬反抗政治所产生的内在矛盾影响的理论化分析……他建议：'如果我们把教学变成一种愤怒的实践，我们就能够实现改革教育学'③ 这诉诸对反抗的复杂性的无耻的误解。尤其被忽视的是那些与作为女性及被贴上社会标签的如种族、阶级、年龄

---

① Mary Ann Doyle, "Peter McLarenand the Field of Critical Pedagogy" *Educational Researcher*, Vol. 25, No. 4, 1996, p. 28.

② Mary Ann Doyle, "Peter McLarenand the Field of Critical Pedagogy" *Educational Researcher*, Vol. 25, No. 4, 1996, pp. 29 – 30.

③ Peter McLaren, *Life in Schools: An Introduction to Critical Pedagogy in the Foundations of Education* (Second Edition), New York: Longman, 1994, p. back cover, p. 299.

和民族所放大的不同的矛盾。"①道尔在评论的总结中承认，麦克拉伦已经从一个在女性主义者、不同的社会理论家及其他的历史上的边缘人群之间的更复杂的团结一致的关系中清晰地表达了愿景。②

在第一版中，"可能性的语言"没有"批判的语言"论述得那么到位。从第二版以后，麦克拉伦更有深度地论述了"可能性的语言"。

《学校生活》这本书颠覆了大家习以为常的教学规则。这种惯常的教学规则提倡将学校生活置于人生之中进行考量。它充分理解学校是学习的地方，也是占有丰富的社会、文化知识的地方，让人生可以在未来绽放光彩。但是学校并不真正关切人生，并不关心实现人生理想所需要的条件，也不主张改造人生。麦克拉伦所倡议的方法来自批判教育理论，他要颠覆这个教育规则。他的教育规则是要把充满动力和矛盾的人生置于学校生活当中。他认为在人生中经济基础影响着阶级地位，政治支持影响着与权力机构的关系，性别特征影响着男性与女性之间所有的差异性和冲突，根本观念影响着生活方式表象下的对生活与世界的感知。他所持的观点与拉丁美洲的解放神学和保罗·弗莱雷的被压迫者的教育学所持的观点一致，都是主张与处在社会边缘的、贫困的和被排斥的人们共存亡。教育事业就是要让这些人走进学校、走进课堂以知识为武器来改变世界。从世界上这些不幸的人所处的社会地位来看，很明显的是仅仅凭学校所预设教导的知识是不足以改变人生的。只有将知识转化为行动，才有可能改变人生。这也具体地界定了实践的含义：在将改造行动转化为知识以及将知识转化为改造行动之间存在辩证的互动关系。这种改造不仅能改变生活还能改变自我，让他们可以自由地思考他们个人状况与社会现实的关系，将自身所在的地区与全球联系起来看待，从人生经历与各种人生知识中找到适合自己人生规划的战略方向。只有像这种重视实践的教育学才可以塑造人类，才能使人类建设出人与自然和谐发

---

① Mary Ann Doyle, "Peter McLarenand the Field of Critical Pedagogy" *Educational Researcher*, Vol. 25, No. 4, 1996, p. 30.

② Mary Ann Doyle, "Peter McLarenand the Field of Critical Pedagogy" *Educational Researcher*, Vol. 25, No. 4, 1996, p. 32.

展的民主社会。①

从1994年开始,麦克拉伦的作品的焦点从教室逐渐向例如政治、文化种族认同、反种族主义多元文化的教育、白人至上的政治学、抵制和流行文化、学校仪式同时作为抵制和顺从的工具、主体性的形成以及解放神学等议题转移。②

三 《学校生活》第四版到第六版——革命性的批判教育学

2003年到2014年是《学校生活》第四版到第六版,麦克拉伦的思想更加激进,发展聚焦了革命性的批判教育学,将批判性分析与乌托邦的想法相结合,明确倡导革命性的批判教育学必须将批判教育学彻底改造,不是要消除阶级对立,而是废除阶级;不是改善现有的社会,而是建立一个新的社会。在1998年版的《学校生活》麦克拉伦用"抗拒的后现代主义"来批评"嬉戏的后现代主义",在2007年版的《学校生活》中,麦克拉伦直接删掉这一章,并以新的章节,强调他转向马克思传统理论取向所处的新立场。

1997年,麦克拉伦出版了第一本明确提到革命的书,书名为《革命的多元文化主义:新千年的异见教育学》(Revolutionary multiculturalism: Pedagogies of dissent for the new millennium)。③ 几年后,他出版了著名的《切·格瓦拉、保罗·弗莱雷与革命教育学》(Che Guevara, Paulo Freire, and the Pedagogy of Revolution)(2000),这本书被普遍认为是他的革命宣言。在《切·格瓦拉、保罗·弗莱雷与革命教育学》的封底鲁道夫·D.托雷斯(Rodolfo D. Torres)写道:"彼得·麦克拉伦对切·格瓦拉、保罗·弗莱雷的遗产进行了清晰而有理论依据的重新评估,为马克思主义理论的更新做出了重大贡献。在批判资本主义似乎已经过时的地方,这

---

① Peter McLaren, *Life in Schools: An Introduction to Critical Pedagogy in the Foundations of Education* (Third Edition), New York: Longman, 1998, pp. xi – xii.

② 王雁:《美国批判教育学者麦克拉伦的学术生命研究》,硕士学位论文,东北师范大学,2013年,第33页。

③ Peter McLaren, *Revolutionary Multiculturalism: Pedagogies of Dissent for the New Millenniura*, Westview, 1997.

本书在'全球化'和日益加剧的阶级不平等的背景下,讲述了两位伟大革命者的生活。"① 在这本书的介绍中,乔·金奇洛给麦克拉伦起了一个绰号,这个绰号将永远伴随着他:"现在或许是宣布彼得·麦克拉伦为'教育左派桂冠诗人'的好时机。在批判性教育领域,没有人有麦克拉伦那样的能力,能够让我们把注意力集中在教育学与非正义之间的关系上,或者让我们在重新审视事物的同时发笑。"②

在他的书《切·格瓦拉、保罗·弗莱雷与革命教育学》中,麦克拉伦强调了切·格瓦拉反资本主义的第三世界国际主义以及保罗·弗莱雷在识字教学方面的激进工作的重要性。麦克拉伦的反资本主义项目呼吁教师在与社会压迫的斗争中,成为有道德和伦理能动性的人,培养和滋养一种"激进的希望"和"乌托邦式的战斗力",这种战斗力将在某一时刻达到顶峰,并促成理论和实践的革命性统一。然而,很明显,对于课堂实践者来说,这本书更像是一本哲学著作,而不是一本"如何做"的书。《切·格瓦拉、保罗·弗莱雷与革命教育学》标志着麦克拉伦自己的激进计划的深刻深化。

回首往事,我们不难发现,麦克拉伦的马克思主义人道主义自童年时代起就一直在发展。然而,他对左派两位标志性人物的评价,最终使这一革命性的转变成为"官方的"。麦克拉伦的转变引起了很多反应,保罗·弗莱雷的妻子妮塔(Nita)可能出最好的总结:"是什么让一个'北方'的金发男人,一个受人尊敬的教授和知识分子,想要写两个来自'南方'的男人?因为(这两个来自'南方'的男人)参与了反抗几个世纪以来每天对拉丁美洲人民的压迫和排斥;这两个人在历史上因相似的勇气和胆识而结合在一起,但主要是在团结、慷慨和谦逊方面。"③

2001年,保拉·奥尔曼出版了《反对全球资本主义的批判教育:卡

---

① Peter McLaren, *Che Guevara, Paulo Freire, and the Pedagogy of Revolution*, Lanhammd Rowman & Littlefield Publishers, 2000.
② Kincheloe J., *Foreword*, in P. McLaren, *Che Guevara, Paulo Freire, and the peda - gogy of revolution*, Lanham, md Rowman & Littlefield Publishers, 2000, p. ix.
③ Araujo Freire A. M., *Foreword*, in P. McLaren, *Che Guevara, Paulo Freire, and the pedagogy of revolution*, Lanham, md Rowman & Littlefield Publishers, 2000, p. xiii.

尔·马克思与革命批判教育》（Critical Education Against Global Capitalism: Karl Marx and Revolutionary Critical Education）① 一书，她在书中引入了"革命性的批判教育学"一词。麦克拉伦立即采用了这个术语，这标志着他的工作进入了一个新的阶段。

此外，麦克拉伦的作品第一次成为专门出版物的主题，例如《国际教育改革杂志》（International Journal of Educational Reform）的特刊《彼得·麦克拉伦的革命性教育学》（The Revolutionary Pedagogy of Peter McLaren）（2001）。

在马克思主义理论的推动下，第四版《学校生活》以马克思的人道唯物主义为出发点，提出了"实践哲学"，麦克拉伦（2003）将理论与传记和历史融合在一起，形成了学生、教师在学校中主观建构自己的交叉点，从而提供一种真实和想象的"希望的教育学"（"pedagogy of hope"）（保罗·弗莱雷的话）；或者用他更喜欢的词来形容，波拉·奥尔曼（Paula Allman，1999，2001）② 提出的"革命性的批判教育学"。麦克拉伦通过向读者提供解释性概念（阶级、意识形态和剥削）和经验工具来实现这一点，从而同时理解和干预正在日益组织和规范日常教育实践的新兴全球结构。通过将这种批判置于社会而不是自我的空间，麦克拉伦将资本主义知识产业的意识形态永远置于守势。根据麦克拉伦和拉明·法拉曼德普尔（2005）的研究，这将要求学生作为具有社会和历史能动性的人，"获得对其智力和体力劳动的控制权"③，这包括找出"从学术界撬开理论，并将其纳入教育实践"④的方法。这在本质上对革命性的批判教育学非常重要，它不是关于自由主义的"赋权"概念，而是针对

---

① Allman P., *Critical Education Against Global Capitalism: Karl Marx and Revolutionary Critical Education*, Westport, CT: Bergin & Garvey, 2001.

② Allman, P., *Revolutionary social transformation: Democratic hopes, political possibilities and critical education*, Westport, CT: Bergin & Garvey, 1999. Allman, P., *Critical education against global capitalism: Karl Marx and revolutionary critical education*, Westport, CT: Bergin & Garvey, 2001.

③ Peter McLaren, Ramin Farahmandpur, *Teaching Against Global Capitalism and the New Imperialism: A Critical Pedagogy*, Rowman & Littlefield Publishers, 2005, p. 180.

④ Peter McLaren, *Life in Schools: An Introduction to Critical Pedagogy in the Foundations of Education* (Fourth Edition), Pearson Publishers, 2003, p. 189.

"废除阶级社会和实现社会主义替代"的集体行动和"权力"①。

在第五版《学校生活》里，由于麦克拉伦介绍了革命性的批判教育学思想，出版商培生集团（Pearson Publishers）最终放弃了对此书的出版，不久标登出版集团（Paradigm Publishers）拿到了这本书的版权。《学校生活》一直表达解放政治学的思想，批判资本主义、种族主义、文化帝国主义以及不对称的权力关系的弊端，但是早期版本中的左倾的后现代主义和政治改革已经被删除了。然而很多读者会抵制以破坏资本主义为前提的"可能性的语言"，不可否认的是革命性的批判教育学将批判性分析与乌托邦的想法相结合，比任何时候都有更多的可能性。《学校生活》所不断体现的并不是通常意义上的学术追求，而是给所有那些为自己和其他人寻求一个更好的世界的人们所提出的建议。

50 多岁时的麦克拉伦是北美批判教育学创始人小团体中广受赞誉的一员，也是美国顶尖大学里一位受人尊敬的教授，麦克拉伦已经拥有了理论背景、生活经历和发展成熟的革命性的批判教育学理论的机会。这一发展建立在麦克拉伦早期马克思主义著作的基础上，如马克思主义反对后现代主义的教育理论②；麦克拉伦对新自由主义等更广泛的社会问题的兴趣反映在《批判理论、激进的教育学和全球冲突中》（Critical Theories, Radical Pedagogies, and Global Conflicts）③，《批判教育学：我们现在在哪里?》（Critical Pedagogy: Where are We Now?）④《革命教育学：全球新自由主义内外的社会正义教育》（Revolutionizing Pedagogy: Education for Social Justice Within and Beyond Global Neoliberalism）;⑤特别是关于麦克

---

① Peter McLaren, *Life in Schools: An Introduction to Critical Pedagogy in the Foundations of Education* (Fourth Edition), Pearson Publishers, 2003, p.191.

② Peter McLaren, Dave Hill, Mike Cole, and Glenn Rikowski, *Marxism Against Postmodernism in Educational Theory*, New York: Lexington Books, 2002.

③ Fischman G., Sunker H., Lankshear C., McLaren P., eds., *Critical theories, radical pedagogies, and global conflicts*, Boulder, co Rowman & Little-field, 2005.

④ McLaren P., Kincheloe J. L., eds., *Critical pedagogy: Where are we now?* New York: Peter Lang Publishing 2007.

⑤ Macrine S., McLaren P., Hill D., eds., *Revolutionizing pedagogy: Education for social justice within and beyond global neo-liberalism*, London: UK Palgrave Macmillan, 2009.

拉伦对资本主义理论和实践的兴趣，反映在以下作品中：《反对全球资本主义和新帝国主义的教学：一种批判的教育学》(Teaching Against Global Capitalism and the New Imperialism: A Critical Pedagogy)[1]、《资本家与征服者：反对帝国的批判教育学》(Capitalists and Conquerors: A Critical Pedagogy Against Empire)[2]、《红色研讨会：教育理论、文化政治和教育学的激进探索》(Red Seminars: Radical Excursions Into Educational Theory, Cultural Politics, and Pedagogy)[3]、《批判消费教育学：“末日启示录”阴影下的生活与学习》(Critical Pedagogies of Consumption: Living and Learning in the Shadow of the "Shopocalypse")[4]、《资本主义的浩劫：公众、教育和环境危机》(The Havoc of Capitalism: Publics, Pedagogies and Environmental Crisis)[5]、《学术压抑：来自学术—工业综合体的反思》(Academic Repression: Reflections from the Academic-Industrial Complex)[6]、《全球工业综合体：统治体系》(The global industrial complex: Systems of Domination)[7]。

在这段时间里，麦克拉伦花了很多时间在拉丁美洲——与委内瑞拉、墨西哥和哥伦比亚的工人和工会，以及萨帕塔的支持者在一起。在2005年，一批学者和活动家在墨西哥北部建立了麦克拉伦批判教育学基金会(La Fundacion McLaren de Pedagogía Critica)，推广批判教育和大众教育的项目。

2006年，麦克拉伦在委内瑞拉玻利瓦尔大学（Bolivarian University of

---

[1] Peter McLaren, Ramin Farahmandpur, *Teaching Against Global Capitalism and the New Imperialism: A Critical Pedagogy*, Rowman & Littlefield Publishers, 2005.

[2] Peter McLaren, ed., *Capitalists and conquerors: A critical pedagogy against empire*, Lanham, MD: Rowman & Littlefield, 2005.

[3] Peter McLaren, *Red Seminars: Radical excursions into educational theory, cultural politics, and pedagogy*, Hampton Press, Inc, 2005.

[4] Sandlin J. A., McLaren P., eds., *Critical pedagogies of consumption: Living and learning in the shadow of the "shopocalypse"*, New York: Routledge, 2009.

[5] Martin G., Houston D., McLaren P., Suoranta J., eds., *The havoc of capitalism: Publics, pedagogies and environmental crisis*, Rotterdam: The Netherlands Sense Publishers, 2010.

[6] Nocella A., Best S., McLaren P., eds., *Academic repression: Reflections from the academic-industrial complex*, Oakland: ca a k Press, 2010.

[7] Best S., Kahn R., Nocella A. J., McLaren P., eds., *The global industrial complex: Systems of Domination*, Lanham, md Lexington Books, Rowman & Littlefield, 2011.

Venezuela）就职。2011 年，麦克拉伦批判教育学研究所（Instituto McLaren de Pedagogía Crítica）在墨西哥的恩塞纳达港（Ensenada）成立。在他多次访问拉丁美洲期间，麦克拉伦会见了乌戈·查韦斯（Hugo Chavez）和洛佩斯·奥夫拉多尔（Lopez Obrador）等重要人物，并为美洲之间的思想和实践交流做出了重要贡献。在这一时期，麦克拉伦也是作品被第一批翻译成俄语的批判性教育学家之一。后来，他应邀到中国讲授马克思主义和批判教育学。麦克拉伦的事业已经走向全球。

麦克拉伦的作品从未受到过当权者的欢迎。然而，他从马克思主义人道主义理论发展到革命性的批判教育学，增加了他与主流的矛盾。2006 年，麦克拉伦在安德鲁·琼斯（Andrew Jones）的进步教育工作者黑名单上名列榜首。这份黑名单上的"肮脏三十人"（Dirty Thirty）[1]旨在骚扰美国大学的左翼教授。为了寻找一个压力较小的工作环境，麦克拉伦在加州大学洛杉矶分校任教 20 年后，2013 年来到查普曼大学任教。

四 后《学校生活》阶段的研究重点——解放神学

麦克拉伦自 2013 年开始他的新工作以来一直留在加州奥兰治市（Orange City）的查普曼大学（Chapman University）。受他多次访问拉丁美洲、少年时对宗教的迷恋以及皈依天主教的启发，麦克拉伦开始在解放神学传统和革命性的批判教育学之间建立起更为明显的联系。拉美解放神学形成于 20 世纪 60 年代末期，其诞生的标志为 1971 年秘鲁神学家古铁雷斯发表了《解放神学》一书。[2] 大多数解放神学家不谈无神论和唯物主义，却接受阶级分析，经济作为主导因素，并愿意接受暴力革命的必要性，也愿意接受某种形式的无产阶级专政。[3] "解放神学是我作品构成的

---

[1] Fassbinder, S., "The 'Dirty Thirty's' Peter McLaren reflects on the crisis of academic freedom [EB/OL]", (2006), http://mrzine.monthlyreview.org/fassbinder060406.html, 2017 – 05 – 14.

[2] 王珊：《解放神学视野下的中国基督教社会主义研究》，博士学位论文，中共中央党校，2017 年，第 32 页。

[3] 王珊：《解放神学视野下的中国基督教社会主义研究》，博士学位论文，中共中央党校，2017 年，第 35 页。

一个重要组成部分,特别是在我 25 岁皈依天主教之后。"① 《反抗的教育学:从复活到革命》(Pedagogy of Iinsurrection: From Resurrection to Revolution)② 是麦克拉伦在这段时间的杰作,后续的对话性文章扩展了它的观点③。

麦克拉伦的解放神学建立在他童年对神学的兴趣,他在马克思主义人道主义和革命性的批判教育学上的理论成就,他在世界各地的实践经验(尤其是在南美洲),以及他生活和思想的各种其他方面。在这个框架内,麦克拉伦产生了一些他最成熟和复杂的见解,并再次违背了主流思想,以朗朗上口、有力的声明激发和震撼了学术主流。这些主张强调了强烈的解放思想,令所有政治派别的人都感到震惊。

如今,对他作品的各种各样的认可实在是太多了——自 2013 年以来,他在包括但不限于希腊、委内瑞拉、哥伦比亚、土耳其、墨西哥、美国、乌克兰、中国、阿根廷和英国在内的国家获得了 30 多个奖项和荣誉职位。麦克拉伦现在坚定地属于世界知识分子,他的公开露面,比如最近与诺贝尔奖得主弗农·史密斯(Vernon Smith)的辩论,引起了社会各阶层的极大的关注。毫不奇怪,他这样的成功也暴露给了许多敌人。2016 年,在他与来自中国的王雁④结婚后,右翼博客指责麦克拉伦是白人种族的叛徒。匿名黑客用俄语对麦克拉伦的一次采访进行了加工,用完全错误的英语翻译代替了他的口头评论。然而,麦克拉伦总是以他独特的谦逊和对他人开放的态度,超越粗暴的诋毁和侮辱。

麦克拉伦在加州奥兰治的查普曼大学(Chapman University)担任批

---

① 来自本书作者对麦克拉伦的访谈。

② Peter McLaren, *Pedagogy of insurrection: From resurrection to revolution*, New York: Peter Lang Publishers, 2015.

③ Peter McLaren, Petar Jandrić, "From Liberation to Salvation: Revolutionary critical pedagogy meets liberation theology" *Policy Futures in Education*, Vol. 15, No. 65, 2017, pp. 620 – 652. &Peter McLaren, Petar Jandrić, "Karl Marx and Liberation Theology: Dialectical materialism and Christian spirituality in, against, and beyond contemporary capitalism", Triple C: Communication, Capitalism & Critique, Vol. 16, No. 2, 2018.

④ 王雁是一位才华横溢的年轻中国女性,她对深化批判教育学和即兴表演之间的关系很感兴趣。

判研究领域的杰出教授,其中包括担任保罗·弗莱雷民主项目(Paulo Freire Democratic Project)的联合主任,以及国际道德和社会正义大使(International Ambassador for Global Ethics and Social Justice)。他广泛出版、编辑、教学,并在世界各地演讲。2018 年,他推出了自己的新书《激进的想象国家:公共教育学与实践》(Radical Imagine-Nation: Public Pedagogy & Praxis)[①]。他的作品现在受到越来越多专门出版物的关注,比如《教育政策未来》(Policy Futures in Education)专刊登载"反抗的教育学"(Pedagogies of Insurrection)的专题。麦克拉伦现在比以往任何时候都更有效率了,我们只能猜测他接下来会想出什么——但我们可以放心,它将是开拓性的、解放性的。

---

① McLaren P., Soohoo S., eds., *Radical Imagine–Nation: Public Pedagogy & Praxis*, New York: Peter Lang, 2018.

第二章

理论渊源与核心理论武器

麦克拉伦的批判教育学思想并不是突发奇想异想天开的空中楼阁，他是站在巨人的肩膀上，批判借鉴了多家理论作为他的理论渊源，如马克思主义、美国进步主义和社会重建主义思想、法兰克福（Frankfurt School）学派批判理论、后现代主义、弗莱雷的解放教育学思想、吉鲁的批判教育学思想。马克思主义人道主义致力于为世界上的居民创造更好的生活，马克思主义人道主义要求改变那些压制性的、阻碍了人类大多数人发挥其潜力的社会安排、制度和关系，最终实现某种社会主义民主替代资本主义的理想。麦克拉伦以马克思主义人道主义作为其批判教育学的理想。麦克拉伦的作品以马克思主义人道主义的概念作为武器去批判全球资本主义下的剥削关系。

第一节 批判借鉴多家理论——麦克拉伦批判教育学的理论渊源

一 马克思主义

马克思主义对麦克拉伦的批判教育学思想的形成发挥了重要影响，而他对教育的关怀最终仍是以马克思主义追求的自由与解放为中心。麦克拉伦对社会革命和解放实践持有高度的期望，他指出："作为我的中心理论和政治立场，我绝对没有放弃、背叛马克思主义。事实上，晚近几年我非常着迷于马克思的'激进的历史观'。我重新发现，马克思主义可以作为建构一个革命性、社会主义工程的方法。"①

其实麦克拉伦的早期作品受到了后现代主义很大的影响。而后他的思想缓慢而坚定地进入了"马克思主义人道主义的轨迹"("the Marxist-humanist trajectory"),影响他的作品从各种带有马克思主义倾向的作品到马克思的原作。② 据麦克拉伦回忆:

> 在20世纪80年代后期我开始阅读对我作品的评论。现在,我在大学里认识的许多教育工作者都不读关于他们作品的评论。我认真对待对我作品的批评。英国有一拨马克思主义者很欣赏我的作品但同时他们也指出了我分析的局限性。我在德国的时候见过他们中的一些人。柏林墙倒塌之后民主德国的教授被赶出大学,取而代之的是联邦德国的教授,有一个会议关于这个,于是我参会去支持民主德国的教授。在那里我遇见了一些英国马克思主义者并与他们热烈交谈。伯明翰当代文化研究学院确实对我产生了影响,但我对其中一些研究的方法进行了批判,如他们研究安东尼奥·葛兰西(Antonio Gramsci)的方法。当然,也确实有很多重要的思想家出自这里,如保罗·威利斯(Paul Willis)、斯图尔特·霍尔(Stuart Hall)等。(来自本书作者对麦克拉伦的访谈)

此外,后现代的麦克拉伦到马克思主义的麦克拉伦的转变已经在例如2006年出版的《愤怒与希望》(Rage and Hope)一书中他与玛西娅·莫拉(Marcia Moraes)和格伦·里科沃斯基(Glenn Rikowski)的对话中进行了相当广泛的阐述。

麦克拉伦最终坚守马克思主义的立场,是因为他认为以马克思主义对于无产阶级的丰富情感来关怀当今社会中的弱势群体,便会认识到种

---

① [美]彼得·麦克拉伦:《校园生活:批判教育学导论》,萧昭君译,台北:巨流图书公司2003版,第393—394页。
② McLaren, P., McMurry. A. & McGuirk, K., "An Interview with Peter McLaren. Waterloo: University of Waterloo [EB/OL]", 2017 - 04 - 14, http://english.uwaterloo.ca/PeterMcLareninterview.pdf.

种压迫者与受压迫者的冲突皆是阶级斗争的变形,因而必须以唯物辩证法的思维方式相信资本主义社会因其内在的矛盾最终会走向灭亡,从而变成更为平等自由的社会。概言之,马克思的历史唯物论、辩证法、阶级冲突论、劳动论、物化和异化等思想,对麦克拉伦的批判教育学思想的形成起到了重要作用。例如,马克思对劳动和实践的重视,使得麦克拉伦认识到人是主动地通过实践来改变世界,从而不断地追求与实现梦想。关于马克思的异化理论,麦克拉伦"始终站在反对资本主义滥用的立场上,支持解放政治"[1]。麦克拉伦从未放松过对社会主义整体观点的关注,由于对差异和代表性政治问题的兴趣,他与后现代左派进行了谨慎的批判性接触,逐渐认同了英国马克思主义者迈克·科尔(Mike Cole)、戴夫·希尔(Dave Hill)和格伦·里科沃斯基的观点,他认识到,左翼后现代主义的私有化领域代表着一个社会死胡同。沉浸在洛杉矶激进的政治文化中,他开始阅读英国马克思主义者的作品,如希尔、科尔(Cole & Hill),并开始熟悉莱雅·杜娜叶夫斯卡亚(Raya Dunayevskaya)的作品[2],这在他的作品中很明显,尤其是在《学校生活》的后几版中。据麦克拉伦口述:

> 我一开始是自发地关注马克思主义,是一种工人阶级的自我行动。最初被诸如安东尼奥·内格里(Antonio Negri)、迈克尔·哈特(Michael Hardt)、拉涅罗·潘泽瑞(Raniero Panzieri)、马里奥·特隆蒂(Mario Tronti)、塞尔吉奥·博洛尼亚(Sergio Bologna)、达拉·科斯塔(Mariorosa Dalla Costa)、弗朗索瓦·贝拉尔迪(Francois Beradi)这些重要的思想家的作品所吸引,虽然我并没有在我教育学的作品中明确地引用他们的作品。后来我又开始关注更经典的马克思主义批判著作,如马斯(Mas'ud Zavarzadeh)、特蕾莎修女艾伯

---

[1] Peter McLaren, *Life in Schools: An Introduction to Critical Pedagogy in the Foundations of Education* (Fourth Edition), Pearson Publishers, 2003, p. 3.

[2] Pruyn, M., & Huerta-Charles, L. (2005), "Teaching Peter McLaren: The scholar and this volume", In M. Pruyn, and L. Huerta-Charles, eds., *Teaching Peter McLaren: paths of dissent*, New York: Peter Lang, pp. xvii – xxxix.

特的作品，然后我开始对彼得·胡迪斯（Peter Hudis）、凯文·安德森（Kevin Anderson）、莱雅·杜娜叶夫斯卡娅、当然还有英国教育家葆拉·奥尔曼（Paula Allman）、戴夫·希尔、迈克·科尔和格伦·里科夫斯基（Glenn Rikowski）等人的马克思人道主义的作品感兴趣。因此我开始对所谓的资本主义发展的新时代——又被冠名为"后工业化主义"（postindustrialism）、"后福特主义"（post-Fordism）或"后现代资本主义"（postmodern capitalism）产生了兴趣。[1]

总结起来，马克思主义对麦克拉伦的影响主要分为三个阶段：（1）平民主义马克思主义者麦克拉伦；（2）后现代主义马克思主义者麦克拉伦；（3）马克思主义人道主义者麦克拉伦。研究者相信这三个麦克拉伦一直且仍然存在于这位爱尔兰的天主教的、加拿大的、北美的激进白人男人身上。研究者也相信这三个麦克拉伦，无论哪一个都是可圈可点的，做出过重要的贡献的。对于我们这些理论者、学者、教育者来说三个麦克拉伦都是有帮助的。当然每一个麦克拉伦也都值得批判。

在20世纪80年代早期及中期处于反抗意识萌芽阶段的平民主义马克思主义者麦克拉伦就已经以分析政治经济的形式与学术界内外的人们开始对话了。但在早期只是在意识层面与马克思的批判理论的相吻合，未上升到理论分析层面。这就是为何他的首部作品《来自走廊地区的呐喊》由于缺乏理论分析而未能达到麦克拉伦的写作初衷。中期麦克拉伦与亨利·吉鲁一起的作品开始延伸、扩展了鲍尔斯（Bowles）、金蒂斯（Gintis）、阿普尔和法兰克福学派的思想。开始运用马克思所描述的上层建筑（Superstructure）以及葛兰西的社会霸权秩序（social hegemonic order）理论解释日常活动和事件。

20世纪80年代晚期及90年代早期麦克拉伦及其作品开始一致地重视后现代主义者或后结构主义者社会理论领域里的理论者和研究者的质

---

[1] Peter McLaren, Petar Jandrić, "An Interview with Peter McLaren – Critical Revolutionary Pedagogy is Made by Walking: in a world where many worlds coexist" *Policy Futures in Education*, Vol. 6, No. 12, 2016, p. 807.

疑、主张和深刻见解。这有助于理解社会、经济、文化环境以及话语在创建、保持或重构人类权利关系中的作用，成为后现代主义马克思主义者。评论家认为麦克拉伦这个时期的学术过于迷恋法国的后现代主义及后结构主义如福柯、鲍德里亚（Baudrillard）、布迪厄（Bourdieu）和德里达（Derrida）的思想。应该注意的是很多批判教育学领域的人都卖弄或试图用后现代主义、后结构主义的重要观点、质疑来分析围绕着权力、话语、能动性等方面的问题。但是他们中的大部分人都是以牺牲之前的马克思主义分析为代价的，但是研究者认为麦克拉伦没有。就麦克拉伦而言，重视多元差异与族群认同的积极民主的主张，将使得差异性团结被分化，而丧失了中心，也去掉了总体性，反而失去了弱势者团结的主体能动性，并将被资本主义用为分化弱势族群的策略，也使批判教育学沦为空谈，而失去解放的可能性。所以，可以说麦克拉伦提出革命性的批判教育学，就是有感于后现代主义太过强调文化的差异，反而忘了探讨压迫产生的最根本原因，是来自资本主义体系剥削的运作。麦克拉伦也认为，当我们忽略了结构性的分析，也是种失去主体能动性的展现。这是因为，激进民主是把抵抗压迫的矛头转向平行的文化差异，却忘却文化差异原本并不会造成压迫或歧视，而是因为文化的差异结合了垂直的阶级压迫，才是压迫的最根本原因。

如果认真仔细地阅读分析他在后现代主义马克思主义者阶段的作品就会发现他所努力尝试的是将后现代主义里的重要经验、教训与他的马克思主义理论基础及对马克思主义的赞同与支持进行协调一致。麦克拉伦从未背弃马克思主义的或历史唯物主义的政治经济分析。事实上，他经常将社会主义导向的教育者行动主义（socialist-oriented educationalist activism）与文化建构的社会关系的理解，非决定性的、非正统的马克思主义理解，非基于压迫但是仍与压迫有关系的社会阶级的理解，如性别主义、种族主义、语言主义等成功地结合。麦克拉伦在看待后现代主义思想的功效时也总是一个谨慎的乐观主义者。他坚持与马克思主义的分析形式保持紧密的联系。这种分析形式看起来能更充分地解释当今的经济现实同时保持后现代主义理论去中心化的集体政治斗争的批判倾向。

英国三位马克思主义教育家——迈克·科尔、戴夫·希尔和格伦·

里科沃斯基,在麦克拉伦早期批判后现代主义的作品中看到了潜力,但他们也从自己的马克思主义视角对其进行了高度批判。最后他们与麦克拉伦成了亲密的同志,合写了很多作品。麦克拉伦从他们身上学到了很多。

麦克拉伦成为马克思主义人道主义者(Marxist-Humanist)是一种偶然也是一种必然,莱雅·杜娜叶夫斯卡亚(1910—1987)和凯文·安德森的作品,以及彼得·胡迪斯对马克思(Marx)和罗莎·卢森堡(Rosa Luxemburg)作品的诠释与评论,对帮助麦克拉伦阅读这些巨匠的作品非常重要。麦克拉伦回忆:

> 我在自己的独立研究中偶然发现莱雅·杜娜叶夫斯卡亚的一本书,并没有谁推荐给我。莱雅是一个有趣的哲学家。她来自乌克兰。她是一个犹太妇女,年轻的时候逃离了乌克兰。我读了莱雅的作品,在我写的关于保罗·弗莱雷和切·格瓦拉的书中,我引用了她的话。一个叫彼得·胡迪斯的哲学家在芝加哥写信联系我说他读了我的书,注意到了莱雅。他逗趣说我是美国的国务卿。彼得·胡迪斯当时正努力使莱雅的运动组织有序,充满活力。莱雅后来去了美国,在芝加哥的底特律向工厂工人传授马克思(Karl Marx)与黑格尔(Hegel)的思想。她发起了马克思主义人道主义运动。我开始追随彼得·胡迪斯和凯文·安德森。凯文·安德森是加州大学圣巴巴拉分校(University of California-Santa Barbara)的教授。彼得·胡迪斯不是学者,但他是我见过的最杰出的马克思主义思想家之一。运动中出现了分裂。另一个小组得到了莱雅去世后留下的钱。彼得·胡迪斯必须找到谋生的途径,所以他很快就在哲学上取得了博士学位,现在他在芝加哥教书。于是我开始和彼得·胡迪斯、凯文·安德森讨论黑格尔的问题。因为我认为如果不理解黑格尔,你就无法充分理解马克思。所以这些年我转向了黑格尔的马克思主义方法,我称之为马克思主义人道主义(Marxist Humanism)。一些人认为马克思主义人道主义(Marxist Humanism)团体是一种邪教,因为它在很大程度上关注了莱雅。但我认为根本不是这样。马克思主义人道主义

运动也在很大程度上涉及罗莎·卢森堡的作品。所以他们已经并正在出版罗莎·卢森堡的所有作品。他们批评卢森堡，但他们也是卢森堡作品的强烈支持者，这就是马克思主义人道主义运动的轨迹。但这与教育有什么关系。因此，当我开始更多地研究资本主义的社会关系时，我开始思考有哪些替代方案。马克思确实已经给了提示。他没有具体地说资本主义之后的世界应该是什么样子，他没有把它写在一本书里。胡迪斯在他的《马克思的选择》（Marx's Choice）一书中所做的是，他读了马克思所有的著作、马克思的书信，他描绘了马克思如何看待一个社会，一个价值生产之外的社会宇宙。他观察到在这个世界里，实际的劳动时间，不是社会必要的劳动时间。所以马克思的伟大发现是劳动和劳动力之间的区别，抽象劳动和具体劳动的区别。他看世界基本上是一种与自由相关的劳动，没有专制，由一种永久革命所驱动，即莱雅所说的绝对否定，否定的否定。例如，你可以说共产主义是对资本主义的否定。你掌握生产资料，你把生产资料从资本家手中夺走，国家拥有生产资料，但这本身需要被否定。因为拥有的概念仍然存在需要被否定。（来自本书作者对麦克拉伦的访谈）

在这个时期的作品里[①]，他已经开始倡导回归马克思主义和葛兰西学派的精髓，重新强调资产阶级对工人阶级的统治与压迫等问题——尤其是在当前全球资本主义企业的权利和控制不断增长、多样化和加强的情况下。他警告说，如果我们忽视阶级关系、阶级剥削在教育及其他领域里起到的核心作用，我们的分析就是不完整的，我们为社会公平所能取

[①] Peter McLaren, Dave Hill, Mike Cole, and Glenn Rikowski. Marxism Against Postmodernism in Educational Theory [M]. New York: Lexington Books, 2002; Peter McLaren. Revolutionary Multiculturalism: Pedagogies of Dissent for the New Millenniura [M]. Westview, 1997; Peter McLaren. Che Guevara, Paulo Freire, and the Pedagogy of Revolution [M]. Lanhammd Rowman & Littlefield Publishers, 2000; Gang of five. In Cole, M., Hill, D., McLaren, P., & Rikowski, G. (Eds. 2001). Red chalk: On schooling, capitalism and politics. London, UK: The Institute for Education Policy Studies; Mclaren, P., Fischman, G, Serra, S. & Antelo, E. The specters of Gramsci: Revolutionary praxis and the committed intellectual [J]. Journal of Thought, 1998 (37), 4: 66.

得的斗争成果将很稀少，成功之路会很漫长。这个"马克思主义人道主义者麦克拉伦"更清晰而直接地看到了回归马克思主义的重要性，重新设想马克思、重新阅读马克思、为马克思重添活力。下面的论述节选自《革命的多元文化主义》(Revolutionary Multiculturalism)："然而一些后现代主义者偶然地断言身份(identity)可以不固定地被重写，重新发明，我觉得这是一种目光短浅且危险的论调。我的观点对于一些读者来说可能有些极端，即特定的文化差异与话语内容不如这些差异是如何嵌入并与更大的社会、经济、政治差异相关联重要。我觉得必须强调这一点。确实，后建构主义和后现代理论极大地扩展了我们对于身份、语言、学校教育之间关系的理解。但是这些话语也经常坍塌、瓦解成去历史化的自满的论述。与这些理论尝试一样基本的是他们经常通过以牺牲权利为代价来关注身份而滥用他们自己的思想见解。"[1]

从麦克拉伦这段论述中，研究者认为麦克拉伦所要表达的是，他的立场从关心后现代主义的文化差异与认同取向，转回关注马克思的历史唯物和阶级分析取向的立场。换言之，他对后现代思潮批判的无力感及虚无化，已感到十分无能为力。研究者认为，马克思从早期人道取向只关心到个人，到后期的经济取向关心人与人之间的关系，其实并不是思想的断裂，而是思想的进展。亦即马克思将主体的能动性置于和结构互为依存的位置，来发展他的理论。麦克拉伦并不是不关心主体而转往结构，而是采取一种由主体扩展到结构并寻求彼此辩证关系的主张。亦即将马克思早期的人道取向和后期的经济取向两者相结合。

在《切·格瓦拉、保罗·弗莱雷与革命教育学》这本书中，麦克拉伦呈现了他最激进的马克思主义，理论化、诗化地明确表达了为了社会公平的教育愿景。书中分析了全球资本主义及其在社会上、政治上及霸权上所建构的上层建筑需要在社会公平与变革的教育斗争下再中心化，但这种再中心化不能忽略超越阶级歧视的压迫形式。需要在全球资本主义的逻辑和背景下理解性别歧视主义、男性至上主义、种族主义、语言

---

[1] Peter McLaren, *Revolutionary Multiculturalism: Pedagogies of Dissent for the New Millenniura*, Westview, 1997, p. 17.

主义、国家主义、排外心理（xenophobia）、年龄歧视主义、外形歧视主义①，这些压迫形式大多都有自己的生命周期，甚至存在于非资本主义时期，但是这些压迫在全球资本主义不断扩张市场、市场份额竞争加剧、没有参加工会及报酬过低的工人越来越多的情况下变得更严重了。

在这本书中他运用墨西哥恰帕斯（Chiapas Mexico）原住民的土地斗争这一案例清晰地解释了这些压迫形式与资本主义的关系。不仅如此，他还成功地将当前的经济、社会状况的马克思主义分析与对后现代主义的细致入微的理解相结合。他通过对这个领域的十年之久的研究做到了恰到好处的赞扬与批判。

麦克拉伦所明确倡导的通过马克思主义视角的社会主义、集体利益及激进民主进行社会重建及重新构想的观点，可以引用他"批判的后现代主义的马克思主义"（critical postmodernist Marxist）时期的一段话来进行最好的总结："所需的是一种新的社会主义构想，这种构想不要基于特定的理性形式而是基于去总体化的机构形式及达到新的社会生活形式的激进民主范围的扩张。"②

麦克拉伦与戴夫·希尔、迈克·科尔和格伦·里科沃斯基合著的《马克思主义反对教育理论中的后现代主义》（Marxism Against Postmodernism in Educational Theory, 2002），兜了圈回到原地，对当今的教育系统、社会和世界状况进行了马克思主义的分析，更重要的是，启发性地解释了我们应该怎样以及我们为何要团结起来为建设更公平的秩序而斗争。

麦克拉伦作为马克思主义者并不是进入学术界那一刻开始的，他个人的理论重点和立足点的变迁，展现给我们的是一个不断学习、跨学科，不断自我否定的学者形象，同时他作为批判教育学的奠基人之一，为批判教育学的理论拓展和发展做出了不可小视的贡献，"尤其是引领批判教育学向马克思主义的转向"③。

---

① 外形歧视主义 Sizeism 指的是对体型过胖或过瘦，身高过高或过矮的人的歧视。
② Peter McLaren, *Critical Pedagogy and Predatory Culture*, Routledge, 1995, p. 24.
③ 王雁：《美国批判教育学者麦克拉伦的学术生命研究》，硕士学位论文，东北师范大学，2013 年，第 8 页。

基本上，就马克思主义而言，麦克拉伦的方法是折中主义和非宗派主义的。① 他对各种各样的人物表示钦佩，比如古巴游击领袖切·格瓦拉、无政府主义者艾玛·戈德堡（Emma Goldberg）、革命民族主义者埃米利奥·萨帕塔（Emilio Zapata），以及印度的甘地（Ghandi）和美国的马丁·路德·金（Martin Luther King）等革命和平主义者。我们也可以把他的批判教育学品牌与约翰·杜威的著作、拉丁美洲大众教育和解放神学的传统以及启蒙运动传统的批判方面联系起来②。马克思主义是麦克拉伦思想的最主要理论渊源之一，马克思主义人道主义是他的批判教育学理想和批判武器。

二 美国进步思想、法兰克福学派批判理论与后现代主义

（一）美国进步主义和社会重建主义思想

除了取经自欧洲法兰克福学派的传统之外，批判教育学同时也受惠于美国自身的独特传统，如约翰·杜威，威廉·H. 基尔帕特里克（William H. Kilpatrick）等人为首的进步主义教育运动，以及20世纪20年代的社会重建主义者如乔治·康茨（George Counts）和休伯纳（Dwayne Huebner）、西奥多·布拉梅尔德（Theodore Brameld）以及詹姆斯·麦克唐纳（James McDonald）等人的贡献。③ 进步主义的教育哲学认为教育的目的在于促进民主的社会生活。教师的角色是问题解决的引导者和科学的探究者。课程的安排必须基于学生的兴趣，包含人类问题、事务的应用、重视跨学科的主题教学。社会重建主义者认为教育的目的在于重建社会、进行社会改革。教师的角色是一个改革的能动者，如同一个方案的引导者、研究的领导者，可以帮助学生觉察到人类社会所面临的问题。麦克拉伦的革命性的批判教育学思想的中心任务就是寻找资本主义体制

---

① Gregory Martin, "Remaking Critical Pedagogy: Peter McLaren's Contribution to a Collective Work" *International Journal of Progressive Education*, Vol. 3, No. 2, 2006, p. 67.

② Gregory Martin, "Remaking Critical Pedagogy: Peter McLaren's Contribution to a Collective Work" *International Journal of Progressive Education*, Vol. 3, No. 2, 2006, p. 67.

③ Peter McLaren, *Life in Schools: An Introduction to Critical Pedagogy in the Foundations of Education* (Second Edition), New York: Longman, 1994.

的替代方案，进行社会重建，实现真正的民主。

(二) 法兰克福学派批判理论

于 20 世纪 30 年代诞生在德国的法兰克福学派的思想理论，是西方最具影响力、传播最广泛的社会思潮之一。批判教育学除了得力于保罗·弗莱雷的启发之外，对于学校教育的批判基础，也受益于欧洲的法兰克福学派，包括西奥多·阿多诺 (Theodor Adorno)、麦克斯·霍克海默 (Max Horkheimer)、赫伯特·马尔库塞等人发展的社会批判理论。[1] 法兰克福学派是在第二次世界大战之前，在德国的社会研究院 (Institute for Social Research) 成立的，成员包括霍克海默、阿多诺、班亚明、洛恩赛尔 (Leo Lowenthal)、弗洛姆 (Erich Fromm) 和马尔库塞，他们曾经发表过非常睿智、道德上振聋发聩的有关《弗洛伊德——马克思主义》(Freudian-Marxist) 的分析。第二次世界大战期间，研究院的一些学者，由于左派和犹太人的身份而逃到美国躲避纳粹迫害。第二次世界大战后，他们在法兰克福重新成立研究院，第二代的批判理论家，例如哈贝马斯 (Habermas)，则到不同的地方继续第一代的研究。在美国，法兰克福学派的社会批判理论也正在重新开始影响社会研究，包括文学批评、人类学、社会学和教育理论。法兰克福学派的思想理论严厉批评现代西方工业文明中工具理性、科学主义、科层体制、资本主义等特质的合理性，他们认为从启蒙以来人类理性的发展，成为资本主义与工业文明的基础，其目的本来是"解放人类理性并征服自然"，然而由于内在逻辑的矛盾，使之反转而走向自我毁灭。因此批判理论认为在科层体制的发达之下，学校教育也是服务于资本主义的，成为工具理性和技术体制宰制个人心灵并控制社会秩序的工具。事实上，法兰克福学派的思想理论对麦克拉伦批判教育学思想中的课程价值、课程内容选择和课程研究方法都产生了重要影响。例如，法兰克福学派理论的文化分析已经成为麦克拉伦分析教育问题的重要工具。法兰克福学派的思想理论侧重于分析社会文化与主流群体及其附属群体之间的关系，并深入分析文化如何传达主流的

---

[1] Peter McLaren, *Life in Schools: An Introduction to Critical Pedagogy in the Foundations of Education* (Second Edition), New York: Longman, 1994.

意识形态，同时，也积极呼吁关注和培养工人阶级、女性、少数族群、学生等群体的语言、知识、沟通技巧和社会关系。法兰克福学派社会批判理论的创始人之一霍克海默指出，批判理论绝非如传统理论一般以知识本身的增长为目标，它乃是一种解放话语，它要改变那些造成不幸的种种状况，把人从奴役状态中解放出来，并为更加公正合理的社会组织而奋斗。[①] 麦克拉伦在《学校生活》中曾言道，批判教育学的理论渊源，就是受到法兰克福学派的批判理论影响很大。

（三）后现代主义

后现代主义是20世纪60年代以来基于对现代哲学的深刻反思而涌现的诸多哲学思潮。这些思潮主要有：以福柯、德里达、利奥塔（J. F. Lyotard）等为代表的后结构主义；以罗蒂（R. Rorty）等为代表的新实用主义；以格里芬（D. R. Griffin）等为代表的"建设性后现代主义"等。后现代主义最重要的特征是对现代主义观念中的整体性、普遍性和理性进行批判。麦克拉伦认为，后现代的反本质主义可以剥离有关性别角色、人性本质、种族偏见等传统思想中所根深蒂固的意识形态，而后现代的反实证主义可以挑战学校教育中信奉客观真理的科学主义迷思。麦克拉伦在访谈中表示："在我最初的学术生涯中，我作为一个左翼自由进步分子，对话语、心理语言学、社会语言学、人类学、社会学、符号学都很感兴趣，然后转向了后现代主义理论。我成为了一名跨学科的学者，我对语言的转变非常感兴趣，并长期将自己描述为一个批判的后现代主义者。"[②] 在诸多后现代主义思潮中，麦克拉伦的批判教育思想主要受到后结构主义的影响，尤其是福柯的思想。福柯被视为马克思以来最全面而透彻剖析权力的思想家。他指出："权力制造知识，权力和知识是直接相互连带的。"[③] 也就是知识与权力二者难以分割，任何知识都包含

---

① 上海社会科学院哲学研究所外国哲学研究室编：《法兰克福学派论著选辑》（上卷），商务印书馆1998年版，第17页。

② 蔡幸芬、杨忠斌：《对后现代主义的反叛——Peter McLaren 的批判教育学后现代主义观点》，Second International Conference on Education and Sports Education, 2011, pp. 499–502.

③ ［法］米歇尔·福柯：《规训与惩罚》，刘北成、杨远婴译，上海三联书店1999年版，第29—30页。

了权力，而任何权力也需要知识才能有效运作。受福柯思想影响，麦克拉伦认为批判教育理论基本上关切的是对"权力—知识"关系的理解。这是因为，主流的教育总是忽视知识和权力的关系，而用纯粹技术性的方式看待知识，这种技术理性的教育使得知识被过度工具化，而忽略了知识的本质是社会建构的，事实上知识绝对不能被视为存在于"权力—知识"的关系之外。

三　保罗·弗莱雷与亨利·吉鲁的教育思想

（一）保罗·弗莱雷的解放教育思想

批判教育学先驱、已故巴西教育家保罗·弗莱雷（1921—1997）被誉为"拉丁美洲的杜威"，他提出了教育的政治性问题，并在《被压迫者教育学》（Pedagogy of the Oppressed）一书中充分完整地阐述了以培养批判意识为目的的解放教育理论。从20世纪70年代开始，这本书帮助唤醒了围绕北美和世界其他地区教育问题的民主活力。他所提出的解放教育学，对第三世界国家的成人识字教育不但具有革命性的影响力，还带动追随者如法拉本多·马蒂（Farabundo Marti）、塞萨尔·奥古斯托·桑迪诺（Cesar Augusto Sandino）、罗莎·卢森堡、切·格瓦拉等人投入拉丁美洲的解放运动。[1] 保罗·弗莱雷肯定个人有发展批判意识的能力，因此，他的教育特色在于将教师与学生视为共同参与意义建构的主体，透过批判式的识字教育（critical literacy），个人得以认知到自身的真实处境，并产生对抗霸权的意识，进而采取行动改变这个世界。[2] 保罗·弗莱雷（1972）对教育赋予积极性的解放意义，并据此批评传统教育有如银行囤积型（banking education），学生只能被动地接受、储存、堆积知识，这样的知识不但容易造成学生疏离感，抹灭其自觉与价值，而且只呈现主流文化的观点。因此他在《被压迫者教育学》一书中提出对话式与质疑式教学，主张"觉醒"（conscientize）的反思，而教师也要时时进行自我反

---

[1] Sleeter, C. E., & McLaren, P. L., *Multicultural education, critical pedagogy and the politics of difference*, Albany, NY: State University of New York Press, 1995, p. 14.

[2] Weiler, K., *Women teaching for change: Gender, class & power*, New York: Bergin & Garvey, 1988, pp. 17–18.

省的工作，以了解自身意识形态背后的预设。保罗·弗莱雷重新定义识字教育（literacy）的概念，将其予以政治化，同时还积极地将教育视为一种自由的实践，一方面显示出新教育社会学的批判色彩，另一方面也可看出解放神学的影响，使其教育哲学蕴含着解放的色彩，可谓同时兼顾批判教育学所提出的"批判性的语言"（language of critique）与"可能性的语言"（language of possibility）。①

事实上，保罗·弗莱雷是对麦克拉伦批判教育思想的形成影响最大的教育学者。麦克拉伦作为保罗·弗莱雷的密友和伙伴，他转向马克思主义社会理论的部分原因是，他阅读了切·格瓦拉的革命政治以及保罗·弗莱雷的作品，尤其是他的《被压迫者教育学》，深受他们的鼓舞。他将保罗·弗莱雷视为开启了批判教育学的先河的学者，认为"保罗·弗莱雷的著作毫无争议地已经成为推动北美批判教育学形成的原动力"。在接受迈克尔·肖内西（Michael Shaughnessy）的采访时，麦克拉伦将保罗·弗莱雷的工作描述为"建立教育学和政治学之间的关键关系，突出教育学的政治方面，并提请人们注意政治领域内教育学的内隐和外显领域"。

麦克拉伦也曾在加州大学洛杉矶分校与流亡到美国的保罗·弗莱雷相遇。他还多次撰写关于保罗·弗莱雷生平和思想的文章，比如《保罗·弗莱雷主义教育学、实践与希望：千禧年的计划》《解放的政治：保罗·弗莱雷之路》（Politics of liberation: Paths from Freire）等。在他的书《切·格瓦拉、保罗·弗莱雷与革命教育学》中，麦克拉伦强调了切·格瓦拉反资本主义的第三世界国际主义以及保罗·弗莱雷在识字教学方面的激进工作的重要性。麦克拉伦认为："保罗·弗莱雷的作品协助我抛开作为一位在西方工业化社会下的教育工作者脑中所具有的殖民观……教育系统其实是被放在帝国主义、父权主义和欧洲中心主义中的论述。更为重要的是，他也协助我发展反抗霸权的策略以及城市教育改革的策

---

① Giroux, H. A. (1985), "Introduction", In P. Freire, *The politics of education* (pp. xi – xxv), South Hadley, MA: Bergin & Garvey, pp. xiv – xviii.

略。"① 实际上，保罗·弗莱雷教育思想中的诸多观点，如"意识觉醒""对话式教学""爱与希望"等都深深影响着麦克拉伦。

麦克拉伦改变写作风格的一个原因是，他越来越关注"批判教育学"的样态与保罗·弗莱雷最初版本的《被压迫者教育学》之间的距离。事实上，对于麦克拉伦来说，这是一个令人担忧的问题："在很多情况下，保罗·弗莱雷的作品通过政治庸俗化和教育驯化，与资本主义达成了和解。保罗·弗莱雷的作品经常被用在批判文学领域以一种令人震惊的方式将文学和教育学与资本主义剥削和阶级斗争分离开来；简而言之，以一种回避革命实践的方式。"②

《被压迫者教育学》的激进主义本身证实了麦克拉伦的断言，即弗莱雷式教育学（Freirean Pedagogy）正朝着被驯化的方向发展——重点是弗莱雷自己的文本是带有60年代革命情绪的文章。他的《被压迫者教育学》第四章很少被引用，它讲述的是如何教导"革命实践"（revolutionary praxis），更具体地说，是如何教导一群人抵制殖民主义。它是专门受切·格瓦拉和菲德尔·卡斯特罗（Fidel Castro）的精神鼓舞而写的。而且，可以论证的是，麦克拉伦的《切·格瓦拉、保罗·弗莱雷与革命教育学》（2000）一书可以被解读为试图将保罗·弗莱雷的书中的同一章节融入语境并加以更新。这本书标志着麦克拉伦重新审视保罗·弗莱雷理论的一个时期，他成为了一个"古典保罗·弗莱雷者"，就像他自己宣称自己是一个"古典马克思主义者"一样。

在麦克拉伦的著作如《资本家与征服者》（Capitalists and Conquerors）（2005）、《红色研讨会》（Red Seminars）（2005）、《反对资本主义和新帝国主义的教学》（Teaching Against Capitalism and the New Imperialism）（2005）以及由一系列采访组成的《愤怒与希望》（2006）中我们可以发现一套回归"古典保罗·弗莱雷主义"的策略。

---

① Peter McLaren, *Life in Schools: An Introduction to Critical Pedagogy in the Foundations of Education* (Fourth Edition), Pearson Publishers, 2003, p. xxix.

② Peter McLaren, ed., *Rage and Hope: interviews with Peter McLaren on war, imperialism, + critical pedagogy*, New York: Peter Lang Publishing, Inc., 2006, p. 25.

(二) 亨利·吉鲁的批判教育学思想

20世纪80年代由亨利·吉鲁、迈克尔·阿普尔、让·安恩（Jean Anyon）、菲利普·韦克斯勒（Philip Wexler）、比尔·派纳（Bill Pinar）、玛德琳·格鲁梅特（Madeline Grumet）等人为批判教育学建立奠基的基础[①]。相关研究可以分为两大范畴：其一是理论基础工作，如彼得·麦克拉伦（Peter Mclaren）、亨利·吉鲁、斯坦利·阿罗诺维茨（Stanley Aronowitz）、比尔·派纳和迈克尔·阿普尔属之；其二则是学校的批判民族志研究和个案研究，从事这方面工作的有保罗·威利斯、凯瑟琳·维勒（Kathleen Weiler）、贝瑞·康柏（Barry Kanpol）及彼得·麦克拉伦（Peter Mclaren）等，这些作品真正触及性别、种族、阶级等范畴的问题。[②]

亨利·吉鲁认为抗拒论虽然超越再制论的悲观决定论色彩，有效地解释了经济关系、文化、意识形态霸权复制过程中主体所拥有的"相对自主性"（relative autonomy），并认知到不同生活面向中意识形态霸权彼此之间存在的矛盾、冲突性格，但是对于批判教育学而言，单单对现象作批判的分析和解释仍是不足、被动的。[③] 因此，亨利·吉鲁认为有必要将抗拒论的观点拉到一种具有解放概念的旨趣当中。亦即，批判教育学认为抗拒行为的性质和意义必须包含解放的可能性。因此，抗拒必须有揭露的功能，它可以有效批判宰制的霸权，也可以达成自我反省、自我解放和社会解放的目的，抗拒必须同时具备批判性的语言和可能性的语言。所以抗拒论可以被视为批判教育学的前身，而批判教育学则在超越抗拒论后，从20世纪80年代逐渐发展出独立的学术造型。

到了20世纪80年代末期，亨利·吉鲁有感于过去批判教育学多将关注的焦点摆放在学校教育之中，如改革师资培育教育、公共学校、高等

[①] Giroux, H. A. & McLaren, P. (1995), "Radical Pedagogy As A Cultural Politics: Beyond the Discourse of Critique and Anti–utopianism", In P. McLaren, Critical Pedagogy and Predatory Culture: Oppositional Politics in A Postmodern Era (p. 29–57), New York: Routledge, p. 30.

[②] Peter McLaren, Life in Schools: An Introduction to Critical Pedagogy in the Foundations of Education (Sixth Edition), Boulder, CO: Paradigm, 2014, p. 128.

[③] Giroux, H. (1983), Theory, Resistance, and Education: A Pedagogy for the Opposition, South Hadley, MA: Bergin & Garvey, 1983, pp. 102–107.

教育和社区教育等领域，虽然这是必要而且正确的着力点。但是，他也发现有许多批判教育者将自己锁在传统学科疆界中，不断反复研究一些旧有的学说思想，忽视了其他领域所产生的重大改变，也无视于外在世界充斥对于民主、社会和学校的威胁。以至于他/她们无法处理现今公立学校、高等教育和广大社会所面临的重要问题。亨利·吉鲁同时也发现多数美国教育者兴起一种反智主义的倾向，只想寻求实用的解决方法，不愿投注于公共教育和高等教育所面临的政治、社会问题。此时，教育的批判论述被化约为一种对于经验的赞扬，理论和实践的对立之声再起，理论变成次要或无用的知识，实践反而变成教育学的权威。因此，他结合了女性主义理论、后结构主义、后现代主义、文化研究和文学理论等，以处理教育学中有关文化差异政治的问题，跨越学科疆界、开启新的联结，为日益恶化的教育领域注入新的希望和养分。如贝尔·胡克斯、康奈尔·韦斯特（Cornel West）、斯图亚特·霍尔、爱德华·萨义德（Said）Edward、钱德拉·莫汉蒂（Chandra Mohanty）、拉里·罗斯伯格（Larry Grossberg）、贾亚特里·C.斯皮瓦克（Gayatri C. Spivak）等人，同时都对"批判教育学"和"文化政治"的概念重新定义。他/她们都拒绝将教育学简化为知识的实践和技术的传输，而是将教育学视为政治、文化生产的一种形式，并认为它与知识、主体性和社会建构有很深的关系。这些不同领域的文化工作者，将教育学从去历史化、无理论性的实践转化为一种文化政治的形式。[1]

为了宣示20世纪90年代批判教育学向文化政治转向的立场，亨利·吉鲁将批判教育学重新定义为：将教育学理解为一组文本的、言语的、视觉的实践结构，以投入人们了解自己的过程，以及他/她们投入他人和其环境的方式。它也认知到符号的表征发生在文化生产的不同领域之中，而生产文化的社会中存在许多竞争性和不平等的权力关系。而教学作为一种文化生产的形式，正与知识、欲望、价值观、社会实践的组织和建构有关。在这个胜败关头，必须发展一种教育学的概念足以对抗主流的

---

[1] Henry Giroux, *Border Crossings: Cultural Workers and the Politics of Education*, Routledge, 1992.

符号生产模式。教育学作为一种文化的实践,以罗杰·西蒙(Roger Simon)的话来说,就是要投入对抗、重塑这些不同形式的影像、文本、说话、动作的建构和呈现,并造成意义的生产,以告知文化工作者、教师和学生,她/他们个人和集体的未来。[1] 为了达成教育的解放目的,亨利·吉鲁对教师寄予深重的期待。因为,若期待教师带领学生一起质疑、对抗"真理政权"(regimes of truth),重要的关键就是要协助教师成为一位转化型知识分子(transformative intellectual),致力于承担社会转化的实践工作。亨利·吉鲁认为身为一位转化型知识分子的教师必须认同以下理念:将教学当作一种解放性实践;将学校创造成一个民主的公共领域;寻回一个可以分享进步观点的社群;强化共同的公共论述,以联结平等、社会正义的民主律令。[2] 如果教师愿意认同自己是转化型知识分子的话,就应致力于将学校转化为一个为民主奋斗的机构。落实到教学实践上,亨利·吉鲁主张教师一定要使课堂知识和学生生活相关,使学生有其声音。也就是说,要肯定学生经验是鼓励师生交流的重要部分,便要提供与学生生活经验有所共鸣的课程内容,并将之意识化与问题化,质疑学生这类生活经验背后埋藏的假设,帮助学生了解其政治、道德意蕴。亨利·吉鲁坚持教师必定要解放知识与经验,促进学生社会幻想和公民勇气,帮助学生型塑自我认同,或进行社会经验与文化意义的再生产。[3]

在《学校生活》一书中,麦克拉伦指出他的许多观点都是受亨利·吉鲁作品的启发而来,尤其是《教育中的理论与抗争》(Theory and Resistance in Education, 1983)、《教育围城》(Education under Siege, 1985)、《教师作为知识分子》(Teachers as Intellectuals, 1985)等作品,亨利·吉鲁提供给他许多具有洞见的研究路线和精神上的鼓励。比如,

---

[1] Henry Giroux, *Border Crossings: Cultural Workers and the Politics of Education*, Routledge, 1992, p. 3.

[2] McMcLaren, P. (1988), "Foreword: Critical Theory and the Meaning of Hope", In H. A. Giroux, *Teachers as Intellectuals* (pp. ix - xxi), Granby, MA: Bergin & Garvey, p. xviii.

[3] McLaren, P. (1988), "Foreword: Critical Theory and the Meaning of Hope", In H. A. Giroux, *Teachers as Intellectuals* (pp. ix - xxi), Granby, MA: Bergin & Garvey, pp. xv - xvii.

在亨利·吉鲁的作品中非常强调批判性的语言和可能性的语言、教师应作为转化型知识分子、学生声音的重要性等。麦克拉伦也使用了亨利·吉鲁的"发声"概念，认为它是一个重要的教学概念，是指个人解读和诉说经验的文化方法，使学生从主流文化的宰制中得以解放，并有能力改造自己和社会。麦克拉伦是这样评价亨利·吉鲁在他心中的位置的："我和亨利·吉鲁一起工作过很久。亨利·吉鲁是我早期的导师，一个非常强大的知识分子。对我来说，和亨利一起工作就像一个初露头角的艺术家和毕加索一起工作。他过去是，现在仍然是一位伟大的导师。"[①]

第二节 马克思主义人道主义——麦克拉伦批判教育学的核心理论武器

一 马克思主义人道主义作为麦克拉伦批判教育学的理想

由于一些学者，不满于经济马克思主义太强调经济决定论的观点，再加上马克思早年的《1844年经济学与哲学手稿》（*Economic and Philosophic Manuscripts of 1844*）在20世纪30年代以后陆续被发现，带动了马克思主义人道主义的研究取向——着重于"人类本质——劳动"能动性展现的观点，反对忽视个体的思想和行动。基本上，此派代表先驱主要有《历史与阶级意识》的作者乔治·卢卡斯（George Luckacs）、"反对只重视手段，而忽略了原先目的"的卡尔·考茨基（Karl Kautsky）、提出"文化霸权"的安东尼奥·葛兰西等人。他们结合了黑格尔（Hegal）对意识的关心旨趣及经济结构决定论者上的旨趣，在思想与行动间带入了个体（individual）、意识（consciousness）和关系（relationship），并在社会革命的实践面向上，强调个体行动的重要性，进而恢复主观性和客观性的辩证性。在此种追求主体性以改造社会的人道马克思主义想法的影响下，麦克拉伦认为批判教育学的目标是一致的——要让没有权力的人，

[①] Engle, S., "Peter McLaren: Connecting Pedagogy to Social Issues" *Forum*, Vol. 7, No. 3, 2005, p. 3.

变得更有能力、有权力,以改变社会不平等和不公义的现象。① 因此,批判教育学对教育领域中勇敢不放弃希望的人,提供历史、文化、政治和道德的方向,并致力于个人自我增能和社会转型改革的解放实践上。整体而言,麦克拉伦自称他是位黑格尔派的马克思主义者,就是立足于这种立场。革命性的批判教育学的理论基础,也是基于此类人道马克思主义的传统。麦克拉伦近年的作品,主要也以马克思人道主义的概念去批判全球资本主义下的剥削关系。

马克思主义人道主义致力于为世界上的居民(人类和非人类)创造更好的生活②。莱雅·杜纳耶夫斯卡娅被誉为美国马克思主义人道主义的奠基人。从莱雅·杜纳耶夫斯卡娅和彼得·胡迪斯③,以及《消极的力量》(The Power of Negative)一书的合著者凯文·安德森那里得到了启发,麦克拉伦(2005)写道:"我自己的马克思主义是由马克思主义人道主义哲学所指导的,它假定,在黑格尔之后,前进的动力来自对障碍的否定。正是对'是什么'的否定和对既定事物的批判,刺激了发展,创造了通往解放的道路。"④

麦克拉伦没有忽视理论与实践之间的冲突,具体地说,也没有忽视学术、工会和革命左派倾向之间的斗争,他认为不存在纯理论的或纯粹的马克思主义。马克思想要的是克服资本主义社会关系对客观世界的异化,回归人性本身。也就是说,人类是其思想的主宰;思想本身不是思想的主宰。人类是理念自我运动的媒介。自我运动通过否定阻碍自我运动的力量而运动。但是彼得·胡迪斯(2012)告诉我们,否定依赖于其否定的对象。不管你否定的是什么,都留下了被否定对象的影子。例如

---

① Peter McLaren, *Life in Schools: An Introduction to Critical Pedagogy in the Foundations of Education* (Fifth Edition), Pearson Publishers, 2007.

② Marx, K., *Economic and Philosophic Manuscripts of 1844*, New York: Prometheus Books, 1988, p. 76.

③ 彼得·胡迪斯(Peter Hudis)是总部位于芝加哥的新闻与信件集团(News & Letters collective)的组织者。

④ McLaren, P. (2005), "Critical Pedagogy in the Age of Neo-liberal Globalization", In P. McLaren, ed., *Capitalists and Conquerors: A Critical Pedagogy Against Empire* (pp. 19-73). Lanham, MD: Rowman & Littlefield, p. 35.

在历史上我们所要极力否定的压迫的形式总是影响我们对于解放的理解与定义。①

麦克拉伦认为:"这就是为什么黑格尔提倡一种以自我作为参照的否定——否定之否定。通过二次否定,建立一种与自己的关系,脱离与之前所要否定的外部客体的联系。因为二次否定不涉及本身之外的外部客体,所以是绝对的——不依赖他者的否定形式。通过自我参照的否定来否定其外部依赖。例如,用集体财产取代私有财产不会确保解放;因为前者仅仅是一种抽象的否定,其本身需要被进一步否定,进而获得解放。集体财产仍然受其否定的对象私有财产的影响,因为他们都无一例外地关注财产,都受所有权或占有权的影响。"② 胡迪斯(2012)写道:"马克思用'否定之否定'原理来解释达到新社会的途径。共产主义对私有财产的取消是对资本主义社会的否定。但是马克思告诉我们,这一否定用集体财产代替私有财产但仍然依赖于私有财产。共产主义没有摆脱所有权这一异化的概念,占有仍然是人类生活中的最重要的一部分;仅仅是另一个层次的占有。当然,马克思同意对私有财产的否定是必要的。但是他坚持认为这一否定本身需要被否定。只有这样才能达到真正的肯定(positive)——一个全新的社会。"杜娜叶夫斯卡娅在她的《哲学与革命》中指出:"被黑格尔称为绝对否定的对'超越'的战胜过程,在马克思看来是达到真正的人类社会的唯一途径,'肯定的人道主义,从自身开始'。"③

如果想要彻底取消资本,对私有财产的否定本身需要被进一步否定,这也是达到肯定的必然过程——肯定的人道主义,从自身开始。也就是说对资本说"不",包含了第一次否定——对私有财产的否定是必要的,不可或缺的。但是如果仅仅满足于第一次否定,那也就是承认拥有(hav-

---

① Hudis, P., *Marx's Concept of the Alternative to Capitalism*, Chicago: Haymarket Books, 2012, pp. 72–73.

② Peter McLaren, "Education Agonistes: an epistle to the transnational capitalist class, Policy Futures in Education" Vol. 12, No. 4, 2014, p. 607.

③ Hudis, P., *Marx's Concept of the Alternative to Capitalism*, Chicago: Haymarket Books, 2012, pp. 71–73.

ing）比存在（being）更为重要。① 麦克拉伦认为："当否定主体开始自我意识到第一次否定，也就是说当主体理解了这一否定的意义并认识到这一否定中的肯定的内涵，那么他就达到了否定之否定层次。"换句话来说，当主体意识到他自己应该是否定的对象，就开始了第二次否定，是对阶级意识的触及。当主体认识到否定性的否定行为本身蕴含的肯定性，她也就认识到她自己作为真正的运动主体的事实。在这个过程中，人类作为自决的主体，倾听他们自己的声音，拒绝压迫和一切恶的行为，宣扬保罗·弗莱雷所说的一种解放的替代形式。麦克拉伦完全同意赖茨（Reitz）② 对批判性知识的定义："批判性的知识推进对人类生活中的主要活动的社会否定，其最核心的内容不是海德格尔强调的向死的存在（being-toward-death），也不是康德口中的从属属性（subservience），而是具有创造力的劳动（creative labor）。"③

麦克拉伦指出："在资本主义社会中寻找替代的社会形态意味着在每日生活中发掘潜在的、被忽视的动力潜能，这就要求教师和教师教育者有意识地，并且刻不容缓地通过自我转化超越每日生活和资本主义之下的人类境遇的限制，并志愿在追求社会公正的过程中引导这一无穷的潜力。也就是说，在追求所有人的人性解放的过程中充分认识到现实中蕴藏的不断壮大的改革潜力，而人性对个体本身的超越不是通过向无法改变的过去或者向受惯性约束的现在寻求避难所，而是通过将主观知识提升到一个独立的和客观的真实的层次，并指向确定的和极具活力的未来——这种知识来自人的思维却又超越思维；这种知识在研究特殊与普遍之间的关系之后从特殊中提取出来；对这种知识的研究永远不会穷尽；这种由探索者创造的知识同时又超越探索者本身。"④

---

① Hudis, P., *Marx's Concept of the Alternative to Capitalism*, Chicago: Haymarket Books, 2012, p. 73.

② Reitz, Charles, *Art, Alienation and the Humanities: a critical engagement with Herbert Marcuse*, Albany, NY: State University of New York, 2000, p. 263.

③ Peter McLaren., "Education Agonistes: an epistle to the transnational capitalist class, Policy Futures in Education", Vol. 12, No. 4, 2014, p. 608.

④ Peter McLaren., "Education Agonistes: an epistle to the transnational capitalist class, Policy Futures in Education", Vol. 12, No. 4, 2014, p. 608.

面对一个不断变化的世界，我们需要对批判和改革的内涵加以进化。马克思指出，被压迫者作为能动主体的任何一种可行的实践都需要工人阶级经历从作为这个阶级的一分子到直面自己所在的阶级的辩证的自我否定的过程，也就是说，这个阶级亟须意识到它的成员是怎样被禁锢在剥削的关系中的，以及他们是怎样作为一种"物种存在"在日常生活中被异化的。当然，这种批判性的转变的最终目的是从劳动的价值形式中解放出来。能够确定的是我们需要打破资本主义自我指涉的谜团——我们每个人都在其中无能为力地受之奴役。消极地将自己暴露于各种媒体之前，等同于心甘情愿屈服于资本主义每日商品生产的仪式，屈服于公式化和惯常的重复和单调，屈服于毫无生气的默许和乏味循环的停滞，而所有这一切都必然将毫无批判能力的我们推进绝望和麻木的深渊中。逃出这一深渊的唯一途径便是对替代价值生产的新型社会形态的不懈追寻。麦克拉伦号召我们："需要不懈地追寻，尽管目标从来都不是预设的或者可以完全实现的。在这个名为解放的宴席上每个人都有一席之地：工会、公民自由主义者、无政府主义者、学生、反战社会活动者、马克思主义者、黑人和拉美社会活动者、教师、生态社会主义者、快餐店员工、工厂工人、动物权利维护者等。我们共同致力于用批判理性取代工具理性，培养更多的持异议者，开创工人和社区委员会，以及社区自决结构。"①

多年来麦克拉伦一直心怀信念——即使世界踽踽走向野蛮，也要始终寻找希望之光，并想象人类社会的新景象，以抵消令人麻木的咒语——别无选择。② 在《学校生活》第五版的序言中，麦克拉伦宣称，他所设想的"未实现的"民主是"社会主义民主"，并以"提倡革命实践

---

① Peter McLaren. , "Education Agonistes: an epistle to the transnational capitalist class, Policy Futures in Education", . Vol. 12, No. 4, 2014, p. 609.
② Valerie Scatamburlo-D'Annibal. , "Imagining the Impossible: Revolutionary Critical Pedagogy Against the 21st Century American Imperium" *International Journal of Progressive Education*, Vol. 3, No. 2, 2006, p. 21.

的马克思主义人道主义者"的身份发言①，鼓励我们思考 21 世纪的新人道主义——在任何意义上都未实现的、反对 21 世纪的美帝国主义的、一个我们可以渴望的人道主义。这种新人道主义将面对资本主义压迫、帝国主义、新法西斯主义和殖民主义的实际情况，而不仅仅是殖民主义、帝国主义等文本。它将表达世界上被压迫者和不幸者的痛苦、悲伤和堕落，以及他们对社会变革的梦想。这种新人道主义将认识到人们挑战和集体改变他们所继承的环境的创造潜力。它将建立在对人类解放和将人类尊严和自由扩大到所有人民的坚定承诺之上——承诺以具体、实际和经济的方式真正普及这些价值观。它将超越自由主义者所接受的社会正义的呼声，而这些呼声往往"与改造资本主义社会关系的计划背道而驰"②。相反，一种新的马克思主义人道主义将要求改变那些压制性的、阻碍了人类大多数人发挥其潜力的社会安排、制度和关系，最终实现某种社会主义民主替代资本主义的理想。虽然这是一个很难实现的理想，但是希望是可能性的解放，可能性是必然性的辩证伙伴。当希望足够强大时，它可以把未来向后推到过去，在过去和现在之间，它可以逃脱不可避免的轨道，打破历史的傲慢的力量，因此，我们为之奋斗的不再是一个停滞在"是什么"的毫无生气的想法，而是把"可能是什么"变成现实。希望是梦想的氧气，是革命斗争的耐力。革命性的梦想是那些梦想者一直梦想到不再有梦想者，而只有梦想自己，每时每刻塑造我们的日常生活，开启可能性的道路，能力的培养不是为了获取利润，而是为了满足需求和充分开发人类潜能。③

在麦克拉伦对马克思主义的阶级斗争与人道主义有了进一步的研究后，他相信能够革除资本主义荼毒，能够重建社会阶级，能够真正平等对待劳动阶级并给以真正价值的唯一途径，就是建立一个社会主义的社

---

① Peter McLaren. , *Life in Schools*: *An Introduction to Critical Pedagogy in the Foundations of Education* (Fifth Edition), Pearson Publishers, 2007, p. 17.

② Peter McLaren, *Life in Schools*: *An Introduction to Critical Pedagogy in the Foundations of Education* (Fifth Edition), Pearson Publishers, 2007, p. 29.

③ Peter McLaren, Ramin Farahmandpur, *Teaching Against Global Capitalism and the New Imperialism*: *A Critical Pedagogy*, Rowman & Littlefield Publishers, 2005, p. 89.

会。对麦克拉伦而言，他的理想和诉求是打倒资本主义，而非请求重新分配。资本的本质是价值，因此，是要去挑战资本，也就是要创造一个社会主义的马克思主义人道主义社会，而这个社会主义的马克思主义人道主义社会不是基于价值，而是基于人类的需要，即作为人应有的人性尊严。①

二 时代呼唤马克思主义人道主义作为麦克拉伦批判资本主义的武器

麦克拉伦认识到资本是我们这个时代占绝对主导地位的社会关系，这使他在批判教育学的著作中注入了马克思主义人道主义的烙印，他认为这是他作品的"基石"。②资本作为一种社会关系，否定了民主，否定了我们的人性，疏远了我们与他人合作自主行动的需要，通过把人类变成累死累活的劳动力来创造和再创造这个世界——把人类束缚在生产和再生产私有财产的同一系统中。"从来没有，"麦克拉伦和拉明·法拉曼德普尔认为，"在这个特殊的历史关头，如此迫切地需要马克思主义对资本主义的分析。"③

麦克拉伦认为，美国多年来对外的军事行动是美国主导的新自由主义的升级，他毫不犹豫地将聚光灯对准了本应成为左翼实质性批评焦点的领域——资本主义制度本身。毫无疑问，在当前的历史关头，美利坚帝国的追求和发展既不是美国的特定领域，也不仅仅是特定国家政策的结果。相反，它是"整个资本主义历史和逻辑的系统结果"④。新自由主义经济措施的扩大，继续使国家在促进社会福利方面的权力"消减"，有利于加强国家对企业福利的奴役，再加上苏联国家的解体，加速了马克

---

① Peter McLaren, Rikiowski, G., "Pedagogy for revolution against education for capital: an e-dialogue on education in capitalism today" *Cultural Logic*, Vol. 4, No. 1, 2001, pp. 1–59.

② David Gabbard, "Peter McLaren & the 3 R's: Reflection, Resistance and Revolution" *International Journal of Progressive Education*, Vol. 3, No. 2, 2006, p. 100.

③ Peter McLaren, Ramin Farahmandpur, *Teaching Against Global Capitalism and the New Imperialism: A Critical Pedagogy*, Rowman & Littlefield Publishers, 2005, p. 15.

④ Foster, J. B., *Naked imperialism: The U.S. pursuit of global dominance*, New York: Monthly Review Press, 2006, p. 13.

思主义学术的衰落。"资本主义,"麦克拉伦和拉明·法拉曼德普尔认为,"从来没有如此盲目地迷恋于自己成功的神话。美国的企业领袖和主流媒体使我们习惯于接受资本主义市场是唯一可能的社会现实。"① 麦克拉伦的作品让我们重新审视资本主义世界秩序丑陋的历史和阴谋诡计,并大胆地用马克思主义的视角来审视这一切,从而加大了激进的力度。这一点尤其大胆,因为马克思主义理论多年来一直被主流的知识权力中心诋毁为"累加的""还原主义的",甚至是"压制性的"。对于那些认同"后马克思主义"的话语工具的人来说,尤其如此,这种工具是为了克服马克思主义假定的不足而建立的。后马克思主义者②试图埋葬马克思的遗产,同时通过写作大量关于其死亡的挽歌来从中受益。

尤其是在北美的学术界,关于马克思和马克思主义的古怪漫画比比皆是。将马克思主义视为一种意识形态的尼安德特人主义(Neanderthalism)的形式而不予理会,是被困在过去时代的精神家具里的人唤起的一种陈旧的记忆,已经变得相当普遍。大多数情况下,这是通过引用学术术语(即普遍化、累加、本质化等)来实现的,这些术语已经流行开来,变得如此普遍,以至于不再需要解释这些术语的含义。人们普遍不愿认真阅读马克思的全部著作,更倾向于依赖于社会学导论教科书中出现的那种扭曲的重现,这激发了一些"后"时代的批判。另一些则尤其令人困惑和矛盾。因为尽管许多后马克思主义者在修辞上赞美差异、特殊性、历史性等,但他们在批判马克思和马克思主义时,并没有把这些立场付诸实践——也就是说,他们没有把他们在理论上拥护的方法付诸实践。相反,他们把马克思主义建构为一种统一的被各种各样的错误和天真的假设所蒙蔽的现象并拒绝接受它。

麦克拉伦提醒我们,后马克思主义者和反马克思主义者一样,从来没有成功地终结马克思主义。正如威廉·格雷德(Willian Greider)所主

---

① Peter McLaren, Ramin Farahmandpur, *Teaching Against Global Capitalism and the New Imperialism: A Critical Pedagogy*, Rowman & Littlefield Publishers, 2005, p. 16.
② 他们通常被称为后现代主义者、后结构主义者、后殖民主义者、激进的多元文化主义者等。

张的,他的幽灵仍然"徘徊在全球的土地上"①,因为随着许多人的条件继续恶化,随着人类苦难在全球化资本主义统治下不断升级,人们越来越难以忽视马克思。事实上,当马克思和恩格斯撰写他们激动人心的小册子《共产党宣言》(The Communist Manifesto)时,资本主义仍然局限于少数国家。今天,资本的统治比以往任何时候都更加绝对,世界许多地方的社会状况正在回归到"19世纪的状况"②。萨德·菲尔奥(Saad-Filho)补充说,《共产党宣言》的关键段落在今天比1848年听起来更真实,因为"19世纪资本主义的关键特征在21世纪早期得到了清晰的认识,并得到了更强有力的发展"③。

我们的世界是一个国际相连的世界,但最终由资产阶级的想法和企业"全球化"的议程所主导;一个利益动机至高无上并存在于社会的各个领域和文化的各个角落的世界;一个为了少数人的利益而压迫多数人的世界。在这个世界上,"自由贸易"只不过是被迫服从,地方对经济的控制已被最强大的全球利益所取代,"世界上100个最大的经济体中有一半是公司"。④ 在这个世界上,"消费者的选择"已经超越了公民的概念成为首要权利,"自由"越来越多地指的是"构建财富分配结构的自由,以及更容易跨越国界剥削工人的自由"。⑤ 在这个世界上,"民主"只不过是"自由世界的妓女"和"帝国对新自由资本主义的委婉说法"。⑥ 在这个世界上,赤裸裸的帝国主义显然已经卷土重来,因为好战的美国政府正在为全球资产阶级摇旗呐喊。在这个世界上,石油等资源正在决定着各国之间全球关系的未来,并影响着无辜民众的生活,他们正陷入帝

---

① Greider, W., *One world, ready or not: The manic logic of global capitalism*, New York: Touchstone, 1998, p. 39.

② Greider, W., *One world, ready or not: The manic logic of global capitalism*, New York: Touchstone, 1998, p. 45.

③ Saad-Filho ed., *Anti-capitalism: A marxist introduction*. London: Pluto Press, 2003, p. 1.

④ Starr, A., *Naming the enemy: Anti-corporate movements confront globalization*, London: Zed Books, 2000, p. 18.

⑤ Peter McLaren, *Capitalists and conquerors: A critical pedagogy against empire*, Lanham, MD: Rowman & Littlefield Publishers, 2005, p. 29.

⑥ Roy, A., *An ordinary person's guide to empire*, Cambridge, Massachusetts: South End Press, 2004, p. 54, p. 56.

国战争的交叉火力、正处于严峻的"结构调整计划"的枪口之下;在这个世界上,自由资本主义点燃了无原则的经济去监管化狂潮,这只会加剧世界上绝大多数穷人的金融贫困和不安全。

几乎在世界上每个国家,随着我们继续以"令人沮丧的规律目睹社会、政治和(最重要的)经济权力在相对少数寡头手中的无耻集中"①,贫富差距已显著扩大。世界上最富有的三个人的财富总和超过了48个最贫穷国家的国内生产总值(GDP)总和,225个最富有的人的财富总和大约等于世界上最贫穷的47%的人口的年收入。②"耐克经济"带来了魔鬼工厂的重生——童工、奴隶般的环境、在出口加工区为微薄收入而工作的年轻女性,她们在那里受到狡猾的新形式的契约奴役,工会成员和劳工组织者经常被解雇、殴打,或者干脆"消失"。在世界主要城市中,大约有1亿遭受虐待和营养不良的"街头儿童",大约有200万5—15岁的女孩被卷入全球性交易。③ 如今,当媒体大肆宣扬企业大亨的净资产,颂扬富人和名人的奢侈时,大约有30亿人每天靠不到2美元的收入勉强维持生计。全球有8.52亿人遭受慢性或急性饥饿。每天都有16000多名儿童死于与饥饿有关的疾病——每5秒钟就有1名儿童。尽管我们所知道的是,美国目前军费开支的一小部分就可以结束饥饿。④

这些是我们世界中存在的具体现实——赤贫和绝望的故事。为什么讲故事的人这么少?愤怒在哪里?难道是许多自称"左派"的学者充当了分散注意力的角色,而不是政治干预的角色?他们是否如此迷恋于他们的"话语激进主义",如此专注于解构文本,以至于未能面对全球化资本主义的更广泛背景?在这个问题上,值得引用麦克拉伦自己的话:"随着穷人数量的增加,无家可归的人涌上城市街头,他们越来越被视为破坏

---

① Peter McLaren and Ramin Farahmandpur, *Teaching Against Global Capitalism and the New Imperialism: A Critical Pedagogy*, Lanham, MD: Rowman & Littlefield Publishers, 2005, p. 195.

② Peter McLaren and Ramin Farahmandpur, *Teaching Against Global Capitalism and the New Imperialism: A Critical Pedagogy*, Lanham, MD: Rowman & Littlefield Publishers, 2005, p. 194.

③ Cole, M., "The 'inevitability of globalized capital' versus the 'ordeal of the undecidable': A marxist critique" in M. Pruyn and L. M. Huerta-Charles, eds. *Teaching Peter McLaren: Paths of dissent* (pp. 101 – 125), New York: Peter Lang, 2005, p. 114.

④ Galeano, E., "Terror in disguise" *The Progressive*, Vol. 67, No. 2, February 2003, p. 19.

了资本主义'自然秩序'的人。在西方学院，我们面对着这个不断解开的历史母体……文化融合的先锋庆典；话语的不可通约性；模仿、不确定性和偶然性……文本滑稽……戏仿……游行抗议……在那里，人们可以避免将政治承诺置于考验之中。在这个学院里，马克思主义被斥为没有复杂性，马克思主义的教育者们也越来越被时尚所包围……对于这些研讨会厅里时髦的恶魔来说，后现代主义是波西米亚之夜的毒害力量，在那里，被禁的、可怜的和悲惨的人只是妨碍了他们的乐趣。"[1] 在这一极具煽动性的声明中，麦克拉伦显然是在挑战那些把"文本"变成政治木偶剧场的人。对许多自称"文化激进分子"的人来说，文本分析在他们的想象中被提升到"与革命行动一样的系统震动水平"。"他们的'话语激进主义'使他们陷入了盲目崇拜语言的死胡同"。[2] 在这里，革命"很大程度上是一场文本革命"，一场"沦为对文学经典和其他形式的话语权威的战争"，而"劳动主体的具体世界"则"在很大程度上是独立存在的"。[3] 在这样的背景下，麦克拉伦的作品让我们想起了历史上那些活着的、受苦的、流血的、贫穷的、无家可归的人们。他提醒我们"理论"的政治含义，它拒绝面对资本主义，它剥夺了人们对其解放可能性的认识，它把理论和实践之间的联系归入非结果性的范畴。麦克拉伦的思想——尤其是他受马克思主义人道主义影响的作品——提醒我们理论主义者、理想主义者和道路主义者在政治上优柔寡断、理论与实践脱节、对历史唯物主义的攻击、否定人类的能动性。[4]

当今人们发现自己深陷帝国战争的残酷和资本全球化带来的不公正之中，人们想看看未来可能会发生什么。在这样的背景下，麦克拉伦拒

---

[1] Peter McLaren, *Che Guevara, Paulo Freire, and the Pedagogy of Revolution*, Lanham, MD: Rowman & Littlefield Publishers, 2000, pp. 24-25.

[2] Harvey, D., "The practical contradictions of marxism" *Critical Sociology*, Vol. 24, No. 1-2, April1998, p. 29.

[3] Peter McLaren, *Life in Schools: An Introduction to Critical Pedagogy in the Foundations of Education (Fifth Edition)*. New York: Pearson Publishers, 2007, p. 13.

[4] Valerie Scatamburlo-D'Annibal, "Imagining the Impossible: Revolutionary Critical Pedagogy Against the 21st Century American Imperium" *International Journal of Progressive Education*, Vol. 2, No. 3, DECEMBER2006, p. 28.

绝承认在马克思主义传统的广泛范围内工作的思想家的洞见已被当今流行的变革性政治议程和社会主义愿景的背信所掩盖。他认识到,在资本主义霸权的裂缝和裂痕中,可以隐约听到他们的声音,他们的幽灵令人不安地提醒我们,必须有所作为。[1]麦克拉伦"既非中立也非无定形"[2]。麦克拉伦不是一个"为资产阶级提供剥削和操纵服务的思想家",他"知道如何勇敢地选择自己希望站在的那一边:生活的那一边,接近那些受压迫的人,被剥夺公平的人"。[3] 像保罗·弗莱雷,像切·格瓦拉一样,人道主义的冲动在麦克拉伦的作品中跳动。毫不奇怪,这种人道主义的冲动已经成为"后时代"反人道主义者嘲笑的对象。[4]

人道主义被批评为一种认识论立场和一种伦理政治立场。人道主义作为一种认识论立场,因其将人性视为一种静止的、永恒的品质而受到攻击;因为它的本质主义和普遍主义,以及它的"形而上学"假设。它还因参与欧洲殖民主义历史而受到严厉谴责。[5] 作为一种伦理和政治叙事,宣称解放信息的人道主义理想,被认为不过是一种意识形态的容器,通过它,某些价值、规范和经验被建构为普遍的,并以"规范"的力量强加于个人。简而言之,按照人道主义批评家的说法,人道主义的论述在理论上是垂死的,在政治上也是破产的。上述反人道主义批判的维度无疑是交织在一起的,但一些更热心的反人道主义小册子,由于种种原因,在智力上是不诚实的,在政治上也是可疑的,尤其重要的是,人们

---

[1] Valerie Scatamburlo-D'Annibal, "Imagining the Impossible: Revolutionary Critical Pedagogy Against the 21st Century American Imperium" *International Journal of Progressive Education*, Vol. 2, No. 3, *DECEMBER*2006, p. 29.

[2] Casali, A. and Freire Ana Maria Araujo, "Peter McLaren: Creative dissent", in M. Pruyn and L. M. Huerta-Charles, eds, *Teaching Peter McLaren: Paths of dissent* (pp. 20 – 29). New York: Peter Lang, 2005, p. 22.

[3] Casali, A. and Freire Ana Maria Araujo, "Peter McLaren: Creative dissent", in M. Pruyn and L. M. Huerta-Charles, eds, *Teaching Peter McLaren: Paths of dissent* (pp. 20 – 29). New York: Peter Lang, 2005, p. 22.

[4] Valerie Scatamburlo-D'Annibal, "Imagining the Impossible: Revolutionary Critical Pedagogy Against the 21st Century American Imperium" *International Journal of Progressive Education*, Vol. 2, No. 3, *DECEMBER*2006, p. 29.

[5] Said, E., *Orientalism*, New York: Random House, 1978.

倾向于创造一幅人道主义的漫画，并把它当作一种存在，或存在着的单一的话语来对待。现代人道主义的这种同质化的表现仅仅是一种压制性的极权主义建构，这暗示了对马利克（Malik）①所作的一维解释，人道主义已经以"从自由主义到马克思主义的各种政治形式"来表达自己。

现在的教育学院课程试图激进，通常会在课程中加入大量的福柯、卢梭（Rousseau）、霍洛威（Holloway）、德勒兹（Deleuze）、哈特、内格里和赛义德（Said）。② 对于福柯来说，不存在必须被挑战的权力核心，因此，解放或解放的概念是不可能的，只有一种更有限的可能性，即作为微观抵抗形式的挑战权力。凯文·安德森坚持认为，哈特和内格里的差异政治也反映了类似的立场，他们认为全球斗争是不可衡量的，因为他们只能在没有任何统一的哲学或组织的情况下，以本地化的生物力量来挑战。③ 卢梭（Rousseau）的抗议是反对由资本家统治的卑鄙和不公正的社会制度并认为如果这些机构所产生的社会矛盾能够被废除或严重削弱，那么自由和主权就有更大的可能性。然而，卢梭无法避免将他所提供的替代选择的条件理想化，因为很明显，他所谴责的矛盾是与资本主义社会本身的客观条件相结合的。④ 毕竟，卢梭认为私有财产是文明生活的根本基础之一。这种基础课程在教育学院中往往侧重于自治的马克思主义、后殖民主义和自我限制革命的战略重要性。总之，这是对马克思主义和革命的否定，是对支持劳动改革而不主张推翻国家政权的主张的肯定。

---

① Malik, K., "The mirror of race: Postmodernism and the celebration of difference." in E. M. Wood and J. B. Foster, eds. *In defense of history: Marxism and the postmodern agenda* (pp. 112 – 133), New York: Monthly Review Press, 1997, p. 112.

② Derek R. Ford. "Revolutionary Critical Pedagogy and the Struggle against Capital Today: An Interview with Peter McLaren". *Education Interview*, 2015 – 7 – 16 [EB/OL]. http://www.hamptoninstitution.org/peter-mclaren-interview.html#.XT6gsi2B3FQ, 2019 – 05 – 22.

③ Derek R. Ford. "Revolutionary Critical Pedagogy and the Struggle against Capital Today: An Interview with Peter McLaren". *Education Interview*, 2015 – 7 – 16 [EB/OL]. http://www.hamptoninstitution.org/peter-mclaren-interview.html#.XT6gsi2B3FQ, 2019 – 05 – 22.

④ Derek R. Ford. "Revolutionary Critical Pedagogy and the Struggle against Capital Today: An Interview with Peter McLaren". *Education Interview*, 2015 – 7 – 16 [EB/OL]. http://www.hamptoninstitution.org/peter – mclaren – interview.html#.XT6gsi2B3FQ, 2019 – 05 – 22.

凯文·安德森和彼得·胡迪斯写过相关文章，麦克拉伦对他们的观点表示认同："我批判自治马克思主义者如哈特和内格里等，他们在《帝国》（Empire）（2001）等书中，认为多数人已经积累了必要的'一般智力'，现在已经形成了抵制资本主义的网络——他们在没有任何统一的实践哲学的情况下，通过拒绝复制资本主义已经简单地抵制了资本主义。马克思人道主义理论家凯文·安德森正确地认为这是对超越的拒绝（如对黑格尔的否定）。他写道：事实上，哈特和内格里经常攻击黑格尔和启蒙哲学家们是保守和独裁的，同时也在赞美前启蒙时期的、根植于马基雅弗利（Machiavelli）和斯宾诺莎（Spinoza）的共和党传统。从而他们将自身与解放的未来与来自现在的辩证观念隔绝。……在这里，我们看到，他们和哈贝马斯一样，拒绝一切形式的激进超越、拒绝用辩证的方法来解释资本主义的另一种选择。正如安德森所指出的那样，这样做会激发人们对乌托邦主义的恐惧，或者更糟糕的，激发独裁主义和殖民主义的傲慢。对于哈贝马斯、哈特和内格里和霍洛威（Holloway）来说，似乎有一种对马克思主义人道主义的恐惧。安德森指出，马克思主义的观点指向了既定的超越。因此，在哈贝马斯的例子中，我们回到了一个改革主义的自由主义，哈特和内格里正朝着后结构主义的激进主义迈进。正如安德森所建议的那样，解决方案就是'直面负面的东西'（引用黑格尔的观点），并在考虑种族、民族、性别、性和青少年的多样化的辩证关系中工作。我们不能像约翰·霍洛韦（John Holloway）和其他人所建议的那样，拒绝接受国家的权力，因为在我们创造出一种新的社会秩序之前，这种有害的统治逻辑将会继续存在，而这种秩序是自由地由世界范围内的相关的劳动力构成的。"[1]

麦克拉伦认识到，哈贝马斯等批判理论家和杜威等人的著作中所蕴含的后现代思想和改革自由主义，不足以挑战跨国资本主义这个庞

---

[1] Peter McLaren and Petar Jandrić, "An Interview with Peter McLaren-Critical Revolutionary Pedagogy is Made by Walking: in a world where many worlds coexist" *Policy Futures in Education*, Vol. 12, No. 6, January2016, pp. 807–808.

然大物。① 许多善意的理论家把他们所反对的异化和物化的条件理想化，肯定了他们最初想要否定的东西，他们通过运用抽象的道德理想来挑战剥削的经济体系，从而使他们的思想不能与社会的物质基础相协调（即生产的社会关系以及决定性的人际关系）。在长期斗争中，一种利益与另一种利益对立，摆脱这种僵局的唯一方法是通过辩证唯物主义分析。②

麦克拉伦主要关注的是从"资产阶级人道主义"的魔爪中拯救批判教育学的工作，"资产阶级人道主义往往使其在功能上有利于现有的社会关系、雇主阶级和国际分工"。③ 很明显，他的提法试图通过复兴的实践理论或麦克拉伦所称的"革命性的批判教育学"来弥合个人与集体之间的鸿沟，从而激活马克思主义人道主义的解放潜力。革命性的批判教育学试图产生新的思维方式来思考"人的能动性的可能性"，因为"人在创造和改造这些结构和关系的同时，也受到结构和社会关系的制约"。④ 但麦克拉伦谨慎地注意到"资本作为一种社会关系的影响"对这种能动性的约束。在这一点上，他与马克思不谋而合也就不足为奇了。

当然，马克思是第一个在启蒙主义启发下的资产阶级人道主义中攻击这一主题概念化的"现代"思想家之一。在《政治经济学批判大纲》（the Grundrisse）中，他认为"主体"的抽象形式是很有问题的，因为它们忽略了自我的特定的、可塑的决定因素。⑤ 此外，自由主体表面上的自由和自主性是马克思所断然否认的，因为人们总是受到个人几乎无法控

---

① Derek R. Ford. "Revolutionary Critical Pedagogy and the Struggle against Capital Today: An Interview with Peter McLaren". *Education Interview*, 2015 - 7 - 16 [EB/OL]. http://www.hamptoninstitution.org/peter-mclaren-interview.html#.XT6gsi2B3FQ, 2019 - 05 - 22.

② Derek R. Ford. "Revolutionary Critical Pedagogy and the Struggle against Capital Today: An Interview with Peter McLaren". *Education Interview*, 2015 - 7 - 16 [EB/OL]. http://www.hamptoninstitution.org/peter-mclaren-interview.html#.XT6gsi2B3FQ, 2019 - 05 - 22.

③ Peter McLaren, *Che Guevara, Paulo Freire, and the Pedagogy of Revolution*, Lanham, MD: Rowman & Littlefield Publishers, 2000, p. 26

④ Peter McLaren ed., *Capitalists and conquerors: A critical pedagogy against empire*, Lanham, MD: Rowman & Littlefield, 2005, p. 9.

⑤ Marx, K., *Grundrisse: Foundations of the critique of political economy*, trans. Nicolaus, Harmondsworth: Penguin, 1973, p. vii.

制的物质和历史条件或"环境"（如马克思在《路易·波拿巴的雾月十八日》中所认为的那样）的限制。然而，应该指出的是，由历史上的具体的能动性的人改变压迫环境的可能性是马克思反复强调的主题。

激发革命性的批判教育学活力的无年龄的人类自我是一种物质的、活生生的、真实的、感性的存在，它总是被理解为与马克思所称的"社会关系的总和"有关，这种"社会关系的总和"制约着每个人，并在历史上发生着变化。① 与许多人声称的相反，马克思主义人道主义拒绝自由主义公式的本质主义。马克思自己也反对黑格尔关于超越历史的人性的观点。当马克思讨论"人的本质"时，他并不是指一种非历史的、不变的人性形式，而是处在现实的、可以通过经验观察到的，在一定条件下进行的发展过程中的人。② 马克思坚持"人的本质不是单个人所固有的抽象物"③。马克思的革命人道主义是建立在这样一种理解之上的，即自我是一个历史上偶然存在的实体，它不能脱离活着的、物质的，因此也不能脱离具体的自我表现。

革命性的批判教育学认识到具体的自我（相对于抽象的哲学概念，如"主体"）是世界上一个实际的、知识渊博的行动者；它认识到"人类的行为塑造了历史"，而不是"抽象的类别"。④ 因此，它并没有把人的能动性和经验的范畴归入话语或文本的阴暗面。然而，它对人的能动性的唯物主义定位告诉我们："人们通过已经饱和的社会关系的联系、冲突的价值观和口音的力量场、之前的惯例和限制可能性的实践活动的调解系统，在内部、反对和通过这种系统创造历史。"⑤ 这一概念显然对资产阶级自由人道主义的自愿性、自主性主体提出了挑战，它使我们注意到资本的力量，因为在当今世界，社会关系的联系在历史上是资本主义特

---

① 《马克思恩格斯选集》第 1 卷，人民出版社 2012 年版，第 135 页。
② 《马克思恩格斯选集》第 1 卷，人民出版社 2012 年版，第 153 页。
③ 《马克思恩格斯选集》第 1 卷，人民出版社 2012 年版，第 135 页。
④ Peter McLaren ed., *Rage and Hope: interviews with Peter McLaren on war, imperialism, and critical pedagogy*, New York: Peter Lang Publishing, Inc, 2006, p. 19.
⑤ Peter McLaren ed., *Rage and Hope: interviews with Peter McLaren on war, imperialism, and critical pedagogy*, New York: Peter Lang Publishing, Inc, 2006, p. 266.

有的。但更重要的是，它提醒我们，没有某种形式的人道主义视角，解放叙事是不可能的。① 对麦克拉伦来说，革命性的批判教育学的目的不在于废除私有财产，而在于废除它所依赖的异化劳动。批判教育学要想超越资本社会关系的统治地位，就必须帮助那些从事教育学的人超越自身的异化。麦克拉伦认为："马克思的思想放在检视现今时代的问题，仍是十分有用的。"他从马克思的"人类本质——劳动"论、"物化和异化"概念、阶级冲突论、辩证法、历史唯物论等思想对全球化资本主义带来的剥削和压迫状况进行分析和批判，并且努力试图将理念落实到真实的生活情境中。麦克拉伦的激进来自通过对马克思的研究与了解，他更加清楚地意识到资本主义下的社会关系已经在全球化、商品化的趋势潮流下，将人对于人的本质与尊严的自我意识吞噬殆尽。麦克拉伦正是在这个资本主义全球化野蛮扩张、新自由主义横行、马克思主义理论被排挤和曲解、资产阶级人道主义露出伪善嘴脸、马克思主义人道主义被污名化的黑暗时代拿起马克思主义人道主义作为批判和反抗资本主义的理论武器，以求最终获得人类的解放。

需要强调指出的是，与抽象的人道主义、资产阶级人道主义、人本主义及其他形形色色的人道主义相比较，马克思主义人道主义在肯定"以人为本"时，坚持了对人的唯物史观分析方法，即对人作社会历史的分析，强调"以人为本"是具体的历史的行为，而不是空洞的理念。② 在马克思看来，历史的主体并"不是处在某种虚幻的离群索居和固定不变状态中的人，而是处在现实的、可以通过经验观察到的、在一定条件下进行的发展过程中的人"③。因为，马克思在开始创立唯物史观的哲学革命与转向中就发现，人类社会存在与发展的前提是"一些现实的个人，是他们的活动和他们的物质生活条件，包括他们已有的和由他们自己的

---

① Malik, K., "The mirror of race: Postmodernism and the celebration of difference" in E.
M. Wood and J. B. Foster, eds., *In defense of history: Marxism and the postmodern agenda* (pp. 112 – 133), New York: Monthly Review Press, 1997, p. 122.

② 黄力之：《"以人为本"：马克思主义的人道主义还是抽象的人道主义？》，《毛泽东邓小平理论研究》2009 年第 1 期。

③ 《马克思恩格斯选集》第 1 卷，人民出版社 2012 年版，第 153 页。

活动创造出来物质生活条件"①。正是立足于现实人的实践活动,马克思将人的本质规定为"一切社会关系的总和",并以此对康德的"理性人"、黑格尔的"理念人"、费尔巴哈的"抽象人"给予了历史唯物主义的改造和扬弃,也正是立足于现实人的实践活动,马克思将人自由而全面发展的人道主义追求与无产阶级彻底解放的命运联系起来,从而在历史观、价值观等方面与历史上形形色色的人道主义彻底地区别开来。② 马克思主义是真正关于实现人类彻底解放的理论,人的自由全面发展是马克思主义价值追求的核心。③ 只有在坚持马克思主义基本原则的指导下,将人道主义的研究融入马克思的唯物史观之中,融入马克思主义的整体研究之中,马克思主义的人道主义才能成长出悦人的绚丽之花。④

---

① 《马克思恩格斯选集》第1卷,人民出版社2012年版,第146页。
② 黄斌:《论整体把握马克思主义与人道主义关系的几个问题》,《科学社会主义》2012年第2期,第42页。
③ 黄斌:《论整体把握马克思主义与人道主义关系的几个问题》,《科学社会主义》2012年第2期,第42页。
④ 黄斌:《论整体把握马克思主义与人道主义关系的几个问题》,《科学社会主义》2012年第2期,第42页。

第 三 章

主　旨

资本主义体制是麦克拉伦批判教育学批判的主要对象,麦克拉伦对合理化剥削与压迫的资本主义全球化、新自由主义导致的教育私有化与市场化、加剧阶级复制与不公平的标准化考试进行了深刻的批判和揭露。由于以往批判教育学的被驯化,麦克拉伦认为他所倡导的革命性的批判教育学是实现资本主义社会替代形式的实践哲学。因为革命的批判教育学的目标就是废除阶级,建立新社会;革命批判教育学是一种哲学,一种敏锐性,一种理解我们所在世界的方式;是在对社会主义的想象中进行的,是帮助我们实现社会、文化、性别公平的教学实践的哲学方向。麦克拉伦的革命的批判教育学指出抵制与替代资本主义的实践方式,即在抗争与行动中养成批判意识、现实揭露、集体行动、阶级斗争、宣扬示范性的革命偶像人物。

第一节　资本主义体制——麦克拉伦批判教育学批判的主要对象

一　合理化剥削与压迫的资本主义全球化

麦克拉伦认为过去由资本主义国家主导的全球化就是一种资本主义变形以及扩张的形式。在此种形式下,资本主义一直都以某种形式存在着,而且在暗地里表露其吸血与压榨的本质。麦克穆尔蒂(McMurty,2001)描述资本主义是种癌症,吞噬着全球人类的身体以及人类赖以生存的水、食物甚至是空气，每个人都无法逃脱资本主义的控制。① 麦克拉伦提出的最重要的见解之一在于他对"全球化是如何代表一种掩盖帝国主义多种行动的意识形态表象"② 的看法。他认为："事实上，全球化的概念有效地取代了特权阶级词汇中的'帝国主义'，因为它夸大了资本主义的全球性质——作为一种无所不包和不知疲倦的力量，显然没有任何一个民族国家具有抵抗或反对的手段。此外，它还欺骗性地暗示，资本主义不再需要民族国家的保护。"③ 麦克拉伦认定资本主义是洪水猛兽、是恶魔，因此不但要击败资本主义，还要击败资本家和资本。④

资本主义借着全球化的背景及主要主张，合理化生产关系的压榨与压迫。在资本主义的社会里，劳工付出努力换取其所该得的价值，表面上似乎是天经地义的事情，是极为平常、公平的社会正义。而资本主义下的阶级产生，经过资本家、政府甚至学校的霸权规范与制度制定，阶级复制也就成了自然而然的必然结果。尽管专治霸权的一方总是打着透过个人努力、社会福利等谎言欺骗着阶级是可以打破与再造的，但结果很明显的是否定的。而且是富者越富、贫者越贫；阶级壁垒更加牢不可破；资本主义更加肆无忌惮地蔓延至全球。在资本主义的价值法则下，市场的自由经济导致社会和经济的不平等，而教育竟成为市场自由化、经济不平等扩张的帮手。全球化不但无法让政治安定与社会经济平等，反而加剧社会和经济的差距。⑤

资本主义也透过海外经济、文化殖民的扩张来巩固财团私有的利益，实质上是一种新帝国主义侵略。为了应对2008年资本主义的结构性危机，

---

① McMurty, J., *Value Wars: the Global Market Versus Life Economy*, Toronto, ON: Garamond, 2001.

② Peter McLaren and Ramin Farahmandpur, *Teaching Against Global Capitalism and the New Imperialism: A Critical Pedagogy*, Lanham, MD: Rowman & Littlefield Publishers, 2005, p.39.

③ Peter McLaren and Ramin Farahmandpur, *Teaching Against Global Capitalism and the New Imperialism: A Critical Pedagogy*, Lanham, MD: Rowman & Littlefield Publishers, 2005, p.39.

④ Peter McLaren ed., *Rage and Hope: Interviews with Peter McLaren on War, Imperialism, and Critical Pedagogy*, New York: Peter Lang Publishing, Inc., 2006, p.248.

⑤ Peter McLare and Farahmandpur, R., "Teaching Against Globalization and the New Imperialism: Toward a Revolutionary Pedagogy" *Journal of Teacher Education*, Vol.52, No.2, March2001, p.139.

跨国资本主义已经在全球资本主义的数字化上投入了数十亿美元,他们的经济冒险正在为建立一个全球警察国家做出贡献。"全球警察国家"指的是无处不在的大规模监视、政治镇压和意识形态操控体系,这些体系控制着大多数民众,以避免人民起义的真正可能性。这些阶级斗争和社会控制系统本身已经成为罗宾逊(2018)所称的"压迫积累"中获取利润的一种手段。全球警察国家也指的是政治体系的崛起,最好的描述是21世纪法西斯主义。[①] 历史上,资本主义总是以新的统治形式应对经济危机[②]。19世纪末后工业革命期间的城市肮脏、农村贫困和流离失所问题,通过扩大美帝国主义和殖民主义得到了解决。[③] 1929年的大萧条通过资本主义新政的阶级妥协得以解决。通过政府干预和向战争经济的转变来开发人力资源,帮助美国资本家"生存"到下一个经济周期。[④] 第二次世界大战后,随着革命阶级意识的增强,资产阶级保证了一份可维持生活的工资——福特主义——以换取有组织的工人的忠诚和服从。然而,20世纪80年代资本家放弃了福特主义,认为它在全球范围内寻找市场和劳动力是不可持续的,资本家抓住技术的新发展来重组工作场所,通过聘用外包工人减少对有组织劳动力的依赖。此外,资产阶级抛弃了凯恩斯主义的经济政策,转而支持无限制的个人主义和自由市场竞争,并在全球南方发起军事干预的新自由主义政策,以挫败支持公平经济做法的民选

---

① Robinson, W. I., "The next economic crisis: Digital capitalism and global police state" *Race & Class*, 2018, 0 (0): 1-16. [EB/OL]. https://doi.org/10.1177/0306396818769016, 2019-05-22.

② Mallot, C. S., "Class consciousness and teacher education: The socialist challenge and the historical context", in A. Darder, R. D. Torres, & M. P. Baltodano eds., *The critical pedagogy reader*. New York: Routledge. Google Scholar (2017) [EB/OL]. http://scholar.google.com/scholar_lookup? title = Class%20consciousness%20and%20teacher%20education%3A%20The%20soc, 2019-07-26.

③ Mallot, C. S., "Class consciousness and teacher education: The socialist challenge and the historical context", in A. Darder, R. D. Torres, & M. P. Baltodano eds., *The critical pedagogy reader*. New York: Routledge. Google Scholar (2017) [EB/OL]. http://scholar.google.com/scholar_lookup? title = Class%20consciousness%20and%20teacher%20education%3A%20The%20soc, 2019-07-26.

④ Mallot, C. S., "Class consciousness and teacher education: The socialist challenge and the historical context", in A. Darder, R. D. Torres, & M. P. Baltodano eds., *The critical pedagogy reader*. New York: Routledge. Google Scholar (2017) [EB/OL]. http://scholar.google.com/scholar_lookup? title = Class%20consciousness%20and%20teacher%20education%3A%20The%20soc, 2019-07-26.

政府。当国际货币基金组织（International Monetary Fund）和世界银行（World Bank）"取消了对跨国资本和货物转移征税的许多规定"[①]时，这预示着跨国贸易为资本家带来了利润。以墨西哥恰帕斯（Chiapas Mexico）为基地的激进社会主义政治运动——原住民萨帕塔（Zapata）起义，就是对这些政策的直接回应。如今，通过数字化实现的资本主义全球化，自2008年的"大衰退"（Great Recession）以来，一直在加剧精英与穷人之间的鸿沟。罗宾逊指出："根据乐施会（Oxfam）[②]的数据，2016年，只有1%的人拥有全球一半以上的财富，而前20%的人拥有其中94.5%的财富，而剩下的80%的人只能靠4.5%的财富勉强度日。"[③] 此外，潜在的经济危机导致生产过剩，导致财富大量集中在跨国资产阶级手中，他们对数字技术的投资不仅增加了潜在的利润，还需要更加复杂的军事化和镇压形式。正如罗宾逊所指出的："从医疗、食品、电话系统等移民拘留中心内的服务，到驱逐制度的其他辅助活动，如政府与私人包机签订合同，将被驱逐者运送回国，打击移民战争的每一个阶段都已成为利润的来源。"[④] 排斥机制包括"大规模监禁和监狱工业综合体的扩张、无孔不入的治安、反移民立法和驱逐制度、涉及城市军事化的边境和其他围

[①] Mallot, C. S., "Class consciousness and teacher education: The socialist challenge and the historical context", in A. Darder, R. D. Torres, & M. P. Baltodano eds., *The critical pedagogy reader*. New York: Routledge. Google Scholar（2017）[EB/OL]. http://scholar.google.com/scholar_lookup? title = Class%20consciousness%20and%20teacher%20education%3A%20The%20soc, 2019 – 07 – 26.

[②] 乐施会，是一个由17个组织组成的国际联盟，在全球大约94个国家开展工作，寻找解决贫困问题的办法，以及解决它认为世界各地存在的不公平现象。乐施会所有行动的最终目标，都是让人们能够行使自己的权利，管理自己的生活。乐施会直接与社区合作，并寻求影响有权势的人，以确保穷人能改善他们的生活和生计，并对影响他们的决定有发言权。每个组织（附属机构）在国际上共同努力，通过集体努力实现更大的影响。

[③] Robinson, W. I., "The next economic crisis: Digital capitalism and global police state" Race & Class, 2018, 0（0）: 1 – 16. [EB/OL]. https://doi.org/10.1177/0306396818769016, 2019 – 05 – 22.

[④] Robinson, W. I., "The next economic crisis: Digital capitalism and global police state" Race & Class, 2018, 0（0）: 1 – 16. [EB/OL]. https://doi.org/10.1177/0306396818769016, 2019 – 05 – 22.

堵墙"，都成为利润的来源。① 麦克拉伦认为资本主义打着自由市场经济的旗号随着全球化的扩张在操纵政府为他们的利益考虑的情形下也形成一种新帝国主义的侵略，进而引发了令人震撼的"9·11"报复事件。美国的海外军事行动表面上是维护世界和平实际是属于新帝国主义的文化与经济侵略，恐怖主义乃是基于美国对其他国家侵略的报复行动。

资本主义制度是残酷的，如今美国各地的社会生活都反映出了节俭资本主义紧缩的迹象，随着量变向质变的转变，世界正处于一个生态临界点。加里·里奇（Garry Leech）称资本主义是种族灭绝的一种形式——因此，我们正在与种族灭绝、生态灭绝和认识论灭绝②的三重威胁作斗争。③ 麦克拉伦认识到：

> 资本主义利用他们毫无人性的野蛮行径作为刻刀，经年累月，积铢累寸地雕凿资本主义那块尚未完成的号称"文明"的丰碑。对于理解"文明"丰碑的真正内涵的人而言，这座丰碑传递给我们不仅仅是难以置信的震惊，还有违之必诛的恐吓。而生态启示录（eco-apocalypse）也不仅仅是科幻片里幻想出的去乌托邦情节，地球大灾难可能就实实在在站在不远的未来向我们挥手示意。在无视质量，单纯参考数字得出的就业率上升的假象之下，我们都被感染了生态法西斯主义的病毒，这种病毒的耀眼的光亮掩盖了隐藏在光华表面之下的恐慌与愤怒。与生态空间一起被侵害的还有我们的社会公共空间，比如公立学校教育中对高风险测试、教师负责制、全面质量管理（total quality management）的狂热追捧，以及对公立学校私立化（往往从公私合营开始）的热衷等，所有这一切如果不加以制止

---

① Robinson, W. I., "The next economic crisis: Digital capitalism and global police state" Race & Class, 2018, 0 (0): 1-16. [EB/OL]. https://doi.org/10.1177/0306396818769016, 2019-05-22.

② 认识论灭绝，指的是土著社区及其语言和生活方式、他们的宇宙观、他们的思维生态遭到破坏。

③ Derek R. Ford. "Revolutionary Critical Pedagogy and the Struggle against Capital Today: An Interview with Peter McLaren". *Education Interview*, 2015-7-16 [EB/OL]. http://www.hamptoninstitution.org/peter-mclaren-interview.html#.XT6gsi2B3FQ, 2019-05-22.

都将成为摧毁美国公立教育系统 200 年根基的决定因素。(节选自麦克拉伦在东北师范大学的讲课材料)

在这种形势下亟须一种基于大众斗争的批判教育学,寻求一种社会替代方案,以取代将数字经济与全球警察国家相结合的全球资本主义政治和经济议程。对麦克拉伦而言,马克思是其心中可以清晰洞视资本主义意图的老师,也启发了他对于全球化资本主义的看法。回顾他在 2001 年与格伦·里科夫斯基的一段对话当中说道:"我是马克思的学生,走的是传统的马克思主义路线。这个有着胡须的老人家对全球化的资本主义有着预言性的看法,没有人比他更能看清资本主义。"通过对马克思的逐步研究与了解,对于资本主义下扭曲的劳动异化、价值转化、意识形态、假自由与假平等之问题,麦克拉伦已经有了更坚定的立场与深入的了解。对于现今受到资本主义侵蚀的社会所产生的问题,麦克拉伦认为必须回到资本主义的面向,而且必须要从马克思的观点,去检视资本主义的意图,如此,才能对抗全球化资本主义。由于全球资本主义只给极少数人带来了巨大的财富,却给大部分人带来了痛苦而且导致了地球上大部分人生活在非人的生活环境,为了让人们可以从霸权压迫中解放出来,麦克拉伦已经重新聚焦分析可替代空间的建设。作为他面对残酷加剧的资本主义的一部分策略,麦克拉伦已经把他的教育行动由之前的"批判教育学"(Critical Pedagogy)转变成了"革命性的批判教育学"(Revolutionary Critical Pedagogy)。

目睹资本主义全球化的种种罪行,麦克拉伦认为革命性的批判教育学必须要优先分析劳工与资本之间的斗争、生产之间的关系、生产的途径以及本质与社会之间的关系。[1] 麦克拉伦主张,批判教育学应该以马克思主义为理论基础,朝向"反资本主义"奋斗,检视美国的教育现状以及全球化的资本主义。[2] 他特别强调,现今有成百上千万的工人被相对少

---

[1] Peter McLaren, *Life in Schools: An Introduction to Critical Pedagogy in the Foundations of Education* (*Fifth Edition*). New York: Pearson Publishers, 2007, p. 35.

[2] Peter McLaren, *Life in Schools: An Introduction to Critical Pedagogy in the Foundations of Education* (*Fifth Edition*). New York: Pearson Publishers, 2007, p. 35.

数的全球富有的统治阶级所剥削,更证明了无情的全球化资本主义之盛行以及资本和劳工之间无法跨越的鸿沟。① 麦克拉伦并不是要通过政治权力让穷人成为统治者或控制财富,也不是要让穷人去掌握军事,而是对于资本主义的社会关系提出质疑和反抗,使被压迫者觉醒,争取自己的权力。麦克拉伦强调,革命性的批判教育学要对资本主义与政府结合的权力无限扩张,对外以军事行动造成暴虐式的屠杀,对内窥探人民的秘密、限制人民的自由权力等情形提出批评和质疑。② 麦克拉伦认为:"如果我们没有思考我们的梦想、欲望和行动是如何被制造出来以及被社会制约,我们就只是消费主义文化下的奴隶。"在全球经济中,革命性的批判教育学在反对跨国资本主义阶级斗争中的中心地位怎么强调都不过分。它是左派不可或缺的资源,可以用来抵抗新兴形式的资本主义剥削和种族压迫、种族迫害及对其他弱势群体的压迫。麦克拉伦认为:"废除资本主义是极为重要的事。我从马克思对于阶级、政治、经济的批判当中获得启发,成为我过去和现在的革命性批判中不可或缺的要件。"③ 革命性的批判教育学的提出,最终希冀能够创造出一个社会主义的公平社会。

二 新自由主义导致的教育私有化与市场化

新自由主义主张开放边界、建立跨地区市场,加速经济与金融交流,是一种通过例如世界银行、国际货币基金组织等双边或多边的国际组织推动、去除政府管理的资本主义。正如麦克拉伦所言,新自由主义"已经变成了新世界秩序的指导原则"④。这种新的世界秩序通过特定的霸权实践和意识形态话语型塑了我们的社会。结果是对人类被非人化、人类只有在被剥削时是有价值的之工作条件的接纳。人被不夸张地认为是可

---

① Peter McLaren, *Life in Schools: An Introduction to Critical Pedagogy in the Foundations of Education* (*Fifth Edition*). New York: Pearson Publishers, 2007, p. 35.

② Michael Pozo, "Towards a Critical Revolutionary Pedagogy", in P. McLaren, ed. *Rage and Hope: An Interview with Peter McLaren*, New York: Rowman & Little-field Publishers, 2006, p. 17.

③ Michael Pozo, "Towards a Critical Revolutionary Pedagogy", in P. McLaren, ed. *Rage and Hope: An Interview with Peter McLaren*, New York: Rowman & Little-field Publishers, 2006, p. 17.

④ Peter McLaren, *Che Guevara, Paulo Freire, and the Pedagogy of Revolution*, Lanham, MD: Rowman & Littlefield Publishers, 2000.

任意处理的或用完即可丢弃的。在新自由主义者的视角里,国家是软弱无力的,是一个放弃社会功能的机构。因此新资本主义社会形式的特征是:激烈竞争的市场、削减的工资、更多临时的工作、全世界范围内被破坏或削弱的工会、不断增长的失业率、更少保障的劳动合同、被削减或破坏的国家福利。[1] 新资本主义通过各种手段促进利润的最大化。换句话说,资本主义全球化和新自由主义已经联合起来吞噬社会和政治经济。[2]

新自由主义思想不仅推动了私有化驱动的经济体系,还进一步令人不安地影响了教育的发展轨迹。在经济全球化以及新自由主义的教育政策下,公立的学校教育受到全球化影响。在资本主义社会下,教育成为一项宣传平等的利器,以标准化为口号,实现平等的幻象。假如你检视公立学校教育,则将发现公立学校教育成为跨国资本家私有化的资源。[3] 在全球化的高度竞争压力下,教育被视为协助经济成长的工具,就以许多发展中国家而言,受过高等教育者和较多技能训练者被视为具有较高的生产力。教育也被视为解决全球化经济下问题的工具,如失业与贫穷之类的问题。[4] 但在追逐高学业成就、高学历、高能力、高生产力与高绩效的方向下,是谁获得了利益?受益者是谁?弱势者、竞争不利者是否受益?[5]

格伦·里科沃斯基指出在资本主义社会中,学校教育的最大功能在于提供资本充足有用途的劳力,且提高生产力,同时剥削劳工的剩余价

---

[1] Peter McLaren, *Life in Schools: An Introduction to Critical Pedagogy in the Foundations of Education* (*Third Edition*), New York: Longman, 1998.

[2] Peter McLaren, *Life in Schools: An Introduction to Critical Pedagogy in the Foundations of Education* (*Third Edition*), New York: Longman, 1998.

[3] Peter McLaren. (2011a: 6) *education and the unchained class struggle in the crisis of global capitalism*, the speech of international conference on higher education management, National Taichung University of Education, Dec, 24, 2011, pp. 1 – 45.

[4] Peter McLare and Farahmandpur, R., "Teaching against globalization and the new imperialism: toward a revolutionary pedagogy" *Journal of teacher education*, Vol. 52, No. 2, March 2001, p. 139.

[5] Peter McLaren, *Life in Schools: An Introduction to Critical Pedagogy in the Foundations of Education* (*Fifth Edition*), New York: Pearson Publishers, 2007, p. 31.

值，达到资本的积累。① 麦克拉伦以及其他的批判教育者，如亨利·吉鲁，已经说明在过去的 10 年间，新自由主义和新资本主义比以往任何时候都全方位地影响了我们的生活。当然也对教育产生了明显的影响。新自由主义企图将所有的企业私有化，推动各级公共教育的私有化与去中心化。麦克拉伦强调，特许学校的爆炸式增长——所有这些学校要么由营利性企业运营，要么由非营利性企业运营——都在努力从国库中吸走公共资金，这是一项系统性的努力，目的是在废除公共教育的同时促进私有化。把公立学校转变成动态管理的私立学校的新自由主义策略非常见效。麦克拉伦指出："新自由主义策略已经让公立教育脑死亡却不愿拔下那根维持躯体组织循环的管子；公立教育曾经的辉煌和骄傲蒙蔽了它的双眼，让它看不到资本主义是置它于死地的罪魁祸首这一事实。关于如何处置公立教育这具将腐的躯体的论争，发生在奢华酒店中那充满花草装饰，铺着挂浆桌布的早餐厅里，由最一流的经纪人论证，以无可争辩的口吻断言对于我们今天的教育体系最重要的便是：推广私立学校的兴建；多元化社区居民的教育选择。事实证明，这些将死的、与排泄物性质相似的教育论争，局限于无限窄化和空洞的概念性词汇，例如'自由选择'、'共同核心'（Common Core）、'基于能力的教育'、'问责制'等，而所有这些词汇都要额外与民主挂钩。'能力'，很明显指代在将学习的目标描述为满足各种工作领域和岗位需求的前提下，学生能够取得的学业进步或达成的高度，例如，学生可以更好地掌握自己的学习节奏，而最终这些能力水平都要转化为可量化的数字。家长通过教育券和选择程序自由地为孩子选择公立学校教育或私立学校教育，这是新自由主义策略为了在自由市场意识形态下'提高'学校质量的一个例子。"② 教育私有化对公共教育的攻击不仅包含在从幼儿园到初高中（K–12）的教育中，而且正如麦克拉伦所表明的，它已经渗透到大学环境中，特别是教师教育。也就是说，由于 K–12 教师被指责在学校表现不佳，全国各地

---

① Rikowski G., "Left alone: end time for Marxist educational theory?" *British Journal of Sociology of Education*, Vol. 17, No. 4, April1996, pp. 415–451.

② Peter McLaren, "Education Agonistes: an epistle to the transnational capitalist class" *Policy Futures in Education*, Vol. 12, No. 4, April 2014, p. 602.

的教师教育项目也受到了同样的指责,因为他们被认为表现不佳,这再次为盖茨基金会和其他机构介入并"改革"教师教育铺平了道路。教师教育的公司化模式更注重培训,而不是批判性教育。①

新自由主义建立教育考核标准,强调绩效责任。这种"卓越"的新标准与批判性思维、批判教育学、不平等以及对影响教与学过程的社会、经济、教育、课程和教学力量的考察并没有多大关系;但是,更准确地说,这个标准是系统性的,目的是集中精力进行让人麻木的培训,以最小化教授职位,更阴险地最终接管教师教育项目,以一种新自由主义的形象将其公司化、贬低终身职位的重要性、摒弃学术自由的概念、取消对高等教育的资助、雇佣更多的临时教师,而这些人没有工作保障,事实上,他们几乎没有发言权。这让麦克拉伦时不时地担忧教师教育者中为数不多的马克思主义者、无政府主义者和革命社会主义者会不会将在未来几年被主要是兼职的临时劳工取代,而只能靠勇气和食品券生存。②这种对教育的公司化阻碍了批判性思维、创造力和各种形式的艺术。学校不再专注于培养民族国家的民主公民……而是帮助民族国家为跨国公司服务。企业投资者对教育拥有越来越多的控制权,学校本身正在变成企业。我们正在训练学生成为消费公民,而不是民主公民。③

麦克拉伦认为要对抗企业私有化及教育私有化,不能让教育沦为资本主义的帮凶。麦克拉伦指出,新自由主义的两个核心是私有化以及市场化,公共教育已经快速地朝向私有化方向发展,教育扮演着工作制造者的角色,生产有纪律、去技能化以及易被取代的劳工,学校从培养民

---

① 虽然接受培训和接受教育之间有一定的联系,但这两种思维和实践的范式有两种不同的目的。从韦氏词典(2012)中可以看出,接受培训的概念意味着一个人学习了从事一项工作或从事一项手艺所必需的技能,而接受教育的概念意味着在大学等地方接受正规教育。换句话说,培训意味着学习方法、技术和技能,简单地指导未来的教师成为工作人员,或者Stokes(1997)所描述的技术人员,他们不加批判地遵循标准化或一刀切的做事模式。的确,正如Freire(1998)正确地提醒我们,教师培养永远不应该被简化为一种形式的培训,而是应该有意识地渗透着批判性,引发认识论的好奇心,是"……根植于自我和历史的伦理形成"(第23页)。

② Derek R. Ford. "Revolutionary Critical Pedagogy and the Struggle against Capital Today: An Interview with Peter McLaren". *Education Interview*, 2015 – 7 – 16 [EB/OL].

③ Peter McLaren, *Pedagogy of insurrection: From resurrection to revolution*, New York: Peter Lang Publishers, 2015, p. 379.

主思想公民的摇床转变为替跨国法人永无止境的利益而服务。[1] 在新自由主义下，教育改革是为了市场的需求，当教育越发市场化，教育将不再是公民的权利，更加深了异化和阶级再制的趋势。学校改革的大部分内容（如果不是全部的话）实际上是关于公立学校的破坏、企业的接管、教师工资和福利的大幅削减，以及削弱学生和公民质疑这个制度的能力。在一代人多的时间里，这个制度一直把越来越多的财富和权力集中在精英阶层的手中。这与已故喜剧演员乔治·卡林（George Carlin）2005年的一段激昂言论极为一致（绝非巧合）："控制一切的大型商业利益集团……不想要什么。"他们不想要有批判性思维能力的公民。卡林阐述：

> 他们不想要见多识广、受过良好教育的人……这些人足够聪明，能够搞清楚自己被一个30年前把他们扔出窗外的体系搞得多么糟糕。你知道他们想要什么吗？听话的工人——足够聪明的人来运行机器和做文书工作，但是需要蠢到被动地接受所有这些越来越糟糕的工作、低工资，工作时间更长，福利减少，年底加班和养老金消失，消失在你能够领取到的那一刻。

尽管劳动阶级的子女可以因为教育扩张开始有机会接受高等教育，但是，所获得的多半是"次等、贬值的文凭"，而很难改变阶级再制的事实。面对高学费的沉重负担，弱势团体或是社会经济地位较低的学生，在原本就无公平的阶级基础下，却要付出更昂贵的学费进入私校，这点也成为他们寄希望通过教育达成社会阶级流动的一大障碍。此外，现在社会弥漫着这样的说法：这是教育机会均等的时代，进入大学不难，人人有机会读大学，若不读就是个人的问题——这也加剧了所谓通过教育就可以打破阶级壁垒的意识形态。所谓的教育机会均等是指要让每个学生都有公平竞争的机会。但是教育机会均等不应当只是入学时的机会均

---

[1] Peter McLaren. (2011a: 5-18) *education and the unchained class struggle in the crisis of global capitalism*, the speech of international conference on higher education management, in National Taichung University of Education, Dec, 24, 2011, pp. 1-45.

等，还应当包括教育的过程以及教育的结果的均等。这对资本主义的社会而言是不易达到的。例如，教育过程包括学校里面的课程、教学环境、设施设备等，对于来自不同阶层的学生都能有公平获取的机会。然而，公私立学校在课程、设备、环境上仍旧存在着差异性；对于教育结果的均等，应当是不同阶层的学生有均等的教育成就，如在未来的就业状况及职场生活中。但是往往来自中下阶层的学生日后所能从事的工作仍然受限，也印证了阶级再制，也再制了贫穷。在教育市场化、商品化之下，不同阶级的子女没有公平竞争的机会，而所谓的推荐、助学贷款等戳破了教育可以促进阶级流动的表象，反而使阶级再制的情况被强化。主流教育符合中产阶级文化的教育，但对于中下阶级或是劳动阶级的子女而言，是一种异化求学的过程。也就是说，他们必须要更加的努力、更加的认真、更加的学习内化与他们本身阶级不同的文化和价值，才能在社会当中生存。学校是传播知识的场所，麦克拉伦认为学校教育的运作一直是将知识产业变成阶级分明合理化的工具，再制了不平等、种族歧视、性别歧视以及通过强调竞争和文化种族优越主义分化民主社会关系。[1]

布迪厄分析在资本主义社会下，教育系统是通过入学机会伪装成成功机会，掩饰淘汰下层阶级的运作方式。他认为，在文化资本概念下，受益者是中产阶级，而中产阶级所强调的文化又有益于中产阶级的子女。因此，学校教育成为复制阶级的场所，教育成为国家机器再制阶级的工具。英国马克思主义教育理论者格伦·里科沃斯基认为学生在求学时要面对异化、竞争化、阶级化、贬值化、新自由主义化的问题。在新自由主义全球化下，教育逐渐被视为一种贩卖的商品，国家对于教育的管控机制逐渐减弱，市场机制导致教育必须要考虑市场的需求性，这会导致阶级的再制。[2] 当代新自由主义和新保守主义教育改革的最终目的是以牺牲民主和公共利益为代价来加强资本关系。相对于自治的（autonomy）民主价值，市场的劳资关系赋予他治（heteronomy）的价值以特权，或由于

---

[1] Peter McLaren, *Life in Schools: An Introduction to Critical Pedagogy in the Foundations of Education* (*Fifth Edition*), New York: Pearson Publishers, 2007, p. 188.

[2] Rikowski, G., "Alien life: Marx and the future of the human" *Historical Materialism*, Vol. 11, No. 2, July2003, pp. 121 – 164.

对外部权威的依赖而屈从于外部权威。① 教师们非常清楚,在《有教无类法案》(No Child Left Behind) 政策下实施的当代学校改革与教育作为公共产品的价值背道而驰,他们因为担心失去工作而拒绝发表言论或采取行动反对这些改革。在一个真正民主的社会里,第一修正案赋予言论自由的权利不会止步于工作场所。相反,言论自由将在工作场所发挥重要作用。但是,资本关系中固有的他治与劳动自治的表述相矛盾,否定了这种表述。麦克拉伦所提出的批判教育学则是要从这个方向努力,针对资本主义所塑造出来的幻象进行批判。

种族隔离在美国的学校是具有普遍性的问题。在纽约市彭博政府(Bloomberg administration) 由于遵循"只有当法律要求时,种族才可能作为学校入学率的一个因素被考虑"的这一政策,已经加剧了公立学校的种族隔离问题。② 然而,正如艾伦·辛格(Alan Singer) 指出的那样,还有其他更有力的因素导致种族分离的学校,包括《共同核心州立标准》(Common Core)、"争创一流"(Race to the Top)、《有教无类法案》、"为美国而教"组织(Teach for America)、营利性学校、学校服务的外包和私有化、诸如培生集团等大企业的影响、新的复杂的老师评价程序等。用艾伦·辛格的话说,"《有教无类法案》和'争创一流'是基于这样的信念,即不需要种族融合就可以实现教育公平"③。艾伦·辛格解释道:"《共同核心州立标准》(Common Core)、'争创一流'、《有教无类法案》以及基于学生成绩的新的教师绩效评价方法都意味着学区、学校和教师尽量避免招收少数民族学生,因为担心他们的成绩不佳及其潜在的破坏

---

① David Gabbard, Karen Anijar. Fearless Speech in Fearful Times: An Essay Review of Capitalists and Conquerors, Teaching against Global Capitalism and the New Imperialism, and Teaching Peter McLaren https://mronline.org/2005/10/30/fearless – speech – in – fearful – timesan – essay – review – of – capitalists – and – conquerors – teaching – against – global – capitalism – and – the – new – imperialism – and – teaching – peter – mclaren/, 2019 – 05 – 22.

② Singer, Alan. (2014, March 31). "Racially Segregated Schools in America: The Bloomberg, Gates, Bush and Obama Legacies." Huffington Post. [EB/OL]. www.huffingtonpost.com/alan – singer/racially – segregated – schoo_b_5059540.html, 2018 – 04 – 02.

③ Singer, Alan. (2014, March 31). "Racially Segregated Schools in America: The Bloomberg, Gates, Bush and Obama Legacies." Huffington Post. [EB/OL]. www.huffingtonpost.com/alan – singer/racially – segregated – schoo_b_5059540.html, 2018 – 04 – 02.

性。"①

  我们知道学校的种族融合是一个值得追求的目标，而且为了达到这个目标，民权运动做出了很多的牺牲。在一个多民族的社会生活和工作可以为所有的学生提供优势。但需要强调的是，对种族融合的破坏与新自由主义资本主义对公立学校的攻击有着直接或间接的联系。艾伦·辛格对这种困境作了如下的总结："美国学校种族隔离的加剧，至少部分或可能大部分，不只是由人口趋势、政策错误或缺乏决心而导致的，而是由于企业、基金会活动及地方、州和联邦政府的有意识的政策决定导致的，是由迈克尔·布隆伯格（Michael Bloomberg）促进城市中产阶级化的努力、比尔·盖茨对小型学校的推动、《共同核心州立标准》、乔治·布什（George Bush）的《有教无类法案》及巴拉克·奥巴马和阿恩·邓肯力推的（Arne Duncan）'争创一流'政策导致的。"②

  学校应该必须要让学生可以有掌握自己命运的能力，可以超脱自己的社会阶级，而不是仅仅作为帮助资本主义生产所需要的文化资本。麦克拉伦警告我们要小心，要反击，要"……做无畏的老师，直到生命的最后一刻……"③ 敦促教育者，甚至整个社会，要意识到新自由主义世界正在发生什么以及新自由主义破坏世界、边缘化并消费整个公共社会的目标。麦克拉伦主张革命性的批判教育学否定教育的中立性，并"拒绝再制所谓的支配的意识形态以及为资本主义下的学校体制服务，相反的，批判教育学要做的是去对抗以及转化"④。

---

① Singer, Alan. (2014, March 31). "Racially Segregated Schools in America: The Bloomberg, Gates, Bush and Obama Legacies." Huffington Post. [EB/OL]. www. huffingtonpost. com/alan – singer/racially – segregated – schoo_b_5059540. html, 2018 – 04 – 02.

② Singer, Alan. (2014, March 31). "Racially Segregated Schools in America: The Bloomberg, Gates, Bush and Obama Legacies." Huffington Post. [EB/OL]. www. huffingtonpost. com/alan – singer/racially – segregated – schoo_b_5059540. html, 2018 – 04 – 02.

③ Peter McLaren, *Pedagogy of insurrection: From resurrection to revolution*, New York: Peter Lang Publishers, 2015, p.436.

④ Peter McLaren. , "This fist called my heart-public pedagogy in the belly of the beast", in Brian, D. , *Handbook of Peter McLaren: education and learning beyond schooling*, pp. 564 – 576, New York: Routledge, 565.

三 加剧人的物化与异化和阶级复制的标准化考试

在竞争、个人主义和消费主义的驱动下，新自由主义思想在应用于教育时，严重地毒害了教育领域，使其陷入扭曲的竞争体系。换句话说，这种体制的基本功能是将所有困扰社会的问题归咎于公立学校的教师，并威胁到学校的校长，如果学生在标准化考试中"表现"不好，学校就有可能关闭。简而言之，威胁和胁迫是新自由主义教育发挥作用的方式，这不仅使许多优秀教师感到沮丧，而且促使许多人离开这个职业。为了要求绩效，量化考评变成了显学，一切东西都要经过量化考评才能证明其价值，教育也被要求拿出绩效。教师在课程和教学上要面对新的评量方式，学校若是没有采用标准化考试、入学考试，则学校有可能面临招生困难的威胁。通过标准化考试，学生的成绩可以被比较、换算和多方的使用。换句话说，适当发展实践的概念被抛出窗外，取而代之的是在以考试为中心的氛围中窒息的学生的物化。

许多教育工作者和心理计量学家一致认为不应该用单一的考试成绩来决定学生的毕业、升学或对教师的聘用。格拉克曼（Gluckman, 2002）指出，标准化考试会让课堂教学让步于它，因为教师会搁置包括文学和社会学等主题学习在内的常规课程而为考试做准备。他还指出，这种做法有违当前的教育研究，即"小型学校能使学生更有效地学习；运用跨学科方法进行主题学习及对学生进行异质分组学习更能提高学生的学习效度"[1]。阿尔法·科恩（Alfie Kohn）在他的经典著作——《反对标准化考试的案例》（The Case Against Standardized Testing）中写道："正如我们所看到的，标准化考试，倾向于衡量学生短期内对于知识和技能的获得，包括考试技能本身，而不是对知识和技能进行真正的理解。在这个意义上，少数民族学生比例越高的学校实施这样的考试越多，这些学校的教学质量就会越差。这种标准化考试的使用只会强调对于考试的重视，结

---

[1] Gluckman Amy, "Testing…Testing…One, Two, Three: The Commercial Side of the Standardized-Testing Boom" *Dollars and Sense*, Vol. 239, 2002, p. 37.

果加速学校对于直接教授技术和无休止的考试练习的依赖。"① 格拉克曼指出:"由哈佛大学的民权项目（Civil Rights Project）做的大量研究都表明这些标准化考试对于课堂教学、学生和教师的士气及辍学率等都有着很大的负面影响。甚至有一些证据表明，那些通过得州学业技能评估考试的毕业生在上大学后他们的实际写作能力要低于几年前没有经历过技能评估考试的那些同龄人。"②

在强调公平竞争的时候却忽视了人类意识的复杂性，而变成抽象的量。将学习简化成考试的分数，在政策方面是让不同的个体学习相同的东西，尝试达到各科的知识均衡原则。将原先就有差异的个体都达到一致，麦克拉伦认为这正是对人性和个别差异暴力的具体化③。依马克思的观点，资本主义将原先不同的物品最后换算成相同的单位代表或衡量，例如金钱。这是将人的复杂性和社会发展的过程以商品的形式呈现，当成如同生产和交换的行径。而这就像是在标准化考试下的成绩，可以将不同的学生、学校或学区拿来作比较。"交换价值"不只体现在资本主义的经济模式中，现在也运用在学校教育中了。如在美国加州，考试分数的进步可以获得较多的财政补助。而两个考试分数接近的学校，在教育的责任下会被认为可以任意的交换其中的老师、学生或课程，仅因为他们在分数上的解释是一样的。④ 就阿多诺的观点来说，这是将两个不同的事物视为一样的，也就是所谓的同一性（identity）的暴力。这意味若两个学生的成绩是一样的，就代表具有相同的知识。但是果真如此吗？这是抹去了个体的特性和差异，没有注意到个别差异的发展；对老师来说，仅是教授相同的课程内容知识给学生而没有注意到学生的兴趣、倾向、

---

① Kohn Alfie, *The Case against Standardized Testing*: *Raising the Scores*, *Ruining the Schools*, Portsmouth, NH: Heinemann, 2000.

② Gluckman Amy, "Testing…Testing…One, Two, Three: The Commercial Side of the Standardized-Testing Boom" *Dollars and Sense*, Vol. 239, 2002, p. 36.

③ Lissovoy N. and Peter McLaren, "Educational 'accountability' and violence of capital: a Marxian reading" *Education policy*, Vol. 18, No. 2, 2003, p. 133.

④ Lissovoy N. and Peter McLaren, "Educational 'accountability' and violence of capital: a Marxian reading" *Education policy*, Vol. 18, No. 2, 2003, p. 133.

天分、资质和个别需求。阿多诺认为这是将全世界同一化或说是整体化[①]，就是将个体的特殊性消融到全体的、普遍当中。

由马克思主义的经济学来看，资本主义的教育仍然是阶级霸权决定的，教育上不应当运用成本效益分析的方法和手段。但是在美国的教育系统中，纳税人就像是债权人，而行政人员、教师甚至是学生都是债务人。债务人必须让债权人在公共政策上的投资有所回馈。就像是州政府对于教育的资助条件是学生必须要达到所谓的"标准"。在这种教育方式下，惩罚多于诊断治疗。而在教育当中"失败"的学生则面临痛苦或异化。[②] 考试本身代表着对行为和责任严格的控制。这不仅是对课程和教育学的干扰，而且使得学生本身的智慧和意愿无法顺势发展，产生异化并使得人格受损。教师为要求学生必须要达到某成就而压迫学生的身体和精神。更值得注意的是对于主体性无意义的影响，既深且远。不仅如此，当今犹如雨后春笋般纷纷出现的各种新型的网上学习平台，例如网上开放课程、自我调整的学习环境、点对点学习平台、第三方服务提供商等，促使教育的重点指向学习的成果和评价，进而忽略了我们为什么要教育学生的最初缘由。在标准化测试的笼罩之下的学生的人性被囚禁在一个集合了工具理性、实证主义和单维目标的特殊的分析结构中。所有这些网上学习平台宣扬的都是关于他律的教条，帮助学生加强控制自己内在和外在的本性，在具体化自我意识的过程中将学生们的隐隐作痛的伤口隐藏在工具理性制成的盔甲之下。学生的自尊、自信心已成为外在、附加的、逐渐朝向非人性，仅是强调技能的方向迈进。[③] 在标准化考试下，难以培养学生批判能力、问题解决能力以及传播有意义的知识。[④]

基于教育绩效责任所运用的标准化考试，许多学者已经指出涉及种

[①] Adorno, T., *Negative dialectics*, trans. E. B. Ashton, New York: Continuum, 1995.

[②] Lissovoy N. and Peter McLaren, "Educational 'accountability' and violence of capital: a Marxian reading" *Education policy*, Vol. 18, No. 2, 2003, p. 140.

[③] Lissovoy N. and Peter McLaren, "Educational 'accountability' and violence of capital: a Marxian reading" *Education policy*, Vol. 18, No. 2, 2003, p. 138.

[④] Peter McLaren. (2011: 5 - 6) *education and the unchained class struggle in the crisis of global capitalism*, the speech of international conference on higher education management, in National Taichung University of Education, Dec, 24, 2011, pp. 1 - 45.

族主义①，毕竟这些考试不是全然中立的，甚至这些考试是对白人中产阶级的学生有利。这些考试是再度复制了阶级以及复制了偏见。以考试当中所使用的语言为例，以英语作为回答的语言可能降低学生母语的语言能力或使用，并不是所有的学生都能成功地通过考试。基本上，这是偏向为白人学生所设计的。因此一些其他肤色的学生可能就无法取得像白人学生一样的优异成绩。②例如，在得州，自从实行标准化考试以来，非洲裔和拉丁裔学生辍学率已经上升。③考试的结果反映出了社会经济与种族的不平等，而不是学生学习或理解的真实状况。麦克拉伦认为这会让其他不是白人的学生感到挫折和遭受到失败。这是让其他肤色的学生在不平等的场域中竞争。甚至，这个场域是相当的不平等，但却又假借着"客观性"（objectivity）试图掩饰其中的真相。

在标准化考试下，教师或是行政人员在有意无意之间常以学生的成绩去判定学生。在标准化考试下，在使用新的标准让大众信服考试是公平的情况下，白人、富有者会强化、增强他们的阶级，而贬抑他者，如贫穷者、黑人和其他少数族裔。标准化考试将学校或学区作排名比较，白人的学校或排名比较靠前的学校是充满荣耀的，而贫民区的学校所能做的仅是无力的挣扎与默默的承受，永远抬不起头。以标准化考试为评价的唯一标准，将使强者更强，弱者更弱，扩大了学校之间不平等的差距，是一场不公平的竞争。美国联邦的教育政策从原先的平等、公平，转向学校自筹资金，并且依据学校的绩效给予奖励或是解雇学校的成员。在课程方面受到财团法人的牵制，至于奖励金是给予表现优异的学校，而非真实需求的学校，因而加剧了阶级的复制。④在标准化考试下，人的

---

① Kohn Alfie, *The Case against Standardized Testing: Raising the Scores, Ruining the Schools*, Portsmouth, NH: Heinemann, 2000.
② Lissovoy N. and Peter McLaren, "Educational 'accountability' and violence of capital: a Marxian reading" *Education policy*, Vol. 18, No. 2, 2003, p. 135.
③ Gluckman Amy, "Testing...Testing...One, Two, Three: The Commercial Side of the Standardized-Testing Boom" *Dollars and Sense*, Vol. 239, 2002, p. 36.
④ Peter McLaren. (2011: 5-6) *education and the unchained class struggle in the crisis of global capitalism*, the speech of international conference on higher education management, in National Taichung University of Education, Dec, 24, 2011, pp. 1-45.

主体性消融在其中,某些学生一直处于受压迫者的状态中。而从福柯的观点来看,规训(Discipline)和绩效(performance)已经成为教育上监视的新工具①。学校的标准化考试变成了确认绩效的唯一标准,强化了控制,其看不见的权力和经济因素都会透过考试而运作着。就教育上而言,借由考试的成就、入学与否不但没有削弱权力;相反地,反而增加或加乘权力的残酷。② 标准化考试也是资产阶级利用意识形态作为社会控制模式的一种方式。如得州有一个学业技能评估(the Texas Assessment of Academic Skills)的考试项目,对高中生物学、代数和美国历史等科目实施标准化结业考试。当然,这些考试限制、占用了分配给学生讨论重要社会问题的时间。它作为一种有效的预防不利意识形态的政策工具,能够控制反对言论和行为进入课堂。③

因此在新自由主义时代,学校改革在左翼思想家和活动人士中声名狼藉是有原因的。当代的学校改革受制于企业支持的学校私有化积极分子,将公立学校、教师和教师工会置于失败的境地,因为他们将学生标准化考试成绩偏低归咎于这些学校,而这些成绩都是学生社会经济地位低下以及相关的种族和民族压迫的产物。它对考试分数的痴迷打击了想象力和批判性思维,缩小了课程和课堂体验的范围。学生成为被动的接受者,接受老师储存在他们大脑中的有限信息,教师被阻止冒险去设计自己的课程,因为产生高分的压力产生了高度照本炮制和严格控制的教学法,其中工作表取代了批判性教学,死记硬背取代了深入思考。在当代国家资本主义和学校内外相关的压迫结构下,学生们无法在道德和政治上挑战他们所面临的可怕环境,也无法想象其他选择。

批判教育者的任务是要剥去伪装成中立的外衣,让人们看到真相。这些有别于白人肤色的其他学生是处于危机当中的,这些学生不是低等

---

① MICHEL FOUCAULT, *Discipline and punish*, trans. A. Sheridan, New York: Pantheon Books, 1977.

② Lissovoy N. and Peter McLaren, "Educational 'accountability' and violence of capital: a Marxian reading" *Education policy*, Vol. 18, No. 2, 2003, pp. 137-138.

③ Gluckman Amy, "Testing... Testing... One, Two, Three: The Commercial Side of the Standardized-Testing Boom" *Dollars and Sense*, Vol. 239, 2002, p. 36.

的、有缺陷的更不是注定要失败的；相反地，要从被定位为失败者当中去反抗。① 看似公平的标准化考试忽略、漠视了个体的差异，僵化了人们的思考更让人们的批判意识无法开展。既有的政权以及既得利益者持续地维持其本身的"正当性"及阶级的复制，继续宣传平等的幻象。当社会当中不平等的问题浮现时，甚至日益严重时，应该考虑到的是资本主义社会的非正义。

第二节 革命性的批判教育学——实现资本主义社会替代形式的实践哲学

一 革命性的批判教育学——一种实践哲学

（一）革命性的批判教育学出现的必要性——以往的批判教育学被驯化

2000 年以来麦克拉伦在他的著作②③④⑤⑥⑦中，坚决拥护以马克思的实践观和历史唯物主义为基础的革命性的批判教育学。麦克拉伦越来越强烈地要求回归马克思人道主义和历史唯物主义，作为发展一种革命性的批判教育学和一个非压迫性社会的乌托邦愿景的一部分。他的革命性的批判教育学通过复兴的实践理论弥合个人与集体之间的鸿沟，将马克思主义人道主义的解放潜力理论化。根据麦克拉伦在第四版《学校生

---

① Lissovoy N. and Peter McLaren, "Educational 'accountability' and violence of capital: a Marxian reading" *Education policy*, Vol. 18, No. 2, 2003, p. 136.

② Peter McLaren, *Che Guevara, Paulo Freire, and the Pedagogy of Revolution*, Lanham, MD: Rowman & Littlefield Publishers, 2000.

③ Peter McLaren and Ramin Farahmandpur, *Teaching Against Global Capitalism and the New Imperialism: A Critical Pedagogy*, Lanham, MD: Rowman & Littlefield Publishers, 2005.

④ Peter McLaren ed., *Capitalists and conquerors: A critical pedagogy against empire*, Lanham, MD: Rowman & Littlefield, 2005.

⑤ Peter McLaren, *Red Seminars: Radical excursions into educational theory, cultural politics, and pedagogy*, New York: Hampton Press, Inc., 2005.

⑥ Peter McLaren ed., *Rage and Hope: interviews with Peter McLaren on war, imperialism, and critical pedagogy*, New York: Peter Lang Publishing, Inc., 2006.

⑦ Peter McLaren, "Fire and Dust" *International Journal of Progressive Education*, Vol. 1, No. 3, October 2006, pp. 34–57.

活》（2003）中的观点，批判教育学有许多不同的分支：自由主义、激进主义和解放主义，而革命性批判性教育学是最近在常规教育和成人教育领域对社会主义斗争的唯物主义干预。正如麦克拉伦在第四版《切·格瓦拉、保罗·弗莱雷与革命教育学》（2000）及《学校生活》（2003）所证明的那样："革命性的批判教育学的祖先 DNA 揭示了它是从对批判教育学的幻灭中产生的，因为批判教育学陷入了自由主义、解构主义、后马克思主义社会变革方法的流沙之中。"① 麦克拉伦（2000）提醒我们："被称为批判教育学的概念网被撒得如此之广，有时又如此漫不经心，以至于它与任何从教育实践的混乱和污染水域中捞上来的东西联系在一起，教育实践泛滥成风，从'对话友好'的课堂到旨在提高学生自我形象的'自我感觉良好'课程，无所不包。换句话说，它已经成为自由人文主义的回归，并被灌输到一种中庸的、市政厅会议式的企业家精神和主日学校的传教活动的结合之中。它的多元文化教育可以与多元化的政治相联系，包括通过庆祝'种族'节日和诸如黑人历史月和五月五日节等主题来'容忍差异'。如果'批判教育学'这个术语被折射到当前教育辩论的舞台上，我们不得不判断，它在很大程度上已经被驯化了，就像它的许多早期倡导者，如巴西的保罗·弗莱雷所强烈恐惧的那样。"②

因此，麦克拉伦基于保拉·奥尔曼（1999，2001）提出的"革命性的批判教育"（revolutionary critical education）这一概念提出了"革命性的批判教育学"的概念。这并不仅仅是为了改变一个理论的名字。这是对不断被成功驯化的批判教育学的回应。如麦克拉伦所言："美国总有各种诱惑的方式合并任何它打不败或改变不了的东西。"③他扩展说，批判教育学已经变成了它原初思想的讽刺漫画，它原本的思想是为了更公平

---

① Martin, G., "You can't be neutral on a moving bus: Critical pedagogy as Community Praxis", (2005) [EB/OL]. http://www.jceps.com/index.php? pageID = article&articleID = 47, 2018 - 06 - 20.

② Peter McLaren, *Che Guevara, Paulo Freire, and the Pedagogy of Revolution*, Lanham, MD: Rowman & Littlefield Publishers, 2000, pp. 97 - 98.

③ Peter McLaren, *Che Guevara, Paulo Freire, and the Pedagogy of Revolution*, Lanham, MD: Rowman & Littlefield Publishers, 2000, p. xxii.

的社会而斗争，为没有权力的人赋权增能，为了解放而斗争。而现在已经被驯化、消减为"学生主导的学习方法"，避免讨论或重新思考"社会批判和革命日程"。①

根深蒂固的社会、政治和经济差异以及对立，促使教育工作者和文化工作者必须要创作出可以替代资本家资本积累的逻辑，然而，这是一项艰巨的任务，毕竟这是一个资本主义市场运作的不平等的社会。因此，对于"衰弱的以及受到驯化的批判教育学，有必要发展所谓的革命的劳动阶级的教育学"②。麦克拉伦再次强调，这也是为何他坚持革命性的批判教育学的立场，针对社会不公平尤其是呈现在学校体制当中的非正义进行高度的批判。他所要澄清的是对于财富的分配不是易如反掌的，而是要去挖掘内在的冲突与矛盾，并且进行讨论，进而去创造一个资本主义之外的社会，使劳动阶级能够发展其自身的价值。③ 因此在以往的批判教育学被驯化、失去作用、幻灭的时候，革命性的批判教育学出现了。

（二）革命性的批判教育学的目标——废除阶级，建立新社会

麦克拉伦和拉明·法拉曼德普尔描述了"改版"了的批判教育学——革命性的批判教育学的一些基本原则：

> 第一，批判教育学必须是一个集体的过程，包括使用对话学习方法（如保罗·弗莱雷式的）。第二，批判教育学必须是批判性的，也就是说，它必须找出阶级剥削和经济压迫的根本原因。第三，批判教育学必须具有深刻的系统性，因为它是以马克思的辩证探究方法为指导的，而马克思的辩证探究方法是从被压迫群众的"真实具体"情况出发的。将理论转化为具体的社会政治活动，重构社会世界，使之具有可理解性。第四，批判教育学应该是参与式的。它包

---

① Peter McLaren, *Che Guevara, Paulo Freire, and the Pedagogy of Revolution*, Lanham, MD: Rowman & Littlefield Publishers, 2000, p. 35.

② Peter McLare and Farahmandpur, R., "Teaching against globalization and the new imperialism: toward a revolutionary pedagogy" *Journal of teacher education*, Vol. 52, No. 2, March 2001, p. 137.

③ Michael Pozo, "Towards a Critical Revolutionary Pedagogy", in P. McLaren, ed. *Rage and Hope: An Interview with Peter McLaren*, New York: Rowman & Little-field Publishers, 2006, p. 15.

括在社区成员、基层运动、教会组织和工会之间建立联盟。第五，批判教育学需要是一个创造性的过程，通过整合流行文化的元素（如戏剧，音乐，口述历史，叙事）作为教育工具，可以成功地提高学生和教师的政治意识水平。[①]

麦克拉伦已经确定了批判教育学与革命性的批判教育学之间的差异："批判教育学实际上是一种辩证的对话的过程，实例化教师与学生之间的相互转化——这种转化致力于重新架构、重新功能化并止于理解问题本身，强调知识的结构和关系维度以及难以根除祸害的权力、知识维度。然而革命性的批判教育学不止于此，它把权力、知识关系与它们自身的内部价值置于冲突状态（a collision course），如此强大的通常难以忍受的冲突催生的不是更高层级的认识论决议而是从过去的奴役中解放的新社会的愿景。"[②]

持有革命教育学观点的教育者必须面对全球资本主义的负面影响。麦克拉伦认为革命教育者应该支持社会变革的集体斗争。运用基于马克思主义的理论框架，革命教育学可以帮助教育者理解或有时战胜一些压迫形式，尤其是那些与学校教育过程有关的压迫。正如保拉·奥尔曼（2002）所说，为了在教室打开替代资本主义的愿景，教师有能力与"红色粉笔"（red chalk）共事。麦克拉伦从这个角度阐释，现在教师有机会也有责任创造体现社会公平原则的教育学的新形式，以便遏制全球资本主义的弊端及其普遍的负面影响。在这种背景下，可以说创建真实的平等的参与性的社会主义运动是革命教育学的主要目标之一。麦克拉伦（2000）表明革命教育学的另一个重要目标是改变造成人类痛苦的条件、带来解放所必需的条件。

因此，革命性的批判教育学试图让我们不断地反思全球资本主义下

---

① McLaren, P. and Farahmandpur, R., "Introduction", in P. McLaren and R. Farahmandpur, eds. *Teaching against global capitalism and the new imperialism: A critical pedagogy* (pp. 1 – 11) Lanham, MD: Rowman & Littlefield, 2005, p. 9.

② Peter McLaren, *Che Guevara, Paulo Freire, and the Pedagogy of Revolution*, Lanham, MD: Rowman & Littlefield Publishers, 2000, p. 185.

的不公平社会关系，并反对由此产生的残酷的生存条件。如果我们聚焦革命性的批判教育学努力提升教学实践，我们可能开始相信世界可以变得更好。革命性的批判教育学仍然是一种探索，一种渗透想象力的过程。麦克拉伦（2006）认为："革命性的批判教育学是在对社会主义的想象中进行的，也就是说，它的运作基于这样一种理解：教育的基础是政治性的，需要创造空间，在那个空间里，学生们可以想象一个不同于资本主义价值法则的世界（即社会劳动形式），可以讨论和辩论资本主义和资本主义制度的替代选择，可以就为什么过去历史上那么多革命变成了它们的对立面展开对话。它希望创造一个社会劳动不再是整个社会劳动的间接部分而是直接部分的世界，其中一种新的分配模式不是以社会需要的劳动时间为基础，而是以实际劳动时间为基础，异化的人际关系被真正透明的人际关系所包容，自由联系的个人可以成功地朝着永久革命的方向努力，精神劳动和体力劳动的界限可以消除，父权关系和其他特权阶级的压迫和剥削可以结束，我们可以真正地实行'各尽所能，各取所需'的原则，我们可以穿越不受必然性束缚的普遍权利的领域，在本体论空间内感性地、流畅地移动，在本体论空间内，主体性作为能力建设和创造性自我活动的一种形式在社会整体内和作为社会整体的一部分在本体论空间内行使；在这个空间里，劳动不再被剥削，而是一种造福全人类的努力；在这个空间里，劳动不再是一种工具化和商品化的活动，不再是一种强制性的活动；在这个空间里，鼓励充分发展人的能力。"[1]革命性的批判教育学必须将批判教育学彻底改造。它的目标不应该局限于消除阶级对立，而是废除阶级，不是改善现有的社会，而是建立一个新的社会。

（三）革命性的批判教育学的本质——一种实践（praxis）哲学

麦克拉伦努力做的是发展实践哲学，以黑格尔马克思主义对历史和政治的理解为基础，并与保罗·弗莱雷方法很好地结合，这是推动他的

---

[1] Peter McLaren, "Fire and Dust" *International Journal of Progressive Education*, Vol. 1, No. 3, October2006, pp. 34–57.

革命性的批判教育学的深层潜流，这与马克思对革命实践的理解是一致的。① 首先，很有必要指出革命性的批判教育学不是一种方法论也不是一系列可遵循的程序。它必须是一种哲学，一种敏锐性，一种理解我们所在世界的方式。② 这是对主体关系的理解——作为一个个体和团体成员——在特定的历史和文化背景下一个人自己的位置。这是一种理解教师与社会、文化和生产力量关系的独特方式。革命性的批判教育学就是帮助我们实现社会、文化、性别公平的教学实践的哲学方向。其次，需要澄清"革命"的意蕴，在教育学上，它与推翻、杀戮统治者的革命无政府主义者无关。它不应该是主人与奴隶之间辩证关系的隐喻，因为奴隶杀了主人之后就变成新的主人，再征服新的奴隶。因此，"革命"需要打破这种二元论。麦克拉伦很清楚这一问题的挑战是创建一种平等的参与的社会主义运动，而不仅仅是实施另一种压迫统治形式。麦克拉伦在课堂上讲道：

> 我们生活在一个同各种症状做斗争的社会，拒绝治疗正在发生的危机的根源——环境、恐怖主义、资源、个人安全、教育等等。在这些令人不安的关系中，最纠结的是资本主义如何以特定的方式构建、组织和调解所有这些对立。在当前的过渡期，无论从哪方面来看，我们实际上是作为人力资本而存在的。我们已经把我们的生活活动卖给了其他人，而部分人口（如被拉美裔人取代的廉价劳动力的非裔美国人），则沦为无法出售劳动力的过剩人口。承认我们生活在资本主义社会就会发抖。今天，我们目睹了监视技术的惊人和恶毒的扩展，技术消除了现实和超现实之间的鸿沟，把我们锁在一个比奥威尔想象的还要糟糕得多的场景中，一个自愿成为资本代理人的场景。

---

① Derek R. Ford. "Revolutionary Critical Pedagogy and the Struggle against Capital Today: An Interview with Peter McLaren". *Education Interview*, 2015 - 7 - 16 [EB/OL]. http://www.hamptoninstitution.org/peter-mclaren-interview.html#.XT6gsi2B3FQ, 2019 - 05 - 22.

② Marc Pruyn and Luis Huerta-Charles, *Teaching Peter McLaren: Path of Dissent*, New York: Peter Lang Publications, 2005, p. xxxvi.

我们为了工资出卖了劳动力，只能用从资本家的利润账上挤出来的银圆来蒙住我们的眼睛。在这个社会中，我们倾向于对基本假设持批判态度，当然，为了保护它们不受攻击，它们被庄严地奉为神圣，并隐藏在宗教特权的背后。正如我几十年来一直主张的那样，资本主义市场是新的上帝。我住在加州奥兰治的老城，对我来说最方便的咖啡店是在富国银行。的确，这座建筑从内部看起来就像一座大教堂。我在加州大学圣巴巴拉分校（UC Santa Barbara）的朋友比尔·罗宾逊（Bill Robinson）指出，反资本主义运动的负面影响，不一定包括另一个后资本主义或社会主义项目的正面影响（在这里我们可以清楚地看到他在呼应黑格尔对否定的否定）。正因为如此，我和我的马克思主义人道主义同志们，长期以来一直呼吁建立在绝对否定基础上的实践哲学。在这里，我深受黑格尔、马克思以及莱雅的国家资本主义理论的影响。我明白了黑格尔的辩证法与这种绝对观念（理论与实践对立的超越）是分不开的。正如黑格尔所建议的那样，我们要始终不断地对用以把握一种现象的基础思想提出质疑，我们需要通过一种建立在绝对否定基础上的实践哲学来打破解放的外部和内部障碍。（节选自麦克拉伦在东北师范大学的讲课材料）

革命性的批判教育学的概念看起来需要一种葛兰西革命，它是一种文化革命，帮助人们明白他们的处境，为人们提供思考他们处境及改变现实的可能性的必要批判空间。安东尼奥·葛兰西（1981）指出，文化不只是经典书籍里的广博知识，它包括组织、纪律本身、世界面前的占位过程、理解我们生活、权利、义务的历史价值的更高层次意识。因此，人们通过教育过程获得文化，通过互动学习，人们实现超我。正如安东尼奥·葛兰西所说，如果我们不懂得自己，就不会真正懂得他人。革命性的批判教育学必须帮助人们获得这种意义上的文化为目标，帮助他们有能力改变世界的情况。葛兰西希望人们以及"有机的知识分子"（organic intellectuals）可以为后代创造一种新的文化、大众的文化。这种文化成为一种新的基于社会公正、公平和共享的霸权，换句话说，与主流霸权是相反的。在那种情况下，统治和压迫的条件会减少或消除。

传统马克思主义的批判教育学所关注的是，资本主义下的学校应该是可以使人的意识觉醒和可能产生改变的场域。异化的过程和意识形态的压迫会让人们顺应在主流文化的阶级意识里面而无法意识到自身的文化与价值。麦克拉伦在建言立说的基础上更强调实践的重要性。他认为在强调阶级抗争时，更加体现出革命实践的必要性。[1] 革命性的批判教育学不是对着政府的政策咆哮或是谩骂，而是不断地朝着革命意识和实践前进。具体说来，实践（praxis）的内涵包含以下两个方面：自我觉醒与行动。

革命的实践并非源自沉思或冥想，而是根据马克思主义，通过集体的革命行动对社会进行改造。[2] 麦克拉伦提到，马克思主义是行动的指导方针，而非形而上学的教条教义，更具体地来说，它是革命性集体抗争的行动指导方针，其目的在于解放人民与增权。[3]

批判的实践是对于殖民主义与资本主义的反击[4]。因而，麦克拉伦疾呼要采取革命行动来改变压迫的来源，而实践正是革命的基本因子。批判不只是可以理解阶级、种族、性别和压迫，还可以改变这些，更重要的是可以建立起解放的主体性去实践革命性的抗争。[5] 马克思在《关于费尔巴哈的提纲》（Outline on Feuerbach）中写道："哲学家的责任在解释世界。然而，重要的是改变世界。"其中强调实践（praxis）精神。马克思主义与社会实践有相当的关联性。从马克思的观点出发，哲学家具有解

---

[1] Peter McLaren, *Life in Schools: An Introduction to Critical Pedagogy in the Foundations of Education (Fifth Edition)*, New York: Pearson Publishers, 2007, pp. 35 – 36.

[2] Peter McLaren, *Life in Schools: An Introduction to Critical Pedagogy in the Foundations of Education (Fifth Edition)*, New York: Pearson Publishers, 2007, p. 35.

[3] Peter McLaren, *Life in Schools: An Introduction to Critical Pedagogy in the Foundations of Education (Fifth Edition)*, New York: Pearson Publishers, 2007, p. 33.

[4] Peter McLaren, "Collisions with otherness: 'Traveling' theory, postcolonial criticism, and the politics of ethnographic practice-the mission of the wounded ethnographer" *Critical theory and educational research*, 1995, p. 290.

[5] Peter McLaren, "Collisions with otherness: 'Traveling' theory, postcolonial criticism, and the politics of ethnographic practice-the mission of the wounded ethnographer" *Critical theory and educational research*, 1995, p. 295.

释世界、改变世界的使命；而哲学与生活、哲学与社会、哲学与教育更是密不可分。麦克拉伦从传统的马克思主义论点出发，认为"所谓的实践（praxis）不是理论化成实际行动（practice）。不是批判地意识到一些理论的重点，然后将那些重点具体化地应用在社会的生活当中。简而言之，是通过改变自身进而改变社会，也就是通过自身的抗争，改变社会"①。此处，麦克拉伦强调的是，实践并不完全等于应用于行动，而是一种自我意识改变的历程。他希望通过辩证的过程，通过意识形态的改变以及抗争的过程，达到批判意识的启发。自我觉醒与认知的提升也是一种行动，这是实践的第一个意思。

麦克拉伦指出，批判教育学的教师被批评是躲在学术的象牙塔中，在教室里所使用的理论与外界的情况有所出入，但他认为教室里也可以发展与实践批判教育学。尽管在教室里批判资本主义是无法让每个人从中获益，但是，这依然是一种方式——从方法论当中去强调并且分享，就像是教师将其所学，诸如文化、课程、意识形态教授给学生，这也是一种理论和实践的结合②，特别是麦克拉伦要将教师和学生的实践引导至政治实践且与社会运动连接，去反对帝国主义以及反对资本主义，去创造多种族和性别平衡的社会。借由历史唯物主义可以批判劳动力何以被转为人类资本、具体的劳工何以被抽象的过程。历史唯物论提供给批判教育学理解物质是源于社会生活的，根植于历史社会关系的，而阶级冲突被伪装是由社会分工所导致。③ 历史的意识不是单独通过冥想和批判的反思就能达成，必须要通过行动才能让想象成真。④ 因此，实践的第二个

---

① Peter McLaren., "This fist called my heart-public pedagogy in the belly of the beast", In Brian, D., *Handbook of Peter McLaren: education and learning beyond schooling*, pp. 564 – 576, New York: Routledge, 2009, p. 571.

② Peter McLaren, *Life in Schools: An Introduction to Critical Pedagogy in the Foundations of Education (Fifth Edition)*, New York: Pearson Publishers, 2007, p. 32.

③ Michael Pozo, "Towards a Critical Revolutionary Pedagogy", in P. McLaren, ed. *Rage and Hope: An Interview with Peter McLaren*, New York: Rowman & Little-field Publishers, 2006, p. 6.

④ Peter McLaren., "This fist called my heart-public pedagogy in the belly of the beast", In Brian, D., *Handbook of Peter McLaren: education and learning beyond schooling*, pp. 564 – 576, New York: Routledge, 2009, p. 571.

意思即是具体的行动。革命性实践是马克思所强调的，麦克拉伦认为所谓的革命实践不是在教室里讨论就行，而是要通过行动才能启发人们的能力，对于环境有所行动以及自我改变。他提道："一些后现代的自以为是的教师，将我所谓的'实践'这个词仅限于是'观念'上的诠释，仅是着重于'差异'或认为是'知识论'的问题。在此，我认为批判教育学要消除后现代主义者的这些论调。"[1]

麦克拉伦认为革命性的批判教育学核心的观点包括：

（1）革命性的批判教育学不承认政治中立。

（2）批判教育学避免让自己降格到教授狭隘的思考技能，摒弃只运用思考技巧的辩论和语境，在意识形态的范畴里，所有的思想、行为和关系都具有政治色彩。

（3）对话是批判的，但是把所有对抗的立场都摆到台面与前后呼应的论点并非一回事。即便把不同意识形态置于相同的组织框架内，他们也不会自己融合为一体。

（4）运用对话的方法来理解世界是至关重要的；学生需要学习在资本主义社会中社会关系有着怎样的内部联系或辩证联系。

（5）教师需要运用社会历史分析法这样的方法论来帮助自身重新建构生产、传播和接受的社会历史条件。

（6）狭隘地关注分层和社会不平等导致了对阶级斗争的抛弃，阶级斗争与劳动有着必然的内在联系。

（7）认识资本主义学校教育中教育的"阶级特征"，倡导"资本主义社会的社会主义重组"。

（8）理论知识很少涉及劳动实践，而革命性的批判教育学教授学生知识与生产和消费是如何在历史、文化以及制度方面产生联系的。

（9）通过马克思主义实现革命实践，不是将思想注入身体的静态仪式，而是重塑社会过程中的动态思考。是一种通过集体革命使物质力量

---

[1] Peter McLaren., "This fist called my heart-public pedagogy in the belly of the beast", In Brian, D., *Handbook of Peter McLaren: education and learning beyond schooling*, pp. 564 – 576, New York: Routledge, 2009, p. 566.

服务于意识的方式。如此,革命实践变成了融合形式与内容、思想与行动的据点。①

从麦克拉伦的著作《愤怒与希望》(2006)当中可知,保罗·弗莱雷的理念很大程度地影响了麦克拉伦的思想,并被他视为推进"革命性的批判教育学"的精神人物之一。对麦克拉伦而言,亨利·吉鲁等人只是停留在空谈理论的层面,缺少行动性,因此他特别强调保罗·弗莱雷的实践概念。在他看来,实践可以说是理论的运用。他是基于废止全球化资本主义无限的扩张以及价值生产而发展的一种实践哲学②。麦克拉伦用革命性实践这个词意指整合阶级斗争的理论与实践,也就是综合了形式与内容、思想与行动。因此,革命性的批判教育学包含理论与实践。③

二 革命性的批判教育学——抵制与替代资本主义的实践方式

(一)在抗争与行动中养成批判意识

意识形态在我们的生活中扮演着重要的角色,资本主义借着意识形态控制了无产阶级的思想,让劳动者误以为是其本身的思想。所谓的意识形态指在思想或意识中,对于处于人们控制之外和个人利益相对的共同利益或是整个生产或分工关系的掌握,而这是脱离人而存在的。④ 马克思用此词来表示社会当中特定的阶级成员所共同拥有的错误意识,举例而言,资产阶级的成员会认为市场的竞争法则是自然的,而在市场竞争下的工人,虽然付出了劳动力,然而也获得薪资与报酬,私有制以及财产制也是正当且合理的。统治阶层首先赋予资产阶级知识分子较高的社会地位,通过控制权威性话语来控制意识形态的生产,然后不断重复专为被压迫群体设计的可以将他们从悲痛中吸引出来的洗脑式的文化产品,

---

① Peter McLaren, *Life in Schools: An Introduction to Critical Pedagogy in the Foundations of Education* (Sixth Edition), Boulder, CO: Paradigm, 2014, pp. 10–14.

② Peter McLaren., "This fist called my heart-public pedagogy in the belly of the beast", In Brian, D., *Handbook of Peter McLaren: education and learning beyond schooling*, pp. 564–576, New York: Routledge, 2009, p. 565.

③ Peter McLaren, *Life in Schools: An Introduction to Critical Pedagogy in the Foundations of Education* (Fifth Edition), New York: Pearson Publishers, 2007, p. 36.

④ 孙善豪:《批判与辩证》,唐山出版社2009年版,第78页。

进而让被压迫群体的诉求看起来越发的不合理、不实际和不爱国。① 统治阶级通过意识形态化了的国家机器，包括学校、宗教、媒体等，稳稳地将造成不平等的因素理性化——利用各种娱乐消遣和谎言欺骗将人民丢进对进取心、忠诚度和目标论的迷信中。因此，麦克拉伦认为有必要让人们具有批判的意识，并借此唤醒人性的尊严，而且他相信人们可以通过自己的解放实践战胜资本主义，因为人们在改变社会的同时也改变了自己的意识。②

在麦克拉伦的很多作品里，他证明了在一些特定的有争议的领域，掌权群体在社会关系生产及教育影响力上的权力是多么的强大。掌权群体运用各种可利用的途径打击、排挤对立面的声音以便取得公众的赞同，创造一种支持全球资本主义的霸权世界观。如公众同意工程（engineering public consent）是有利于政府或掌权群体操纵影响公众意见的一种手段。霸权是通过一些场域如教堂、学校、大众媒体、政治体系以及家庭等地方的意见一致的、两相情愿的社会实践（consensual social practices）保持统治的过程。这些过程展现了这个体制延续自己的能力。

在霸权斗争的过程中权势群体获得被压迫者的支持，这些被压迫者通常没有意识到他们通过接受权势群体建立的价值观和社会实践在增强压迫者的统治。统治集团通过给定的符号、建构的知识、特定的语言和隐藏了不平等权力关系和特权的社会实践把他们的世界观强加给被压迫者群体（Chomsky, 1998；McLaren, 1989）。如此，统治集团建立与自己思想相似的同盟团体以便压制对手的声音。通过这种方式他们获得控制部署他们世界观的手段。所以意识一直是批判教育学关注的中心问题。麦克拉伦非常重视意识在创造一个更人性化、激进和平等的社会主义的世界的过程中所起的重要作用。

麦克拉伦已经相当透彻地分析了这些过程，对我们理解这些问题做

---

① Best, S., Kahn, R., Nocella, A. and McLaren, P., *The Global Industrial Complex: systems of domination*, Lanham, MD: Lexington Books, 2011.

② Derek R. Ford. "Revolutionary Critical Pedagogy and the Struggle against Capital Today: An Interview with Peter McLaren". *Education Interview*, 2015 - 7 - 16 [EB/OL]. http://www.hamptoninstitution.org/peter-mclaren-interview.html#.XT6gsi2B3FQ, 2019 - 05 - 22.

出了巨大的贡献。他已经向我们展示了来自全球资本主义世界观的话语和社会实践已经引导人们自然地吸纳了资本主义意识形态。正如麦克拉伦所言（1998），资本主义已经被自然化（naturalized）了，已经成为了自然本身的一部分。在20世纪80年代和90年代，新资本主义（neo capitalism）变成了理解世界的一种方式。新自由主义（neo-liberalism）和新资本主义通过组织社会实践把个人与社会作为一个整体进行控制和征服。新自由主义作为新资本主义的理论基础，变成了我们当今时代的引导性意识形态。

马克思试图将意识和物质世界结合在一起，意识形态是人所创作出来的，但反倒变成与人对立，甚至于是控制人的。无产阶级无法意识到自己，其主要的原因在于资产阶级的意识形态，通过教育、文化的媒介，让无产阶级无法意识到自己的利益和使命。马克思认为在人类的历史中，是社会存在（social being）决定意识。他在《德意志意识形态》（German Ideology）当中提到，不是意识决定生活，而是生活决定意识，此处马克思的思想正转向后期的经济决定论，逐渐离开了早期的人道主义立场。在此论点下，他翻转了黑格尔的观点，是从唯物主义的角度出发去看待意识形态。对后期马克思而言，意识形态虽然也起着某些作用，但其实不是重点，打破经济的生产关系才会获得解放的核心关键。但麦克拉伦则认为直接的批判那些意识形态、结构和迷思是很重要的，因为意识形态、结构和迷思不但助长了现存文化的复制现象，也持续维持着社会的不公不义的现象。[1] 而且没有任何一种深层结构、理论是可以免予意识形态的影响的。麦克拉伦一再提及他自己的马克思主义观点来自马克思主义的人道主义哲学。

在意识形态之下，主流意识引导着社会，也使得主流阶级的地位更加巩固。革命性的批判教育学尝试着让劳工可以享有个体的职业自由以及可以成为自由的生产者，不再受到资本家的压迫与血汗工厂的压榨[2]，

---

[1] Peter McLaren, *Life in Schools: An Introduction to Critical Pedagogy in the Foundations of Education (Fifth Edition)*, New York: Pearson Publishers, 2007, p. 176.

[2] Michael Pozo, "Towards a Critical Revolutionary Pedagogy", in P. McLaren, ed. *Rage and Hope: An Interview with Peter McLaren*, New York: Rowman & Little-field Publishers, 2006, p. 26.

故而自由必须是突破阶级樊篱的，唯有资本主义对于劳动阶级的剥削不再，唯有劳动者能够借由批判资产阶级进而产生出自我意识，那自由才能真正地体现，也才是真正的自由。而自我意识的产生有赖于批判意识的觉醒。

麦克拉伦呼吁，身为批判教育学者要营造一个批判意识的情境，而这本质上是政治意蕴的意识，而这意识终将成为革命性的，可以介入帝国主义和殖民化的运作当中。① 但是要期望工人革命是不大合理的，唯有透过提升工人的批判素养，才能遏止当代资本日益恶化的状况。②

保罗·弗莱雷认为不是透过自我意识达到批判性的抗争，而是通过抗争才具有批判性的意识。③ 这种唯物主义的批判思维正是马克思、麦克拉伦对于实践的体现。也正是麦克拉伦一直认为真正的革命性的批判教育学必须是学生亲身的自觉，主动的对现今的资本主义提出批判，而不是单单仅在教室里接受教师知识的灌输。批判意识是必须要通过真正的参与抗争才能从过程中养成或建立。

资本和劳工的关系是资本主义社会当中的核心问题，而学校教育则扮演着一个支持与发展的角色。教育对资本而言极为重要。透过教育，培养出工人，而工人必须要不断地通过学习以取得其技术以保证自己不被取代。但是，这是资本对于工人的迷惑，也让工人无法发挥其批判意识。④ 对资本主义辩证的批判需要批判的意识。批判的意识是最为基础的，因为通过批判的意识可以将日常的生活解码，让学生可以知道在资本主义的运作下，他们是无法自由地选择其生活、身份、梦想和行动。

---

① Peter McLaren., "This fist called my heart-public pedagogy in the belly of the beast", In Brian, D., *Handbook of Peter McLaren: education and learning beyond schooling*, pp. 564 – 576, New York: Routledge, 2009, p. 571.

② Michael Pozo, "Towards a Critical Revolutionary Pedagogy", in P. McLaren, ed. *Rage and Hope: An Interview with Peter McLaren*, New York: Rowman & Little-field Publishers, 2006, p. 23.

③ Peter McLaren., "This fist called my heart-public pedagogy in the belly of the beast", In Brian, D., *Handbook of Peter McLaren: education and learning beyond schooling*, pp. 564 – 576, New York: Routledge, 2009, p. 570.

④ Peter McLaren, *Life in Schools: An Introduction to Critical Pedagogy in the Foundations of Education (Fifth Edition)*, New York: Pearson Publishers, 2007, p. 34.

严肃地说，商品化控制了人们的社会生活。

麦克拉伦认为即使是号称民主自由的美国大学，仍充满意识形态。以他自己为例，不管是在研究所受到的攻击或是身为一位受邀学者而被无理的批判，都显示出是虚假意识的表现。① 他提到，近年来，右翼团体把他关于保罗·弗莱雷、切·格瓦拉、以马克思人道主义对于资本主义社会进行分析和将社会理论的斗争运用到批判教育学上的这些相关著作，当成是箭靶。甚至于他在委内瑞拉、墨西哥等的活动，赢得了"左翼偏见"这个臭名，一部分的美国人对他是嗤之以鼻。②

这些对于左翼教授的上课内容的录音、攻击，其实所反映出的是资本主义社会下对于观念的支配。③ 也就是借由意识形态来控制劳动阶级，让其无法通过自身的意识觉醒来威胁资本主义对劳动阶级剥削的合理理由。而批判教育学是资产阶级所畏惧的，他们害怕批判教育学的力量以及所提出的不同看法与意见。④ 当右翼分子把批判教育学和共产主义画上等号，左翼分子则在无法直接挑战资本主义以及国家权力下臣服时，麦克拉伦坚持对抗资本主义和殖民主义的火花是永不熄灭的，批判教育学作为革命性实践是不会低头的。

学习是一种社会和文化建构活动，由一系列如社会、经济、文化、政治和历史因素型塑和决定。这些因素通过社会实践、统治群体使用的塑造人们主观性的标准和规则与霸权话语交织在一起。这样人们逐渐给自身的潜意识灌输某些通常并不属于他们的创造和身份的思想和世界观。

---

① Peter McLaren., "This fist called my heart-public pedagogy in the belly of the beast", In Brian, D., *Handbook of Peter McLaren：education and learning beyond schooling*, pp. 564 - 576, New York：Routledge, 2009, p. 569.

② Peter McLaren., "This fist called my heart-public pedagogy in the belly of the beast", In Brian, D., *Handbook of Peter McLaren：education and learning beyond schooling*, pp. 564 - 576, New York：Routledge, 2009, p. 568.

③ Peter McLaren., "This fist called my heart-public pedagogy in the belly of the beast", In Brian, D., *Handbook of Peter McLaren：education and learning beyond schooling*, pp. 564 - 576, New York：Routledge, 2009, p. 568.

④ Peter McLaren., "This fist called my heart-public pedagogy in the belly of the beast", In Brian, D., *Handbook of Peter McLaren：education and learning beyond schooling*, pp. 564 - 576, New York：Routledge, 2009, p. 569.

并且他们相信这些思想和世界观是不可改变的,自然的,就像事情本就该这样一样。在学习的过程中,一定立场的主体(positioned subjects)建构知识并赋予事物、状况、事件特定的意蕴。因此,当学习发生时,学习者会以他们所在立场的角度和世界观来解读任何事情,即人们用其之前的知识来处理学习中的任何事实或关系。然而,学习并不仅仅发生在学校里,学习无处不在,个体在每一种情境中,每一种互动中接触的任何客体知识都是学习。学习可以发生在大街上、在家里、在工厂里、在教堂里,或更明显的在学校里。因此,可以说,学习是社会建构的。

麦克拉伦说曾经有学生批评他的授课内容是空洞的、无益的,只是个雄辩家,听他的课简直就是浪费时间。事实上,批判教育学不是仅给予知识,而是去澄清一些观点。比如,虽然意识到我们的社会存在着不公平、种族歧视以及性别偏见,而这些其实是可以被改变的,批判教育学正是让我们正视这些议题,通过辅以相关理论使这些对社会现状缄默的人民可以反思、改革与实践。唤醒批判意识是要洞识资本主义的本质与种种恶行,去除人的异化,找回人性的尊严。就教育而言则是让学生了解资本主义的问题,争取劳动阶级的平等权益,返回教育与人性的本质。

(二)质疑与揭露

麦克拉伦信奉苏格拉底式的承诺(Socratic Commitment),即质疑对任何民主社会都至关重要的问题,但又被太多的教育学家们所长期回避的问题,这些教育家对考试成绩和研究经费的盲目追求使我们无法再确定公共教育的生存,更不用说它未来的发展方向了。此外,这些教育学家缺乏批判性的质疑,使他们无法认识到,威胁公共教育生存的各种力量的根源,与现在威胁民主生存的根源相同,不仅威胁到美国,而且威胁到全世界,以及地球的生存。麦克拉伦为我们做出示范,即只有彻底遵循古希腊苏格拉底式质疑的伟大传统,即"对自己、权威、教条、狭隘主义和原教旨主义的质疑",才能认识到这些威胁的共同来源和联系。当然,苏格拉底式的质疑从来都不是为了装腔作势,对质疑的恐惧破坏了最基本的民主承诺,会让人们走上一条众所周知的"滑坡",滑向任何一个善意的诡辩,这种思想和话语通过错误的疏忽的、厌恶或恶意的诡辩，助长了不公正和压迫的重现，这种思想和话语通过为权力的利益服务而为自己的私利服务。显然象牙塔里的很多教育者都缺乏质疑的勇气和行动，他们在揭露事实真相方面做得还不够，因此在过去30年里民主教育的条件受到了极大的破坏。激进的苏格拉底式的麦克拉伦不畏恐惧与威胁，他大胆地提出质疑和问题，挑战在这个可怕的时代对民主构成最大威胁的三大主导信条：市场原教旨主义（market fundamentalism）、帝国主义、军国主义的抬头以及独裁主义。麦克拉伦对市场原教旨主义提出了激进的苏格拉底式的质疑，质疑市场原教旨主义是如何催生了军国主义的崛起，并伴随着新帝国主义和威权主义的崛起。无论是《资本家与征服者：反对帝国的批判教育学》(*Capitalists and Conquerors: A Critical Pedagogy Against Empire*)，还是《反对全球资本主义和新帝国主义的教学：一种批判教育学》(*Teaching Against Global Capitalism and the New Imperialism: A Critical Pedagogy*)，都包含了无数的例子，表明他愿意谴责资本主义关系所带来的各种形式的不公正。

根据新自由主义的逻辑，市场应当而且实际上就是教育及教育改革的资助者，私人利益应该在市场过程中得到回报。事实证明，是那些为数极少的富有者控制着公共与社会生活。许多未取得终身教席的教育者，在大学课堂里通过教学开辟了反对全球资本主义和新帝国主义的新阵地，但是，质疑、更不用说揭露帝国主义和教育之间关系，对他们来说，变得日益危险了。[①] 在此情况下，有些教育者却害怕面对政治和意识形态矛盾，为了保护自己，他们躲进了学术象牙塔。然而，仍有一些教育者如麦克拉伦勇敢地面对着这种现实继续对现实进行揭露。就像马克思当年通过对"血腥的、肮脏的"资本的分析来揭露早期资本主义的特征那样，麦克拉伦通过对当前"非人道的"资本及这种资本的新形式——跨国集团的分析来揭露全球资本主义的特征，以唤醒人们的反抗意识。

马克思主义教育者面临的最大批评之一是批判教育学对公共政策领域几乎没有影响。因为对于普通读者来说，革命性的批判教育学的作品，

---

① Peter McLaren and Ramin Farahmandpur, *Teaching Against Global Capitalism and the New Imperialism: A Critical Pedagogy*, Lanham, MD: Rowman & Littlefield Publishers, 2005, p. 7.

除了极少数的例外，即使出现在知名的教师教育期刊上或由著名的学术出版社出版，这类文学作品的读者也主要局限于学术团体内的读者群。但这是对形势的静态和一维的看法，这种情况忘记了麦克拉伦等马克思主义者和一群"赤脚"教育工作者正在进行的广泛而灵活的工作，他们在社会运动组织的左翼运动层中，揭露工人阶级所处的真实境况，并以革命的观点看待各个文化领域在发展中国家的形势。认识到公众舆论存在严重分歧，认识到美帝国主义面临的危机更加严重，像麦克拉伦和他的同事们这样的马克思主义教育家，通过列宁所说的"政治揭露"，把马克思主义的路线"延伸"到各种社会运动中，为革命形势的可能性奠定了实际基础。这些政治揭露集中在资产阶级犯下的"可耻暴行"的"活生生的例子"上，并被组织起来对资本主义的"内部运作"提出质疑。[①]在列宁的政治小册子《怎么办？》（*What is to be Done?*）中，他认为这种"全面的政治鼓动"形式构成了"全面的政治教育"，应该把重点放在日常生活和思想中最多样化的领域中的社会问题和世界事件上[②]。他认为工人阶级的意识不可能是真正的阶级意识，除非工人们从具体的，尤其是从时事的政治事实和事件中，学习观察每一个其他社会阶级的知识、道德和政治生活的一切表现形式；除非他们学会在实践中应用唯物主义对所有阶级、阶层和人群的生活和活动的各个方面的估计。……这里重要的是，工人阶级斗争的发展将取决于无产阶级"对一切暴政、压迫、暴力和虐待做出反应"的自觉能力。[③] 因此革命性的批判教育学要把群众的自发性转变为意识，转变为批判意识，把社会主义作为一种思想力量，为生态革命、经济平等、资本价值形态之外的社会宇宙创造条件，创造一个没有种族主义、性别歧视、父权制、白人至上和军国主义的社会。

麦克拉伦拒绝接纳和迎合极右翼边缘，他敢于质疑权威，公开表达

---

① Lenin, V. I., "What is to be done? Burning questions of our movement" in Tucker, R., ed. *The Lenin anthology*, New York: W. W. Norton & Company, 1975, p. 43.

② Lenin, V. I., "What is to be done? Burning questions of our movement" in Tucker, R., ed. *The Lenin anthology*, New York: W. W. Norton & Company, 1975, p. 57.

③ Lenin, V. I., "What is to be done? Burning questions of our movement" in Tucker, R., ed. *The Lenin anthology*, New York: W. W. Norton & Company, 1975, p. 42.

对社会主义的支持，这使他在琼斯的布鲁因校友会（Bruin Alumni Association）"肮脏三十人"（Dirty Thirty List）排行榜上名列第一，该榜单引起了国际社会的关注。麦克拉伦在美国和世界各地的工作场所和社区与工人、工会成员和学生进行讨论时，谴责了目前的右翼镇压浪潮。当他谈到对激进学术界的攻击时，他把火力集中在那些他认为直接致力于压制学术界言论自由的新保守主义组织身上。在指认敌人时，麦克拉伦关注的是事实，将其程式化，以揭示世界上是如何存在权力的，以及真实的个人是如何使用权力的。麦克拉伦从事教育的那一刻开始就从未停止过对现实的揭露，从对加拿大肮脏的教育丑闻进行了富有说服力的人种志宣传到之后的每一本专著每一篇文章到每一次讲座都在揭露社会现实中各种不公平的现象。如在《学校生活》的第六版中麦克拉伦对世界上最具挑战性的问题如军国主义、新自由主义、资本主义、金融化、技术、环境恶化等给予了最新的揭露和批判。如在《反抗的教育学：从复活到革命》（Pedagogy of Insurrection：From Resurrection to Revolution）中麦克拉伦揭露了跨国资本主义对教育的影响，尤其是对美国教育的影响，包括各种企业私有化学校的举措所带来的毁灭性影响，其中有一章是对新数字技术的激烈批判。如在大学课堂上，麦克拉伦讲道："在我的很多关于批判教育学的著作中一直呼吁的是一种批判的爱国主义，而批判教育学所作的是揭露和谴责美国犯下的反人类罪行，防止这样的悲剧继续发生。在高中的历史课堂上，我们看不到发生在1899—1902年的美菲战争中美军的暴行；或者智利政变；或者皮诺切特的恐怖政策；还有在瓜太马拉的克萨尔特南戈省、韦韦特南戈省、圣马科斯以及索洛拉发生的对天主教教父的暗杀；或者2002年对查韦斯政府的颠覆计划的失败；或者美国中央情报局对发生在拉美和中东地区的持续一个世纪的不稳定应负的责任；或者美国历史上作为单边定向进攻的首席大师和其坚定不移的黩武精神将美国推上有史以来最恐怖的国家的位置；我们也不会在历史课上看到发生在墨西哥的反对政府压迫的萨帕塔主义者（Zapatista）起义。"

不论是通过课堂、讲座、研讨会、网上刊物、传单、报纸或小册子，麦克拉伦认为，这些"生动的揭露"所产生的对话、反思和批判的持续循环，将通过打破资产阶级思想的阶级结构，对今天在这一领域运作的各种阶级力量产生巨大的影响，从而为革命思想的发展创造必要的教育条件，并创造一整套能够使人们自觉地反对这一压迫性制度的做法。革命性的批判教育学似乎是乌托邦式的吗？正如麦克拉伦提醒我们的那样，只有当我们盲目或愤世嫉俗地接受资本主义的统治及其剥削关系的暴政，即系统性地剥夺人类充分发挥其创造能力和潜力的时候，我们才会承认这一点。

（三）集体行动

现在，在全球资本主义的背景下，主流的教育学将世界上不同的民族变成说英语的消费者，麦克拉伦致力于建立一个反社区，旨在打破这种将人们束缚在整个资本主义制度之下的商品关系的魔咒。他认为：

> 老师的功能不能只是停留在批评社会而已。他们必须尝试形塑一种希望的语言，在实践自由和正义的原则下倡导新的社会和物质关系，他们也必须主动地介入人类的行为。批判论述必须不只是一种文化失调的形式，不只是将主流意义和社会关系的能力加以削弱而已。批判论述的运作，必须可以创造一种民主的社群，建立在一种公共联结的语言与社会改造的责任上。批判论述必须倡议一种新的论述，让社会大众可以想象一个比较有品质的世界，并且努力让想象得以实现。我们必须在困难重重的现实下团结一致，我们所做的教学，必须能够扩展人类的能力，对抗宰制的力量，同时，又能够让我们有能力对抗绝望，拒绝向现实投降。[1]

此外，麦克拉伦也认为批判教育学应该扩展到教室之外，成为一种国际性和区域性的新的社会运动。他被邀请去帮助批判教育学更好地融入委内瑞拉的玻利瓦尔革命。在米拉弗洛雷斯宫（Miraflores Palace）会见乌戈·查韦斯后，他开始意识到任何革命都不能孤立存在。那次会面

---

[1] Peter McLaren*Life in Schools: An Introduction to Critical Pedagogy in the Foundations of Education* (*Sixth Edition*), Boulder, CO: Paradigm, 2014, p. 191.

进一步激发了他与激进团体建立尽可能多的联系，他的想法是把批判教育学转变为一场跨国社会运动。[1] 他认为年轻人需要建立一个具有明确社会主义议程的新政党，一个能够与拉丁美洲和其他地方的左翼政党结成跨国联盟的政党，并为人类规划一个新的全球未来。[2] 他说："困难在于，批判性文化的媒体很少有机会挑战企业媒体的谎言、欺骗和常识无知。我们需要赢得这场地位之战，当然，这意味着左派需要创造一个可行的替代紧缩资本主义的方案——一个社会主义的方案——大多数人可以在理性和情感上进行投资，建立和加强他们的主观能动性和变革意愿。在委内瑞拉，国有媒体绝大多数由富人拥有和控制，支持统治阶级的观点，现在仍然如此。尽管如此，人民还是取得了胜利，选举乌戈·查韦斯和他的继任者尼古拉斯·马杜罗（Nicolas Maduro）上台。在大多数国家，富人庆祝，穷人抗议，而在委内瑞拉，穷人庆祝，富人抗议。也许类似的事情会在美国发生。让我们希望美国的局势不要像委内瑞拉那样绝望时这样的事情才会发生。"[3]麦克拉伦认为："教学是一种可以期待、希望的事业，建立在辩证的逻辑之上，以批判和社会主义改革作为其核心挑战。摆在我们眼前的重大工程，就是要投入到被压迫团体真正需要的工作上，并且发展一种持久的责任感帮助他们增能。我们必须努力奋斗以改变当代每况愈下的道德水平，改变社会不断诱发的人性精神的颓丧。年轻的一代在面对需求和成就之间的鸿沟所展现的愤怒，必须在教室、法院、立法和街头等场域，用一种充满责任感和热忱的救赎教学加以解决。只有通过这种参与、投入，作为改革和希望的媒介，我们才可能开始去真正感觉和了解世界的苦难和疏离，也才有可能获得一种意志力、

---

① Derek R. Ford. "Revolutionary Critical Pedagogy and the Struggle against Capital Today: An Interview with Peter McLaren". *Education Interview*, 2015 - 7 - 16［EB/OL］. http: //www. hamptoninstitution. org/peter-mclaren-interview. html#. XT6gsi2B3FQ, 2019 - 05 - 22.

② Derek R. Ford. "Revolutionary Critical Pedagogy and the Struggle against Capital Today: An Interview with Peter McLaren". *Education Interview*, 2015 - 7 - 16［EB/OL］. http: //www. hamptoninstitution. org/peter-mclaren-interview. html#. XT6gsi2B3FQ, 2019 - 05 - 22.

③ Derek R. Ford. "Revolutionary Critical Pedagogy and the Struggle against Capital Today: An Interview with Peter McLaren". *Education Interview*, 2015 - 7 - 16［EB/OL］. http: //www. hamptoninstitution. org/peter-mclaren-interview. html#. XT6gsi2B3FQ, 2019 - 05 - 22.

目标感和理解力，来战胜这些苦难和疏离。"①

正如麦克拉伦在他最近的政治著作中明确指出的那样，当前的"反恐战争"表明，帝国主义的内在矛盾现在以罗莎·卢森堡所称的"社会主义或野蛮主义"②的历史选择的形式出现了。只要看看过去五年发生了什么，就像列宁所说的"垂死的资本"一样，通过增加国家干预和帝国主义战争来解决利润率下降所引发的混乱和危机。③麦克拉伦认为，在一片次等公民不满的海洋中，随着世界范围内帝国主义制度的矛盾浮出水面，引发了自发的抗议和反抗，革命工作的机会正在打开。然而，在政治层面上，我们很难忽视这样一个事实：尽管最近出现了反对伊拉克战争的抗议浪潮，目前的局势的特点并不是有大量的人对一个社会制度进行积极的辩论和采取行动，这是导致在整个星球上的野蛮行径的根源。根据国家的不同，部分问题在于资本主义退化的症状，统治阶级及其支持的国家机构创造了新的网络指挥结构来粉碎和雾化工人的意识，使社会处于一种疯狂的平衡状态。④

尽管这些打击工人阶级的意识，麦克拉伦认为资本主义不会永远持续。面对资本主义权威，我们很容易失去希望，把当前的形势看成是静止和暗淡的，麦克拉伦敦促我们把每一次抗议和叛乱的爆发都看作是为将来的革命机会做准备的训练场。面对新的世界局势，这将需要政治和组织上的战术变得更有灵活性。很明显，关于如何建立革命性的组织存在着很多争论，没有蓝图或配方。虽然在帝国主义大本营"革命时机尚未成熟"，我们生活在一个充满机遇的时代，工人阶级的运动可以借鉴其他国家和势力的丰富经验，特别是在亚洲、拉丁美洲和非洲被压迫的资

---

① Peter McLaren, *Life in Schools: An Introduction to Critical Pedagogy in the Foundations of Education* (Sixth Edition), Boulder, CO: Paradigm, 2014, p. 191.

② Martin, G., *I see red: The revolutionary critical pedagogy of Peter McLaren*, Aula Critica, Numero Especial Julio-Septiembre de, 2004, pp. 13 – 14.

③ Lenin, V. I., *Imperialism: The highest stage of capitalism*, New York: International, 1977.

④ Martin, G., *I see red: The revolutionary critical pedagogy of Peter McLaren*, Aula Critica, Numero Especial Julio-Septiembre de, 2004, pp. 13 – 14.

本主义国家。① 要理解这一点，还需要做更多的工作，但是，导致先进资本主义国家革命危机的条件，也是由今天进行的成千上万的小冲突和斗争所准备的。②

这里的重点不是成为经济主义、实用主义或宗派主义的牺牲品，而是在任何时期都保持灵活和准备，通过响应各种社会运动对政治和教育行动的要求，无论是在思想上还是在实践上，无论是在建立社区抗议运动的小型活动中，还是在建立或重建国际主义组织的大规模动员中，有意识地干预阶级斗争。虽然社会主义建设不是一条直线，但我们有希望。在反对资本主义的最明显的社会斗争中，激进分子和左翼运动的趋势正在发展，而且越来越明显的是，激进分子的新阶层对采取切实措施恢复、重建左派非常感兴趣。

为了摆脱机构赞助和资本社会的束缚，麦克拉伦认为，一种革命性的批判教育学"将主体性的非殖民化作为其目标，并将其作为资本主义社会关系的物质基础"③。麦克拉伦（2003）对格伦·里科沃斯基（2000，2001）④ 关于马克思劳动价值论的著作进行了阐述，认为"阶级斗争是社会整体内部矛盾力量和驱动力的冲突，是一种主体化和集体化的斗争"⑤。为了澄清这一点，麦克拉伦（2003）引用了格伦·里科沃斯基⑥的观点：

---

① Percy, J and Lorimer, D., *The democratic socialist party and the Fourth International*. Chippendale, NSW: Resistance Books, 2001, p.11.

② Martin, G., "You can't be neutral on a moving bus: Critical pedagogy as Community Praxis", (2005) [EB/OL]. http://www.jceps.com/index.php?pageID=article&articleID=47, 2018-06-20. &Percy, J. and Lorimer, D. *The democratic socialist party and the Fourth International*, Chippendale, NSW: Resistance Books, 2001.

③ Rizvi, M. "Educating for social justice and liberation: Peter McLaren interviewed by Mashhood Rizvi", [EB/OL]. http://www.zmag.org/content/showarticle.cfm?ItemID=2229, 2017-05-12.

④ Rikowski, G., "Messing with the explosive commodity: School improvement, educational research, and labour-power in the era of global capitalism. If we aren't pursuing improvement, what are we doing?" (2000) [EB/OL]. http://www.leeds.ac.uk/educol/documents/00001610.htm, 2016-07-14. & Rikowski, G. *The battle in Seattle: Its significance for education*, London: Tufnell Press, 2001.

⑤ Peter McLaren, *Life in Schools: An Introduction to Critical Pedagogy in the Foundations of Education (Fourth Edition)*, New York: Pearson Publishers, 2003, p.30.

⑥ Rikowski, G., *The battle in Seattle: Its significance for education*, London: Tufnell Press, 2001.

"阶级关系贯穿于我们的人格之中。它对我们来说是内在的;我们是劳动力,我们是资本。我们是社会人,包含着对立的社会驱动力和力量。这一事实引发了我们生活中的矛盾,而它们的解决只能来自我们自身作为资本和劳动力的解体,以及我们作为一种新的、非资本主义的生活形式的出现。"[1]

正如格伦·里科沃斯基(2002)所说,我们社会存在的潜在矛盾"把我们个人和集体搞砸了",他认为,我们需要克服我们在劳动过程本身的异化,抵制我们在金钱和国家的外来和敌对力量下,把自己贬低为人力资本的"特殊"形式。[2] 格伦·里科沃斯基写道:"我们需要一种人类反抗的政治。这是一种旨在抵制将我们的人格降低为劳动力(人力资本),从而抵制人性的资本化的政治。这种政治也有真正消极的一面:消除那些使我们陷入混乱、迷惑和沮丧的矛盾。然而,只有集体才能消除这些构成人格和社会的矛盾。它们的终结取决于产生它们的社会关系(资本主义社会关系)的消灭,在社会现象中制约其发展的社会力量,包括'人'(资本)和资本社会宇宙实质(价值)的消解。一项人类抵抗的集体政治计划是必要的,这与共产主义政治,一项社会和人类重建的积极政治是相辅相成的。"[3]

有鉴于此,一种革命性的批判教育学,将个人的发展(主体的内心生活)与旨在社会变革的集体参与形式联系起来,旨在抵制主体性的"资本化"。[4] 在集体行动这一层面,麦克拉伦看到了青年一代所作出的努力,他指出:

---

[1] Peter McLaren, *Life in Schools: An Introduction to Critical Pedagogy in the Foundations of Education* (*Fourth Edition*), New York: Pearson Publishers, 2003, p. 30.

[2] Rikowski, G., "Methods for researching the social production of labour power in capitalism" (2002) [EB/OL]. http://www.ieps.org.uk.cwc.net/rikowski2002b.pdf, 2018-04-02.

[3] McLaren, P. and Rikowski, G., "Pedagogy for revolution against education for capital: An e-dialogue on education in capitalism today" (2001) [EB/OL]. http://eserver.org/clogic/4-1/mclaren&rikowski.html, 2018-04-02.

[4] Peter McLaren, *Life in Schools: An Introduction to Critical Pedagogy in the Foundations of Education* (*Fourth Edition*), New York: Pearson Publishers, 2003, p. 25.

在这个前所未有的历史时刻,资本主义描绘出一条分界线,线的一边是世界银行、国际货币基金组织、世界贸易组织以及美国帝国等,资本主义通过这些国家或机构对界限另一边的机构和人民实施压迫,我们年轻的社会活动者终于意识到他们不可能在这个被资本主义文化覆盖的分化的大陆上寻求一个整体。他们需要重新开始一个新世界。犹如从煤油灯中跳出来的小精灵,一群生态无产主义者呼吁国际联合和跨国抵制,从推翻资本主义政体的积累方式开始,发誓改写人类历史进程。虽然我们不能肯定社会主义一定是替代资本主义的救赎方式,但是在我们的年轻人之间存在着对新的主张和斗争方式的热烈地追寻。尽管我们正在面临不断加密的政府监控,越发强硬的对外政策,街边警察频繁的拦截盘查,蔓延扩展的黑帮势力,以及节节高升的青少年犯罪率等等;我们同时也可以看到青年人努力改变现状的决心——他们参与美国民权运动,参与"LGBTQ"运动,参与各种形式的女权运动、环保主义和环境公正运动,还有工会、反战、移民权利运动等;在国际范围内的青年见证和参与的抵制运动例如——他们参与"反峰会会议"①,参与萨帕塔主义者组织的"遭遇"活动②;他们认识到社会实践创造的使用价值不是经济计算和与他人的竞争关系可以涵盖的,受到团结行动的启发,他们在保证和推动市场规律的权力的纵向网络之外寻求横向的国际团结;他们通过草根民主、共识、对话和相互了解达成社会合作,以及非固定关系为前提的权威和社会合作,以互动为前提的自决;通过与他人的更深层的交往超越地区、工种、社会条件、性别、年龄、文化、性取向、语言、宗教、信仰的限制。总之,他们支持一个全球的社区网络。如果年轻一代决心挣脱资产阶级用几个世纪

---

① 反峰会会议(counter-summit,会议全称:Counter-Summit for Peace & Economic Justice)于2012年5月在芝加哥举行,目的是与同一时间同一地点在芝加哥举行的北大西洋公约组织首脑峰会相抗衡,呼吁取缔北约,推进世界和平和经济公正。

② Zapatista Encuentros:1996年7月萨帕塔主义者召集美洲大陆以及全球的社会活动者、知识分子、革命者等在墨西哥恰帕斯(Chiapas)商讨在全球范围内抵制新自由主义政策的策略,吸引来自5大洲42个国家的近3000人参与。

的教条炼成的锁链，我们不会将这个任务仅仅丢给他们。我们需要展现给他们希望，但是不真实的希望可以将乐观转变成无所不能的错觉，并可能导致致命的狂妄自大。我们应该将希望与对公正的追求相结合，即便冷酷的现实往往不怀好意，也许永远都会这样。（节选自麦克拉伦在东北师范大学的讲课材料）

关于麦克拉伦的工作还有很多没有被提及，但我可以说它是由一种深深的激情、希望和革命性的爱所驱动的。这些态度的核心是麦克拉伦工作各个方面的政治态度，这是一个更大的集体努力的一部分。作为麦克拉伦的一名学生和朋友，研究者可以证明，他从不羞于让自己变得脆弱，也从不羞于在社交场合表露自己的内心。也许正是因为这个原因，他的革命信息得到了如此巨大的反响。在过去的 5 年里，研究者感受到了他的日常关怀以及他对地球居民的巨大的爱，这些都建立在他的支持团结社群的基础上。麦克拉伦在一个集体的框架下运作，帮助他人发挥领导作用，鼓励他的学生尽最大努力，并为其他同志和全体工人运动的成功和胜利感到高兴和自豪。麦克拉伦似乎已经积累了一群盟友。当然，这反映在他在世界各地的积极努力中；如他与英国的戴夫·希尔一起发展教育政策研究所（The Institute for Education Policy Studies），2003 年起更创刊电子杂志半年刊《批判教育政策研究杂志》（Journal for Critical Education Policy Studies）（http：//www.jceps.com/），并与由英国的戴夫·希尔和巴西的巴勃罗·真蒂利（Pablo Gentili）一起担任主编。目前该所的作者群有 6 位，包括英国的葆拉·奥尔曼、戴夫·希尔、迈克·科尔和格伦·里科沃斯基和美国的麦克拉伦以及加拿大的山鲁佐德（Shahrzad Mojab）。如果要用文字来诠释麦克拉伦的团结精神，可以从他很多的作品中发现，如作品集《红色研讨会》（Red Seminar）是由 22 位不同的合著者共同撰写的。也可以在麦克拉伦的作品中阅读到大量的文献强调引文，这本身也是一种社区建设功能。150 年前，马克思给了革命的希望，但他也写道，思想本身不能改变社会。从长远的历史观点来看，麦克拉伦的主要论点是，若想摧毁资本主义就需要重建我们的内部和社会关系，而不是宣传一套特定的理念。在一个只能被描述为"战区"的无法忍受的世界背景下,需要通过集体行动将理论与实践之间建立一种新的关系来与统治阶级的暴行做斗争。麦克拉伦说,尽管有存在着诸多的理论和思想家的观点,但是他学会的最重要的是我们需要正视人类的真实处境,只有通过集体的抗争才能达到权力的解放。①

(四)阶级斗争

阶级是马克思主义当中很重要的议题,麦克拉伦认为后现代主义忽略了阶级的问题,甚至于避谈,他(2001)表示:"我的任务是要去强调阶级的重要性以及要废止所有形式的压迫。"②因此,他寄希望从马克思主义当中可以获得对抗资本主义的利器,因此,他顺着马克思主义的思路,论述社会阶级再制的问题,期望通过阶级斗争而建立社会主义的社会,朝向乌托邦蓝图迈进。他认为:"在根本上,批判教育学是一种阶级斗争的教育学,它以各种形式展开——反种族主义、反性别主义、批判的残疾人研究,等等。"③

何为社会阶级?如果说有人属于上层阶级、下层阶级,则势必有中产阶级,而这正是资本主义的阶级观点。资本主义对于阶级所编织的神话——通过勤奋的努力工作、刚毅和坚忍不拔的努力可以提升身份和阶级。将劳动和阶级区分,是意图让阶级的关系模糊化。例如,当我们说到"白领"和"蓝领"工人时,事实上是隐藏劳动阶级和阶级的利益。麦克拉伦一再强调,"阶级"这个议题在批判教育学当中太常被忽视。他指出,近年来批判教育学转到文化以及政治的层面探讨,在这当中,阶级被简化为"结果"而不是"起因"。事实上,阶级中所谓的压迫,涉及

---

① Peter McLaren., "This fist called my heart-public pedagogy in the belly of the beast", In Brian, D., *Handbook of Peter McLaren*: *education and learning beyond schooling*, pp. 564 – 576, New York: Routledge, 2009, pp. 564 –565.

② Peter McLaren. (2011a: 34) *education and the unchained class struggle in the crisis of global capitalism*, the speech of international conference on higher education management, in National Taichung University of Education, Dec, 24, 2011, pp. 1 – 45.

③ Peter McLaren, "Education Agonistes: an epistle to the transnational capitalist class" *Policy Futures in Education*, Vol. 12, No. 4, April 2014, p. 604.

控制，是资本主义社会关系当中权力的扩增。① 因此，麦克拉伦认为主流阶级或者说统治阶级具有经济权力和政治利益极大的支配权，而所谓的"阶级流动"是神话。

麦克拉伦在研究生课堂上曾向学生建议阅读乔尔·克沃尔（Joel Kovel）关于为何突出强调阶级与进行阶级斗争的原因，他本人非常认同这段论述：

> 接下来的讨论或许可以帮助澄清困扰左派已久的一个问题，那就是，被称为"绝对性分歧"（dominative splitting）的关于性别、阶级、种族、民族和国家排他性，还有生态危机、物种危机这些议题的优先性排列的分歧。现在的问题是，在什么样的标准之下的优先性？如果以时间为首要标准的话，性别议题自然夺魁，而且，考虑到历史是在过去基础之上的叠加而不是对过去的完全替代，所以至少我们可以将性别议题作为一个线索来进一步研究其他从属关系。如果我们以存在的意义（existential significance）作为首要标准的话，那么任何一种基于某一人类群体的直接的历史推动力的分类都说得通，因为这是某一人类群体亲身经历的：例如对生活在上个世纪30年代德国的犹太人来说，反犹论调毫无疑问是首要的矛盾，就好像反阿拉伯种族歧视论调之于生活在以色列控制区的巴勒斯坦人，或者是恶劣无情的性别歧视之于例如生活在阿富汗的妇女。至于哪一种矛盾具有政治上的优先性，从谁的变革在实践上更加具有紧迫性这个意义上说，要取决于先后关系（the preceding），同时也受一个真实情境中各种活跃因素的配置关系影响——但是，如果我们从效能（efficacy）的角度来看，也就是说哪一种矛盾冲突具有"牵一发而动全身"的特质，那么一定是阶级矛盾了，最简单的解释便是阶级关系决定了国家作为强制和控制的工具的属性，而国家同时又形

---

① Peter McLaren and Ramin Farahmandpur, "Teaching Against Global Capitalism and the New Imperialism: toward a revolutionary pedagogy" *Journal of teacher education*, Vol. 52, No. 2, March 2001, pp. 136 – 137.

塑和组织人类生态体系中的各种矛盾。所以阶级在逻辑上和历史上都与其他形式的排他矛盾不同（因此我们不应该将"阶级主义 classism"与"性别主义""种族主义""物种主义"等并列）。首先，因为阶级实质上是一个人为的（man-made）分类，甚至不存在一个迷思化的生物学根基。也就是说，我们不能想象一个不存在性别区分的社会——当然我们可以想象一个没有性别歧视的社会。但是不存在阶级区分的社会是完全可以想象的——的确，在人类历史的大部分时间中不存在阶级关系，然而对性别的讨论却是一致存在的。历史上，差异的出现是因为阶级在国家机器中产生影响，而国家机器的控制和规范方式造就了种族关系以及性别关系。因此只要是阶级社会存在一天，种族歧视问题就不会得到有效解决，因为一个种族歧视的社会意味着森严的阶级区分作为隐含的行动规范。同样，只要阶级社会要求对女性劳动力进行剥削，性别歧视问题就可能通过立法得到解决。阶级社会一刻不停地制造性别、种族、民族等压迫形式，这些压迫形式各自独立的同时，又都在深刻影响着具体的阶级关系。阶级政治需要在这些活跃的社会对抗中得以解决。正是对这些对抗种类的有效掌控保证了国家社会（state society）的正常运行。因此虽然每一个处于这个阶级社会中的个人都从他/她可以成为什么开始被化约，不同的化约结果与历史的分层政权相结合——这个人将成为勇猛的战士，那个人是个循规蹈矩的办公室职员，那个是顺从的女裁缝，等等，直到我们达到对资本的人格化，成为工业领袖。然而，不论阶级社会有多么的功能化，它所造成的生态破坏的严峻性确保了一个推进历史前进的基本对抗的存在。历史是阶级社会的历史——因为不管如何改良，这一分裂都是要注定显现的，进而激发抵制行动，例如"阶级斗争"，导致权力的交替。[①]

对麦克拉伦来说，教育对当今的反资本主义运动极具重要性，激进

[①] Kovel, J., *The Enemy of Nature: the end of capitalism or the end of the world?*, London: Zed Books, 2002, pp. 123 – 124.

的教育学和反资本主义的抗争是密切相关的。麦克拉伦（2000）呼吁致力于工人阶级斗争，这是革命的核心。① 革命性的批判教育学质疑官方霸权式所推动的教育改革，就像是目前美国所推动的"卓越竞争计划""力争上游计划"等。作为革命性批判教育工作者必须要理解到资本主义已经成为跨国性的资本主义，冲击到教育制度和方法。对于全球的重建以及对资本主义的紧缩应该要始于教师认真的分析教育。麦克拉伦称之为革命性的阶级斗争，也就是社会重组必须要根源于教师……此外，最重要的是要通过集体的力量，克服资本主义的压迫，打破资本主义社会的铜墙铁壁。② 他极力强调批判的重要性，也认为要对习以为常的事物进行批判。③ 否则劳动阶级的学生通过教育和社会的运作，会被再制成劳工阶层。④

麦克拉伦认为马克思主义关注到统治阶级的压迫。对马克思来说，国家是异化的一种形式，而国家是作为一种工具来创作出国际性的公民。在麦克拉伦看来，不是将问题单纯地视为仅是阶级问题，他认为在遍及全球的资本主义下，因为社会阶级的对立以及当代的薪资与酬劳日益凸显出阶级问题的重要性。⑤ 革命性的批判教育学认为倘若没有阶级的斗争，则批判教育学所能做的人类行为学的改变是有限的。因此，革命性的批判教育学要从世界上古往今来的历史实践、意识形态以及每日的生

---

① Eryaman, Mustafa Yunus. , "Editorial Statement (English) : Understanding Critical Pedagogy and Peter McLaren in the Age of Global Capitalism" *International Journal of Progressive Education*, Vol. 2, No. 3, October2006, p. 8.

② Peter McLaren and Glenn Rikiowski, "Pedagogy for revolution against education for capital: an e-dialogue on education in capitalism today" *Cultural Logic*, Vol. 4, No. 1, January2001, p. 44.

③ Peter McLaren. , "This fist called my heart-public pedagogy in the belly of the beast", In Brian, D. , *Handbook of Peter McLaren: education and learning beyond schooling*, pp. 564 – 576, New York: Routledge, 2009, p. 570.

④ Peter McLaren, *Life in Schools: An Introduction to Critical Pedagogy in the Foundations of Education (Fifth Edition)*, New York: Pearson Publishers, 2007, p. 35.

⑤ Peter McLaren. , "This fist called my heart-public pedagogy in the belly of the beast", In Brian, D. , *Handbook of Peter McLaren: education and learning beyond schooling*, pp. 564 – 576, New York: Routledge, 2009, p. 570.

活当中的生产面向去实践。① 麦克拉伦认为：

> 很多对资本主义制度的批判之所以能够进入主流的话题领域是因为它们避免将自由市场作为罪魁祸首，而是将批评的视角转向金融资本主义背景之下强盗资本家的不断强化的贪婪行径、弱肉强食的市场规则、家族王朝、无限高薪，以及我们正在和一直在面临的经济不平等背后的谎言。诚然，开门见山地指出政府和各种组织在当下数字经济时代履行社会责任时表现出的暴力倾向和道德惰性是很有必要的。但是我想要强调的是资本主义不平等的结构性暴力以及营造一个替代资本主义社会的社会主义社会的必要性是我们这个正在飞速断裂以致无可挽回的破碎的世界的最亟须和悲壮的呼声。阶级抗争是走向社会主义的必要途径。然而我在这里有必要重申国际马克思主义人道主义组织的重要论述——阶级抗争必须与实践哲学并行，而实践哲学是一种具体化的哲学，它直面，而不是放弃辩证理论。辩证哲学可以帮我们脱下资本主义意识形态的伪装的外衣，帮助我们意识到我们是如何一边期盼一个解放的未来，一边不加批判地接受社会改革，任由资本主义的剥削关系蒙蔽我们的双眼。（节选自麦克拉伦在东北师范大学的讲课材料）

事实上，美国在崇尚经济自由、民主的资本主义社会下，社会呈现出种种不平等的现象。社会福利制度、社会救济等各项措施都是尝试去解决资本主义下所衍生的社会问题。就麦克拉伦而言，现今的社会充满着不公正的现象，美国的现实社会状况与政治、经济有关。② 麦克拉伦感受到资本主义除了在政治、经济上产生压迫，更体悟到在教育上资本主义霸权的威权与思想的钳制，因此提出革命性的批判教育学予以反

---

① Michael Pozo, "Towards a Critical Revolutionary Pedagogy", in P. McLaren, ed. *Rage and Hope: An Interview with Peter McLaren*, New York: Rowman & Little-field Publishers, 2006, p. 16.

② Peter McLaren, *Life in Schools: An Introduction to Critical Pedagogy in the Foundations of Education (Fifth Edition)*, New York: Pearson Publishers, 2007, p. 261.

击。①革命性的批判教育学是一个革命前的准备，预备学生考虑外在于资本社会领域的生活，去"瞥见超越资本主义视觉下人类可能的未来"②。发展革命性的批判教育学能够使劳动阶级的团体发现其劳动力的使用价值如何被资本所剥削，并且劳动阶级的倡议与权力如何被这种决定力量的形态所诋毁；凭借着阶级关系的重组，直接在多重面向上挑战资本主义。

麦克拉伦从阶级的抗争作为切入点，说明革命性的批判教育学的立场，为此，他说道："我们的抗争并非冷血的，不是在别处，也不会为了错失真理而哀悼，革命性的批判教育学是始于阶级抗争的立场。麦克拉伦（2000）呼吁致力于工人阶级斗争，这是革命的核心。③ 最终目的是，我们必须要剥去各种人类处境的伪装，理解到要与资产阶级的意识形态进行对抗，直到社会关系的再制消失为止。"④麦克拉伦遗憾地表示："社会主义本身不会造成动荡，但是在美国，社会主义一词被污蔑为让人民不安、引起恐慌，会造成社会大众惊恐的名词。"他特别强调："虽然是沿着社会主义的路径，试图对于消除阶级或是从劳工的立场去推翻资本社会制度，但是还是要小心谨慎地避免流血事件。当人民意识到整个教育系统是必须照顾他们的利益以及有所变革，这就是革命性的批判教育学的力量所在。在某种意义上，革命性的批判教育学的工作就是凸显出阶级，进而认清现实生活中私有化和商品化的残酷，并且试图改造资本的运作方式，这也是革命性的批判教育学的目标。"⑤

---

① Peter McLaren, *Rage and Hope*, New York: Peter Lang Publishing, Inc., 2006.

② Allman, P., *Critical education against global capitalism: Karl Marx and revolutionary critical education*, Westport, CT: Bergin & Garvey, 2001, p.219.

③ Eryaman, Mustafa Yunus. "Editorial Statement (English): Understanding Critical Pedagogy and Peter McLaren in the Age of Global Capitalism" *International Journal of Progressive Education*, Vol.2, No.3, October2006, p.8.

④ Peter McLaren., "This fist called my heart-public pedagogy in the belly of the beast", In Brian, D., *Handbook of Peter McLaren: education and learning beyond schooling*, pp.564-576, New York: Routledge, 2009, p.566.

⑤ 彼得·麦克拉伦和周霖：《革命的批判教育学：教师教育项目的解毒剂》，《东北师大学报（哲学社会科学版）》2009年第2期。

（五）宣扬示范性的革命偶像人物

麦克拉伦是北美传播保罗·弗莱雷作品和思想的最重要的大使[1]。除了大力宣传保罗·弗莱雷，他还比较善于并乐于挖掘别人忽略的教育界人物、在教育左翼的文献中几乎从未被讨论过的人物如古巴革命家切·格瓦拉、古巴共和国、古巴共产党和古巴革命武装力量的主要缔造者菲德尔·卡斯特罗、委内瑞拉前总统乌戈·查韦斯、墨西哥的革命家埃米利亚诺·萨帕塔（Emiliano Zapata）等，来扩展教育领域的界限。在其作品中和演讲中宣扬这些示范性的革命偶像。他选择在学校和教育的背景下讨论这些人物，并不是因为他们的职业是教师或从事与教育相关的行业，而是因为他认为对这些人物的讨论将为批判教育学的理论提供合适的象征性笔触，如像切·格瓦拉一样，"对战胜资本主义充满信心"，并给它一个"坚定而英勇"的视角。[2]

麦克拉伦对切·格瓦拉这样的政治英雄充满敬意，对他的知识分子兄弟兼朋友保罗·弗莱雷有着最高的评价。他很欣赏乌戈·查韦斯并评价他确实是一个有机知识分子。查韦斯使他认识到，批判教育学对玻利瓦尔革命有多么重要，在观花宫（Miraflores Palace）会见查韦斯是他永远不会忘记的经历。在墨西哥的社区里，支持萨帕塔主义者（Zapatistas，一群墨西哥革命运动者）对他的影响超过了他的预期。他在家里和办公室里摆满了革命纪念品和艺术品，包括列宁、马克思和毛泽东的半身像。他右肩上纹有古巴革命家切·格瓦拉，左肩上纹有墨西哥的革命家埃米利亚诺·萨帕塔。

在《切·格瓦拉，保罗·弗莱雷与革命教育学》这本书中，麦克拉伦追溯了切·格瓦拉和保罗·弗莱雷这两位20世纪最重要的左翼成员的生活和工作的历程。在《反抗的教育学：从复活到革命》（Pedagogy of Insurrection: From Resurrection to Revolution）中麦克拉伦讨论了一些在美国媒体上被钉在十字架上的历史人物，——保罗·弗莱雷、切·格瓦拉、

---

[1] Peter McLaren, *Red Seminars: Radical excursions into educational theory, cultural politics, and pedagogy*, New York,: Hampton Press, Inc., 2005, p.509.

[2] Peter McLaren, *Che Guevara, Paulo Freire, and the Pedagogy of Revolution*, Lanham, MD: Rowman & Littlefield Publishers, 2000, p.107.

菲德尔·卡斯特罗和乌戈·查韦斯。麦克拉伦认为他们为人类的自由和解放所做的贡献值得我们认真地思考。① 他的目标是"利用这些人物的思想和实践作为教育学的源泉,创造出一种批判的能动性,来对抗和改变当前的全球剥削和压迫关系"②。麦克拉伦认为,这些教育家和革命者的思想和示范可以帮助教育工作者把学校改造成社会正义和革命社会主义实践的场所。

当麦克拉伦写《切·格瓦拉、保罗·弗莱雷和革命教育学》时,他将切·格瓦拉和保罗·弗莱雷视为马克思主义人道主义立场的典范。如切·格瓦拉对反资本主义努力的启发,或许比拉美任何一位标志性人物都要大,他的面部形象早已经在(资本主义)世界的壁画、T恤衫和其他地方传播开来。然而,切·格瓦拉并不是完美的象征。正如乔恩·李·安德森(Jon Lee Anderson)的传记《切·格瓦拉:革命的一生》(Che Guevara: A Revolutionary Life)中所述,切·格瓦拉的革命战略低估了"进行革命"所需的适当条件。葛兰西对"运动之战"和"立场之战"进行过区分,前者涉及列宁所完成的对国家的征服,后者是为人民意识而进行的意识形态之战。当切·格瓦拉工作的国家(当然是古巴以外的国家)的"立场之战"还没有结束时,也许他太急于进行"运动之战"。这也影响了他的声誉;皮埃尔·卡尔丰(Pierre Kalfon)的《切·埃内斯托·格瓦拉》(Che Ernesto Guevara)的封底把切·格瓦拉称为一个浪漫的非现实主义者。那些在T恤上印有切·格瓦拉形象的人并不是提倡切·格瓦拉所做的一切,而是一种浪漫的反资本主义,将格瓦拉(Che Guevara)的形象作为一种情感的基础。麦克拉伦在宣扬这些革命偶像人物时不是提倡这些人所做的一切,不是盲目地崇拜,他对切·格瓦拉等人的标志性颂扬并不意味着任何教义或宗教。也许,如果我们把偶像和标志性的话语理论化,从而对批判性思维产生敌意,我们就低估了

---

① Kenneth Zeichner. "Book Review: Peter McLaren, Che Guevara, Paulo Freire, and the Pedagogy of Revolution. Roman & Littlefield, Lanham, Maryland, USA, 2000. 264 pages, ISBN 0847695336" *Journal of Educational Change*, No. 2, 2001, p. 181.

② Peter McLaren, *Che Guevara, Paulo Freire, and the Pedagogy of Revolution*, Lanham, MD: Rowman & Littlefield Publishers, 2000, p. xxvi.

偶像。显然，我们自己的社会充满了偶像。我们崇拜这些偶像是因为他们的象征价值。金钱本身就是我们的偶像；在它的纸质和金属形式上，印有总统头像的图片。我们对它的尊重是象征性的；作为一种物质的存在，它仅仅是纸币、金属光盘或屏幕上的像素点，它们本身作为物体并不重要。然而，不知何故，我们认为金钱是我们工作生活的动力，事实上是一种"使世界运转"的东西。从理论上讲，货币是交换价值的一种标志性形式。因为我们对金钱的迷恋，我们可以用它买到的任何东西都有"交换价值"。这确实是商品崇拜的意义所在。我们使用货币形式（金、银）来制作珠宝，并将它们形象地展示在我们的身体上。在学校我们教偶像崇拜；国旗每天早晨受到敬礼。2001年9月11日上午，飞机撞向纽约世贸中心的意义在于，这些直耸云霄的高楼被劫机者视为美国的象征，美国力量的象征。偶像的力量以及符号形式的沟通和行为的确构成了"咒语"，尤其是商品关系的咒语。麦克拉伦对我们的偶像存在的回应是将反偶像引入讨论，以显示其颠覆性的价值。例如，他在加州大学洛杉矶分校（UCLA）和查普曼大学的办公室和他的家中是马克思、恩格斯、乌戈·查韦斯以及任何具有偶像价值的人物的圣地，这些人物在他的联想链中具有颠覆主流范式的价值。麦克拉伦认为这些人物把建立一个更公正的世界置于个人利益之上，他们对社会正义事业的献身精神和实践应该得到发扬光大，为后人提供榜样的力量。

麦克拉伦在作品中和讲学中对这些革命人物进行宣传是很有必要的，否则在像美国这样的资本主义国家这些人物是鲜为人知的。如，威斯康星大学麦迪逊分校（University of Wisconsin-Madison）的教师肯尼斯·蔡克纳（Kenneth Zeichner）在文章中写道："读完《切·格瓦拉、保罗·弗莱雷和革命教育学》本书后，我随机询问了威斯康星大学麦迪逊分校（University of Wisconsin-Madison）不同专业的教师教育学生，他们是否听说过切·格瓦拉和保罗·弗莱雷，如果听说过，他们对切·格瓦拉和保罗·弗莱雷的生活和工作了解多少。即使在这所相对进步的教育学院，与我交谈过的学生中，也很少有人能告诉我关于这两个人的很多情况。有些人在历史课上听说过切·格瓦拉，但几乎没有人知道保罗·弗莱雷的生活和工作。这是一种非常可悲的情况。与十几名学生的短暂接触让我确信，麦克拉伦在书的开头所说的是正确的——我们有必要复兴切·格瓦拉和保罗·弗莱雷的作品，并把批判实践的理念带回批判教育学的讨论中。鉴于当今世界上许多人所经历的贫困和苦难，这是一项非常严肃而重要的事业。"[1]

---

[1] Kenneth Zeichner. "Book Review: Peter McLaren, Che Guevara, Paulo Freire, and the Pedagogy of Revolution. Roman & Littlefield, Lanham, Maryland, USA, 2000. 264 pages, ISBN 0847695336" *Journal of Educational Change*, No. 2, 2000, p. 184.

第四章

立场、特色与评价

与亨利·吉鲁、迈克尔·阿普尔等北美的主要批判教育家的思想相比,麦克拉伦批判教育学思想有着本质的不同。其马克思主义人道主义的立场倡导通过教育实现某种资本主义社会形式的替代,而亨利·吉鲁、迈克尔·阿普尔等人倡导通过教育改革资本主义。麦克拉伦的批判教育学思想体现出坚守质疑与希望、兼顾理论与实践的特色。学界对麦克拉伦在学术成就与贡献、其学者与教师身份及革命激情与行动等方面进行了充分的肯定,而且世界各地、社会各界授予了麦克拉伦数量相当可观的奖项。当然麦克拉伦也受到了各种批判与攻击。无论如何麦克拉伦知行合一、做有献身精神的知识分子、拒绝故步自封等品质可作为世界各地教育者的表率。

第一节 麦克拉伦批判教育学的立场与特色

一 麦克拉伦批判教育学的马克思主义人道主义立场

发展自中南美洲与北美洲的批判教育学,深受保罗·弗莱雷在巴西所进行的成人识字教育影响。并由北美亨利·吉鲁、麦克拉伦等人所倡议之"批判教育学",自20世纪80年代以来已成为西方世界里头左派知识分子用以批判新右派、新保守主义、新自由主义、教育市场化的主要论述利器,同时也为富有批判、解放色彩的教育实践开启另一扇希望之窗。而在批判教育学传统底下的学者,为了因应此时代潮流的转变,纷纷从事理论转型的工作,进而生产出形形色色的相关词汇：如亨利·吉鲁（1992）的"边界教育学"（border pedagogy）、麦克拉伦 2000）的"革命的教育学"（revolutionary pedagogy）、贝尔·胡克斯（1994）的"交融教育学"（engaged pedagogy）等。不管名称为何，基本上，它们都同意批判教育学的理念：将教育视为一种增益权能（empowerment）的催化剂，并希望透过此途径达成社会的整体转化。

作为早期在北美倡导批判教育运动的领军人物或批判教育学的奠基人，作为当今北美批判理论界的三巨头之一的麦克拉伦与另外两位——亨利·吉鲁和迈克尔·阿普尔对世界许多国家的教育改革和民主教育进程发挥着重要影响。① 在批判教育思想上，他们彼此观点同中有异、异中有同，既有相似之处又有本质区别。

除了认同学校再制不平等和不公正之外，当代的批判理论家在许多分析的观点上其实各持己见。当前批判传统的论述大约可以分成两派：一派人相信可以按照工人阶级的利益改革资本主义，例如亨利·吉鲁、迈克尔·阿普尔等；另一派人认为只有废除阶级社会实现社会主义社会替代资本主义社会才能真正取得社会公平，例如彼得·麦克拉伦（Peter McLaren）和保拉·奥尔曼、麦克·科尔（Mike Cole）、柯里·马洛特（Curry Malott）、格伦·里科沃斯基、戴夫·希尔、达德尔（Antonia Darder）、理查德·布劳斯（Richard Brosio）、拉明·法拉曼德普尔等。②无论是哪一派都是希望通过发挥教育过程中的人的主体性的那一面，挖掘出教育过程中的反抗因素，进而实现人的解放。换句话说这些批判理论家的目标是一致的：赋予无权力者以权力，以改变社会不平等和不公正的现象。③

---

① 王占魁：《阿普尔批判教育研究的批判逻辑》，《教育研究》2012 年第 4 期，第 134 页。
② Peter McLaren, *Life in Schools: An Introduction to Critical Pedagogy in the Foundations of Education* (Sixth Edition), Boulder, CO: Paradigm, 2014, p. 128.
③ Peter McLaren, *Life in Schools: An Introduction to Critical Pedagogy in the Foundations of Education* (Sixth Edition), Boulder, CO: Paradigm, 2014, p. 122.

迈克尔·阿普尔是美国最早的新马克思主义学者①并被称为知识社会学领域的教育学者之一。亨利·吉鲁曾被美国媒体称为"批判教育学之父"。麦克拉伦是马克思主义人道主义教育理论代表人物之一，也是世界范围内批判教育学的主要倡导者之一。

迈克尔·阿普尔受到了英国学者巴兹尔·伯恩斯坦（Basil Bernstein）、迈克尔·杨（Michael Young）和杰夫·惠蒂（Geoff Whitty）的影响。亨利·吉鲁受到社会学家斯坦利·阿罗诺维茨和法兰克福批判理论学派（Frankfurt School of Critical Theory）的影响。麦克拉伦最初受到人类学家维克多·特纳（Victor Turner）的比较符号学的影响，后来又受到"新马克思主义"学术的影响，包括安东尼奥·葛兰西和法兰克福批判理论学派。1995年，麦克拉伦与英国马克思主义者格伦·里科夫斯基、戴夫·希尔和迈克·科尔进行了对话，他们说服他重新审视马克思的著作。麦克拉伦受到黑格尔马克思主义传统的影响。

亨利·吉鲁和麦克拉伦在20世纪80年代和90年代初一同在迈阿密大学（Miami University）并肩作战，引领了北美批判教育学的成长，都深受文化研究领域的影响，致力于文化政治学部分的研究，提出批判的多元文化主义的观点，引领批判教育学向文化政治转向的立场，当时他们把自己定义为批判的后现代主义者。90年代中后期之后麦克拉伦不再把自己归为后现代主义者，而是常常把自己称为古典马克思主义者或马克思主义人道主义者。国内外教育哲学学者普遍认为应当将阿普尔定名为"新马克思主义者"。②迈克尔·阿普尔自己也曾公开承认自己是一名新马

---

① "新马克思主义"：1960—1980年，法兰克福学派在西奥多·阿多诺、麦克斯·霍克海默、赫伯特·马尔库塞等人的开创下逐渐茁壮。他们也吸纳了拉丁美洲、非洲的解放神学，东欧的华沙学派、布拉格学派、南斯拉夫实践学派等不同地区发展出来的马克思主义思想，而脱胎成为"新马克思主义"学派。关心的主题有别于西方马克思主义的上层结构和意识形态，还纳入了语言与文化分析、生态与沟通理论、资本主义全球化、新帝国主义与世界体系等概念。此外，"新马克思主义"除了使用历史分析和辩证法外，还融入了语言分析、文化分析、心理分析、行为学等不同的方法论基础。简单来说，"新马克思主义"呈现了一种内容与方法混杂的现象。

② 王占魁：《价值选择与教育政治——阿普尔批判教育研究的实践逻辑》，教育科学出版社2014年版，第9页。

克思主义者。① 亨利·吉鲁则认为自己是激进的民主主义者，他并不认为自己是马克思主义者或新马克思主义者。

亨利·吉鲁认为，后现代主义尽管有一些缺点，但它毕竟为批判教育学的形成提供了很多见识，特别是后现代主义有关文化、边界、差异性、主体性的观点，为激进批判教育的发展提供了更多的丰富性与可能性。②在后现代语境中亨利·吉鲁极力把后现代主义、新马克思主义、后马克思主义③、批判理论等整合到"抵抗理论"中来，试图发展一种教育的后现代理论。④ 可以说，后现代主义的存在，构成了吉鲁批判教育哲学产生、发展的理论沃土与哲学语境。他创建了带有鲜明个性特征和时代特点的"亨利·吉鲁式"抵抗理论，为其分析学校和社会的关系提供了一个重要的理论视角和工具，形成了他分析教育活动的基本问题域和框架。在抵抗理论的视野下，亨利·吉鲁将教育视为一种文化和政治的实践，从政治、文化两种维度阐释了他对教育的理解。⑤

迈克尔·阿普尔对于自己的学术道路，他却拒不接受为保罗·弗莱雷、亨利·吉鲁和麦克拉伦等人所共同使用的"批判教育学"的说法，而坚称自己的学术为"批判教育研究"。⑥ 迈克尔·阿普尔"批判教育研究"的首要价值追求，并不在于"否定"或者"贬低"什么，而是旨在通过对资本主义世界经济杠杆背后有悖教育理论问题的揭露，唤起人们对教育内外现实世界的确切理解。进而，为人们探寻和建构那种"更好

---

① 王占魁：《阿普尔批判教育研究的理论来源》，《华东师范大学学报（教育科学版）》2012 年第 2 期。

② Henry Giroux and Stanley Aronowitz, *Postmodern Education: Politics, Culture and Social Criticism*, Minnesota: University of Minnesota Press, 1991, pp. 80 - 81.

③ 后马克思主义：1985 年受到语言分析学影响的阿根廷学者拉克劳（Laclau）和墨菲（Mouffe）两人，将马克思主义和后现代主义融合，并声称社会与经济型构（socio-economic formation）已被论述型构（discursive）所取代，世上没有物质利益的东西，只有透过论述所构成的指涉到物质利益的理念。他们主张激进民主关怀广大被剥削、被压迫的团体与个人，例如妇女、有色人种、环保人士、移民、消费大众，才是马克思主义的反资产阶级压迫的策略。激进民主是把抵抗压迫的矛头转向平行的文化差异，却忘却文化差异原本并不会造成压迫或歧视。

④ 杨昌勇：《新教育社会学：连续与断裂的学术历程》，中国社会科学出版社 2004 年版，第 187 页。

⑤ 祁东方：《吉鲁批判教育哲学思想研究》，博士学位论文，山西大学，2015 年。

⑥ 王占魁：《阿普尔批判教育研究的批判逻辑》，《教育研究》2012 年第 4 期，第 134 页。

的可能",提供重要的认识论前提和价值基础。[1] 迈克尔·阿普尔所要追求的不仅仅是批判和揭露,更是为了改变和建构,这是后来他的新马克思主义取向与亨利·吉鲁的后现代取向发生分野的关键。[2]他提出"非改革主义的改革"与"厚民主"的学校教育。"非改革主义的改革",即国家应该正视政治系统和文化系统与经济系统危机的本质区别,进而对社会各系统的危机做出其所应当的结构性调整。[3] "厚民主"的学校教育,即从根本上加强民主,给沉默的大多数赋权、创造新的方法将学校内外的人们联系在一起……地方对课程做出决定的权力来自下层,而非上层,它将越来越多地回应被压迫者、有色人种和穷人们的需要、历史和文化。[4]

麦克拉伦离开迈阿密大学转至加州大学洛杉矶分校(UCLA)后,他的思想开始转往更激进的路线。麦克拉伦指出,后现代学派里所重视的"激进民主"一直强调文化差异与文化认同,并主张这就是一种正义的展现,麦克拉伦认为后现代主义着重在尊重所有的差异,马克思主义则强调阶级的不平等问题。但如果没有消除阶级的不平等,所有的差异也得不到尊重,无法解决阶级宰制的问题。[5]这促使他的批判教育学的立场从关心后现代主义的文化差异与认同取向,转回关注马克思的历史唯物和阶级分析取向。鉴于后现代潮流的多元论述已被资本主义渗透与利用,以及考虑到重视多元差异与族群认同的激进民主的主张将使得差异性团结被分化,而丧失了中心,也去掉了总体性,反而失去了弱势者团结的主体能动性,并将被资本主义用为分化弱势族群的策略,也使批判教育学沦为空谈,而失去了解放的可能性,麦克拉伦指出面对资本主义的全

---

[1] 王占魁:《价值选择与教育政治——阿普尔批判教育研究的实践逻辑》,教育科学出版社2014年版,第9页。

[2] 王占魁:《价值选择与教育政治——阿普尔批判教育研究的实践逻辑》,教育科学出版社2014年版,第9页。

[3] 王占魁:《价值选择与教育政治——阿普尔批判教育研究的实践逻辑》,教育科学出版社2014年版,第226页。

[4] 王占魁:《价值选择与教育政治——阿普尔批判教育研究的实践逻辑》,教育科学出版社2014年版,第232页。

[5] Peter McLaren, *Rage and Hope*, New York: Peter Lang Publishing, Inc., 2006.

球化及其对公共教育的影响,应该在后现代思潮下急迫的发展革命性的批判教育学,以避免全球化资本主义对教育的破坏性影响。他大声提出呼吁指出,批判教育学必须回到马克思人道主义的传统与历史唯物论的分析,关注经济阶级的压迫以及生活实践的层面的探讨,并将他批判教育学思想正名为——革命性的批判教育学。麦克拉伦以恰切的方式打开了批判教育学的新视角,开创了批判教育学的新领域。麦克拉伦从马克思人道主义出发,从一个完全不同于资本主义的视角,剖析我们习以为常的日常生活,关注资本主义下的弱势群体,再通过不断的辩证与反思过程,揭示资本主义社会下的问题所在。麦克拉伦致力于把学校发展成学生可以开始想象资本主义以外的社会替代形式(如社会主义)的地方。尽管美国绝大多数教育工作者呼吁在更"富有同情心"的资本主义体制下重新分配经济资源。麦克拉伦相信,只有在社会主义社会中才能实现民主。[1] 批判教育学要恢复活力,必须要回到马克思主义。如此,教育工作者才能在全球化的社会下发展出具有革命性的民主社会模式并达成教育实践。

马克思主义和后现代主义都承认阶级、种族和性别间的相互联系,但是他们的政治和意识形态倾向性是极为不同的。后现代教育家们接受了市场经济而未能挑战新自由主义的经济观和资本主义的剥削关系,在他们茫然的眼神中,社会发展已经迷失了它的方向和可能性;他们的社会策略充斥着无法解决的矛盾;他们在立场上滑向了与新右派自由市场经济的意识形态相似的个人主义的教育消费主义。[2] 在马克思主义者看来,历史是人们在自己的社会环境中追求他们的目的的具体活动。马克思主义理论的目的,不仅要解释世界,还要改变

---

[1] Peter McLaren, *Red Seminars: Radical excursions into educational theory, cultural politics, and pedagogy*, New York: Hampton Press, Inc., 2005, p. 509.

[2] Junrui Chang, Changyong Yang, "Book Review: McLaren, Peter & Farahmandpur, Ramin (2005). Teaching against Global Capitalism and the New Imperialism: A Critical Pedagogy. Lanham Maryland: Rowman & Littlefield Publishers" *International Journal of Progressive Education*, Vol. 2, No. 3, October 2006, p. 132.

世界。[1]迈克尔·阿普尔与亨利·吉鲁的批判理论虽然都受马克思主义影响，但是立场都不同程度地倾向于后现代主义立场，提倡改革资本主义；麦克拉伦虽然赞同后现代主义的一些理念，但是其立场从20世纪90年代中期开始由后现代主义倾向的立场转变为马克思主义人道主义或古典马克思主义的立场，竭力主张以其他形式如社会主义替代资本主义。但是以这三巨头为代表的北美批判教育理论思想还是有很多共同点的，那就是他们都深化了教育的目标，使其不止于标准化的读和写；他们丰富了教育的价值取向，使其脱离了狭隘的消费主义和功利主义；他们都在为了一个更美好的、更公平的未来，思考并承担着教育的使命和责任。

二 麦克拉伦批判教育学的特色

麦克拉伦具备了从教师到作家、到社会运动者，甚至是充满宗教家的热忱与毅力的多重角色。他既是马克思主义者、民主社会主义者又是天主教徒，所有的这三个维度塑造了麦克拉伦的批判教育学思想，打开了批判教育学的新视角，开创了批判教育学的新领域。研究者认为可以从以下两个方面概括麦克拉伦批判教育学思想的特色。

（一）坚守质疑与希望

三十多年来，麦克拉伦一直用带有苏格拉底式的质疑与对希望的悲喜剧性承诺的声音的向外界发声。苏格拉底式的麦克拉伦总是表现出非凡的无所畏惧的表达能力，对最根本的问题提出质疑——总是成功地使那些不加批判地梦游的教育家们感到不安、紧张和不适；他的语言总是带有悲喜剧色彩，在绝望之中给人以希望。麦克拉伦的每一本书、每一篇文章、每一次演讲都能让受众感受到他在苏格拉底式的质疑和对希望的悲喜剧性承诺的方面都做得非常出色。

自从业以来麦克拉伦一直具有苏格拉底式的质疑精神，即他质疑对

---

[1] Junrui Chang, Changyong Yang, "Book Review: McLaren, Peter & Farahmandpur, Ramin (2005). Teaching against Global Capitalism and the New Imperialism: A Critical Pedagogy. Lanham Maryland: Rowman & Littlefield Publishers" *International Journal of Progressive Education*, Vol. 2, No. 3, October 2006, p. 132.

任何民主社会都至关重要的根本问题，但又被太多的教育家所长期回避的问题，使人们认识到威胁公共教育生存的各种力量的根源，与现在威胁民主生存的根源相同，不仅威胁到美国，而且威胁到全世界，以及地球的生存。麦克拉伦认为批判教育学是对抗资本主义最为有效的武器，但是他的理论基础是几经更迭，越来越激进。从最初的马克思主义的启蒙，到后现代主义，最终还是回到了马克思主义思想，这个转变意味着麦克拉伦并不是为了独树一帜而偏执于某一个学派或是理论。对麦克拉伦而言，著书立说并不是其所最看重的，在他心中，真正能够解决资本主义所造成的伤害的学说、理论才是麦克拉伦所在乎与追求的。有人说麦克拉伦的批判教育学思想太激进（radical）。尽管"激进"（radical）一词带有贬义，但《牛津英语词典》将radical定义为"寻根或起源；触及或作用于本质和基本的东西；彻底"。因此，对于那些说麦克拉伦"太激进"的人，我们必须假设他们的意思是，他太接近他所解决问题的根源。如果是这样，我们必须扪心自问，仅仅在边缘地带提出问题有什么意义？不追问核心问题有什么意义？唯有像麦克拉伦这样激进的教育学思想才能提出最核心的问题，接近问题的本质。

苏格拉底式的麦克拉伦提出质疑，悲喜剧的麦克拉伦一定跟随。他将这种悲喜剧般的承诺与"希望"联系在一起。就像是非裔美国人布鲁斯和爵士乐的伟大传统所体现的一种非凡的乐观的能力，并保留着一种生活乐趣的感觉，即使面对仇恨和虚伪，也要保持希望，以免陷入使人麻痹的绝望的虚无主义。麦克拉伦就是这样，即使是在他对不公正的预言性谴责中，他对语言的悲喜剧性运用也总能激发我们的希望，帮助我们保留自己面对痛苦时开怀大笑的能力。麦克拉伦在他的作品中和演讲中都呼吁人们把希望的信念从愤世嫉俗、自满和冷漠的深渊中拯救出来，并将其应用于想象某种类似于社会主义民主形式的东西。他号召我们要有革命性的梦想——梦想者一直梦想到不再有梦想者，而只有梦想自己，每时每刻塑造我们的日常生活，开启可能性的道路。[1]他提倡我们保护在

---

[1] Peter McLaren and Ramin Farahmandpur, *Teaching Against Global Capitalism and the New Imperialism: A Critical Pedagogy*, Lanham, MD: Rowman & Littlefield Publishers, 2005, p. 89.

战争废墟中燃烧的希望的余烬,并在希望之火可能燃烧的任何地方进一步点燃希望之火。最重要的是,他向我们提出挑战,要让希望永存——无论情况如何——用传奇的美国历史学家、学者和活动家斯图兹·特克尔(Studs Terkel)的话来说,就是要确保希望永存。

(二) 兼顾理论与实践

麦克拉伦以他所处时代的美国社会为背景,以马克思主义为核心理论支撑,对后现代主义理论以及以往的激进教育理论进行了选择与吸收,将他的批判教育学思想与哲学、经济学、政治学与社会学等一系列观点和思想进行融合与交锋,以独特的视角对教育、政治、经济、文化之间的错综复杂关系进行分析,综合运用多学科理论,站在教育之外省察教育,却又时刻不忘回归教育,这使他敏锐地把握了教育与相关学科理论以及社会之间互动的真实现状。在麦克拉伦的研究生涯中,他拒绝偏执与独断,尊重多元与差异,他不仅借鉴了欧洲如德国、法国、英国诸多学者的知识传统,也借鉴了拉丁美洲如巴西以及美国等学者的理论观点,使其思想呈现出丰富的知识结构。作为一位富有责任感与献身精神且具有敏锐政治视角的杰出公共知识分子,麦克拉伦以深厚的理论功底和行动经验,对资本主义社会关系做出了极具综合性的分析。

麦克拉伦的批判教育学既是一种"乌托邦"理想,又根植于鲜活的教育实践之中,他的教育乌托邦并不是虚无缥缈的空中楼阁,而是基于美国社会和教育的种种现实。麦克拉伦提出了革命性的批判教育学的目的就是对抗资本主义,所以批判的对象涉及经济、政治、教育、文化等面向。麦克拉伦通过对马克思主义的研究与了解,更加清楚地指出,资本主义下的社会关系已经在全球化、商品化的趋势潮流下,将人对人的本质与尊严的自我意识吞噬殆尽;压迫产生的最根本原因,是来自资本主义体系剥削的运作。因为注重实践,革命性的批判教育学不再仅是纸上谈兵的理论文字,它已经成为对抗资本主义,唤起人民批判意识、重视人性尊严的、改变社会阶层的学说。当民众渐渐自觉其生命价值与人性尊严不应当被商品化时,就是资本主义受到挑战与被质疑的时候;当人民逐渐接受、理解社会主义可以不再复制阶级、可以重视个别差异与实现社会正义、公平时,就是资本主义的垮台之日。

理论的发展永无止境，在不断变化的时代背景下，每一代人都面临着新的现实，都要继续理论探索的步伐。在这一过程中，仅仅依靠对前人理论的继承是远远不够的，还必须在继承的基础上有所创造，麦克拉伦正是这样做的。从坐而言的理论家，麦克拉伦努力成为起而行的实践家，姑且不论其成功与否，但他致力于教育学的研究与实践活动之精神，足以值得教师和教育工作者学习借鉴。梦想的实现是必须通过行动得以落实与实践的。这也正是革命性的批判教育学的最终精神之所在。

第二节　学界对麦克拉伦及其思想的肯定与批判

一　对麦克拉伦的肯定与赞誉

（一）对麦克拉伦学术成就与贡献的肯定

作为美国批判教育的代表人物之一，麦克拉伦聚焦于教育的根本性问题，突破了不同权力、学科间的界限，以经典马克思主义为核心理论基础构建了一种激进的批判教育哲学。他直面教育实践，致力于发展学生的权能与批判性思维，建设一个更加民主公正的社会，对美国教育理论与实践的发展产生了深远的影响。近 40 年来他所取得的学术成就与做出的学术贡献得到了学术界极大的认可：

玛丽亚·尼古拉卡（Maria Nikolakaki）评价彼得·麦克拉伦是批判教育学的先驱，他的贡献是杰出和独特的。[①] 穆斯塔法·尤努斯·厄利曼指出，在过去的 30 年里，麦克拉伦在这个领域做出了重要的贡献，包括他为批判教育学和激进政治阐述了伦理基础；他关于全球资本主义和后现代性对人类身份和集体斗争影响的观点；他对学校教育的民族志探索以及仪式、阈限（liminality）和充实（enfleshment）的关键概念；以及他的批判或革命的多元文化主义和教育学的概念作为教育和社会彻底变革

[①] Luis Charles-Huerta and Marc Pruyn, *This Fist Called My Heart*: *The Peter McLaren Reader*, *CHARLOTTE NC USA*: Information Age Publishing Inc, 2015, advance praise.

的政治基础。① 马克·普鲁恩和路易斯·M. 韦尔塔·查尔斯（2005）认为，当今任何想研究教育左派的思想、政治、哲学、意识形态或研究的人都必须读麦克拉伦的作品。很多人都是从读他的作品开始的。② 亨利·吉鲁（Henry Giroux，1995）评价他："作为一名作家，他（麦克拉伦）将稀有的精明的理论家天赋与著名的瓦尔特·本雅明的讲故事方式结合起来。"③安东尼娅·达尔德（2005）评价道："他极具想象力的语言及雄辩的修辞风格让我毫无疑问地认为麦克拉伦的激情真正地值得'燃烧的文字'这样的荣誉。"④ 威廉·F. 派纳（1995）写道："麦克拉伦能够准确地感知什么是重要的，他的杰出的学术成就使他成为当今这个领域的核心政治理论家。"⑤ 保拉·奥尔曼（2000）描述了麦克拉伦的作品：麦克拉伦的作品是激情、承诺和批判性分析和洞察力的绝妙结合。他的作品像是一种跳着亲密舞蹈的诗歌和散文，能够立刻触及读者的心灵和思想。麦克拉伦的朋友保罗·弗莱雷（1995）写道："彼得·麦克拉伦（Peter McLaren）是我在诸多杰出的'知识分子'中发现的，反过来我又被他发现。"⑥到目前为止，他是当今学术界最多产的作家之一。他在世界范围内发表期刊数百篇，其书籍和文章被翻译成多种语言，在这个跨国经济残酷剥削无权无势的穷人的时代，他以其革命性的批判教育学大大地扩展了我们的批判视野。⑦ 雷蒙（Ramon Grosfoguel，2015）指出，彼

---

① Eryaman, Mustafa Yunus., "Editorial Statement (English): Understanding Critical Pedagogy and Peter McLaren in the Age of Global Capitalism" *International Journal of Progressive Education*, Vol. 2, No. 3, October2006, p. 6.

② Marc Pruyn and Luis Huerta-Charles, *Teaching Peter McLaren: Path of Dissent*, New York: Peter Lang Publications, 2005, Foreword. p. xxxvi.

③ Giroux, H., "Preface", in P. McLaren, *Schooling as a Ritual Performance: towards a political economy of educational symbols and gestures*, Lanham, MD: Rowman & Littlefield, 1999.

④ Marc Pruyn and Luis Huerta-Charles, *Teaching Peter McLaren: Path of Dissent*, New York: Peter Lang Publications, 2005, Foreword. p. xvi.

⑤ Pinar, W. F., "Back Cover", in P. McLaren, *Critical Pedagogy and Predatory Culture*, London: Routledge, 1995.

⑥ Freire, P. "Preface", in P. McLaren, *Critical Pedagogy and Predatory Culture* (p. ix – xi), London: Routledge, 1995, p. x.

⑦ Marc Pruyn and Luis Huerta-Charles, *Teaching Peter McLaren: Path of Dissent*, New York: Peter Lang Publications, 2005, Foreword. p. xvi.

得·麦克拉伦的作品不仅在北美，而且在全世界都具有影响力。他对批判教育学、人道主义马克思主义和革命理论的许多贡献，是全球南方解放斗争的根本。对于许多北美、拉美和亚洲的活动家来说，麦克拉伦的作品是他们的教学实践和解放斗争的重要参考。……任何有兴趣改变这个破坏性的全球资本主义、殖民世界的人，都必须阅读彼得·麦克拉伦革命性的批判教育学。[1] 格伦·里科沃斯基（2015）评价："彼得·麦克拉伦的著作在这个动荡的时代引起了深刻的共鸣。这本书（《这拳头呼唤我的心：彼得·麦克拉伦读本 第一卷》）（*This Fist Called My Heart: The Peter McLaren Reader*）的读者是那些对人类进步抱有希望的人，是那些对提高生活质量的教育抱有希望的人，而不是那些对资本运作缺乏思考和行动能力的人。资本主义教育已经过时，迫切需要其他的教育选择。这本书的章节将批判教育学从自满的自由主义中拯救出来，并把它作为一种革命和人类福祉的力量。"[2] 斯坦利·阿罗诺维茨（2015）认为："彼得·麦克拉伦的作品处于教育理论和实践的前沿。这部作品（《这拳头呼唤我的心：彼得·麦克拉伦读本 第一卷》）的与众不同之处在于其广博的视野、严谨的思维以及对真正教育的清晰愿景。而且，不像许多人被禁锢在狭窄的思想走廊里，麦克拉伦能够把许多通常被忽视的哲学和社会理论传统带入他的话语中。任何关心当前教育危机的人都应该读这本书。"[3] 切·格瓦拉是左派的灯塔，指路明灯，他吹响了马克思主义者团结的号角，尤其是在那些新自由主义、结构调整、极度剥削的时期，麦克拉伦在教育左派与切·格瓦拉的作用是一样的。当然，对于那些真正对左派教育学感兴趣的人来说，麦克拉伦的作品是必读的。麦克拉伦是从读切·格瓦拉和保罗·弗莱雷开始研究左派教育学的。有些是从读保罗·弗莱雷、比奇洛（Bigelow）魏乐尔（Weiler）、洛温（Loewen）、金

---

[1] Luis Charles-Huerta and Marc Pruyn, *This Fist Called My Heart: The Peter McLaren Reader*, CHARLOTTE NC USA: Information Age Publishing Inc, 2015, advance praise.

[2] Luis Charles-Huerta and Marc Pruyn, *This Fist Called My Heart: The Peter McLaren Reader*, CHARLOTTE NC USA: Information Age Publishing Inc, 2015, advance praise.

[3] Luis Charles-Huerta and Marc Pruyn, *This Fist Called My Heart: The Peter McLaren Reader*, CHARLOTTE NC USA: Information Age Publishing Inc, 2015, advance praise.

奇洛（Kincheloe）、斯坦伯格（Steinberg）、斯莱特里（Slattery）开始的。当今，任何想研究教育左派的思想、政治、哲学、意识形态或研究的人都必须读麦克拉伦的作品，很多人都是从读他的作品开始。①

（二）对麦克拉伦学者、教师身份的肯定

麦克拉伦作为一位国际知名学者和教师从来没有过高高在上的时候，纵有这么高的权力、信誉和地位麦克拉伦还能保持谦卑，实属难能可贵。他对周围的同事、学生总是平易近人，尽力扶持与帮助，在业界享有盛誉。总有人仅仅是满足于写一些关于团结一致的激进话语，但是从不考虑这些在现实世界意味着什么。而麦克拉伦是真的关心建立生活中团结的关系，不论是与较高权威的国际学者还是与他指导的研究生、大学课堂里听他课的学生。②麦克拉伦愿意参与大学生活的各个方面，这使得很多教职员工都很惊讶。他参加学术委员会会议并提供午餐讲座（brown bag presentations）的出版资料。奥兰治县组织的关于针对特雷文·马丁（Trayvon Martin）以及种族与教育之间的关系问题的讨论由于麦克拉伦的参与达到了顶峰。他无论是对朋友、牧师、当地社区积极分子还是对授予他荣誉教授的中国东北师范大学的领导、新西兰奥克兰大学的领导都是一样的亲切有礼、风度翩翩。作为麦克拉伦的同事既希望与他交朋友又希望与他在专业上共同合作③。我们永远不要低估他对学生、同事、社会正义的忠诚和奉献。④

由于受到麦克拉伦的启发，很多学者和博士生都给他寄来感谢信。麦克拉伦会认真地回复他们的每一封信。他欢迎学生们对他正在写作的新论文进行反馈，也表现了他对学生的充分尊重。他通过给学生讲明他

---

① Marc Pruyn and Luis Huerta-Charles, *Teaching Peter McLaren: Path of Dissent*, New York: Peter Lang Publications, 2005, Foreword. p. xviii.

② Marc Pruyn and Luis Huerta-Charles, *Teaching Peter McLaren: Path of Dissent*, New York: Peter Lang Publications, 2005, Foreword. p. xvi.

③ Peter McLaren, *Life in Schools: An Introduction to Critical Pedagogy in the Foundations of Education (Sixth Edition)*, Boulder, CO: Paradigm, 2014, p. xvi.

④ Marc Pruyn and Luis Huerta-Charles, *Teaching Peter McLaren: Path of Dissent*, New York: Peter Lang Publications, 2005, Foreword. p. xvi.

的思考过程并邀请每个学生参与思考来达到这一互动。①如今,互联网让学者和活动人士面对面交流变得更加容易,但考虑到麦克拉伦每天收到来自世界各地学生、学者的大量问题,可以想象以个人的方式回答每一位崭露头角的年轻左翼分子提出的一大堆紧迫问题是多么困难。但是麦克拉伦从不怠慢每一封认真写给他的信,在研究者对他的访谈中得知他之所以一直坚持这么做的原因之一是他在年轻不知名的时候一些知名的学者也曾这样帮助过他答疑解惑。他回忆说:

> 如果你足够幸运的话,理论不仅仅是通过书本,也可以通过与这些书的作者的接触来获得。我很幸运,在我早期的思想形成过程中,有个别学者抽出时间来承认我对他们工作的兴趣,我对此印象深刻,比如,在多伦多读博士的时候,我旁听了米歇尔·福柯的一堂课,福柯在他的课上给了我时间与他交谈。还有一些人,他们对我那些幼稚的问题彬彬有礼、热情耐心地给予解答:最让我印象深刻的是让·弗朗索瓦·利奥塔(Jean Francois Lyotard)、安东尼·威尔登(Anthony Wilden)和埃内斯托·拉克劳。当我还是一个年轻的学者的时候,他们愿意和我面对面地交流,尽管时间很短,但这无疑影响了我80年代中期到90年代早期的"批判后现代主义"时期的思想,因为我更倾向于在和他们交谈后被他们的作品所吸引。亨利·吉鲁是另一位学者,他在我读博士的时候就和我成为了朋友,后来我有幸在俄亥俄州迈阿密大学和他一起工作了8年,收获颇多。斯坦利·阿罗诺维茨的指导对我早期左派思想的形成有重要意义。因此,无论是在我的后现代时期,还是在我当前的马克思主义时期,我的定位都在很大程度上归功于那些谦逊而亲切的人,他们与一位相对不知名的我成为了朋友。(节选自本书作者对麦克拉伦的访谈录)

---

① Peter McLaren, *Life in Schools: An Introduction to Critical Pedagogy in the Foundations of Education* (*Sixth Edition*), Boulder, CO: Paradigm, 2014, p. xvi.

他现在所做的算是对那些帮助、提携后辈学者的知名学者们的精神传承。瓦莱丽（2006）在他的论文中提道："我刚刚开始探索麦克拉伦的一些独立作品，以及他与亨利·吉鲁的合作时，他的学术成就以及他的写作激情和强度给了我很大的启发。在一位教员的鼓励下，我向我的研究生同学建议，我们邀请麦克拉伦教授来我们的校园演讲，作为上述系列讨论会的一部分。他当时住在俄亥俄州的迈阿密大学，在收到我们的请求后没几天就接受了邀请。1991年9月，他来到我们的校园，发表了一篇振奋人心的演讲，题为《批判教育学与政治正确性的政治》（Critical Pedagogy and the Politics of Political Correctness），该演讲被当地和地区作了新闻报道。讲座结束后，在晚餐中，我有机会和麦克拉伦交谈。他热情、风趣、善于自嘲。他几乎马上就问了我的研究兴趣。当我告诉他我正在研究他演讲的主题时，他说他会寄给我一些他在准备讲稿时使用过的资料。当时，我认为他的提议是慷慨的，但从未期望他会跟进。但是他真的跟进了。大约一周后，一个包裹送到了我的校园邮箱。信中有他答应过的资料和一封邀请我保持联系的信。那是一段已经超过15年的师徒关系和友谊的开始。这是终身课程的第一天，——希望的政治课程和激进想象的可能性课程。"[①] 大卫·盖博（David Gabbard，2006）回忆："我总是被麦克拉伦的作品所吸引，当我请他为各种各样的项目贡献自己的力量时，他从来没有拒绝过我的邀请，是我自己愚蠢的不安全感使我在他面前不能完全自在——部分原因是他是当今批判教育理论中最具国际知名度的人物，我们很容易对他产生敬畏之感。"[②] 尽管他多年来获得了国际和国内的奖项和荣誉，我们这些认识麦克拉伦的人认识到，他最大的荣誉来自他的学生和同事能和他一起工作的特权。正如安东尼娅·达尔德早些时候写道的那样，她虽然欣赏他的修辞天赋、独特的语言及有力量的写作，但她多年来一直与麦克拉伦保持着距离。然而，最终，

---

① Valerie Scatamburlo-D'Annibal, "Imagining the Impossible: Revolutionary Critical Pedagogy Against the 21st Century American Imperium" *International Journal of Progressive Education*, Vol. 2, No. 3, 2006, p. 2.

② David Gabbard, "Peter McLaren & the 3 R's: Reflection, Resistance and Revolution" *International Journal of Progressive Education*, Vol. 2, No. 3, 2006, p. 98.

她对他的"耐心和坚持"表示了感激。"随着时间的推移,我了解到,"她写道,"彼得·麦克拉伦是我在学术界遇到的最善良、最慷慨的人之一。是的,就像我们许多可怜的人一样,他永远都在与个人的不安全感和自我怀疑做斗争——但和很少人一样,他永远愿意伸出援手,为寻求他支持的同志和奋斗中的年轻学者创造机会。"① 雪莉·斯坦伯格认为:"麦克拉伦是我们这个文化、教育荒诞现实中乏味的三幕戏剧中一个独特的角色。他的幽默、风格、投入、才智和为人成就了这出戏剧中其他的角色。因为他促使他们更深入地挖掘他们教育上的和政治上的灵魂。他很自豪地宣布自己对教育事业的忠诚并请求其他学科要注意批判教育学的深度和本质。他是教师的教师。"②

(三) 对麦克拉伦革命激情与行动的肯定

麦克拉伦不仅是一位激进的教育哲学家,也是一位国际活动家和有远见的梦想家。他的工作体现了对人类福祉的承诺,对真理的追求,对其他观点的尊重,以及保护弱者和穷人的义务。他永远充满革命激情并积极行动、投身实践。我们承认,作为人类我们具有多面性。我们知道麦克拉伦是一位多产的、慷慨的、谦逊的活动家。但是他的真诚与真实、他的人道主义精神有时还是不被人所知。有的人认为他是一个摇滚明星、是"肮脏的三十人"("Dirty Thirty",加州大学洛杉矶分校最危险的左翼教授团体)的成员之一、是切·格瓦拉的革命追随者、是说唱王子、是马克思主义者。无论说他是谁,我们最好以眼见为实。正如阿利皮奥·卡萨里(Alipio Casali)和安娜·玛丽亚·奥霍·保罗·弗莱雷(Ana Maria Aaujo Freire)在马克·普鲁因和路易斯·韦尔塔-查尔斯(Luis Huerta-Charles)的新书《教授彼得·麦克拉伦:异见之路》(Teaching Peter McLaren: Paths of Dissent)的一章中如此准确地描述了他:"在人群中不可能不注意到彼得·麦克拉伦,就像不可能不被他的形象完全吸引一样:他个性独特的衣着、凌乱的头发、文身、迅捷而突然的动作、专注的态

---

① Marc Pruyn and Luis Huerta-Charles, *Teaching Peter McLaren: Path of Dissent*, New York: Peter Lang Publications, 2005, Foreword. p. xv.

② Marc Pruyn and Luis Huerta-Charles, *Teaching Peter McLaren: Path of Dissent*, New York: Peter Lang Publications, 2005, Foreword.

度和明亮的气场。起初，他似乎是一幅漫画，是20世纪60年代反主流文化的残迹。"① 虽然这些文身是在我们辛辛那提的岁月之后才出现的，但我也被麦克拉伦"吸引"了，但吸引我的不是他的外表和举止，而是他对工作的热情和投入。②

当他与院长和校长相遇，三个人都超越了对彼此感官上的认识，无论是穿西装的（意指领导）还是摇滚明星（意指行为放荡不羁的人）都不重要了，他们看重的是他们共同的对学术严谨与学术改革的兴趣和尊重。③ 麦克拉伦的同事汤姆·威尔逊（Tom Wilson）和苏珊娜·苏霍（Suzanne SooHoo）认为："无论是否喜欢麦克拉伦的方法，是否认同他的观点，他不能、也不应该被忽视，因为他一直与志同道合的人走在对新语言及对教育目的重建的深入理解的道路上，所有这些都是为了一个不同的未来、一个真正公正的、批判的、民主的社会现实。"④他不是"土生土长的民主党人……支持布什的战争…在做出需要诚实和勇气的政治行为之前，会静观风向，并认为好的民主党人是土生土长的"⑤。在资产阶级学院错综复杂的迷宫中，麦克拉伦的沮丧、愤怒和政治最大化让世界知道，"抗议基因"是活跃的。⑥ 安东尼娅·达尔德（2005），当我看见鲁米（Rumi）的诗句"我要说出能够燃烧的文字"，我马上想到了麦克拉伦，自从我第一次见到他我就看见了麦克拉伦身上一种罕见的激情，

---

① Marc Pruyn and Luis Huerta-Charles, *Teaching Peter McLaren: Path of Dissent*, New York: Peter Lang Publications, 2005, p. 21.

② David Gabbard, "Peter McLaren & the 3 R's: Reflection, Resistance and Revolution" *International Journal of Progressive Education*, Vol. 2, No. 3, 2006, p. 98.

③ Peter McLaren, *Life in Schools: An Introduction to Critical Pedagogy in the Foundations of Education* (Sixth Edition), Boulder, CO: Paradigm, 2014, p. xvii.

④ Peter McLaren, *Life in Schools: An Introduction to Critical Pedagogy in the Foundations of Education* (Sixth Edition), Boulder, CO: Paradigm, 2014, p. xv.

⑤ Denzin, N. K., "Homegrown Democracy, Homegrown Democrats" *International Journal of Progressive Education*, Vol. 1, No. 1, 2005, p. 47.

⑥ Ng, D., "Paris loves a riot: France is a democracy where dissent is not only tolerated but expected" (2006) [EB/OL]. http://www.villagevoice.com/news/0614, ng, 72715, 2.html, 2018-09-27.

他是能够说出燃烧文字的那种人。① 他有意地避免北美教育界把保罗·弗莱雷的思想驯化成没有威胁的"可爱存在"（loving presence），他运用保罗·弗莱雷谴责种族主义、阶级主义和性别主义的原始资料来支持21世纪的学校生活。

麦克拉伦的学生对他的评价与认识，列举如下："作为麦克拉伦的一名前学生，我可以证明，他从不羞于让自己变得脆弱，也从不羞于在社交场合表露自己的内心。也许正是因为这个原因，他的革命信息得到了如此巨大的反响。出于某种奇怪的原因，学者们应该对他们的学生采取一种冷静而疏远的态度，但我很感激麦克拉伦从未如此。在过去的8年里，我感受到了他的日常关怀以及他对地球居民的巨大的爱，这些都建立在他的支持网络的基础上，这些网络为成长和团结提供了不受阻碍的机会。"② "作为一个学术新手，我非常渴望见到麦克拉伦，即使在那时，他也是批判教育学研究中的重要人物。当他真的出现时，他也热情地欢迎我们，像我们相识多年一样接待我们，就像我们的到来对他和对我们来说都是一件大事一样。在过去的15年里，随着我对麦克拉伦的了解不断加深，我学会了信任和欣赏他的直接随性，把它作为他生活中更普遍的激情的一部分。同样的激情毫无疑问地反映在他的作品中，同样的激情在他自己、他的学生和我们与他共事的其他人之间产生了如此巨大的共同忠诚和团结纽带。"③ "我不仅认为麦克拉伦是我的导师，而且是我的同志，一个亲爱的和特殊的朋友。和麦克拉伦一起工作彻底改变了我的生活，这不仅仅是因为他是我的学术导师，教会了我很多关于学术的来龙去脉以及如何得到奖学金。我从麦克拉伦身上学到了很多，更是因为他的内在。这是他的精神，他的心，他的忠诚，他对革命实践的想象力和无畏的防御，这教会了我最多。在过去的3年里，我有机会与麦克拉

---

① Marc Pruyn and Luis Huerta-Charles, *Teaching Peter McLaren: Path of Dissent*, New York: Peter Lang Publications, 2005, Foreword. p. xv.

② Gregory Martin, "Remaking Critical Pedagogy: Peter McLaren's Contribution to a Collective Work" *International Journal of Progressive Education*, Vol. 2, No. 3, 2006, p. 74.

③ David Gabbard, "Peter McLaren & the 3 R's: Reflection, Resistance and Revolution" *International Journal of Progressive Education*, Vol. 2, No. 3, 2006, p. 98.

伦密切合作，我很幸运。我很幸运能和他在一起，和世界各地的人们在一起，为我们所有人把这个地方变得更美好而奋斗。"①

麦克拉伦作为一名教师、诗人、革命家、革命性的批判教育学的理论家，关于他的工作还有很多没有被提及，但我可以说这是由一种深深的激情、希望和革命性的爱所驱动的。事实上，他接过了保罗·弗莱雷手里的火炬，把这种彻底的爱和批判政治带入了21世纪真实的及隐喻性的飓风之中。②他在拥有支持社会平等的政治人权及经济民主方面所贡献和付出的心智和才华无论何时，当人们谈起麦克拉伦的时候，他的卓越功绩都值得被认可、被颂扬。

（四）奖项所代表的肯定

在过去的十几年里世界各地、社会各界授予了麦克拉伦数量相当可观的奖项：2002年查普曼大学授予他"保罗·弗莱雷社会公平奖"。2006年教育政策研究所在马克思主义理论与实践发展领域授予他"国际活动家学者奖"。2007年国际创价学会③授予他自由奖章。纽约中部和平研究协会授予他"和平研究终身成就奖"、批判研究协会（希腊·雅典）授予他"2013年度批判研究成就奖"、安提俄克大学（洛杉矶）教育学院授予他首届"社会公平和教育道德奖"、美国教育研究协会（American Educational Research Association）的一个特殊利益团体 – 马克思主义社会、学校和教育研究所授予他"公共教育的社会与经济公平奖"、保罗·弗莱雷研究中心（芬兰）授予他"保罗·弗莱雷国际社会公平奖"、美国教育研究协会授予他"保罗·弗莱雷杰出学者奖"、委内瑞拉教育部授予他"国际批判教育学奖"。多伦多中心大学教育工作研究所授予他"安·克里斯廷·皮尔森教育经济奖"、全国教育与社会公平会议创建成员颁发给他"教育公平奖"、全国教育工会（米却肯）授予他"与墨西哥教师团结一致战斗奖"。除此之外，为了纪念保卫森林两周年，社区政府高级委员

---

① David Gabbard, "Peter McLaren & the 3 R's: Reflection, Resistance and Revolution" *International Journal of Progressive Education*, Vol. 2, No. 3, 2006, p. 102.

② Peter McLaren, *Life in Schools: An Introduction to Critical Pedagogy in the Foundations of Education* (*Fifth Edition*), New York: Pearson Publishers, 2007, xii.

③ 国际创价学会，是一个在全世界拥有1200万名成员的佛教组织。

会、民政事务委员会、米却肯教育委员会授予他"保卫原著居民权力奖"。21世纪批判理论教育学会议的创会会员授予他"韦斯切斯特大学首届杰出反全球资本主义教育与行动奖"。由于在社会科学及劳工与民主斗争方面的贡献，2013年麦克拉伦在土耳其的安卡拉大学获得教育与科学工会授予的"学术荣誉奖"以及成人教育与终身学习部授予的"批判教育学荣誉奖"。2013年他获得拉丁美洲和加勒比地区的教育工作者协会授予的"杰出教育工作者奖"。墨西哥教育工人全国联合会授予麦克拉伦"与墨西哥抗争的教师们的团结友谊奖"；委内瑞拉玻利瓦尔共和国教育部授予麦克拉伦在批判教育学领域的国际奖，为了表彰他在委内瑞拉为社会主义教育学理论和实践所做出的贡献；希腊雅典批判研究协会授予麦克拉伦在批判研究领域的成就奖；最近，麦克拉伦已经加入了密歇根州全球高级研究中心的批判教育研究所。2017年美国教育研究协会（AERA）授予麦克拉伦终身成就奖。以上列举的所获奖项只是他所获奖项中的一小部分，但已经可见其在学术、民主运动等各个领域在全世界多地被推崇、被认可的程度。

二 对麦克拉伦的批判与攻击

相对于麦克拉伦著作的范围和批判深度来说，任何评论，即使在乐观的条件下，也都很难做到公正。尽管麦克拉伦对教育的批判和论述有着深厚而博学的理论基础，有着犀利而独到的视角，但这并不意味着他所有的研究成果都无懈可击，同样要经受批判和考验。必须承认，首先麦克拉伦的全部作品都是既有挑战性又难懂的。事实上，一些学者（Apple，1999；Huerta, Horton&Scott，2001）已经指出，一些批判理论家的阐释语言如麦克拉伦过于抽象、令人费解。此外，麦克拉伦的全部作品都要求特殊的信念并致力于建设一个更好的、更人性化的更公平的世界。[①]阿里皮奥·卡萨里和安娜·玛丽亚·奥霍·弗莱雷（2005）认为他思考和写作的方式总是复杂的，深刻的，不容易理解的。他的写作风格不符

---

① Marc Pruyn and Luis Huerta-Charles, *Teaching Peter McLaren: Path of Dissent*, New York: Peter Lang Publications, 2005, p. xxxii.

合标准的学术格式。① 阿里皮奥·卡萨里和安娜·玛丽亚·奥霍·弗莱雷（2005）指出，对于不熟悉辩证推理的读者，追随麦克拉伦的理论进出和他丰富的思想也是很困难的。对于缺少一定的哲学、社会学、教育学背景知识的读者来说，阅读他的作品也是很大的挑战，因为麦克拉伦在他的作品里通过确证或反驳提到了很多相关人物，对于初次阅读他作品的学生来说确实是困难的、不容易理解的。② 难怪著名的美国教育研究员迈克尔·阿普尔发现麦克拉伦和"批判理论家"的语言是如此"抽象和令人困惑"。试着想象一下，在麦克拉伦《来自走廊地区的呐喊》中的贫民区儿童和年轻人，会对他最近写的一些关于"革命性的批判教育学"和"新自由主义霸权"的"总体性"的著作做何感想。"如果我们要真正面对当今内城和郊区学校的年轻人所面临的非常真实、根深蒂固的问题，说同样的语言可能是一个很好的起点。"③

一些评论家赞扬麦克拉伦在学术上的大胆和勇气，另一些评论家以各种方式攻击他的思想，几乎达到了使用憎恨的语言的程度。麦克拉伦的作品已经面对了大量的尖锐的、轻蔑的批判。一些读者指控他使用旧式的马克思主义语言是一种极权主义；一些人负面地认为他是"来自60年代的嬉皮"④。包华士批判："批判教育学的支持者们把他们的文章重新印刷成书，然后把这些书作为一种开拓性的努力，这种做法具有不小的讽刺意味。保罗·弗莱雷的《教育政治学》就是这种做法的一个可悲的例子；这两篇旨在为其他文章提供理论依据的文章，结果是1970年出版的再版。除了把期刊文章和专论的部分变成可以付两倍钱的商品，还有

---

① Eryaman, Mustafa Yunus, "Editorial Statement (English): Understanding Critical Pedagogy and Peter McLaren in the Age of Global Capitalism" *International Journal of Progressive Education*, Vol. 2, No. 3, October2006, p. 6.

② Marc Pruyn and Luis Huerta-Charles, *Teaching Peter McLaren: Path of Dissent*, New York: Peter Lang Publications, 2005, p. 20.

③ Anonymity, "Life in Schools: Whatever Happened to Peter McLaren and Cries from the Corridor?" [EB/OL]. https://educhatter.wordpress.com/2015/07/11/life-in-schools-whatever-happened-to-peter-mclaren-and-cries-from-the-corridor/, 2018-09-27.

④ Marc Pruyn and Luis Huerta-Charles, *Teaching Peter McLaren: Path of Dissent*, New York: Peter Lang Publications, 2005, p. xxxiv.

其他更严重的问题。其中之一就是要使一篇期刊文章的初衷与一本书更复杂的目的相适应。把期刊上的文章拼凑在一起，即使是经过最仔细的编辑，也很少会产生一幅关于问题的重叠和不均匀展开的讨论的马赛克。以亨利·吉鲁的《老师作为知识分子》（Teachers as Intellectuals）和麦克拉伦《学校生活》为例，这是令人失望的马赛克，而不是对一本书的综合和逐步发展的分析。"① 由于他对马克思主义人道主义的开放接受，麦克拉伦成为了上述右翼攻击机器的目标。右翼意识形态网络的一个组成部分——《华盛顿时报》（Washington Times），发表了一篇由肯尼斯·劳埃德·比林斯利（Kenneth Lloyd Billingsly）撰写的文章，总体上抨击了批判教育学家，尤其是麦克拉伦。在胡佛研究所（Hoover Institute）（新保守主义智库已成为右翼煽动家戴维·霍洛维茨（David Horowitz）的大本营），出版的《教育下一步》（Education Next）杂志上发表的另一篇文章中，罗彻斯特（J. Martin Rochester）可笑地指责麦克拉伦"智力薄弱"，而他首先攻击的是批判性教育学："它强调情感规范领域，而忽视了认知经验领域（这根本不是真的，反映出罗切斯特对批判教育学的无知，或者他愿意对此撒谎。）——它更感兴趣的是让学生理解世界应该是什么样的，而不是世界是怎样的（这又是一个谎言。）其次，因为它接受了等级分明、主观评判的课堂，教师的角色不是促进无价值的探究，而是利用讲坛来宣讲教条主义的福音（事实正好相反，批判教育者总是特别自觉地防范这种行为），学校发挥的不是政治社会化的功能，而是反社会化的功能。这样的学校即使不是一个政府的部门，至少也是一个政党。"而麦克拉伦针对这样的攻击却很欣慰："对于我们这些左翼作家来说，在受欢迎的右翼出版物中受到攻击是一种荣誉"。② 因为他认为正是由于他所提出的批评和反对意见具备巨大的解放潜力，才能引发如此咄咄逼人的诋毁或攻击。

重新思考、反思自己的置身所在或者换句话说重新思考自己作为社

---

① Bowers, C. A., "Review: Some Questions about the Anachronistic Elements in the Giroux-McLaren Theory of a Critical Pedagogy" *Curriculum Inquiry*, Vol. 21, No. 2, 1991, p. 239.

② David Gabbard, "Peter McLaren & the 3 R's: Reflection, Resistance and Revolution" *International Journal of Progressive Education*, Vol. 2, No. 3, 2006, p. 101.

会的一部分的处境,那意味着我们的"自我鉴定、自我评价"(self-inventory)。这是一项艰巨的任务,因为这暗含着自我否定,认识到是什么样的事件或境况导致我们成为现在的自己。当一个人开始这样的自我评价程序时,他或她就必须明白他们需要审视他们自己的价值观和信仰。这是最难的一部分,因为大多数时候我们的信仰是在我们童年时期建构或型塑的,代表我们家庭的传统和社会化。如此,质疑信仰就像是质疑和拒绝或抛弃家庭灌输给我们的信条。因此,对我们很多人来说,怀疑批判性的阐述或假设更容易——或者理所当然地认为我们现在的全球社会对我们所有人来说都运行良好。在这种背景下,通常通过否定麦克拉伦的理论来批判他是容易的,因为他的这些理论让我们感到疼痛。说"麦克拉伦陷入了60年代"比重新思考自己的置身所在更容易。说"他是一个不合时宜的守旧的马克思主义者"比分析他所进行的无情、坚定地挑战我们的思想更容易。麦克拉伦已经意识到了那些肤浅的批判。我说"肤浅"并不是低估忽视或边缘化那些不接受批判立场的人而是因为那些攻击者并没有提供回应麦克拉伦在书中所提出的问题的解释和反思性的论证。

由于麦克拉伦所受的学界关注以及得到的评论过多无法一一列举与呈现,因此,无论是肯定抑或批判尤其是肯定方面以上虽只是管中窥豹,但可见一斑。

第三节 麦克拉伦对世界各地教育者的影响

一 知行合一

知行合一,是由明朝思想家王守仁提出来的,根据汉语词典的解释,即认识事物的道理与在现实中运用此道理,是密不可分的。知是指良知,行是指人的实践,知与行的合一,既不是以知来吞并行,认为知便是行,也不是以行来吞并知,认为行便是知。它是中国古代哲学中认识论和实践论的命题,主要是关于道德修养、道德实践方面的。中国古代哲学家认为,不仅要认识("知"),尤其应当实践("行"),只有把"知"和"行"统一起来,才能称得上"善"。麦克拉伦的革命性的批判教育学中出现频率最高、也代表他批判教育学思想核心观点的词汇之一是 praxis,翻译成汉语就是将理论与实践相结合,相当于知行合一。麦克拉伦多年来一直践行他所倡导的理论,做到了知行合一。

近 40 年来,麦克拉伦笔耕不辍地出版专著、发表文章宣扬其革命性的批判教育学,迄今为止,他出版了 45 本书和数百篇学术文章和章节,为一百多本书撰写序言、刊后语、介绍、结束语、编后记,这些文章和章节被翻译成土耳其语、西班牙语、葡萄牙语、汉语、韩语、波兰语、俄语、希腊语、德语等 20 多种语言,他的作品得到在墨西哥、委内瑞拉、巴西、土耳其、希腊、中国、波兰、匈牙利、德国、巴基斯坦、印度、以色列、巴勒斯坦、克罗地亚、塞尔维亚和其他大大小小的国家里对批判教育学感兴趣的人们的关注。他的名字慢慢地成为当代批判教育项目的代名词。可以说麦克拉伦的事业已经走向全球,麦克拉伦的论点和学说受到世界的瞩目,如墨西哥、阿根廷都开设了许多麦克拉伦的批判教育学机构[1]。但是麦克拉伦不仅仅做到了"知",更是很好地将学术工作与政治行动相结合。他在世界各地讲课,积极参与各种政治斗争,积极践行革命性的批判教育学的理论和实践。他说:"我的大部分旅程都与建立一个理论框架和政治路线有关。但旅行和会见活动人士远比我自己反思的时候给我带来更有的勇气和政治敏锐性。与那些在激烈的斗争中塑造了自己人生的人见面——有些人是知名人士,有些人则是无名小卒——让我停下来思考,单凭书本你能真正学到多少东西。"[2]

他已经获得了向世界各地的政治和教育活动人士发表演讲的能力,无论他走到哪里,都受到热烈的欢迎。这部分是由于他的人道主义激进情怀,部分是由于他的深情和始终警惕的性格。他的信息不会使任何人

---

[1] 墨西哥的恩塞纳达港(Ensenada)的彼得·麦克拉伦批判教育学基金会与研究所(La Fundacion McLaren de Pedagogia Critica and Instituto Peter McLaren in Mexico),以及委内瑞拉加拉斯玻利瓦尔大学的彼得·麦克拉伦基金会(La Catedra Peter McLaren at the Bolivarian University in Caracas)。

[2] Derek R. Ford. "Revolutionary Critical Pedagogy and the Struggle against Capital Today: An Interview with Peter McLaren". *Education Interview*, 2015 – 7 – 16 [EB/OL]. http://www.hamptoninstitution. org/peter-mclaren-interview. html#. XT6gsi2B3FQ, 2019 – 05 – 22.

平静，他的声音会被听到，因为他无论往哪里去，都能遇见志趣相投的人，他们也能找到他。正如他宣布的激进希望的信息：即使在最困难的时期，当人们走到一起，参与到责任感的过程中，资本主义的弊病也不是不可克服的。自1987年以来，麦克拉伦受邀到瑞典、澳洲、南非、中国、巴基斯坦、巴勒斯坦、以色列、英国、德国、韩国、墨西哥、古巴、委内瑞拉、哥伦比亚和巴西等大约30个国家（其中许多国家他继续访问，有些国家他定期访问，例如墨西哥和委内瑞拉）向学者、教师和社会活动家作主题演讲或为当地大学的研究生作系列讲座（详见附录一），并在许多情况下结成积极的联盟。在他作为客座教授的写作和旅行中，他游历了每一个大陆，尤其是拉丁美洲，麦克拉伦把他革命性的批判教育学作为批判理论的一个变种，用霍克海默和阿多诺在2000年修订的《启蒙辩证法》(Dialectics of Enlightenment) 序言中说，它是一个"通往真理的暂时核心，而不是……真理是历史运动中永恒不变的东西"。麦克拉伦的革命性思维与集体社会专业知识的建立有着内在的联系，因为在他的公共事务中，他以激进的成人和大众教育的精神发展了一种革命性的公民参与理论。他不仅扩大了自己的受众范围，而且把自己的理论和实践推向了政治形成的新高度。他的听众过去是，现在仍然是，在他洛杉矶的家乡机构里，最重要的是，在拉丁美洲的许多国家里，在那里，他与他的合作教育工作者、行政人员、政治家、社会运动积极分子、政治煽动者和普通人一起进行了许多研讨和对话。许多活动都是由麦克拉伦批判教育学基金会①赞助的。麦克拉伦还与委内瑞拉的学者建立了联系，这些学者认可他的工作，并重视他对批判教育学的贡献。应他们的邀请，麦克拉伦前往加拉加斯和全国各地，在一系列演讲活动中向学者和教师发表演讲，2006年，麦克拉伦在委内瑞拉玻利瓦尔大学（Bolivari-

---

① 麦克拉伦批判教育学基金会是一个由一群墨西哥的教授和教育活动家发起和发展的非营利组织。采用多种族、性别均衡、反资本主义、反种族主义和反帝国主义的教学议程，这个基金会的成立是为了推进一些目标，包括在墨西哥和美洲培养和发展革命批判教育学，开展行动研究项目，组织会议，建立批判教育学中心，建立公共论坛，进行辩论、讨论和政治活动。该基金会目前正在用西班牙语出版一本名为《Aula Critica》的杂志，并计划出版葡萄牙语、法语和英语版本。

an University of Venezuela) 成为客座教授。在他多次访问拉丁美洲期间，麦克拉伦会见了乌戈·查韦斯和洛佩斯·奥夫拉多尔等重要人物，并为美洲之间的思想和实践交流做出了重要贡献。与众多纸上谈兵的学者不同，麦克拉伦一直在践行批判教育学理论的最前线，2015年麦克拉伦其轰动性著作——《反抗的教育学：从复活到革命》（Pedagogy of Insurrection: From Resurrection to Revolution）中写道：

> 在与众多国家的教师、教育学者、政治活动家以及革命者的合作交流过程中，我拜访了太多的苦涩而孤独的街区：布达佩斯的吉普赛人街区；麦克拉伦德林（哥伦比亚城市）市郊贫民区的街道；贩毒集团控制的墨西哥城市莫雷里亚（Morelia）或者华瑞兹市（Juarez）；里约热内卢或者圣保罗的棚户区；旧德里那些拥挤的房屋和狭窄的街道；又或者洛杉矶中南部的黑人区。不要问我是不是跟困在暴风雪中的试图搭便车的旅人有过交谈；或者是不是看到了越来越多的越战老兵流落街头；还有依靠政府发放的食物券艰难度日的老人躲进紧急取暖中心，因为共和党的减少食物券发放的决议让他们的日常口粮不知去向；费城的冬日，一群群无业男女躺在下水道井盖上，试图利用那徐徐飘出的充满馊味的热气温暖他们冻僵了的身体和心肠；还有那群十来岁的孩子，身着褪色而斑驳的出售打折麦芽酒的衣裳在红灯区游荡；再或者是一小搓日工在简陋的比萨房前吆喝出售廉价比萨——在不同的时间和空间中，我听到了相同的呼喊与绝望。然而，即使是在这样实实在在的经济灾难面前，我还是要宣讲哲学的重要性。简而言之，在阶级抗争中培养实践哲学。（麦克拉伦，2015）[1]

这里我们看到了麦克拉伦对被压迫者深深的爱，他用自己的行动宣扬自己的理念，用自己做得到的方式，落实革命实践的精神。他对保

---

[1] Peter McLaren, *Pedagogy of insurrection: From resurrection to revolution*, New York: Peter Lang Publishers, 2015, p. 59.

罗·弗莱雷批判教育学档案所①捐赠的海报、政治艺术品和手工制品记录了他在全世界很多国家如墨西哥、塞尔维亚、委内瑞拉、土耳其、中国等国家的足迹。在国际上屡次获得社会公平奖,经常被邀请去作演讲、作咨询、写书甚至是拍电影,经常被世界各地的博士生请教等这些都说明了麦克拉伦的全球影响力及其理论与实践相结合的典范作用。路易斯·M. 韦尔塔·查尔斯(2005)认为麦克拉伦是言行一致的人,换句话说,他是一位知行合一的学者,他按照他的理论生活。② 乔·金奇洛(2007)指出,简单地曝光不为人所见的东西,说出不可言说的事件是一回事,作为批判理论家他把这种行动还推向了实践领域,他将他的思想表达与社会和教育行动结合起来。拥有如此行动能力的头脑在本质上是十分重要的,也是难能可贵的,因为它点燃了黑暗岁月的希望之光,在阴暗的学校地狱里点燃了可能之光。③ 教育者仅仅关注课堂是狭隘的、悲哀的,麦克拉伦超越了很多教育界人士对于教育理想实现方式的想象。

二 做有献身精神的知识分子

在知识分子的各种分类中,有传统知识分子(traditional intellectual)、特定知识分子(specific intellectual)、有机知识分子(organic intellectual)等。传统知识分子是"产生去语境化思想的人",不受地域和实践的限制,仿佛这些"知识产品被感知……属于一个特别高的领域"。④ 福柯笔下特定的知识分子,他们不愿意告诉别人需要做什么,也不愿意塑造人们的政治意愿。相反,他们通过在自己领域的分析,对共同的假设和惯常的工作和思维方式提出了质疑,并通过这样做,作为公民参与政治意愿的形成。葛兰西有机知识分子通常是工人阶级出身,他们参与实际生

---

① 隶属于美国查普曼大学。
② Marc Pruyn and Luis Huerta-Charles, *Teaching Peter McLaren: Path of Dissent*, New York: Peter Lang Publications, 2005, p. xxvi.
③ Peter McLaren, *Life in Schools: An Introduction to Critical Pedagogy in the Foundations of Education (Fifth Edition)*, New York: Pearson Publishers, 2007, p. xi.
④ Collins Randall, *Sociology of Philosophies: A Global Theory of Intellectual Change*, Cambridge: Belknap Press of Harvard University Press, 1998, p. 19.

活,帮助建立一种破坏现有社会关系和资本主义生产的反霸权。然而,这并不是在意识形态上是盲目的,但总是伴随着通过问一个人到底是什么的自我反思。麦克拉伦作为一位激进知识分子与安东尼奥·葛兰西的有机知识分子最为接近,作为其延伸,麦克拉伦与他的同伴们所阐述的"有献身精神的知识分子"(committed intellectual)的概念:"有献身精神的知识分子不仅对抵制和击败文化统治形式感兴趣,而且对他们来说,结束一切形式的剥削是他们致力于改造世界的焦点。"[1] 麦克拉伦就是这样一位有献身精神的知识分子。在致力于改造世界的过程中,他不惧生命危险地勇于口诛笔伐地揭露黑暗真相、质疑威权、四处演讲、参与游行,不仅体现了他对革命性的批判教育学的深刻信仰,也为革命的批判教育的实践树立了一个真实的榜样。

麦克拉伦是一位知识分子和政治风险承担者;他愿意走出教育领域,面对具有挑战性的新理论,与保守主义和新自由主义的政治攻击和议程做斗争。[2] 麦克拉伦总是能以其独特的方式质疑、揭露出被我们大多数人所忽视的我们大部分人都无能力言说的事情。他指出了人类无法立刻感知的推动社会、政治、经济、文化和教育事件的极其复杂、隐形及阴险的势力因素。这种天才般的识察力与呈现力向我们展示了这些隐藏的模糊的因素是如何型塑我们在学校及其他地方的日常生活。随着经年累月的积累麦克拉伦这种能力和智慧变得越来越强大。在当今这个世界,已建立的权力机构总是试图把民族、社会、国家、宗教分类成"好的"或"坏的",他经常选择写一些能够打乱或煽动当今世界的东西,提出各种质疑,如"为什么美国拥有世界上最大的国防支出、发达国家中最高的经济不平等水平以及世界上最高的人均医疗支出……而且,为什么在

---

[1] McLaren Peter, Fischman, Gustavo, Serra, Silvia and Antelo, Estanislao, "The Specter of Gramsci: Revolutionary Praxis and the Committed Intellectual", in McLaren, Peter and Companeras y Companeros, *Red Seminars. Radical Excursions into Educational Theory, Cultural Politics, and Pedagogy*, Cresskill: Hampton Press, 2005, p.277.

[2] Eryaman, Mustafa Yunus. "Editorial Statement (English): Understanding Critical Pedagogy and Peter McLaren in the Age of Global Capitalism" *International Journal of Progressive Education*, Vol.2, No.3, 2006, p.6.

发达国家中，美国人的预期寿命最低。为什么这样一个富裕的国家在机会平等方面的标准最低？"[1] 麦克拉伦总是在寻找一些不太容易追随的路径，他以敏锐的识察力铸就了反映他深刻而宽广的知识构成的路径。[2] 罗伯特·拜罗斯（Roberto Bahruth，2005）讲道："我很喜欢麦克拉伦率直有亲和力的声音，揭露话语背后的人有时好像是生气的，但是向人们展示学术话语极少让读者知道的东西。他作品的力量展示的是'道德愤怒'而不是生气。"[3] 他在一定程度上受到了麦克拉伦在教育学上的大胆精神的影响，也将这种大胆运用在他的教学之中。"麦克拉伦运用阶级结构分析对教育的解构使我清晰地明白了教育的政治"。[4]

虽然学术界的工作环境大不相同，但从事这类政治工作并非没有危险。在加州大学洛杉矶分校工作期间，麦克拉伦受到安德鲁·琼斯[5]及其右翼支持者的攻击，他们把麦克拉伦的作品视为炭疽一样的致命传染病，在任何情况下都不能对毫无戒心的民众，尤其是对学生造成影响。[6] 如果你身上文着切·格瓦拉的刺青，你就成了恐怖主义嫌疑人，而穆斯林和阿拉伯人则被视为邪恶、危险的二等公民，这对美国来说是一个可悲的命运。麦克拉伦拒绝接纳和迎合极右翼边缘，他敢于质疑权威，公开表达对社会主义的支持，这使他在琼斯的布鲁因校友会（Bruin Alumni Association）"肮脏三十人"（Dirty Thirty List）排行榜上名列第一，该榜单引起了国际社会的关注。尽管麦克拉伦的工作是有争议的，但是他从规

---

[1] Peter McLaren, *Breaking free: the life and times of Peter McLaren, radical educator*, Gorham, ME: Myers Education Press, 2019, p. 68.

[2] Marc Pruyn and Luis Huerta-Charles, *Teaching Peter McLaren: Path of Dissent*, New York: Peter Lang Publications, 2005, p. 20.

[3] Marc Pruyn and Luis Huerta-Charles, *Teaching Peter McLaren: Path of Dissent*, New York: Peter Lang Publications, 2005, pp. 5 – 6.

[4] Marc Pruyn and Luis Huerta-Charles, *Teaching Peter McLaren: Path of Dissent*, New York: Peter Lang Publications, 2005, pp. 5 – 6.

[5] 安德鲁·琼斯（Andrew Jones），加州大学洛杉矶分校毕业生，前加州大学洛杉矶分校共和党人，大卫·霍洛维茨（David Horowitz）的研究助理。

[6] Younge, G "Silence in class" (2006) [EB/OL]. http://www.guardian.co.uk/usa/story/0,,1746227,00.html, 2017 – 05 – 14. &Fassbinder, S., "The 'Dirty Thirty's' Peter McLaren reflects on the crisis of academic freedom" (2006) [EB/OL]. http://mrzine.monthlyreview.org/fassbinder060406.html, 2017 – 05 – 14.

模更大的大规模工人运动的国际支持网络中汲取内部和集体力量。需要理解的是,这场麦卡锡式的运动是与政府有关的右翼势力发起的一场规模更大的运动的一部分,目的是通过将被认为"不爱国"的教授列入黑名单,将左派赶出大学。

意识到统治阶级会不惜一切代价保护自己的特权和利益,麦克拉伦在美国和世界各地的工作场所和社区与工人、工会成员和学生进行讨论时,谴责了右翼镇压浪潮。从麦克拉伦的角度来看,这种学术压制既需要道德上的愤怒,也需要反霸权的回应。尤其是,有一种策略似乎是典型的麦克拉伦式的,那就是拒绝逃离那些诋毁、反对甚至禁止他发声的人。麦克拉伦并没有忽视他的敌人的尖刻言辞或诽谤,事实上,他的方法往往是勇敢地协助传播和广泛传播这类攻击,把它们转变成一种手段,通过这种手段对当今教育政治的反动方面进行批判性干预,并组织反对力量,同时,从战略上向其他人强调,他所提出的批评和反对意见,因为具备巨大的解放潜力,才能引发如此咄咄逼人的抵抗。换句话说,对于那些称他为社会危险分子的人来说,他一定是特别危险的。①

麦克拉伦不惧右翼言论的诽谤,也不惜冒着生命危险在生活中进行持续的批判实践:从大学期间为征兵抵抗者提供住房,揭露简·芬奇走廊孩子们的遭遇,与墨西哥塔拉乌马拉(Tarahumara,Mexico)人民一起抗议,加入土耳其学生反对叙利亚边境爆炸案的游行,到最近(2018)在奥兰治县的法庭上冲向一名持刀的右翼法西斯分子等。多年来麦克拉伦在拉丁美洲的工作、演讲中过着危险的生活。如 2006 年在委内瑞拉加拉加斯举行的世界社会论坛和世界教育论坛结束后,他访问了哥伦比亚,几名目击者告诉他,当地准军事组织的敢死队是如何追捕和暗杀教师和教师工会领导人的。就在他抵达加拉加斯前不久,一名教师在自己的学生面前被暗杀。麦克拉伦虽然几乎总是在严密的安全保护下,仍然被抢劫了他的随身物品。当他在墨西哥的莫雷里亚(Morelia)举行的一次会

---

① Mustafa Yunus Eryaman. *Peter McLaren, Education and the Struggle for Liberation*,New York:Hampton Press,Inc. 2009,p. 161.

议上发表讲话，La Familia Michoacana①袭击了这座城市，点燃了公交车，封锁了城市的出口，当时，幸好有一名激进的出租车司机将他从危险中救了出来。偶尔，在演讲之前，麦克拉伦会在酒店里收到匿名的死亡威胁信。但是在这些极度绝望的地方，麦克拉伦没有停止发表他的演讲，他与老师和工会积极分子分享了他的悲伤，但也分享了希望和奋斗的精神。麦克拉伦在访谈中说："世界各地的活动人士每天都在冒着生命和肢体的危险，在我能够回到美国舒适的工作单位和家的时候，他们的奉献精神令我深感钦佩。这些瞬间凝结在记忆中，成为我作品情感层次的一部分。它们形成我通往自己心灵的道路，当然也与理论工作纠缠在一起——这是一种头脑与心灵之间的辩证法，多年来，这让我相信，除了让社会主义替代资本主义价值生产之外，我们别无选择。"②

总的来说，麦克拉伦的意识形态驱动的好斗与他的同情心和敏感的性格格格不入，这种好斗是由无产阶级的行动的愿景所激发的，旨在克服腐败和崩溃的不公正制度。无论是在文字里，领奖台上，还是在战壕里，麦克拉伦都保持着惊人的良好状态，各种威胁似乎并没有让他感到害怕。在过去的40年里，他一直是一个敏锐的政治观察家，是一位有献身精神的知识分子，试图揭开资产阶级意识形态的神秘面纱，从而清晰地揭露资本主义文化的利益和运作。

三　拒绝故步自封

虽然过去几十年里，很多左派学者都被引人注目的后现代理论吸引住，麦克拉伦还是努力走出迷雾，很有勇气地从自己的作品中以及其他批判教育理论家的作品中撤回，开始拿起马克思主义人道主义这个武器直截了当地批判资本主义及其视线障碍和这个国家的民主教育实践，回归到了最根本、最中心的问题：当今资本主义的结构和阶级构成是如何

---

① La Familia Michoacana（LFM）：是一个墨西哥贩毒集团和有组织的犯罪集团，总部设在墨西哥米却肯州。

② Derek R. Ford. "Revolutionary Critical Pedagogy and the Struggle against Capital Today：An Interview with Peter McLaren". *Education Interview*，2015 - 7 - 16 [EB/OL]. http：//www.hamptoninstitute.org/peter-mclaren-interview.html#.XT6gsi2B3FQ，2019 - 05 - 22.

继续建构和保护美国学校和社会顽固的不平等的。安东尼娅·达尔德（2005）这样评价麦克拉伦：他因炽热而勇猛的作品以及他深刻抓住资本主义问题而在这个领域所产生的广泛影响在各地批判教育者的话语中成为重要转折的标志。[1] 路易斯·M. 韦尔塔·查尔斯认为："麦克拉伦是一位反思性行动的思想开放的学者。因为他会倾听不同的见解、关注不同的替代方案并考虑自己的基本理念会是错误的可能性。我也相信麦克拉伦在他的行动中也是负责的、诚实的，因为他敢于定期地检视、评价这些行动并相信他可以从中学到新的东西。对我来说，他就是这种道德崇高的知识分子。"[2]

麦克拉伦的理论和学识的发展向我们展示为了让这个世界变得更好，他一直在不断探索建构理解、解释世界的理论。他不是一个静态的个体，因为处于静态会让他认为世界理所当然就该如此，就像这个世界是不能被改变的，是必然如此的。如果做一个静态的个体他就冒着成为一个不顾史实的家伙的风险，完全不能通过行动来做出改变，因为否则就看起来很奇怪。这样思考是冒很大的风险的。我们会关上让世界呈现另外样态的希望之门。如果我们不冒这样的风险去想象事情可以是不同的，我们就无法开始改变之路，就无法追寻我们的乌托邦社会之梦。路易斯·M. 韦尔塔·查尔斯认为："由于麦克拉伦一直注意自己的设想与自己的致力于社会平等、建设民主社会的价值观、理论的关系，我们已经看到他从批判理论转向了后现代主义分析架构。现在，我们又看到他从批判教育学——一个他帮助建构的理论——转向了他所称之为的'革命教育学'（pedagogy of revolution），由此，我说他是知行合一的。因为，在他一直寻找不会破坏他的理论的新视角的过程中，同时他一直生活在偶然性和不确定性中。"[3]

---

[1] Marc Pruyn and Luis Huerta-Charles, *Teaching Peter McLaren: Path of Dissent*, New York: Peter Lang Publications, 2005, Foreword. p. xvi.

[2] Marc Pruyn and Luis Huerta-Charles, *Teaching Peter McLaren: Path of Dissent*, New York: Peter Lang Publications, 2005, Foreword. P. xxviii.

[3] Marc Pruyn and Luis Huerta-Charles, *Teaching Peter McLaren: Path of Dissent*, New York: Peter Lang Publications, 2005, Foreword. p. xxvi.

王雁指出，麦克拉伦作为马克思主义者并不是进入学术界那一刻开始的，他个人的理论重点和立足点的变迁，展现给我们的是一个不断学习，跨学科，不断自我否定的学者形象，同时他作为批判教育学的奠基人之一，为批判教育学的理论拓展和发展做出了不可小视的贡献，尤其是引领批判教育学向马克思主义的转向。①

莱昂纳多指出麦克拉伦受到了许多人物和思想传统的影响，其中包括马克思和激进的人道主义马克思主义、后现代主义、结构主义、文化研究、女权主义、后殖民主义、象征人类学、种族和民族理论、保罗·弗莱雷教育学、法兰克福批判理论、批判民族志和批判媒体研究。② 埃尔亚曼（2006）指出，麦克拉伦的作品根植于丰富而深刻的文献中，他借鉴了保罗·弗莱雷、卡尔·马克思、切·格瓦拉、路易斯·阿尔都塞（Louis Althusser）、皮埃尔·布尔迪厄（Pierre Bourdieu）、莱雅·杜纳耶夫斯卡娅、埃里希·弗洛姆、黑格尔（G. W. F. Hegel）、约翰·杜威、安东尼奥·葛兰西等激进进步主义政治哲学理论家的著作。③ 这一系列的影响给了他"阅读文字和世界"的视角，并在不同的情况下保持批判性的推理。据麦克拉伦回忆：

> 当我十几岁的时候，我受到了威廉·布莱克（William Blake）、迪伦·托马斯、莎士比亚（Shakespeare）、米尔顿（Milton）、乔叟（Chaucer）、诺斯罗普·弗莱的新批判主义作品的启发。在20世纪60年代末和70年代初，我受到了垮掉一代的（Beat）诗人、哈莱姆文艺复兴（Harlem Renaissance）以及詹姆斯·鲍德温（James Baldwin）和杜波依斯（Du Bois）作品的影响。当然，还有黑人权力运动

---

① 王雁：《美国批判教育学者麦克拉伦的学术生命研究》，硕士学位论文，东北师范大学，2013年，第8页。

② Marc Pruyn and Luis Huerta-Charles, *Teaching Peter McLaren: Path of Dissent*, New York: Peter Lang Publications, 2005, p. 43.

③ Eryaman, Mustafa Yunus, "Editorial Statement (English): Understanding Critical Pedagogy and Peter McLaren in the Age of Global Capitalism" *International Journal of Progressive Education*, Vol. 2, No. 3, 2006, p. 6.

和安吉拉·戴维斯（Angela Davis）、马尔科姆·艾克斯（Malcolm X）等人的作品。玛格丽特·兰德尔（Margaret Randal）的著作无疑具有影响力。后来我被埃内斯托·切·格瓦拉、弗朗茨·范恩（Frantz Fanon）、卡尔·科西克（Karel Kosik）、大主教奥斯卡·罗梅罗（Oscar Romero）、马尔科姆·艾克斯以及卡尔·马克思和罗莎·卢森堡、诺姆·乔姆斯基、威利斯（P. Wills）、伯恩斯坦（P. Bernstein）、皮埃尔·布尔迪厄、莱雅·杜纳耶夫斯卡娅、埃里希·弗洛姆、黑格尔、约翰·杜威、安东尼奥·葛兰西斯坦利·阿罗诺维茨的教导和学说所吸引。解放神学是我作品构成的一个重要组成部分，特别是在我25岁皈依天主教之后。彼得·胡迪斯对马克思和罗莎·卢森堡作品的诠释与评论，以及凯文·安德森的作品，对帮助我阅读这些巨匠的作品非常重要。保罗·弗莱雷的思想当然一直是我作品的核心。霍华德·津恩、伊斯特万·马埃斯特斯（Istvan Maestros）、何塞·卡洛斯·玛丽亚特（Jose Carlos Mariategui）、马尔库塞、沃尔特·本杰明，莱昂纳多·波夫，当然还有恩斯特·布洛赫（Ernst Bloch）都对我产生了很大的影响。像恩里克·杜塞尔（Enrique Dussel）和阿尼巴尔·奎杰罗（Anibal Quijano）和雷蒙这样的去殖民化思想家（Decolonial thinkers）以及威廉·罗宾逊（William I. Robinson）在跨国资产阶级方面的作品，在我最近的思考中占据了重要的位置。我也非常喜欢何塞·波菲里奥·米兰达（Jose Porfirio Miranda）关于社会主义和圣经的作品。（来自本书作者对麦克拉伦的访谈）

读书与写作占据了麦克拉伦大部分的生命活动，书不离手，笔耕不辍。他的知识非常渊博，从平凡琐碎的知识到庄严的大问题无所不知。麦克拉伦不是想要崇拜者证明其地位的偶像教师，而是我们灵魂深处不可或缺的角色。[1] 他不断虚心学习各家之言，在他的研究中他经常引用

---

[1] Marc Pruyn and Luis Huerta-Charles, *Teaching Peter McLaren: Path of Dissent*, New York: Peter Lang Publications, 2005, Foreword. p. xiii.

这些学者的研究和观点作为他分析问题的基础。成功地将这些理论和观点整合应用于他的研究。同时，对于不合理的理论观点，他也能运用相关研究提出修正和批评。麦克拉伦拒绝故步自封，不断调整、改变和学习，应该是他如今著作等身，成为批判教育领域一位顶尖学者的主要原因。

结　　语

麦克拉伦的批判教育学的形成是由内部因素包括自身的经历与他人的影响、勤奋及对教育事业的忠诚与热爱和外部因素包括资本主义全球化导致的严重负面后果、以往批判教育学的被驯化等共同促成的。以《学校生活》为代表的麦克拉伦批判教育学思想对当下的教育理论与实践都产生了重要的影响与启示，但是也存在其自身的局限性。同时本书也存在着一定的研究局限，需要未来作进一步的补充。

第一节　麦克拉伦批判教育学的形成因素

一　内在因素

（一）自身的经历与他人的影响

父亲的被迫过早退休并过早离世，前往美国反对越战的经历，简·芬奇走廊的孩子及他们的家庭的境况与遭遇，让麦克拉伦切身地感受到他们在资本主义的大环境下受到了资本家的剥削、受到了社会阶级再制、教育资源不均等种种不平等现象的摧残。因而，麦克拉伦之所以成为资本主义的反对者，其中的很重要的原因就是他本人及他身边的人就是资本主义的受害者。

从一个小学教师到一个大学教授，麦克拉伦深感到了培养学生批判意识的重要性以及批判教育学必须从校园舞台跨入社会舞台的必要性。此外，由于一直身在教育领域，麦克拉伦有机会遇见、结识许多代表性人物如保罗·弗莱雷、亨利·吉鲁、保拉·奥尔曼等批判教育学领域的知名学者。这些学者的著作和思想都深深地吸引并影响了麦克拉伦批判教育学思想的不断发展。多次深入拉美地区讲学、参与抗争游行、与委内瑞拉前总统查韦斯的会面等,都强化了他进一步发展革命性批判教育学的决心。

(二)博览群书、思考不停、笔耕不辍

麦克拉伦独树一帜的批判教育学思想的形成绝非偶然、更非一日之功。他自小就博览群书吸收各家思想,如前所述,十几岁的时候就读了各种关于哲学、政治学的名家作品,受到各种思潮的影响,几十年来书不离手早已成为他的生活习惯。由于互联网的高度发达,很多信息和书籍直接可在网上获取,最近十几年电脑不离手成为了麦克拉伦的另一个生活习惯。毫不夸张地说除了睡觉,他一天中的大部分时间都在阅读与写作,包括吃饭的时候他都经常一边看电脑里的资料一边进餐,他每天除了阅读专业领域的资料还会把美国的各大主要报纸网、新闻网都浏览一遍,所以我们在他的作品里经常能够看到当今世界发生的大事或各种政策措施的最新的数据和资讯作为论证他观点的材料。几十年来他把自己活成了百科全书。但是尽信书则不如无书,他并没有拘泥于书上的信息或迷信书本,他一直在不停地思考、批判地吸收或借鉴各种信息,然后加工、整理他所吸纳的各种信息,形成自己的思想并落实于笔端。他的写作上的勤奋是惊人的,自从业以来他的作品层出不穷,平均每年出品一两本书,以及几十篇文章(见附录三)。在课程设置、教育政策、基层政治、教育和文化运动等领域,他撰写编辑了50多部著作,并独撰或与他人合作撰写了数百篇有关批判教育学的文章,主题涉及诸如反战运动、多族裔劳工斗争、土著和新殖民主义解放运动、争取环境正义的斗争、国际巴勒斯坦团结运动和学生行动主义等多个方面。可以说,除非极特殊的情况,他每天都在写作。让研究者极为震撼的一个例子是,在2017年年末麦克拉伦做膝盖手术住院的3天时间里他忍受着手术后极大的不良反应和疼痛完成了一篇杂志社的邀约稿。正是这种孜孜不倦才使得他如此多产,才得到目前为止著作等身的成就,才在北美乃至全世界的批判教育学领域成为不可或缺的代表人物。

(三) 对教育事业的忠诚与热爱

麦克拉伦自从教以来从来没有离开过教育这个领域。尽管他被许许多多的其他学者批判，尽管他甚至被自己的学生指责上课无趣、内容空洞，尽管他遇到过各种各样的恐吓和威胁，尽管他被诋毁为"肮脏三十"（Dirty Thirty）之首，尽管他在 UCLA 被右派排挤而提早离职，麦克拉伦从来没有放弃过他希望将批判教育学深植于校园的理念。他一直心系莘莘学子与劳动阶级，所以不顾自己的名誉与安危痛斥和揭露资本主义的罪恶。以他目前的社会地位与经济条件，他是不属于受压迫、受剥削的阶级，反而是当前资本主义的受惠者，但是麦克拉伦非但没有维护资本主义虚伪的面具，反倒竭力拆穿资本的糖衣，甚而希望打倒资本主义社会建立社会主义社会。以他目前的学术成就，他本不需要再辛苦写作，但是他说人能留给这个世界的东西很少，如果他的作品和思想能够为社会的发展哪怕做出一点点的贡献他就要一直以笔为戎，与资本主义抗争到他生命的尽头。以他目前的学术地位，他去某些机构随随便便一场讲座或演讲都能让他获得颇丰的收入，但是他从来都拒绝不符合或违背他思想立场的但是收入丰厚讲学邀请，反而他经常去拉丁美洲的一些国家如巴西、墨西哥等地（见附录）不计任何报酬地去给当地的学生、教师或工人团体等讲学，因为他觉得这些地方才更需要他，才更值得去，在这样的地方讲学或演讲才是真正有意义的。麦克拉伦从未离开过他的讲台，在世界各地留下了他讲学的身影。对于教育的热情与执着，是其即使有时身体状况欠佳却依然继续奔走各地继续在发光发热的主要原因。麦克拉伦知道教育是百年树人的功夫，而学生更是具有无限的可能性，唯有将批判的种子播于学生的心田里，将来才有可能长成大树，进而开花结果。正是麦克拉伦对教育的强烈使命感使得他一直在无私的付出与奉献。

二 外在因素

(一) 资本主义全球化导致的严重负面后果

资本主义借着全球化的背景及主要主张，合理化生产关系的压榨与压迫。导致富者越富、贫者越贫；阶级壁垒更加牢不可破；资本主义更加肆无忌惮地蔓延至全球。在资本主义的价值法则下，市场的自由经济导致社会和经济的不平等，而教育竟成为市场自由化、经济不平等扩张的帮手。全球化不但无法让政治安定与社会经济平等，反而加剧社会的动荡和经济的差距。资本主义也透过海外经济、文化殖民的扩张来巩固财团私有的利益，实质上是一种新帝国主义侵略。美国的海外军事行动表面上是维护世界和平实际是属于新帝国主义的文化与经济侵略。在这种形势下亟须一种基于大众斗争的批判教育学，寻求一种社会替代方案，以取代将数字经济与全球警察国家相结合的全球资本主义政治和经济议程。对麦克拉伦而言，马克思是其心中可以清晰洞视资本主义意图的老师，也启发了他对于全球化资本主义的看法，进而逐步提出了他的革命性的批判教育学，一种实现资本主义社会替代形式的实践哲学。

（二）以往批判教育学的被驯化

麦克拉伦认为美国总有各种诱惑的方式合并任何它打不败或改变不了的东西。他认为批判教育学已经变成了它原初思想的讽刺漫画，它原本的思想是为了更公平的社会而斗争，为没有权力的人赋权增能，为了解放而斗争。而现在已经被驯化、消减为"学生主导的学习方法"，避免讨论或重新思考"社会批判和革命日程"。

根深蒂固的社会、政治和经济差异以及对立，促使教育工作者和文化工作者必须要创作出可以替代资本家资本积累的逻辑，然而，这是一项艰巨的任务，毕竟这是一个资本主义市场运作的不平等的社会。因此，对于衰弱的以及受到驯化的批判教育学，有必要发展所谓的革命的劳动阶级的教育学。麦克拉伦强调，这也是为何他坚持革命性的批判教育学的立场，针对社会不公平尤其是呈现在学校体制当中的非正义进行高度的批判。他所要澄清的是对于财富的分配不是易如反掌的，而是要去挖掘内在的冲突与矛盾，并且进行讨论，进而去创造一个资本主义之外的社会，使劳动阶级能够发展其自身的价值。因此在以往的批判教育学被驯化、失去作用、幻灭的时候，革命性的批判教育学出现了。

第二节 《学校生活》为代表的麦克拉伦批判教育学的影响与局限性

一 影响

社会公平是推动当代教育研究与教师教育的主要概念之一。财富、机会及特权的不平等经常与学习教育问题相关联，但是通常都是被彼此分开地处理，既没有历史化也没有政治化。在《学校生活》中麦克拉伦提出了很多被其他人忽略的问题，为读者呈现了一个从整体到部分的世界观，即从资本主义体系到考试体系（如不平等）来探究每一个部分的适用性和功能。他对于学校、教育及社会的辩证分析方法使我们可以将马克思主义视为：（1）科学（描述资本主义如何运行）；（2）批判（资本主义的有害影响）；（3）愿景（后资本主义世界的乌托邦想象）；（4）战略（从这儿到那儿，"应该做什么"）。就像保拉·奥尔曼（2003）提出的那样，大多数对于马克思的解释者都只强调这些主题中的一个或几个，但是《学校生活》尤其是革命性的批判教育学阐释了这些元素的每一项是如何影响并为其他各项做出贡献的。

马克思主义者对学校和教育的分析已经在英国及印度繁荣很久了，但是自从鲍尔斯、金帝斯（Gintis）的《资本主义美国的学校教育》（Schooling in Capitalist America）（1996）出版以来，北美教育界似乎对马克思主义分析产生了免疫。在2008年全球金融危机的觉醒中，人们开始对马克思及其分析重新产生了兴趣［比如伊格尔顿（Eagleton, 2011）］[1]，在北美慢慢地增加了马克思主义教育分析的兴趣，这在很大程度上是由于麦克拉伦，尤其是他的《学校生活》的影响。毫无疑问，今天的批判教育学深受麦克拉伦的影响，他的政治激进主义已经牢牢地聚焦于促进阶级意识及革命改革的组织。

保拉·奥尔曼（2003）写到，大多数反对马克思主义对资本主义分析的人并非简单地反对，而是"无视马克思所谈论的资本主义"。资本主

---

[1] Eagleton, *Marx was right*, New Haven, CT: Yale University Press, 2011, p.201.

义并非是看不见的，但是像保拉·奥尔曼所指出的那样，也不是立刻就很明显的："资本主义尚待被发现，更何况说被理解，应该吸引人们关注一些并不明显的要素关系。但是如果大多数处于资本主义中的人甚至都看不到资本主义及其系统的话，呈现资本主义的面貌，简单地展示它是存在的及其本质为何与解释资本主义如何运作同样需要巨大的努力。因此，解决对于马克思作品的普遍忽视问题与解释马克思主义是同样至关重要的。事实上，没有前者后者是不可能的。"[1]

虽然"本书没有对开国先父的甜美赞歌，没有慷慨陈词给出如何培养企业精神和缩小数字鸿沟的建议，也没有关于教师如何提高学生标准化测试成绩的妙招"，但是书中提出的对教育问题的这种分析通常涉及教育学的根本。而这种从批判角度来写的教育学教材基本从20世纪80年代起就没有了。《学校生活》的诞生是为了在北美这块资本主义占支配地位的土地上挑战种族、阶级和性别特权，这正是《学校生活》强有力的卖点。[2]

然而，尽管《学校生活》收获了成功与诸多赞美，但是2014年发行的第六版将是该书付梓问世的最后一版。麦克拉伦解释道："不是因为我认为该书表达的观点将会过时，而是因为我的政治观点变得日益激进。除少数例外（《学校生活》正是其中之一），激进的政治和教师的教科书历来水火不容也无法长存。"[3] 但是《学校生活》第六版继续向读者和教师们提出挑战：他们站在谁的立场上；他们怎样通过这本书使孩子们、教育者们及文化工作者们的生活产生不同；他们应该提出什么问题及解决对策。麦克拉伦提醒读者"当你读这本书的时候请谨记保罗·弗莱雷的话：阅读不仅仅是一目十行的阅过文字本身，而是要抓住文字所要表达的灵魂"。这一版的《学校生活》并不是向革命社会主义致敬，而是像

---

[1] Ollman, B., *Dance of the dialectic: Steps in Marx's method*, Urbana: University of Illinois Press, 2003, p. 67.

[2] Peter McLaren, *Life in Schools: An Introduction to Critical Pedagogy in the Foundations of Education (Sixth Edition)*, Boulder, CO: Paradigm, 2014, p. 4.

[3] Peter McLaren, *Life in Schools: An Introduction to Critical Pedagogy in the Foundations of Education (Sixth Edition)*, Boulder, CO: Paradigm, 2014, p. 4.

一首唱给资本主义的战歌，一次对教育者的挑战，通过努力联合社会工厂之外或资本社会的劳工为批判教育学强筋健骨。①

除了《学校生活》在北美以及世界很多地方成为教育学及相关专业的教科书，麦克拉伦的很多著作，现在也已经成为很多学校教学的参考书，他的批判教育学在世界各地的大学都有教授。随着数字革命未能点燃民主之火，未能给知识、经济和社会自由注入活力，人们认识到，我们迫切需要新的方法来对抗我们当前的新自由主义数字化国家和令人作呕的法西斯主义崛起。麦克拉伦革命性的批判性教育学，为这个黑暗的时代提供了一线希望的曙光。麦克拉伦在总结自传时呼吁读者"挣脱束缚"②，最终留给我们一个选择：我们会继续像旅鼠一样接受特朗普（Trump）的暴行和跨全球资本主义，还是会接受这位哲人的革命性呼吁，寻求将我们自己和人类从历史上、并持续束缚我们的霸权枷锁中解放出来？

《学校生活》对于资本主义、学校和教育体系有着一种持续不断的、不断演化发展的影响。可见，这本书绝不仅如书名所呈现的，只限在学校生活。它鼓励批判教育工作者可以运用新增的检视不平等权力关系的理论分析，例如后殖民主义和社会主义，来分析他的教学日志中所呈现的议题。可以说这本书提供学生、批判教育工作者和这位有名的教育理论家难得的机会，在一个资本主义、父权当道和种族歧视的社会可以针对学校教育和民主中有关的道德议题进行对话、发表异见、互相质疑，并且拓展彼此的思考和行动。

二 局限性

（一）语言抽象难懂

麦克拉伦批判教育学表达思想所使用的很多词汇较为生僻，有些甚至是古英语词汇，访学期间研究者从查普曼大学的博士生口中得知，母

---

① Peter McLaren, *Life in Schools: An Introduction to Critical Pedagogy in the Foundations of Education* (Sixth Edition), Boulder, CO: Paradigm, 2014, p. 5.

② Peter McLaren, *Breaking free: the life and times of Peter McLaren, radical educator*, Gorham, ME: Myers Education Press, 2019, p. 103.

语为英语的这些高才生对其使用的一些词汇都表示不认识,不明所以;其所使用的语言也过于诗歌化,抽象难懂。研究者认为,为无产阶级发声的批判教育学应该让无产阶级看得懂才能更好地发挥它的功效。

(二) 解决策略模糊

麦克拉伦批判教育学虽然对资本主义进行了全方位的、深刻的批判,指出了资本主义社会诸多亟待解决的问题,但是对于解决这些问题的策略却比较模糊,缺乏具体的指导方案,容易陷入乌托邦式的空想。

(三) 对中国的适用性有限

批判教育学的最终理想都在于追求社会的公平与正义,并致力于人性主体的解放。但是西方的批判教育学思想,如果要作为我国的参考时,并不能完全一成不变的移植,而要考虑到我们东方的本土民情以及条件限制,才不会造成水土不服的严重后遗症。由于麦克拉伦所生活、工作及批判的背景为资本主义国家,所以对于社会主义中国的适用性还是比较有限的。而且也有必要指出,麦克拉伦虽然坚持马克思主义,并大量地使用了马克思主义的理论观点和方法,但是麦克拉伦基于马克思主义人道主义的革命性批判教育学思想与中国所坚持的马克思主义唯物主义教育思想还是有所不同的,因此需要批判地审视其作用,取其精华,弃其糟粕。马克思主义唯物主义教育思想必然应是社会主义教育事业的科学指导思想。

参考文献

一 相关中文著作和论文

（一）著作

S. 鲍尔斯、H. 金蒂斯：《美国：经济生活与教育改革》，王佩雄等译，上海教育出版社1990年版。

保罗·弗莱雷：《被压迫者教育学》，顾建新等译，华东师范大学出版社2001年版。

彼得·麦克拉伦：《校园生活——批判教育学导论》，萧昭君、陈巨擘译，台北：台湾巨流图书公司2003年版。

布尔迪厄：《文化资本和社会炼金术》，包亚明译，上海人民出版社1997年版。

布尔迪厄：《再生产：一种教育系统理论的要点》，刑克超译，商务印书馆2002年版。

李锦旭、王慧澜：《批判教育学——台湾的探索》，台北：心理出版社2006年版。

卢朝佑：《美国批判教育学的批判解释性研究》，科学出版社2018年版。

马克思：《1844年经济学哲学手稿》，北京：人民出版社2000年版。

马克思、恩格斯：《德意志意识形态》（节选本），人民出版社2003年版。

《马克思恩格斯选集》第1卷，人民出版社2012年版。

米歇尔·福柯：《规训与惩罚》，刘北成、杨远婴译，上海三联书店1999年版。

上海社会科学院哲学研究所外国哲学研究室编：《法兰克福学派论著选

辑》(上卷),商务印书馆 1998 年版。

孙善豪:《批判与辩证》台北:唐山 2009 年版。

王占魁:《价值选择与教育政治——阿普尔批判教育研究的实践逻辑》,教育科学出版社 2014 年版。

杨昌勇:《新教育社会学:连续与断裂的学术历程》,中国社会科学出版社 2004 年版。

(二) 论文

彼得·麦克拉伦、于伟:《学者对于正义的追寻——彼得·麦克拉伦(Peter McLaren)访谈录》,《外国教育研究》2015 年第 6 期。

彼得·麦克拉伦、周霖:《革命性的批判教育学:教师教育项目的解毒剂》,《东北师大学报(哲学社会科学版)》2009 第 2 期。

蔡幸芬:《Peter McLaren 的批判教育学后现代主义观点》,Intelligent Information Technology Application Association. Proceedings of the 2011 Second International Conference on Education and sports Education (ESE 2011 V3)[C]. Intelligent Information Technology Application Association:智能信息技术应用学会,2011:4。

蔡幸芬、杨忠斌:《对后现代主义的反叛——Peter McLaren 的批判教育学后现代主义观点》,second international conference on education and sports education,2011。

邓志伟:《后现代主义思潮与西方批判教育学》,《外国教育资料》1996 年第 8 期。

黄斌:《论整体把握马克思主义与人道主义关系的几个问题》,《科学社会主义》2012 年第 2 期。

黄力之:《"以人为本":马克思主义的人道主义还是抽象的人道主义?》,《毛泽东邓小平理论研究》2009 年第 1 期。

李宝庆、樊亚峤:《麦克莱伦的多元文化教育观及其启示》《比较教育研究》2012 年第 5 期。

李宝庆、靳玉乐:《麦克莱伦的批判课程理论及其启示》,《西南大学学报(社会科学版)》2014 年第 6 期。

李家永:《保罗·弗莱雷成人扫盲的理论与实践》,《比较教育研究》1996

年第 6 期。

彭静：《批判教育学视域中的教师角色分析》，《教育理论与实践》2004 年第 10 期。

祁东方：《亨利·吉鲁批判教育哲学思想研究》，博士学位论文，山西大学，2015 年。

田友谊：《教育即解放：试析保罗·弗莱雷的"解放教育学"》，《外国教育研究》2004 年第 4 期。

王珊：《解放神学视野下的中国基督教社会主义研究》，博士学位论文，中共中央党校，2017 年。

王彦斌：《吉鲁克斯批判教育学师生观概述》，《中国教育学刊》2007 年第 12 期。

王雁：《美国批判教育学者麦克拉伦的学术生命研究》，硕士学位论文，东北师范大学，2013 年。

王占魁：《阿普尔批判教育研究的理论来源》，《华东师范大学学报（教育科学版）》2012 年第 2 期。

王占魁：《阿普尔批判教育研究的批判逻辑》，《教育研究》2012 年第 4 期。

辛治洋：《批判教育学的困境与出路》，《比较教育研究》2004 年第 9 期。

辛治洋：《批判教育学解读》，《比较教育研究》2006 年第 7 期。

徐湘荷、赵占强：《社会正义抑或生态正义——批判教育学和生态正义教育学之争》，《比较教育研究》2011 年第 4 期。

阎光才：《批判教育研究的学术脉络与时代境遇》，《教育研究》2007 年第 8 期。

阎光才：《批判教育研究在中国的境遇及其可能》，《教育学报》2008 年第 3 期。

杨昌勇：《"西方马克思主义"思潮与"新"教育社会学理论的关系分析》，《华东师范大学学报（教科版）》1998 年第 1 期。

于向化：《保罗·弗莱雷的教育思想述评》，《华东师范大学学报（教科版）》1995 年第 3 期。

张聪：《为了儿童的解放和自由——麦克莱伦（Peter McLaren）〈反抗教

育学〉（Pedagogy of insurrection）的价值意蕴》，《外国教育研究》2017年第2期。

张华：《美国当代批判课程理论初探（上）》，《全球教育展望》1998年第2期。

张华：《美国当代批判课程理论初探（下）》，《全球教育展望》1998年第3期。

张华：《批判理论与批判教育学探析》，《外国教育资料》1996年第4期。

张琨：《论保罗·弗莱雷的希望教育哲学》，《外国教育研究》2006年第5期。

郑富兴：《美国批判教育学的道德教育思想述评》，《比较教育研究》2007年第12期。

郑金洲：《美国批判教育学之批判——吉鲁的批判教育观述评》，《比较教育研究》1997年第5期。

郑蕾：《批判教育学视野下的美国多元文化教育——访美国加州大学洛杉矶分校Peter Mc Laren教授》，《全球教育展望》2012年第3期。

周勇：《忧伤与愤怒：教育社会学的情感动力——以涂尔干、麦克拉伦为例》，《教育学术月刊》2014年第9期。

二 麦克拉伦的主要著作和论文

（一）独著

Peter McLaren, *Breaking free: the life and times of Peter McLaren, radical educator*, Gorham, ME: Myers Education Press, 2019.

Peter McLaren, *Capitalists and Conquerors: A Critical Pedagogy Against Empire*, Rowraan & Littlefield Publishers, 2007.

Peter McLaren, *Che Guevara, Paulo Freire, and the Pedagogy of Revolution*, Lanham MD: Rowman & Littlefield Publishers, 2000.

Peter McLaren, Colin Lankshear, *Politics of Liberation*, Routledge, London, 1994.

Peter McLaren, *Cries from the Corridor: The New Suburban Ghettoes*, Markham, Ontario, Canada: Paperjacks, 1981.

Peter McLaren, *Cries from the corridor: The new suburban ghettos (revised with new Afterword)*, Markham, Ontario, Canada, 1982.

Peter McLaren, *Critical Pedagogy and Predatory Culture*, New York: Routldge, 1995.

Peter McLaren, *Critical pedagogy and predatory culture: Oppositional politics in a postmodern era*, New York: Routledge, 1995.

Peter McLaren, *Critical pedagogy and predatory culture—oppositional politics in a postmodern era*, London: Routledge, 2004.

Peter McLaren, *Life in Schools: An Introduction to Critical Pedagogy in the Foundations of Education (Fifth Edition)*, Pearson Publishers, 2007.

Peter McLaren, *Life in Schools: An Introduction to Critical Pedagogy in the Foundations of Education (Fourth Edition)*, Pearson Publishers, 2003.

Peter McLaren, *Life in Schools: An Introduction to Critical Pedagogy in the Foundations of Education (Second Edition)*, New York: Longman, 1994.

Peter McLaren, *Life in Schools: An Introduction to Critical Pedagogy in the Foundations of Education (Sixth Edition)*, Boulder, CO: Paradigm, 2014.

Peter McLaren, *Life in Schools: An Introduction to Critical Pedagogy in the Foundations of Education (Third Edition)*, New York: Longman, 1998.

Peter McLaren, *Life in Schools: An lntroduction to Critical Pedagogy in the Foundations of Education (First Edition)*, New York: Longman, 1989.

Peter McLaren, *Pedagogy of insurrection: From resurrection to revolution*, New York: Peter Lang Publishers, 2015.

Peter McLaren, *Postmodernism Postcolonialism and Pedagogy*, Albert Park: Australia, James Nicholas Publishers, 1995.

Peter McLaren, *Red Seminars: Radical excursions into educational theory, cultural politics, and pedagogy*, Hampton Press, Inc., 2005.

Peter McLaren, *Revolutionary Multiculturalism: Pedagogies of Dissent for the New Millenniura*, Westview, 1997.

Peter McLaren, *Schooling as a ritual performance: Toward a political economy of educational symbols and gestures (3rd ed.)*, Lanham, MD: Rowman and

Littlefield, 1999.

Peter McLaren, *Schooling as a Ritual Performancefirst*, London: Routledge & Kegan Paul, 1986.

Peter McLarened. , *Capitalists and conquerors: A critical pedagogy against empire*, Lanham, MD: Rowman & Littlefield, 2005.

Peter McLaren ed. , *Rage and Hope: interviews with Peter McLaren on war, imperialism, +critical pedagogy*, New York: Peter Lang Publishing, Inc. , 2006.

（二）合著

Best S. , Kahn R. , Nocella A. J. , McLaren P. eds. , *The global industrial complex: Systems of Domination*, Lanham, MD: Lexington Books, Rowman & Littlefield, 2011.

Cole, M. , Hill, D. , McLaren, P. , Rikowski, G. eds. , *Red chalk: On schooling, capitalism and politics*, London, UK: The Institute for Education Policy Studies, 2001.

Fischman G. , Sunker H. , Lankshear C. , McLaren P. eds. , *Critical theories, radical pedagogies, and global conflicts*, Boulder, CO: Rowman & Littlefield, 2005.

Henry Giroux, Peter McLaren (editors), *Critical Pedagogy, the State, and Cultural Struggle*, State University of New York Press, 1989.

Henry Giroux, Peter McLaren eds. , *Between Borders: Pedagogy and the Politics of Cultural Studies*, New York: Routledge, 1994.

Lankshear C. , McLaren P. eds. , *Critical literacy: Politics, praxis, and the postmodern*, Albany, New York: Suny Press, 1993.

Leonard P. , McLaren P. eds. , *Paulo Freire: A critical encounter*, New York: Routledge, 1993.

Macrine S. , McLaren P. , Hill D. eds. , *Revolutionizing pedagogy: Education for social justice within and beyond global neo-liberalism*, London, UK: Palgrave Macmillan, 2009.

Martin G. , Houston D. , McLaren P. , Suoranta J. eds. , *The havoc of capitalism: Publics, pedagogies and environmental crisis*, Rotterdam: The Netherlands Sense Publishers, 2010.

McLaren P., Hammer R., Sholle D., Reilly S., *Rethinking media literacy: A critical pedagogy of representation*, New York: Peter Lang Publishing, 1995.

McLaren P., Kincheloe J. L. eds., *Critical pedagogy: Where are we now?*, New York: Peter Lang Publishing, 2007.

McLaren P., Soohoo S. eds., *Radical Imagine-Nation: Public Pedagogy & Praxis*, New York: Peter Lang, 2018.

McLaren P. L., Lanshear C. eds., *Politics of liberation: Paths from Freire*, NewYork, NY: Routledge, 1994.

Nocella A., Best S., McLaren P. eds., *Academic repression: Reflections from the academic-industrial complex*, Oakland, CA: AK Press, 2010.

Peter McLaren, Colin Lankshear, *Critical Literacy: Politics Praxis and the Postmodern*, State University of New York Press, 1993.

Peter McLaren, Dave Hill, Mike Cole, Glenn Rikowski, *Marxism Against Postmodernism in Educational Theory*, New York: Lexington Books, 2002.

Peter McLaren, Peter Leonard (editors), *Paulo Freire: A Critical Encounter*, London: Routledge, 1993.

Peter McLaren, Ramin Farahmandpur, *Teaching Against Global Capitalism and the New Imperialism: A Critical Pedagogy*, Rowman & Littlefield Publishers, 2005.

Sandlin J. A., McLaren P. eds., *Critical pedagogies of consumption: Living and learning in the shadow of the "shopocalypse"*, New York: Routledge, 2009.

Sleeter, C. E., McLaren, P. L., *Multicultural education, critical pedagogy and the politics of difference*, Albany, NY: State University of New York Press, 1995.

（三）论文

Lissovoy N., Peter McLaren, "Educational 'accountability' and violence of capital: a Marxian reading", *Education policy*, Vol. 18, No. 2, 2003, pp. 131–143.

Peter McLaren, "Collisions with otherness: 'Traveling' theory, postcolonial criticism, and the politics of ethnographic practice-the mission of the wounded ethnographer", *Critical theory and educational research*, 1995, pp. 271 – 300.

Peter McLaren, "Conservation, Class Struggle, or Both: A Response to C. A. Bowers", *Capitalism Nature Socialism*, Vol. 18, No. 1, 2007, pp. 99 – 108.

Peter McLaren, "Critical literacy and postcolonial praxis: A Freirian Perspective", *College Literature /Double issue*, Vol. 19, No. 3, 1992, pp. 7 – 27.

Peter McLaren, Donna Houston, "Revolutionary Ecologies: Ecosocialism and Critical Pedagogy", *Educational Studies*, Vol. 36, No. 1, 2004, pp. 27 – 45.

Peter McLaren, "Education Agonistes: an epistle to the transnational capitalist class, Policy Futures in Education", Vol. 12, No. 4, 2014, pp. 583 – 610.

Peter McLaren, *Education and the unchained class struggle in the crisis of global capitalism*, "the speech of international conference on higher education management, on Dec, 24, 2011", in National Taichung University of Education. 2011, pp. 1 – 45.

Peter McLaren, Farahmandpur, R., "Teaching against globalization and the new imperialism: toward a revolutionary pedagogy", *Journal of teacher education*, Vol. 52, No. 2, 2001, pp. 136 – 150.

Peter McLaren, "Fire and Dust", *International Journal of Progressive Education*, Vol. 1, No. 3, 2006, pp. 34 – 57.

Peter McLaren, Michael Dantley, "Leadership and a Critical Pedagogy of Race: Cornel Peter McLaren", Petar Jandrić, "Critical revolutionary pedagogy is made by walking-in a world where many worlds coexist", *Policy Futures in Education*, Vol. 12, No. 6, 2014, pp. 805 – 831.

Peter McLaren, Petar Jandrić, "From Liberation to Salvation: Revolutionary critical pedagogy meets liberation theology", *Policy Futures in Education*, Vol. 15, No. 65, 2017, pp. 620 – 652.

Peter McLaren, Petar Jandrić, "Karl Marx and Liberation Theology: Dialectical materi – alism and Christian spirituality in, against, and beyond contemporary capitalism", *Triple C: Communication, Capitalism & Critique*, Vol. 16, No. 2, 2018.

Peter McLaren, Rikiowski, G., "Pedagogy for revolution against education for capital: an e-dialogue on education in capitalism today", *Cultural Logic*, Vol. 4, No. 1, 2001, pp. 1 – 59.

Peter McLaren and Henry Giroux, "Leon Golub's Radical Pessimism: Towards a Pedagogy of Representation", *Exposure*, Vol. 28, No. 2, 1991, pp. 18 – 34.

Stuart West, "Hall and the Prophetic Tradition", *Journal of Negro Education*, Vol. 59, No. 1, 1990, pp. 29 – 44.

三 其他相关英文著作和论文

（一）著作

Adorno, T., *Negative dialectics*, trans. E. B. Ashton, New York: Continuum, 1995.

Allman, P., *Critical education against global capitalism: Karl Marx and revolutionary critical education*, Westport, CT: Bergin & Garvey, 2001.

Allman, P., *Revolutionary social transformation: Democratic hopes, political possibilities and critical education*, Westport, CT: Bergin & Garvey, 1999.

Allman P., *Critical Education Against Global Capitalism: Karl Marx and Revolutionary Critical Education*, Westport, ct Bergin & Garvey, 2001.

Apple, M., *Educating the "Right" Way: Markets, Standards, God and Inequality*, New York London: Routledge Falmer, 2001.

Best, S., Kahn, R., Nocella, A. & McLaren, P., *The Global Industrial Complex: systems of domination*, Lanham, MD: Lexington Books, 2011.

B. J. Portfilio, D. Ford, *Leaders in Critical Pedagogy: Narratives for Understanding and Solidarity*, Rotterdam, Sense, 2015.

Brian, D., *Handbook of Peter McLaren: education and learning beyond schooling*, New York: Routledge, 2009.

Discipline and punish, trans. A. Sheridan, New York: Pantheon Book, 1997.

E. M. Wood, J. B. Foster eds., *In defense of history: Marxism and the postmod-*

ern agenda, New York: Monthly Review Press, 1997.

E. M. Wood, J. B. Fostereds. , In defense of history: Marxism and the postmodern agenda, New York: Monthly Review Press, 1997.

Eryaman M. ed. , Peter McLaren, education, and the struggle for liberation, New York, NY: Hampton Press, 2009.

Fay, B. , Critical social science, Ithaca, NY: Cornell University Press, 1978.

Foster, J. B. , Naked, Imperialism: The U. S. pursuit of global dominance, New York: Monthly Review Press, 2006.

Giroux, H. , Theory, resistance, and education: A pedagogy for the opposition, South Hadley, MA: Bergin & Garvey, 1983.

Greider, W. , One world, ready or not: The manic logic of global capitalism, New York: Touchstone, 1988.

H. A. Giroux, Teachers as intellectual, Granby , MA: Bergin & Garve, 1988.

Henry Giroux, Border Crossings: Cultural workers and the politics of education, Routledge, 1992.

Hudis, P. , Marx's Concept of the Alternative to Capitalism, Chicago: Haymarket Books, 2012.

J. L. De Vitis ed. , Popular educational classics: A reader, New York, Peter Lang, 1985.

Kohn, A. , The case against standardized testing, Portsmouth, NH: Heinemann, 2000.

Kohn Alfie, The Case against Standardized Testing: Raising the Scores, Ruining the Schools, Portsmouth, NH: Heinemann, 2000.

Lenin, V. I. , Imperialism: The highest stage of capitalism, New York: International Publishers, 1977.

Luis Charles – Huerta, Marc Pruy, This Fist Called My Heart: The Peter McLaren Reader, Information Age Publishing Inc. , 2015

Marc Pruyn, Luis Huerta – Charles (editors) , Teaching Peter McLaren: Path of Dissent, New York: Peter Lang Publications, 2005.

Martin, G. , I see red: The revolutionary critical pedagogy of Peter McLare,

Aula Critica, Numero Especial Julio – Septiembre de, 2004.

Marx, K., *Economic and philosophic manuscripts of* 1844, New York: Prometheus Books, 1988.

Marx, K., *Grundrisse: Foundations of the critique of political economy*, trans. Nicolaus, Harmondsworth: Penguin, 1973

McMurty, J., *Value wars: the global market versus life economy*. Toronto, ON: Garamond, 2001.

McNeil, L., *Contradictions of School Reform: Educational Costs of Standardized Testing*, New York: Routledge, 2000.

Michael Peters, Colin Lankshear, Mark Olssen eds., *Futures of Critical Theory: Dreams of Difference*, New York: Rowman and Littlefield, 2003.

Mustafa Yunus Eryaman, Peter McLaren, *Education and the Struggle for Liberation*, Hampton Press, Inc., 2009.

Neumann, M., *What's Left? Radical Politics and the Radical Psyche*, Peterborough, Ontario: Broadview Press, 1988.

Norman K. Denzin, Yvonna Lincoln eds, *Handbook of Qualitative Research*, Sage, 1994.

Paulo Freire, Donaldo Macedo, *Literacy: Reading the Word and theWorld*, Bergin & Garvey, 1987.

Paulo Freire, *Pedagogy of Indignation*, Boulder, CO: Paradigm Publishers, 2004.

Paulo Freire, *Pedagogy of the Oppressed*, trans, M. Bergman Ramos, New York: Continuum, 1996.

Paulo Freire. *The politics of education*, South Hadley, MA: Bergin & Garvey, 1985.

Percy, J., Lorimer, D., *The democratic socialist party and the Fourth International*, Chippendale, NSW: Resistance Books, 2001.

Petras, J., Veltmeyer, H., *Globalization unmasked: Imperialism in the 21st century*, New York: Zed Books, 2001.

P. Jandrić, D. Boras eds., *Critical Learning in Digital Networks*, New York, Springer, 2015.

R. C. Tuckered. , *The Marx – Engels reader（Second Edition ed.）*, New York：W. W. Norton & Company, 1978.

Reitz C. ed. , *Crisis of commonwealth：Marcuse, Marx, McLaren*, Lanham, md：Lexington Books, Rowman & Littlefield, 2013.

Rikowski, G. , *The battle in Seattle：Its significance for education*, London：Tufnell Press, 2001.

Roy, A. , *An ordinary person's guide to empire*, Cambridge, Massachusetts：South End Press, 2004.

Saad – Filho ed. , *Anti – capitalism：A marxist introduction*, London：Pluto Press, 2003.

Said, E. , *Orientalism*, New York：Random House, 1978.

Schrag, F. , *Thinking in school and society*, London：Routledge, 1988.

Sears, James T. , *Sexuality and the Curriculum*, Teachers College Press, 1992.

Starr, A. , *Naming the enemy：Anti – corporate movements confront globalization*, London：Zed Books, 2000.

Tucker, R. ed. , *The Lenin antholog*, New York：W. W. Norton & Company, 1975.

Turner Victor, *Process, Performance and Pilgriraage*, New Delhi：concept, 1979.

Turner Victor, *The Ritual Process：Structure and Anti – structure. Chicago*, Aldine, 1969.

Weiler, K. , *Women teaching for change：Gender, class & power*, New York：Bergin & Garvey, 1988.

Yali Zou, Enrique T. Trueba（editors）, *Ethnography and Schools：Qualitative Approaches to The Study of Education*, Rowman & Littlefield Publishers, 2002.

（二）期刊论文

Berlak, "Race and the achievement gap", *Rethinking Schools*, Vol. 15, No. 4, 2001.

Bojesen E. , "Special Issue：Pedagogies of Insurrection", *Policy Futures in Education*, Vol. 15, No. 5, 2017.

Bowers, C. A. , "Review：Some Questions about the Anachronistic Elements in the Giroux – McLaren Theory of a Critical Pedagogy", *Curriculum Inquiry*,

Vol. 21, No. 2, 1991.

Bowers C. A., "Silences and Double Binds: Why the Theories of John Dewey and Paulo Freire Cannot Contribute to Revitalizing the Commons", *Capitalism Nature Socialism*, *Vol.* 17, No. 3, 2006.

David Gabbard, "Peter McLaren & the 3 R's: Reflection, Resistance and Revolution", *International Journal of Progressive Education*, Vol. 2, No. 3, 2006.

David Gabbard, "Peter McLaren & the 3 R's: Reflection, Resistance and Revolution ", *nternational Journal of Progressive Education*, Vol. 2, No. 3, 2006.

Denzin, N. K., "Homegrown Democracy, Homegrown Democrats", *International Journal of Progressive Education*, Vol. 1, No. 1, 2005.

Derek R. Ford, "Book review: Life in Schools: An Introduction to Critical Pedagogy in the Foundations of Education (6th edition). Peter McLaren. Boulder and London: Paradigm Publishers, 2014", *Educational Studies*, *Vol.* 51, No. 5, 2015.

Derek R. Ford, "Book review: Life in Schools: An Introduction to Critical Pedagogy in the Foundations of Education (6th edition). Peter McLaren. Boulder and London: Paradigm Publishers, 2014" *Educational Studies*. Vol. 51, No. 5, 2015.

Engle, S., "Peter McLaren: Connecting pedagogy to social issues", *Forum*, Vol. 7, No. 3, 2005.

Eryaman, Mustafa Yunus, "Editorial Statement (English): Understanding Critical Pedagogy and Peter McLaren in the Age of Global Capitalism", *International Journal of Progressive Education*, Vol. 2, No. 3, 2006.

Eryaman, Mustafa Yunus, "Editorial Statement (English): Understanding Critical Pedagogy and Peter McLaren in the Age of Global Capitalism", *International Journal of Progressive Education*, Vol. 2, No. 3, 2006.

Gluckman Amy., "Testing… Testing… One, Two, Three: The Commercial Side of the Standardized – Testing Boom." *Dollars and Sense*, Vol. 239, 2002.

Gregory Martin, "Remaking Critical Pedagogy: Peter McLaren's Contribution to a Collective Work", *International Journal of Progressive Education*, Vol. 2, No. 3, 2006.

Gregory Martin, " Remaking Critical Pedagogy: Peter McLaren's Contribution to a Collective Work", *International Journal of Progressive Education*, Vol. 2, No. 3, 2006.

Gregory Martin, "Remaking Critical Pedagogy: Peter McLaren's Contribution to a Collective Work", *International Journal of Progressive Education*, Vol. 2, No. 3, 2006.

Harvey, D., "The practical contradictions of marxism", *Critical Sociology*, Vol. 24, No. 1 &2, 1998.

International Journal of Educational Reform, "Special Issue: The Revolutionary Pedagogy of Peter McLaren", *International Journal of Educational Reform*, Vol. 10, No. 2, 2001.

John P. Portell, "From Text to Textuality: 'Reading' McLaren's Life in Schools", *Journal of Education*, Vol. 173, No. 3, 1991.

John Smyth, "Book Review: Life in Schools: An Introduction to Critical Pedagogy in the Foundations of Education by Peter McLaren, New York: Longman, 1989", *Educational Theory*, Vol. 40, No. 2, 1990.

Junrui Chang, Changyong Yang, "Book Review: McLaren, Peter & Farahmandpur, Ramin (2005). Teaching against Global Capitalism and the New Imperialism: A Critical Pedagogy. Lanham, Maryland, Rowman & Littlefield Publishers", *International Journal of Progressive Education*, Vol. 2, No. 3, 2006.

Kenneth Zeichne, "BOOK REVIEW: Peter McLaren, Che Guevara, Paulo Freire, and the Pedagogy of Revolution. Roman & Littlefield, Lanham, Maryland, USA, 2000. 264 pages, ISBN 0847695336", *Journal of Educational Change*, Vol. 2, 2001.

Mary Ann Doyle, "Peter McLaren and the Field of Critical Pedagogy", *Educational Researcher*, Vol. 25, No. 4, 1996.

Purpel, D., "Review article – Schooling as a Ritual Performance", *Education-

al Theory, Vol. 38, No. 1, 1988.

Rikiowsk, G., "Alien life: Marx and the future of the human", *Historical Materalism*, Vol. 11, No. 2, 2003.

Rikiowski, G., "Left alone: end time for Marxist educational theory?" *British Journal of Sociology of Education*, Vol. 17, No. 4, 1996.

Samuel Day Fassbinder, "Book Review: Life in Schools: An Introduction to Critical Pedagogy in the Foundations of Education by Peter McLaren, Boulder, CO: Paradigm, 2014 ", *Journal for Critical Education Policy Studies*, 2014.

Samuel Day Fassbinder, "Interview with Peter McLaren, on his Work, on his Visit to Turkey and on Ongoing Popular Struggles", *Policy Futures in Education*, Vol. 11, No. 6, 2013.

Ursula A. Kelly, "From Text to Textuality: 'Reading' McLaren's Life in Schools", *Journal of Education*, Vol. 173, No. 3, 1991.

Valerie Scatamburlo – D'Annibal, "Imagining the Impossible: Revolutionary Critical Pedagogy Against the 21st Century American Imperium", *International Journal of Progressive Education*, Vol. 2, No. 3, 2006.

Walter Werner, "Book Review: Life in Schools: An Introduction to Critical Pedagogy in the Foundations of Education by Peter McLaren, New York: Longman, 1989", . *Pedagogy + Phenomenology*, No. 7, 1989.

West, G., "Book Review: Cries from the Corridor: The Suburban Ghettoes", *Canadian Journal of Education*, No. 6, 1981.

(三) 英文电子文献

Anonymity, Life in Schools: Whatever Happened to Peter McLaren and Cries from the Corridor? [EB/OL], https: //educhatter.wordpress.com/2015/07/11/life – in – schools – whatever – happened – to – peter – mclaren – and – cries – from – the – corridor/, 2018 – 09 – 27.

Caroline G. Whitcomb (2019), Review of Peter McLaren. Breaking Free: The Life and Times of Peter McLaren, Radical Educator, Illustrated by Miles Wilson, Gorham, ME: Myers Education Press, 120 pp, ISBN 1975501691,

(Paperback) Postdigital Science and Education [EB/OL], https: // doi. org/10. 1007/s42438 – 019 – 00061 – y, 2019 – 07 – 26.

Caroline G. Whitcomb (2019), Review of Peter McLaren. Breaking Free: The Life and Times of Peter McLaren, Radical Educator, Illustrated by Miles Wilson. Gorham, ME: Myers Education Press, 120 pp. ISBN 1975501691. (Paperback)《Postdigital Science and Education》[EB/OL], https: // doi. org/10. 1007/s42438 – 019 – 00061 – y, 2019 – 07 – 26.

David Gabbard, Karen Anijar, Fearless Speech in Fearful Times: An Essay Review of Capitalists and Conquerors, Teaching against Global Capitalism and the New Imperialism, and Teaching Peter McLaren, https: //mronline. org/2005/10/30/fearless – speech – in – fearful – timesan – essay – review – of – capitalists – and – conquerors – teaching – against – global – capitalism – and – the – new – imperialism – and – teaching – peter – mclaren/, 2019 – 05 – 22.

Davis C. , An Interview with a Revolutionary, Professor Peter McLaren, Huffington Post, 3 August 2015 [EB/OL], https: //www. huff – ingtonpost. com/creston – davis/an – interview – with – a – revol_b_6825766. html, 2019 – 05 – 22.

Derek R. Ford, "Revolutionary Critical Pedagogy and the Struggle against Capital Today: An Interview with Peter McLaren", *Education Interview*, 2015 – 7 – 16 [EB/OL] .

Fassbinder, S. (2006)., The "Dirty Thirty's" Peter McLaren reflects on the crisis of academic freedom [EB/OL], http: //mrzine. monthlyreview. org/fassbinder060406. html, 2017 – 05 – 14.

Fassbinder S. C. , McLaren P. , The "Dirty Thirty's" Peter McLaren Reflects on the Crisis of Academic Freedom,《MRonline》, 6 April 2006 [EB/OL], https: //mronline. org/2006/04/06/the – dirty – thirtys – peter – mclar – en – reflects – on – the – crisis – of – academic – freedom/, 2017 – 05 – 30.

Jandrić, P. (2018), Peter McLaren: Portrait of a revolutionary. Rassegna Di Pedagogia, 76 (1 – 2), 139 – 158, [EB/OL], https: //doi. org/

10. 19272/201802102010/, 2018 – 04 – 02.

Mallot, C. S. (2017), "Class consciousness and teacher education: The socialist challenge and the historical context" In A. Darder, R. D. Torres, & M. P. Baltodano, eds. *The critical pedagogy reader*. NewYork: Routledge. GoogleScholar [EB/OL]. http: //scholar. google. com/scholar _ lookup? title = Class% 20consciousness% 20and% 20teacher% 20education% 3A% 20The% 20soc, 2019 – 07 – 26.

Martin, G. (2005), You can't be neutral on a moving bus: Critical pedagogy as Community Praxis [EB/OL], http: //www. jceps. com/index. php? pageID = article&articleID = 47, 2018 – 06 – 20.

McLaren, P., & Jandrić, P. (2014), Critical revolutionary pedagogy is made by walking: in a world where many worlds coexist, Policy Futures in Education, 12 (6), 805 – 831, [EB/OL], https: //doi. org/10. 2304 / pfie. 2014. 12. 6. 805/, 2018 – 04 – 02.

McLaren, P., & Rikowski, G. (2001), Pedagogy for revolution against education for capital: An e – dialogue on education in capitalism today [EB/OL], http: //eserver. org/clogic/4 – 1/mclaren&rikowski. html, 2018 – 04 – 02.

McLaren, P., McMurry. A. & McGuirk, K., An Interview with Peter McLaren, Waterloo: University of Waterloo [EB/OL], http: //english. uwaterloo. ca/PeterMcLareninterview. pdf, 2017 – 04 – 14.

McLaren P., Smith V., What Unites Us [EB/OL], Retrieved 2 April 2018 fromhttps: // blogs. chapman. edu/magazine/2017/03/15/what – unites – us/, 2018 – 04 – 02.

Ng, D. (2006), Paris loves a riot: France is a democracy where dissent is not only tolerated but expected [EB/OL], http: //www. villagevoice. com/ news/0614, ng, 72715, 2. html, 2018 – 09 – 27.

Peter McLaren, "Revolutionary critical pedagogy: Staking a claim against the macrostructural unconscious", *Critical Education*, Vol. 7, No. 8, 2016, [EB/OL], http: //ojs. library. ubc. ca/index. php/criticaled/article/view/

186144, 2019 - 05 - 22.

Pozo M., Toward a Critical Revolutionary Pedagogy: An Interview with Peter McLaren, 2003 [EB/OL], http://facpub.stjohns.edu/~ganterg/sjureview/vol21/mclaren.html, 2018 - 04 - 02.

Rikowski, G. (2000), Messing with the explosive commodity: School improvement, educational research, and labour - power in the era of global capitalism. If we arent pursuing improvement, what are we doing? [EB/OL], http://www.leeds.ac.uk/educol/documents/00001610.htm, 2016 - 07 - 14.

Rikowski, G. (2002)., Methods for researching the social production of labour power in capitalism [EB/OL], http://www.ieps.org.uk.cwc.net/rikowski2002b.pdf, 2018 - 04 - 02.

Rizvi, M. Educating for social justice and liberation: Peter McLaren interviewed by Mashhood Rizvi. [EB/OL], http://www.zmag.org/content/showarticle.cfm?ItemID = 2229, 2017 - 05 - 12.

Robinson, W. I., "The next economic crisis: Digital capitalism and global police state", *Race & Class*, 2018, 0 (0): 1 - 16, [EB/OL], https://doi.org/10.1177/0306396818769016, 2019 - 05 - 22.

Singer, Alan. (2014, March 31), "Racially Segregated Schools in America: The Bloomberg, Gates, Bush and Obama Legacies." Huffington Post, [EB/OL], www.huffingtonpost.com/alan - singer/racially - segregated - schoo_b_5059540.html, 2018 - 04 - 02.

Wikipedia, Peter McLaren [EB/OL], https://en.wikipedia.org/wiki/Peter_McLaren, 2018 - 04 - 02.

Younge, G (2006), Silence in class, [EB/OL], http://www.guardian.co.uk/usa/story/0,, 1746227, 00.html, 2017 - 05 - 14.

Younge, G (2006)., Silence in class [EB/OL], http://www.guardian.co.uk/usa/story/0, 1746227, 00.html, 2017 - 05 - 14.

附　　录

附录一　访谈麦克拉伦提纲

	访谈时间	访谈地点	访谈内容
1	2014年5月11日	东北师范大学	*对美国社会现状的看法。 *对美国教育现状的看法。
2	2014年5月23日	东北师范大学	*对美国批判教育学发展现状的看法。 *关于教育公平的看法。
3	2015年5月15日	东北师范大学	*《学校生活》的写作缘由及您对这本书的看法。 *《学校生活》各个版本之间最大的差异。
4	2015年5月17日	东北师范大学	*《来自走廊地区的呐喊》（Cries from the Corridor）这本书的写作缘由及对这本书的看法。 *《学校生活》所获得主要赞誉与批判。
5	2015年6月2日	东北师范大学	*其青少年时期的经历和故事。 *齐克对您的影响。
6	2016年5月17日	东北师范大学	*与吉鲁一起在迈阿密大学工作八年的主要经历及印象深刻的事件。 *对吉鲁的思想的认识及对您的影响。
7	2016年5月29日	东北师范大学	*在中小学阶段的学习经历和社会实践活动及感受。 *父母对您的影响。

续表

	访谈时间	访谈地点	访谈内容
8	2016年6月4日	东北师范大学	* 与保罗·弗莱雷的私交。 * 对保罗·弗莱雷的思想的认识及对您的影响。
9	2017年5月20日	东北师范大学	* 研究生阶段的主要收获和影响人物。 * 惯用一些生僻词汇表达思想的理由。 * 《学校教育作为一种仪式表演》（Schooling as A Ritual Performance）后停止批判民族志方面的研究与写作的原因。
10	2017年5月24日	东北师范大学	* 在UCLA工作二十年的主要经历及印象深刻的事件。 * 对被UCLA右翼团体列为"肮脏三十"教授之首事件的看法。
11	2017年5月27日	东北师范大学	* 对后现代主义的看法，以及放弃后现代主义的原因。 * 对抵制理论的看法。
12	2017年8月31日	美国查普曼大学	* 您的博士论文《教育是一种仪式表演》（Schooling as a Ritual Performance）的选题缘由和研究过程。
13	2017年9月5日	麦克拉伦家中	* 您的博士导师理查德·考特尼（Richard Courtney）对您的影响。 * 福柯对您的影响。
14	2017年9月11日	美国查普曼大学	* 如何看待"可能性的语言"与"批判的语言"之间的关系。 * 对美国进步主义和社会重建主义思想的理解。
15	2017年9月20日	美国查普曼大学	* 马克思主义人道主义的理论内核以及主要代表人物。 * 莱雅·杜娜叶夫斯卡亚的作品对您的影响。
16	2017年10月10日	美国查普曼大学	* 您对研究者博士论文研究框架的建议和意见。

续表

	访谈时间	访谈地点	访谈内容
17	2017年10月20日	麦克拉伦家中	*凯文·安德森对您成为马克思主义人道主义者的影响。 *罗莎·卢森堡对您成为马克思主义人道主义者的影响。 *彼得·胡迪斯对您成为马克思主义人道主义者的影响。
18	2017年10月27日	美国查普曼大学	*对马克思主义的认识。 *主要阅读了哪些马克思的经典作品。
19	2017年11月3日	美国查普曼大学	*切·格瓦拉对您的人生、对您的批判教育学思想的影响。 *影响您走上批判教育学这个领域的主要人物。
20	2017年11月19日	美国查普曼大学	*对您影响最大的著作书籍。 *英国教育家马克思主义者葆拉·奥尔曼对您理论形成的影响。
21	2017年11月23日	麦克拉伦家中	*英国的马克思主义者戴夫·希尔、迈克·科尔和格伦·里科夫斯基等人与您的私人关系及对您理论的影响。
22	2017年11月28日	美国查普曼大学	*《切·格瓦拉、保罗·弗莱雷与革命教育学》(Che Guevara, Paulo Freire, and the Pedagogy of Revolution) 的写作背景及其与革命性批判教育学之间的思想关联。
23	2017年12月6日	美国查普曼大学	*在简·芬奇走廊的工作感受及印象深刻的事件。 *校长吉姆·蒙哥梅力对您的影响。
24	2017年12月15日	美国查普曼大学	*您的三部曲《来自走廊地区的呐喊》(Cries from the Corridor)、《学校教育作为一种仪式表演》(Schooling as A Ritual Performance)、《学校生活》(Life in Schools) 之间的阶段性转变。

续表

	访谈时间	访谈地点	访谈内容
25	2017年12月26日	美国查普曼大学	*参与的国际性的进步教育实践活动。 *在委内瑞拉与查韦斯总统见面的感受和收获。
26	2018年1月10日	麦克拉伦家中	*您对自己思想理论的阶段性划分。 *由后现代主义转向马克思主义的主要标志。
27	2018年1月19日	美国查普曼大学	*青年时期参加反战行动的经历与感受。 *青年时期在约克维尔的反主流叛逆生活对您的影响。 *滑铁卢大学和多伦多大学的教授们对您的影响。
28	2018年1月24日	美国查普曼大学	*马克思主义与新马克思主义之间的区别和联系。 *如何看待自治马克思主义者如哈特和内格里。
29	2018年2月05日	美国查普曼大学	*您由人文主义者彻底变成一个主张革命实践的马克思主义人道主义者的转变背景、原因和关键节点。
30	2018年2月13日	麦克拉伦家中	*对布什政府提出的《有教无类法案》和奥巴马政府提出的《争创一流》政策的看法。 *如何看待美国的教育私有化。 *当今资本主义的结构和阶级构成与美国学校和社会不平等之间的关系。
31	2018年2月26日	美国查普曼大学	*如何看待美国的特许学校。 *如何看待芬兰的教育。 *批判意识养成的重要性。
32	2018年3月14日	美国查普曼大学	*如何看待所获得的数量众多的来自世界各地的奖项。 *如何看待在右翼出版物中受到学术攻击并作何回应。

续表

	访谈时间	访谈地点	访谈内容
33	2018年3月18日	美国查普曼大学	*如何看待保罗·弗莱雷把您归为一个完全相同的"知识分子家族"("intellectual family")。
34	2018年3月26日	麦克拉伦家中	*墨西哥的彼得·麦克拉伦批判教育学基金会与研究所的基本情况及发展方向。 *委内瑞拉加拉加斯玻利瓦尔大学的彼得·麦克拉伦基金会的基本情况及发展方向。
35	2018年4月7日	美国查普曼大学	*认真回复来自世界各地学者或学生发来的邮件的动力与原因。 *为拉美国家的很多教育机构作免费讲座的动力与原因。
36	2018年4月18日	美国查普曼大学	*有机知识分子(organic intellectual)、"有献身精神的知识分子"(committed intellectual)与传统知识分子(traditional intellectual)的区别与联系。 *葛兰西的"有机知识分子"与您的"具有献身精神的知识分子"之间的关系。
37	2018年4月28日	美国查普曼大学	*由"批判教育学"更名为"革命性的批判教育学"的背景及原因。 *革命性的批判教育学与以往的革命性的批判教育学的本质不同之处。 *革命性批判教育学的价值立场。
38	2018年5月8日	美国查普曼大学	*基督教和天主教对其思想的影响。 *对学校教育的政治立场问题的看法。
39	2018年5月17日	美国查普曼大学	*您作为查普曼大学保罗·弗莱雷民主项目的联合主任所作的主要努力和开展的主要活动。 *您如何看待您作为查普曼大学国际道德和社会正义大使的角色。

续表

	访谈时间	访谈地点	访谈内容
40	2018年5月22日	美国查普曼大学	*对"实践"（praxis）这个词的理解。 *对"激进"（radical）这个词的理解。 *对"革命"（revolution）这个词的理解。
41	2018年5月29日	美国查普曼大学	*在AERA参与学术交流活动的情况。 *精力和时间如何分配才能高效地产出作品。
42	2018年6月8日	麦克拉伦家中	*您在中国各地讲学的感受与收获。 *您在拉丁美洲各地讲学的难忘经历。 *您在欧洲、亚洲、澳洲、拉丁美洲、北美讲学的主要不同感受。
43	2018年6月21日	美国查普曼大学	*保罗·威利斯的《学做工》与《学校生活》的异同。 *鲍尔斯和金蒂斯的著作对您的理论影响。
44	2018年6月26日	美国查普曼大学	*新自由主义的特征及问题。 *全球化资本主义的特征及问题。 *《反对全球资本主义和新帝国主义的教学：一种批判教育学》（Teaching Against Global Capitalism and the New Imperialism: A Critical Pedagogy）的写作背景与主要思想。
45	2018年6月30日	美国查普曼大学	*对于受到的学术批判与攻击的看法。 *对于受到人身威胁与攻击的看法。 *您作为一位"有献身精神的知识分子"所肩负的责任。
46	2018年7月9日	麦克拉伦家中	*如何看待资产阶级人道主义。 *改革主义的自由主义和后结构主义的激进主义在挑战全球资本主义中的局限性。
47	2018年7月18日	美国查普曼大学	*马克思的阶级冲突论、辩证法、历史唯物论等思想在其革命性批判教育学形成中的作用。
48	2018年7月20日	美国查普曼大学	*对资本主义全球化的看法。 *革命性的批判教育学把资本主义全球化作为最主要的批判对象的原因。

续表

	访谈时间	访谈地点	访谈内容
49	2018年7月27日	美国查普曼大学	*市场原教旨主义、帝国主义军国主义的抬头以及独裁主义与资本主义全球化的关系。 *《资本家与征服者：反对帝国的批判教育学》（Capitalists and Conquerors: A Critical Pedagogy Against Empire）的写作缘由及主旨。
50	2018年8月1日	美国查普曼大学	*在其作品中为何把古巴革命家切·格瓦拉、菲德尔·卡斯特罗、委内瑞拉前总统乌戈·查韦斯、墨西哥的革命家埃米利亚诺·萨帕塔等扩展到教育领域。
51	2018年8月22日	美国查普曼大学	*皮埃尔·布尔迪厄、埃里希·弗洛姆、黑格尔、约翰·杜威、安东尼奥·葛兰西的思想对您的影响。
52	2018年8月24日	美国查普曼大学	*研究生阶段修习米歇尔·福柯、翁贝托·艾柯、埃内斯托·拉康和其您批判理论家的课程主要收获。
53	2018年8月28日	美国查普曼大学	*保拉·奥尔曼的《反对全球资本主义的批判教育：卡尔·马克思与革命批判教育》（Critical Education Against Global Capitalism: Karl Marx and Revolutionary Critical Education）对您革命性批判教育学的影响。
54	2018年9月4日	麦克拉伦家中	*如何看待以墨西哥恰帕斯（Chiapas Mexico）为基地的激进社会主义政治运动——原住民萨帕塔（Zapata）起义。 *如何看待美国作为"全球警察国家"。

续表

	访谈时间	访谈地点	访谈内容
55	2018年9月7日	美国查普曼大学	*阶级斗争与建立社会主义的社会之间的关系。 *革命性的批判教育学的目标及实现目标的途径。
56	2018年9月16日	美国查普曼大学	*如何看待迈克尔·阿普尔"非改革主义的改革"与"厚民主"的学校教育。 *如何看待后现代主义的"激进民主"。
57	2019年5月21日	东北师范大学	*您的批判教育学和吉鲁的批判教育学、阿普尔的批判教育研究的异同。 *如何看待贝尔·胡克斯的"交融教育学"(engaged pedagogy)。
58	2019年5月24日	东北师范大学	*漫画体自传的创作背景和用意。 *您不惧生命危险地勇于口诛笔伐地揭露黑暗真相、质疑威权、参与游行的动力与原因。
59	2019年5月26日	东北师范大学	*如何看待自己既是马克思主义者、民主社会主义者又是天主教徒的多重身份。 *您的研究立场与您白人身份的关系。
60	2019年6月3日	东北师范大学	*您与英国的戴夫·希尔一起创刊的《批判教育政策研究杂志》(Journal for Critical Education Policy Studies)的现状及今后的方向。 *革命的希望在哪里。

附录二　麦克拉伦世界各地讲学年表（1987—2022）

麦克拉伦1985年离开加拿大后的世界各地的讲学及演讲足迹

年份	日期	国家	地点/机构	讲学或演讲主题
1987	6.28—7.3	古巴	哈瓦那泛美心理学会	学校教育、主体性和经验政治
1988	4	葡萄牙	葡萄牙法罗理工学院	超越批判与反乌托邦的话语
	6.7	墨西哥	墨西哥城的大学生中心	批判理论与教育改革
	6.8	墨西哥	阿拉贡国立埃斯库埃拉大学	批判民族志与课程：趋势与可能性
	11.15	墨西哥	墨西哥城墨西哥自治国立大学	批判理论、文化霸权与社会正义之争：拉丁美洲的视角
	11.17	墨西哥	墨西哥托卢卡州第一师范学院（电视直播）	构建社会公正课程体系
	11.22	墨西哥	墨西哥瓜达拉哈拉大学	教育学理论、知识生活和争取民主改革的斗争
1989	5	墨西哥	墨西哥瓜达拉哈拉大学	辩证地梦想与葛兰西的精神
	5	墨西哥	桂塔罗大学	拉丁美洲的开放脉络：南北之间的关键对话
	5	墨西哥	墨西哥城自治大学	走向抗争与希望的教育学
	5.22—26	墨西哥	墨西哥城瓜达拉哈拉大学，米却肯科学研究与发展研究所	社会、文化和教育
1991	4.22—26	墨西哥	墨西哥城国际研讨会	课程与21世纪
1992	8	巴西	阿雷格里港巴西儿童神经精神病学协会、南里约热内卢教育与医学协会	1. 学校：解放还是统治？ 2. 主观性和情景性暴力
	8	巴西	巴西阿雷格里港的南里约热内卢联邦大学	后殖民主义教育学、跨文化主观性和解放政治
	8	巴西	巴西阿雷格里港的罗马天主教大学	抗拒与反叙事

续表

年份	日期	国家	地点/机构	讲学或演讲主题
1992	8	阿根廷	帕拉纳国立大学教育科学学院——国际研讨会：21世纪大学课程展望	1. 对抗记忆和文化阻力 2. 仪式/反仪式：拉康、德里达、福柯、哈贝马斯以及他们的工作对发展一种批判的抵抗教育学的影响
	8	阿根廷	布宜诺斯艾利斯社会科学研究所	主体性与文化反抗的反叙事
	8	墨西哥	普埃布拉的伊比利亚美洲大学，教育研究研讨会：2000年的成就和挑战	批判多元文化主义与反叙事的解放
	11.23—26	墨西哥	夏拉帕市韦拉克鲁斯纳师范大学研讨会	批判教育学与后现代主义
	12	波兰	波兰托伦哥白尼大学社会科学研究	批判理论与解放政治
	12	波兰	华沙	课程改革的政治学
	12	波兰	波兹南	后现代主义与教育学：北美视角
1993	7.4—8	巴西	巴西圣玛利亚大学艺术与文学中心国际跨学科研讨会	研讨会邀请致辞
	8	荷兰	格罗宁根国际人文科学会议	主题演讲
	9.8—10	葡萄牙	法罗第二届国际教育社会学会议	民主公民和发展的主题演讲
	12.6—9	马来西亚	槟城	后现代时代的传播与发展：对弗赖尔遗产的重新评价
1994	5.6	墨西哥	夏拉帕市韦拉克鲁斯纳师范大学博物馆礼堂	高等教育课程日：对韦拉克鲁斯纳大学的影响
	5.23—27	墨西哥	索诺拉大学和墨西哥工人工会	批判教育学与后现代主义
	6.11	墨西哥	墨西哥城大学第三届国际研讨会：课程和21世纪	面对21世纪挑战的课程前景

续表

年份	日期	国家	地点/机构	讲学或演讲主题
1994	6.12—14	墨西哥	韦拉克鲁斯纳市夏拉帕市	批判性教育学的理论基础
	6.16	墨西哥	墨西哥普埃布拉英语西班牙语大学	环境、人权和教育
	6.17	墨西哥	墨西哥国立自治大学，墨西哥城阿拉贡国家职业研究学院	霸权文化和民主课程的进程
	9.5—9	巴西	佛罗里达波利圣卡塔琳娜联邦大学教育科学中心集训20小时课程	教育硕士课程
	9.14	巴西	巴西阿雷格里港的南里约热内卢联邦大学教育学院教育研究生课程	1. 批判教育学和流行文化 2. 后现代教育学
	9.14	巴西	圣保罗天主教大学教育心理学的研究生课程	学校的仪式
	9.15	巴西	圣保罗天主教大学教育学院教学理论和学校实践	学校的仪式
	10	墨西哥	墨西卡利国家教育学院	当前社会背景下教育研究面临的巨大挑战
1995	2.16—18	德国	维滕贝格黑尔的马丁·路德大学国际会议	全球社会正义教育的政治
	2.22—24	波多黎各	圣胡安第四届波多黎各教育研究大会	1. 全球主义：教育和研究的挑战 2. 教育研究中的方法论与不断变化的世界并行不悖
	7.24	墨西哥	特皮克纳亚里特高等师范学校	主题演讲
	8	德国	柏林亚历山大第二届理论文化与社会大会	文化与身份：城市、民族、世界
	9.8	巴西	佛罗里达波利圣卡塔琳娜联邦大学	多元文化和批判性主观性
	9.27—30	德国	维滕贝格黑尔的马丁·路德大学	批判教育学与社会分析

1996	1.26—29	墨西哥	华雷斯自治大学	学校改革的关键途径
	5.8	巴西	佛罗里达波利圣卡塔琳娜联邦大学	批判的多元文化主义
	5.13	巴西	里约热内卢的联邦大学	葛兰西，弗莱雷和哈贝马斯：批判的观点
	6.14	阿根廷	罗萨里奥批判教育学研究中心	教师和文化：新的教学视野
	6.15	阿根廷	罗萨里奥国际研讨会	批判教育与学术自由——拉丁美洲的经验
	6.18	阿根廷	圣达菲联合国文化论坛	新的教学视野
	7.22—27	墨西哥	纳亚里特师范学院，纳亚里特州第四届文化教育学会议	主题演讲
	9.20—22	日本	联合国大学东京国立语言研究所第四届国际专题讨论会	1. 语言学、多元文化主义和民主 2. 多元文化社区的语言管理：文学、话语和身份的焦虑
	11.27—29	墨西哥	阿拉贡墨西哥国立自治大学	教育与文化多样性
	12.2—6	墨西哥	墨西哥城大学第四届国际研讨会：课程与21世纪	1. 面对技术变革的大学 2. 成为一名批判教育家：为正义而战
1997	1.17—18	墨西哥	华雷斯	不假思索的白人，反思民主
	4.28	墨西哥	蒂华纳大学中心墨西卡利校园教育博士课程指导	葛兰西、马尔库塞、哈贝马斯：批判理论与教师的形成
	4.29	墨西哥	蒂华纳大学中心墨西卡利校园教育博士课程指导	争取发言权的斗争：教育中的种族、阶级和性别
	4.30	墨西哥	蒂华纳大学中心墨西卡利校园教育博士课程指导	教育中的主体性与同一性
	5.1	墨西哥	蒂华纳大学中心墨西卡利校园教育博士课程指导	教育与民主：迈向新千年的批判教育学

续表

年份	日期	国家	地点/机构	讲学或演讲主题
1997	5.2	墨西哥	蒂华纳大学中心墨西卡利校园教育博士课程指导	不假思索的白人：瓦解教育中的白人至上主义意识形态
	5.29	巴西	萨尔瓦多，巴伊亚，由NGO组织的批判性教育学国际会议：文化与教育	教育、文化和社会
	5.30	巴西	萨尔瓦多，巴伊亚，由NGO组织的批判性教育学国际会议：文化与教育	当代学校的批判教育学
	5.31	巴西	萨尔瓦多，巴伊亚，由NGO组织的批判性教育学国际会议：文化与教育	学校仪式
	6.5	阿根廷	阿根廷罗萨里奥大学的公开演讲	教育和解放斗争
	6.6	阿根廷	罗萨里奥国立大学文化教育学院，罗萨里奥大学师范学院	国际课程：身份
	6.7	阿根廷	罗萨里奥大学	文化研究
	8.8	墨西哥	阿瓜斯卡达特斯，教育和人权课程和讲习班：民主和人权会	无意识的白人，重新思考民主和教育
1998	1.16	墨西哥	华雷斯，由奇瓦瓦州教育服务、危险学生教育研究中心、约翰霍普金斯大学和霍华德大学发起的会议	切·格瓦拉的教育学

续表

年份	日期	国家	地点/机构	讲学或演讲主题
1998	3.26	墨西哥	圣路易斯波提索,国立师范大学	批判教育学;后现代主义和切·格瓦拉的遗产
	3.27	墨西哥	圣路易斯波提索,国立师范大学	白人至上(盎格鲁－撒克逊人)、身份和多元文化的概念
	5.19	芬兰	芬兰教育部,批判教育学博士研讨会	"全球化时代的批判教育学"公开讲座
	5.20	芬兰	赫尔辛基大学,芬兰教育部	"受伤的人种志学者"博士研讨会讲座/讨论
	5.22	芬兰	赫尔辛基大学,芬兰教育部	赫尔辛基"全球化时代的批判教育学"公开讲座
	7.6	巴西	阿雷格里港市教育局	保罗·弗莱雷教育学
	7.8—11	巴西	阿雷格里港市教育局	资本的创伤:全球市场的教育学、政治学和实践
1999	1.26—28	哥斯达黎加	圣何塞,哥斯达黎加大学	哥斯达黎加的小学教育前景分析
	5	墨西哥	蒂华纳大学	教育博士课程
	9.7	巴西	圣克鲁斯南部,社区大学邀请研讨会	
	11.8	以色列	海法,以色列海法大学	教育共存
	11.21	芬兰	罗凡尼米,拉普兰大学	主题演讲
	11.23	芬兰	坦佩雷,坦佩雷大学	邀请讲座
	11.26	芬兰	芬兰社会心理学家年会:下一千年的社会心理学	社会心理学家作为批判的社会代理人
	12.13—15	墨西哥	恩塞纳达港,蒂华纳大学	教育博士研讨会
	12.19—21	墨西哥	蒂华纳,蒂华纳大学库利亚坎校区	教育博士研讨会

续表

年份	日期	国家	地点/机构	讲学或演讲主题
2000	1.17—19	古巴	哈瓦那,哈瓦那高等艺术学院	1. 革命领导与教育实践:切·格瓦拉的遗产 2. 从左翼看当今的马克思主义
	7.7	澳大利亚	墨尔本,墨尔本理工大学,第七届国际识字与教育研究网络学习会议	新自由主义与政治的终结:走向违禁品的皇家教育学
	7.12—13	澳大利亚	珀斯,由西澳大利亚大学、默多克大学和《澳大利亚人报》赞助的教育学院部门研讨会系列	1. 不假思索的白人:重新思考民主 2. 多元文化教育的政治
	8.22	巴西	圣保罗,圣多明戈斯学院	邀请讲座
	8.23—24	巴西	桑托斯,巴西桑托斯蒙特塞拉特中央大学,6年级教师培训,3年级学生培训	教育的作用:语言和语境
	8.25	巴西	里约热内卢,高等教育学院	巴西文化对教育的影响
	8.26	巴西	里约热内卢	幼儿教育工作者培训
	9.29—30	阿根廷	布宜诺斯艾利斯,布宜诺斯艾利斯大学哲学与文学学院,关于识字和批判教育学的讲习班	向扫盲工作者发表主题演讲:第三阶段的识字和公民建设
	11.16—17	墨西哥	墨西哥城,墨西哥城国立教育大学	批判教育学
	11.18	墨西哥	瓜达拉哈拉,国家教育大学	全球化、新自由主义和教育政策
	11.27	中国	台湾,屏东师范学院	新自由主义、教育学、全球化:边缘的批判
	11.28	中国	台湾,台湾师范大学	反对全球化和新帝国主义的教学
	11.29	中国	台湾,台北市立师范学院	向批判性公民教育迈进
	11.30	中国	台湾,花莲师范学院	新自由主义、教育学及全球化:边缘的批判

续表

年份	日期	国家	地点/机构	讲学或演讲主题
2000	12.1	中国	台湾，台湾社会科学学会年会	革命性的多元文化主义与希望的政治：政治、文化与经济转型教学
	12.27—29	墨西哥	蒂华纳，蒂华纳大学中心的恩塞纳达校园	批判教育学与政治的终结
2001	6.20—24	德国	伍珀塔尔，德国伍珀塔尔大学，政治社会化、参与和教育会议	全球化与教育政策的政治学
	11.30	墨西哥	瓜达拉哈拉，瓜达拉哈拉世博会，瓜达拉哈拉国际图书节	"9·11"事件后的社会正义斗争
	12.27—30	墨西哥	蒂华纳，蒂华纳大学，教育博士论坛	"9·11"事件后的批判教育学
2002	3.21—22	墨西哥	恩塞纳达港，墨西哥蒂华纳中央理工大学	1. 全球化时代的批判教育学 2. 墨西哥教育的未来
	7.24—8.3	墨西哥	韦拉克鲁斯，韦拉克鲁斯教育研究，多元文化教育研讨会	四次专题讲座
	9.3	南非	比勒陀利亚，威特沃特斯兰德大学	新自由主义全球化时代的批判教育学：对学校生活的反思
	9.4	南非	比勒陀利亚，南非大学	批判多元文化主义：多元文化和非种族主义教育的新方向
	9.5	南非	比勒陀利亚，南非大学	游击教育学与恐怖主义辩证法
	9.6	南非	比勒陀利亚大学，南非教师教育学院（格伦克洛夫校区）	教育研究批判理论
	11.5	巴西	里约热内卢，高等教育学院	革命教育学

续表

年份	日期	国家	地点/机构	讲学或演讲主题
2003	4.11	墨西哥	蒂华纳，蒂华纳大学，多元文化教育国际会议	开幕式主题演讲
	4.12	墨西哥	蒂华纳，蒂华纳大学，多元文化教育国际会议	闭幕式主题演讲
	8.21—22	墨西哥	维拉克鲁斯，维拉克鲁斯师范大学，批判教育学第八次研讨会	四次主题讲座
	11.2	韩国	首尔，首尔国立大学	新自由主义全球化时代的批判教育学
	11.27—29	德国	奥尔登堡，人权教育与保罗·弗莱雷教育取向会议	帝国时代的批判教育学：挑战布什政府的帝国议程
2004	4.5	英格兰	普利茅斯，话语、权力、抵抗：全球问题会议	全球帝国时代的批判教育学
	7.30	墨西哥	蒂华纳，麦克莱伦教育基金会成立开幕式	主题演讲
2005	4.1—2	西班牙	巴塞罗那，重新审视批判教育学会议	主题演讲
	4.13—16	委内瑞拉	向世界学习和传播我们的知识：声援玻利瓦尔革命国际会议	主题演讲
	4.14	委内瑞拉	巴里纳斯，西平原国家实验大学	资本主义者与征服者：反对帝国的批判教育学
	4.17	委内瑞拉	加拉加斯电台	建立跨国联盟
	4.18	委内瑞拉	加拉加斯，委内瑞拉中央解放大学	野兽腹中的批判教育学
	4.19	委内瑞拉	加拉加斯	科学与技术教育部的政治
	4.20	委内瑞拉	加拉加斯，委内瑞拉玻利瓦尔共和国大学	布什政府的教育政策

续表

年份	日期	国家	地点/机构	讲学或演讲主题
2005	5.29—6.2	以色列	耶路撒冷范里尔学院和海法大学，冲突社会公民教育国际会议	主题演讲
	6.2	以色列	海法，海法大学	批判教育学与批判的公民
	6.3	巴基斯坦	比尔泽特大学	批判教育学与为社会主义抗争
	6.27—29	巴基斯坦	卡拉奇，理解高质量教育研讨会	主题演讲
	6.30	巴基斯坦	教育质量再设想会议	作为专家组成员参会
	7.28—30	委内瑞拉	加拉加斯，批判教育学研讨会，委内瑞拉玻利瓦尔大学	主题演讲
	7.30	委内瑞拉	加拉加斯电台	解放斗争与联盟建设
	8.28	中国	台湾，中正大学	主题演讲
	8.29	中国	台湾，屏东师范大学	演讲
	11.11	墨西哥	奇瓦瓦	主题演讲
	11.12	墨西哥	奇瓦瓦	与本土教育工作者对话
	11.12	墨西哥	帕拉尔，国立师范大学	社会运动与批判教育学：一种分析
	11.13	墨西哥	克里尔	与本土教育工作者对话
2006	1.24	委内瑞拉	加拉加斯，委内瑞拉玻利瓦尔大学	新人文主义的批判教育学
	1.25	委内瑞拉	巴尔加斯，国立大学	作为马克思主义人本主义的批判教育学
	1.26	委内瑞拉	巴尔加斯，国立大学	作为政治方案的批判教育学
	1.27	委内瑞拉	加拉加斯，世界社会论坛	切·格瓦拉的马克思主义与21世纪的社会主义
	1.31	哥伦比亚	波哥大	批判教育学：展望与基础

续表

年份	日期	国家	地点/机构	讲学或演讲主题
2006	2.1	哥伦比亚	波哥大,哥伦比亚教育工作者联合会及其教育研究中心	全球化与批判教育学
	2.2	哥伦比亚	卡利	民主与教育
	2.2	哥伦比亚	麦德林,安蒂奥基亚大学	民族志、教育学与政治学
	2.3	哥伦比亚	麦德林,安提奥基亚研究所	主体性、权力和教育学
	2.21-22	墨西哥	墨西哥城,墨西哥自治大学	作为有组织的实践的批判教育学
	2.24	墨西哥	墨西哥城,墨西哥国立自治大学	批判教育学:概述
	5.22	南非	开普敦,西开普大学	社会运动中的批判教育学——当代背景下意味着什么?
	5.23	南非	开普敦,西开普大学	正规教育中的批判教育学——当代背景下意味着什么?
	5.24	南非	德班,夸祖鲁-纳塔尔大学	主题演讲
	5.25	南非	哈罗德·沃尔普纪念讲座	弗莱雷的批判教育学与当代解放斗争
	5.29—6.2	南非	夸祖鲁-纳塔尔大学,保罗·弗莱雷研究中心	5天的演讲和讨论
	6.5—6.7	南非	约翰内斯堡,南非工会联盟冬季学校	讨论批判教育学,进行性别及阶级斗争相关主题小组报告
	7.17	墨西哥	赫莫西洛	批判教育学:保罗·弗莱雷和解放教育学
	7.19	墨西哥	蒂华纳,蒂华纳大学	批判教育学:保罗·弗莱雷和解放教育学
	8.10	澳大利亚	黄金海岸,格里菲斯大学应用语言及文化交流中心	批判教育学:我们现在身处何地?

续表

年份	日期	国家	地点/机构	讲学或演讲主题
2006	8.30	哥伦比亚	波哥大，批判教育学国际研讨会	主题演讲
	9.14	委内瑞拉	拉加拉斯，米兰达国际中心	从批判教育学到革命教育学
	9.15	委内瑞拉	拉加拉斯，委内瑞拉玻利瓦尔大学	作为争取解放的政治斗争的教育
	11.1—4	委内瑞拉	拉加拉斯，世界教育专题论坛	批判教育学与争取社会正义
	11.9	墨西哥	蒙特雷	作为教育学专家参与 50 名教师组成的工会
2007	1.29	古巴	哈瓦那，古巴电视台	两个小时的电视访谈
	2.13—14	墨西哥	蒂华纳，第二十六届拉丁美洲社会学协会大会	主题演讲
	4.25—27	墨西哥	瓦哈卡，第十一次教育研究区域会议	主题演讲
	4.28	墨西哥	塔瓦斯科州和塔瓦斯科州华雷斯自治大学	主题演讲
	5.14	瑞典	文化研究中心；布罗斯大学	文化研究于批判教育学；当代社会中的批判教育学
	5.15	瑞典	哥德堡大学	当代社会中的批判教育学
	7.21	墨西哥	蒂华纳大学，国际研讨会	主题发言
	10.7	希腊	沃洛斯，塞萨利亚大学特殊教育学院，第一届民主、教育与文化国际会议	批判教育学与民主危机
	11.20	芬兰	坦佩雷，坦佩雷大学保罗·弗莱雷研究中心	开幕式演讲
	11.22	芬兰	瓦萨，芬兰教育研究协会年会	帝国时代的批判教育学
	12.3—7	墨西哥	墨西哥城，墨西哥国立自治大学	从批判教育学到解放的批判教育学

续表

年份	日期	国家	地点/机构	讲学或演讲主题
2008	3.14	泰国	曼谷，泰国商会大学，社会动态中的语言会议	主题演讲
	3.29	奥地利	维也纳	自我教育的原理和方法论
	4.24—26	加拿大	多伦多，约克大学，第一届国际唯物史观会议	今日批判教育学：我们现在身处何处？
	5.21	哥伦比亚	麦德林，安蒂奥基亚教师工会	拉丁美洲背景下的批判教育学
	5.22	哥伦比亚	麦德林，教师和教师管理新道路：批判教育学和教育的阻力研讨会	顺从时代的批判教育学
	5.23	哥伦比亚	麦德林，教师和教师管理新道路：批判教育学和教育的阻力研讨会	批判教育学及其可能性
	5.23	哥伦比亚	麦德林，安蒂奥基亚大学	批判教育学讨论
	6.28	葡萄牙	米尼奥大学	解放的政治
	8.7	巴西	桑塔纳费拉大学	全球化时代下的多元文化主义
	8.9—12	巴西	萨尔瓦多	革命的多元文化主义和批判教育学
	8.17	巴西	尤伯兰迪亚联邦大学，国家和教育政治研讨会	帝国主义时代下的批判教育学
	8.19	巴西	尤伯兰迪亚联邦大学	主题演讲
	9	希腊	塞萨利	批判教育学的政治
	9.19—20	中国	长春，教师教育国际会议	主题演讲
	9.26	加拿大	滑铁卢，滑铁卢大学艺术学院，2008年度学术演讲系列	为社会转型的教育：为什么教授需要成为社会正义的积极分子
	10.2	委内瑞拉	加拉加斯，米兰达国际中心	批判教育学与新理论视角
	10.2	委内瑞拉	加拉加斯，米兰达国际中心	批判教育学和新理论视角
	11.27—29	希腊	雅典，潘泰昂大学	帝国时代下的文化差异和革命实践问题

续表

年份	日期	国家	地点/机构	讲学或演讲主题
2009	1.20	新西兰	瓦卡坦，新西兰教育研究协会	主题演讲
	1.28–30	墨西哥	阿瓜斯卡连特斯自治大学和国立师范大学，批判教育学和批判民族志研讨会	主题演讲
	2.28	墨西哥	蒂华纳大学	主题演讲
	4.20	加拿大	三角洲温哥华机场酒店，多元文化教育国际会议	重新思考社会和种族正义：跨越资本主义鸿沟
	5.2	土耳其	康纳卡莱大学	新自由主义时代下的批判教育学：冲突与挑战
	5.6	土耳其	伊斯坦布尔，博加齐奇大学	批判教育学
	5.8	土耳其	安卡拉，教师工会	新自由主义危机下的批判教育学
	6.21—24	克罗地亚	扎达尔，第三届国际批判研究会议	主题演讲
	7.11—13	墨西哥	墨西加利	回到马克思
	8.5 & 8.9	秘鲁	利马	与教育工作者非正式讨论
	8.6	秘鲁	利马，批判教育学国际研讨会	主题演讲
	8.8	秘鲁	利马，国立圣马科斯大学	主题演讲
	8.29	墨西哥	图卢卡国际大学	批判教育学和资本主义危机
	9.1	阿根廷	布宜诺斯艾利斯，第二十七届拉丁美洲社会学协会国际会议	作为一种社会运动的批判教育学
	9.2	阿根廷	布宜诺斯艾利斯，第二十七届拉丁美洲社会学协会国际会议	批判知识的生产
	9.4	阿根廷	布宜诺斯艾利斯，面对200名工人、艺术家、诗人和学生演讲	批判教育学与抵制后资本主义未来的阶级斗争
	9.5	阿根廷	布宜诺斯艾利斯，神学与社会研究方法研讨会	危机时代下的批判教育学

续表

年份	日期	国家	地点/机构	讲学或演讲主题
2010	3.9	墨西哥	瓜达拉哈拉，回到马克思会议	主题演讲
	3	墨西哥	帕丘卡	寻找正规教育研究的经验
	3.13	墨西哥	第六个教育文化日	主题演讲
	4.8	西班牙	马拉加，第三届艺术与视觉教育国际会议	主题演讲
	5.11	阿根廷	布宜诺斯艾利斯，萨尔瓦多大学	主题演讲
	5.11—14	丹麦	第六届国际人权教育论坛（视频会议，预先录制）	为了社会变革的人权教育
	5.12	阿根廷	波萨达斯，国立米西奥内斯大学	主题演讲
	5.13	阿根廷	布宜诺斯艾利斯	接受大学教师联合会的奖励
	5.14	阿根廷	萨莫拉洛玛斯大学和布宜诺斯艾利斯大学	主题演讲
	5.19—21	墨西哥	奇瓦瓦，批判教育学研讨会	主题演讲
	5.22	墨西哥	奇瓦瓦	批判教育学的基础
	7	墨西哥	米考坎，第十八届全国教育工作者联合会议	主题演讲
	7.12—13	墨西哥	塔巴斯科	主题演讲
	10.1	墨西哥	帕丘卡，第七届全国教育研究会议	主题演讲
	11	西班牙	萨弟瓦，继续教育中心	进行为期5天的研讨会
	11	西班牙	瓦伦西亚	主题演讲
	11.24	苏格兰	格拉斯哥大学	为了后资本主义未来的革命的批判教育学
	12.9—12	墨西哥	米考坎，回到马克思	主题演讲

续表

年份	日期	国家	地点/机构	讲学或演讲主题
2011	4.14—17	瑞典	斯德哥尔摩，南塔大学，跨文化教育与批判教育学国际会议	主题演讲
	5.4—6	委内瑞拉	马克思主义与非殖民化研讨会	主题演讲
	7.23	墨西哥	恩塞纳达	介绍与讨论
	7.24—30	墨西哥	恩塞纳达，麦克拉伦批判教育研究所	主题演讲
2012	5.7—14	墨西哥	麦克拉伦批判教育研究所	讲授为期一周的研讨会
	5.23	墨西哥	米考坎，教育研究工会中心	公开演讲
	5.25	墨西哥	贾利斯科	公开演讲
	5.26	墨西哥	米考坎，国立师范大学，从神学到改革实践的教育论坛	公开演讲
	5.27	墨西哥	全国反塔利班抵抗运动会议	参与其中
	8.30	中国	长春，批判教育学国际会议	介绍批判教育学（第一部分）
	8.31	中国	长春，批判教育学国际会议	介绍批判教育学（第二部分）
	10.3—5	墨西哥	圣路易斯波托西	主题演讲
	11.26	新西兰	怀卡托大学，保罗·弗莱雷：全球遗产大学	占据批判教育学：复兴弗莱雷的遗产
	11.28	新西兰	奥克兰理工大学	参与研讨会

续表

年份	日期	国家	地点/机构	讲学或演讲主题
2013	5.3—5	墨西哥	墨西哥城,回到马克思研讨会	主题演讲
	5.15—19	土耳其	安卡拉,批判教育国际会议	通过批判教育学实现和平
	7.7—21	墨西哥	恩塞纳达	麦克拉伦研究所小型课程
	10.9—11	塞尔维亚	贝尔格莱德,民族博物馆	创造民主未来的网络
	11.20—22	墨西哥	帕丘卡,伊达尔戈州自治大学	批判教育学与民主的创造
	12.7	墨西哥	巴亚尔塔港	从批判教育学看作为一种片面的政治决策的大学评价
	12.19—22	墨西哥	莫雷利亚	麦克拉伦研究所小型课程
2014	1.16	墨西哥	蒂华纳大学	主题演讲
	3.14	墨西哥	瓜达拉哈拉,瓜达拉哈拉大学	重新思考21世纪的马克思
	3.20—22	印度	南亚大学,教育转型与转型的教育:教育危机的可能性和替代方案国际会议	恐怖时代的批判教育学与阶级斗争
	3.24	印度	尼赫鲁大学,新自由主义的资本主义对教育的战争与新出现的抵抗形式	批判教育学与国家安全
	4.15	匈牙利	欧洲教师教育协会会议:教师教育中的社会正义与多样性	主题演讲
	5.26—6.24	中国	东北师范大学	讲授硕士研究生课程
	6.12	中国	北华大学	批判教育学与资本主义危机
	6.17	中国	长春师范大学	批判教育学与资本主义危机
	6.26	中国	浙江师范大学	新自由主义的资本主义时代下的批判教育学;批判教育学与去殖民化

续表

年份	日期	国家	地点/机构	讲学或演讲主题
2014	6.30	中国	浙江大学	批判教育学与资本主义危机
	7.20—8.2	墨西哥	恩塞纳达	麦克拉伦研究所小型课程
	7.27	墨西哥	恩塞纳达	教育的总体质量和社会质量：克服危机的路线
	8.18	墨西哥	瓦哈卡市，瓦哈卡自治大学	新自由主义全球化时代的教育和阶级斗争；革命的批判教育学的今天：从玻利瓦尔革命开始的一些思考
	8.19	墨西哥	瓦哈卡市	革命的批判教育学和教师培训
	9.23—27	墨西哥	墨西哥城	主题演讲
	11.6—8	德国	奥尔登堡大学，国际和跨学科会议	进入黑暗：为了社会主义社会的革命的批判教育学
	11.23—28	墨西哥	恰帕斯，恰帕斯自治大学	主题演讲
2015	3.22	美国	查普曼大学	为儿童、学校、家庭和社区而崛起
	5.7	美国	俄勒冈州波特兰，波特兰州立大学和美国大学教授协会	教会人们改变世界
	5.28—30	美国	性别与教育：批判的主题，政策和实践国际会议	以劳动为标志：性别和跨国资本主义
	6.1—7.1	中国	东北师范大学	教授硕士研究生课程
	6.15—18	波兰	弗罗茨瓦夫，《校园生活》（波兰版）出版	重获教育：革命的批判教育学；改变世界意味着什么？批判教育的新旧视角
	7.23—25	加拿大	雷吉纳大学，夏季研讨会	耶稣同志：辩证法的恢复，人民的解放——走向革命的批判教育学
	7.27	加拿大	英属哥伦比亚，汤普森河大学	革命的批判教育学
	7.30	加拿大	英属哥伦比亚，汤普森河大学	革命的批判教育学

续表

年份	日期	国家	地点/机构	讲学或演讲主题
2015	10.10—11	中国	东北师范大学，第一届批判教育学国际研讨会：马克思、毛泽东、弗莱雷与批判教育学	批判教育学与国际马克思主义人本主义的方案
	10.31	阿根廷	布宜诺斯艾利斯	向工厂工人、教师和积极分子演讲
	11.2	阿根廷	奇莱西托	批判教育学：当代的紧张形势与挑战
	11.3	阿根廷	奇莱西托	当今世界的教育与为社会正义而斗争
	11.4	阿根廷	奇莱西托	与奇莱西托国立大学的学生和研究人员讨论
	11.6	阿根廷	布宜诺斯艾利斯	主题讲座
	12.2	美国	圣安娜	《反抗教育学》一书出版
2016	2.15	美国	洛杉矶，洛约拉马利蒙特大学	爱与暴动的伦理：为了社会正义而教育
	4.9—12	美国	华盛顿，美国教育研究协会会议	圆桌会议：非法者、边境和野蛮人：公民教育中的界限；超越感觉：保罗·弗莱雷《被压迫者教育学》中的黑格尔辩证法
	4.26	芬兰	赫尔辛基	与当地的成人教育工作者会面并交谈
	4.27	芬兰	赫尔辛基，赫尔辛基大学	介绍批判教育
	4.28	芬兰	赫尔辛基，赫尔辛基大学	主题演讲
	5.24—7.2	中国	长春，东北师范大学；四平，吉林师范大学	教授研究生课程；讲座
	6.15—22	中国	香港，香港教育大学	革命的批判教育学与社会正义的抗争；与教授交谈
	7.30—31	墨西哥	恩塞纳达，二十一世纪比较教育国际研讨会	主题演讲并参与小组讨论：危机中的教育

续表

年份	日期	国家	地点/机构	讲学或演讲主题
2016	8.10—13	英国	伦敦，米德尔塞克斯大学，第六届批判教育国际会议	1. 主题演讲：人民的批判神学——走向基督教共产主义 2.《反抗教育学》与《这个拳头名为我的心：彼得·麦克拉伦读本》两本书出版 3. 主持研讨会：女性学者将批判教育学理论化及其他
	11.3—5	加拿大	多伦多，多伦多大学，去殖民化会议	赔偿、和解与记忆的政治
2017	2.25	美国	南佐治亚大学，第五届批判媒体素养会议	超越被动抵抗：处在十字路口的批判教育学
	3.29—4.1	美国	安纳海姆，加州双语教育协会会议	主题演讲
	4.28	美国	圣安东尼奥市，美国教育研究协会会议	专题研讨会：转型的教育学中的课程路线：新自由主义时代的阻力
	4.28	美国	圣安东尼奥市，美国教育研究协会会议	专题研讨会：共产主义研究：批判教育学的理论化与实践
	4.28	美国	圣安东尼奥市，美国教育研究协会会议	专题研讨会：通过基于社区的研究和项目来改变关系：保罗·弗莱雷民主项目
	4.28	美国	圣安东尼奥市，美国教育研究协会会议	会议：社会、学校和教育的马克思式分析
	4.29	美国	圣安东尼奥市，美国教育研究协会会议	圆桌会议：想象教育：超越新自由主义资本主义的逻辑与学习
	5.1	美国	圣安东尼奥市，美国教育研究协会会议	圆桌会议：兴趣、欲望和身份：通过种族和种族主义的意识形态理解教育政策和实践
	5.1	美国	圣安东尼奥市，美国教育研究协会会议	专题研讨会：社会公正的标准：核心价值是否为批判教育学留出空间？

续表

年份	日期	国家	地点/机构	讲学或演讲主题
2018	4.14	美国	纽约，美国教育研究协会会议	后真理世界中的批判教育与哲学；参加激进的梦想和变革性的实践：庆祝保罗·弗莱雷的《被压迫者教育学》50周年活动
	4.15	美国	纽约，美国教育研究协会会议	数字化理性时代的学习：重塑对话
	5.20—6.20	中国	长春	面向东北师范大学的硕士和博士研究生进行10场批判教育学讲座
	6.15—16	中国	长春，第二届批判教育学国际会议：教育与儿童的美好生活	革命的批判教育学的挑战：替罪羊机制与社会主义的障碍
	12.5	美国	圣安娜，社区教育中心	美国的法西斯主义与巴西的情况有何相似之处？了解世界尤其是美国的法西斯主义的兴起
2019	3.2	美国	拉文大学	邀请演讲
	3.14—15	美国	伊利诺伊州埃文斯顿，神学院	主题演讲
	3.28	美国	查普曼大学，哈辛格系列讲座：走向无限，绝望时代的希望之路	由查普曼大学学生组织和参与，与麦克拉伦围炉对话
	4.6	加拿大	多伦多，美国教育研究协会会议	参与讨论：挑战假新闻时代特朗普的仇外的法西斯主义：展现集体战线；论文发表：马克思与解放神学：走向道德良知与解放的辩证方法
	4.7	加拿大	多伦多，美国教育研究协会会议	参与讨论：重新思考教育的马克思主义；可选择的教育与组织：作为阻力的教学
	4.8	加拿大	多伦多，美国教育研究协会会议	参与讨论：后真理时代的保罗·弗莱雷与批判教育学 受邀参加会议：开始、延续和沉思：关于课程和文化研究中批判性问题的对话
	5.21—6.22	中国	长春，东北师范大学	批判教育学系列讲座
	6.3	中国	成都，四川师范大学	保罗·弗莱雷与批判教育学

续表

年份	日期	国家	地点/机构	讲学或演讲主题
2019	7.8	美国（网络）	拉美教育国际会议	美国对批判教育学的抵制势力：对教育政治化的恐惧
	11.15—16	中国（网络）	广州，第三届国际批判教育学年会	批判教育学的未来
2020	6	智利（网络）	塞雷娜大学	邀请演讲：社会运动，疫情与教育
	6	土耳其（网络）	安卡拉大学 教育科学学院	3小时关于批判教育学的会议报告
	6	美国（网络）	德克萨斯州，贝勒大学	博士生课堂（基督教信仰与教育）上，2小时报告：用解放神学与社会正义对抗美国正在抬头的法西斯主义潮流
	7	秘鲁（网络）	批判教育学与比较教育大会，圣奥古斯汀国家大学，阿雷帕基	特邀报告嘉宾
	7	南美洲（网络）	南美教师工会大学（参与的有来自巴西，阿根廷，智利，哥伦比亚等国的教师）	参与报告，会议主题：教师工会在支持南美洲公立教育中的重要作用
	7.30	委内瑞拉（网络）	委内瑞拉政府资助，玻利维亚大学举办的国际教育会议	邀请演讲：站在历史关头的革命的批判教育学
	8	爱尔兰（网络）	都柏林学院的进修国际中心	受邀参与学生毕业典礼
	8	苏格兰（网络）	"反种族歧视教育者"博客	受邀对话嘉宾
	9	委内瑞拉（网络）	委内瑞拉国际研究中心：教育中的边缘者的声音	邀请演讲

续表

年份	日期	国家	地点/机构	讲学或演讲主题
2020	10	以色列（网络）	犹太信仰与社会研究院举办的2021社会愿景大学	邀请演讲，会议围绕菲利普·韦克斯勒的著作（社会愿景：犹太教仪式派成员的范式革新对世界的启示）展开讨论
	11	巴基斯坦（网络）	齐亚丁大学，卡拉奇	第一届关于多样化，包容，平等的多学科视角国际网络会议。报告题目：疫情之下的协同与挑战
2021	3.16	英国（网络）	高等教育研究协会	会议主题：蓄意欺骗：后数字时代关于欺骗的认识论以及高等教育的批判使命
	3	国际网络会议	冷战真相考察委员会	会议主题：教育一瞥，证词与行动演讲：在拉美军事独裁组织暗杀传播解放神学的天主教神父和修女这一历史事件中，美国政府对其在组织和策略上的支持。
	5	Youtube网络会议		保罗弗莱雷100年诞辰纪念大会（与会者包括保罗的遗孀尼塔弗莱雷）
	11	智利（网络）	拉美包容教育研究中心	麦克拉伦被授予荣誉博士学位的报告：一百年：主题，革新，现实与弗莱雷
	11	加拿大（网络）	英属哥伦比亚大学（批判教育研究机构）	参与博士研讨会
	11	秘鲁（网络）	科学与人文大学，利马	第五届社会与人文国际研讨会：永不过时的保罗弗莱雷：对事实与意义的反思
2022	3	巴西（网络）	半干旱地区联邦大学	报告题目：认知，技术和机构 研讨会主题：认知，影响和技术：面对文明的混乱

附录三　麦克拉伦学术作品列表（1979—2022）

1979 年（31 岁）

期刊论文 1 篇

Immigrant children in the schools, *Centerfold*, Vol. 4, No. 1, October/November 1979.

1980 年（32 岁）

学术著作 1 部

McLaren, P. *Cries from the Corridor*. London, UK: Methuen Publications, 1980.

参著篇章 1 篇

published in Replay: A Canadian College Reader. Toronto: Methuen, 1980.

期刊论文 1 篇

The corridor kids. Today Magazine, April, Vol. 12, 1980.

1981 年（33 岁）

期刊论文 1 篇

They called it Metro's worst school. Mudpie, Vol. 2, No. 2, 1981.

1982 年（34 岁）

期刊论文 1 篇

Bein' tough: Rituals of resistance in the culture of working-class schoolgirls. Canadian Woman Studies, 1, Fall 1982.

书评论文 2 篇

Core: Stories and Poems Celebrating the Lives of Ordinary People Who Call Toronto Their Home. Compiled by Ruth Johnson and edited by Enid Lee. Ontario Public School Teacher's Federation News (December 1982).

The Practical Rebel: An Essay Review of Jonathan Kozol's "On Being a Teacher." Orbit, Vol. 13, No. 3, October 1982. Reprinted in Ontario Public School Teachers' Federation

News (February 1983).

1983 年（35 岁）

书评论文 1 篇

The Police and the Blacks. A Review of Home Feeling: Struggle for Community (National Film Board Documentary). Mudpie Magazine, Vol. 4, No. 7, September 1983.

1984 年（36 岁）

期刊论文 2 篇

Schooling and the culture of pain. International Newsletter for Prison Alternatives, 2 (2/3), winter 1984 – 1985.

Natural justice for justice agencies. Canadian Dimension, Vol. 18, No. 4, 1984.

书评论文 1 篇

Rethinking ritual. Etc.: A Review of General Semantics, Vol. 41, No. 3, 1984.

1985 年（37 岁）

参著篇章 2 篇

From ritual to reasoning: A prolegomena towards linking ritology and schooling. In J. Kase – Polisini (ed.), Creativedrama in a developmental Context. Washington, DC: University Press of America, 1985.

The politics of student resistance. In R. Common (ed.), New forces in educational policymaking. Brock University Occasional Publications, 1985.

期刊论文 6 篇

Classroom symbols and the ritual dimensions of schooling. Anthropologica, 27 (1/2), 1985 Special issue – Victor Turner: A Canadian Tribute.

A Tribute to Victor Turner (1920 – 1983). Anthropologica, 27 (1/2), 1985. Special issue – Victor Turner: A Canadian Tribute.

The ritual dimensions of resistance: Clowning and symbolic inversion. Journal of Education, Vol. 167, No. 2, 1985.

The pursuit of excellence in education: A reaction. Insights: The John Dewey Society for the Study of Education and Culture, Vol. 21, No. 2, June 1985.

Radical and pragmatic politics of education: The possibility of rapprochement. Insights: The John Dewey Society for the Study of Education and Culture, Vol. 21, No. 1, May 1985.

In memoriam: Jim Montgomerie, 1930 – 1985. Ontario Public School Teacher's Federation News, June 1, 1985.

书评论文 1 篇

Contemporary ritual studies: A post – turnerian perspective. Review article, Beginnings in ritual studies by Ronald L. Grimes. Semiotic Inquiry, Vol. 5, No. 1, 1985.

1986 年（38 岁）

学术著作 1 部

McLaren, P. (1986). *Schooling as A Ritual Performance: Toward A Political Economy of Educational Symbols and Gestures* (1st ed.). New York, NY: Routledge.

期刊论文 12 篇

(with Henry A. Giroux). Reproducing reproduction: An essay review of keeping track by Jeanie Oakes. Metropolitan Education, 1, Spring 1986.

Interrogating the conceptual roots of invitational education. An essay review of inviting school success by William Watson Purkey and John Novak. Interchange, Vol. 17, No. 4, 1986.

Postmodernism and the death of politics: A Brazilian reprieve. An essay review of the politics of education by Paulo Freire. Educational Theory, Vol. 36, No. 4, 1986.

An essay review of education under siege by Stanley Aronowitz and Henry Giroux. Educational Studies, Vol. 71, No. 2, 1986.

(with Henry A. Giroux). Teacher education as cultural politics: Towards a counterpublic sphere. New Education (Australia), Vol. 8, No. 1, 1986 (lead article).

Making Catholics: The ritual production of conformity in a Catholic junior high school. Journal of Education, Vol. 168, No. 2, 1986.

(with Henry A. Giroux). Teacher education and the politics of engagement: The case for democratic schooling. Harvard Educational Review, Vol. 56, No. 3, 1986 (lead article).

Pirandello on education: An interview with Richard Courtney. In Teacher Education (University of Toronto Faculty of Education), 28, April 1986.

(with Henry A. Giroux). Resurrecting the spirit of John Dewey and the challenge of critical pedagogy. Insights: The John Dewey Society for the Study of Education and Culture, Vol. 22, No. 22, 1986.

(with Henry A. Giroux). Rejoiner to Rodman Web and Robert Sherman. Insights: The John Dewey Society for the Study of Education and Culture, Vol. 22, No. 22, 1986.

(with Henry A. Giroux). Rejoiner in which Professors Giroux and McLaren Reply to Mr. Lunn's Concern About Languages. Ontario Public School Teachers' Federation News, February 1, 1986.

Is there a reviewer in the house? A Reply to Terry Barker. Ontario Public School Teachers' Federation News, June 1, 1986.

1987年（39岁）

参著篇章2篇

(with Henry A. Giroux). Teacher education and the politics of engagement: The case for democratic schooling. In M. Okazawa – Rey, J. Anderson, and R. Traver (eds.), Teaching, teachers, and teacher education. Cambridge, MA: Harvard Educational Review, 1987.

(with Henry A. Giroux). Teacher education as a counterpublic sphere: Notes toward a redefinition. In T. Popkewitz (ed.), Critical studies in teacher education: Its folklore, theory, and practice. Philadelphia: Falmer Press, 1987.

期刊论文10篇

Radical pedagogy and the dream of emancipation. Social Education, Vol. 51, No. 2, February, 1987.

The anthropological roots of pedagogy: The teacher as liminal servant. Anthropology and Humanism Quarterly, Vol. 12, No. 304, 1987.

(with Henry A. Giroux). Teacher education as a counterpublic sphere: Radical pedagogy as a form of cultural politics. Philosophy and Social Criticism, Vol. 12, No. 1, Spring 1987.

Ideology, science and the politics of Marxian orthodoxy: A response to Michael Dale. Educational Theory, Vol. 37, No. 3, 1987.

Schooling for salvation: Christian fundamentalism'sideological weapons of death. Journal of Education, Vol. 169, No. 2, 1987.

Education as counter – discourse. Review of Education, Vol. 3, No. 1, 1987.

(with Henry A. Giroux). Review of the management of ignorance by Fred Inglis. Canadian Journal of Sociology, Vol. 12, No. 3, 1987.

The writer as social agent. University of Toronto Review, No. 11, 1987, Reprinted in Que Ondee Sola, Vol. 20, No. 12, June 1987.

Peter McLaren and Brian Powers debate theory in education. Letters Section, Socialist Review, 17, May – August 1987.

Response to Salvatore D'Urso. Educational Studies, Vol. 18, No. 1, 1987.

书评论文 1 篇

Review of Culture wars by Ira Shor. Educational Policy, Vol. 1, No. 4, 1987.

外文（除英文外）出版物 1 篇

Paulo Freire e o Postmoderno. Educaçao & Realidade, Vol. 12, No. 1, 1987. (Portuguese)

1988 年（40 岁）

学术著作 1 部

Giroux, H. A. & McLaren, P. (1988). *Sociedad, cultura y escuela.* Madrid and Buenos Aires: Mino y Davila Editors (originally published by Universidad Nacional Autónoma de México).

参著篇章 2 篇

(with Henry A. Giroux). Reproducing reproduction: The politics of tracking. In H. A. Giroux (ed.), Teachers as intellectuals. South Hadley, MA: Bergin and Garvey Publishers, 1988. Previously published in Metropolitan Review.

(with Henry A. Giroux). Teacher education and the politics of democratic reform. In H. A. Giroux (ed.), Teachers as intellectuals. South Hadley, MA: Bergin and Garvey Publishers, 1988. Previously published in New Education and Philosophy and Social Criticism.

期刊论文 6 篇

Culture or Canon? Critical Pedagogy and the Politics of Literacy. Harvard Educational Review, Vol. 58, No. 2, 1988.

(with Richard Smith). Televangelism as pedagogy and cultural politics. Curriculum and Teaching, Vol. 3, No. 1/2, 1988.

The liminal servant and the ritual roots of critical pedagogy. Language Arts, Vo. 65, No. 2, February 1988.

No light but rather darkness visible: Language and the politics of criticism. Curriculum

Inquiry, Vol. 18, No. 3, 1988.

On ideology and education: Critical pedagogy and the politics of education. Social Text, 19/20, Fall 1988.

Language, social structure, and the production of subjectivity. Critical Pedagogy Networker, Vol. 1, No. 2/3, 1988.

书评论文 2 篇

Review of Paul Atkinson'sLanguage, structure and reproduction. Language in Society, Vol. 17, 1988.

Review of Theology and Praxis: Epistemological Foundations by Clodovis Boff. Small Press, Vol. 5, No. 4, April 1988.

著作前言 1 篇

Foreword. Critical theory and the meaning of hope: Henry Giroux's pedagogy of the concrete. In Henry A. Giroux, Teachers as intellectuals South Hadley, MA: Bergin and Garvey Publishers, 1988.

1989 年（41 岁）

学术著作 1 部

McLaren, P. (1989). *Life in Schools. An Introduction to Critical Pedagogy in the Foundations of Education* (1st ed.). New York, NY: Longman (Pearson PLC).

主编书籍 1 部

Giroux, H. A., & McLaren, P. (Eds.). (1989). *Critical Pedagogy, the State, and Cultural Struggle*. Albany, NY: SUNY Press.

参著篇章 3 篇

(with Richard Smith). Televangelism as pedagogy and popular culture. In Henry A. Giroux and Roger Simon (eds.), Popular culture and critical pedagogy. South Hadley: Bergin and Garvey, 1989.

(with Henry A. Giroux). Schooling, cultural politics, and the struggle for democracy: Introduction. In H. A. Giroux and P. McLaren (eds.), Critical pedagogy, the state, and cultural struggle. New York: SUNY Press, 1989.

On ideology and education: Critical pedagogy and the cultural politics of resistance. In Henry A. Giroux and Peter McLaren (eds.), Critical pedagogy, the state, and cultural struggle. New York: SUNY Press, 1989.

期刊论文 4 篇

Schooling the postmodern body: Critical pedagogy and the politics of enfleshment. Journal of Education, Vol. 170, No. 3, 1988. (Published in 1989)

(with Rhonda Hammer). Critical pedagogy and the postmodern challenge: Towards a critical postmodernist pedagogy of liberation. Educational Foundations, Vol. 3, No. 3, 1989.

(with Pam Smith). Review of Ivor Goodson's School subjects and curriculum change. Educational Studies, Vol. 20, No. 2, 1989.

Broken dreams, false promises, and the decline of public schooling. Journal of Education, Vol. 170, No. 1, January 1989 (lead article).

书评论文 1 篇

Review of NancyLesko's Symbolizing society. Anthropology and Education Quarterly, Vol. 20, 1989.

1990 年（42 岁）

参著篇章 1 篇

The blue – eyed mistress of the keys. In Richard Davies and Glen Kirkland (eds.), Relating (2nd ed.). Toronto: Gage, 1990.

期刊论文 5 篇

(withMichael Dantley). Leadership and a critical pedagogy of race: Cornel West, Stuart Hall and the prophetic tradition. Journal of Negro Education, Vol. 59, No. 1, 1990.

Radical pedagogy: Constructing an arch of social dreaming and a doorway to hope. Social Environment and Adult Learning, Center for Adult Learning Research, Montana State University, May, 1990.

Critical social theory and its implications in educational thought: A prospectus for the nineties. Insights: The John Dewey Society for the Study of Education and Culture (August 1990).

The arch of social dreaming: Teaching radical pedagogy under the sign of postmodernity. Social Environment and Adult Learning. Center for Adult Learning Research. Montana State University, May 1990.

Commentary: An academic chain – letter on postmodernism and education. Educational Foundations, Vol. 4, No. 3, 1990.

书评论文 1 篇

Review of Freire in the classroom by Ira Shor. Journal of Urban and Cultural Studies,

Vol. 1, No. 1, 1990.

1991年（43岁）

参著篇章6篇

Culture or canon? Critical pedagogy and the politics of literacy. Previously published in Harvard Educational Review. In Masahiko Minami and Bruce P. Kennedy (eds.), Language: Issues in literacy and bilingual/multicultural education. Cambridge, Mass: Harvard Educational Review, 1991. Reprint.

(with Henry A. Giroux). Radical pedagogy as cultural politics: Beyond the discourse of critique and anti-utopianism. In D. Morton and M. Zavarzadeh (eds.), Theory/Pedagogy/Politics. Chicago: University of Illinois Press, 1991.

Decentering culture: Postmodernism, resistance, and critical pedagogy. In N. Wyner (ed.), Current perspectives on school culture. Brookline Books, Massachusetts, 1991.

(with Henry A. Giroux). Language, schooling, and subjectivity: Beyond a pedagogy of reproduction and resistance. In Kathryn Borman, Piyush Swami and Lonnie P. Wagstaff (eds.), Contemporary issues in U. S. education. New Jersey: Ablex Publishing Corporation, 1991.

Schooling the postmodern body: Critical pedagogy and the politics of enfleshment. In Henry A. Giroux (ed.), Postmodernism, feminism and cultural politics. Albany, New York: SUNY Press, 1991.

Field relations and the discourse of the other. In Stebbins and Shaffir (eds.), Experiencing fieldwork. Newbury Park, CA: SAGE, 1991.

期刊论文6篇

Critical pedagogy: Constructing an arch of social dreaming and a doorway to hope. Boston University Journal of Education, Vol. 173, No. 1, 1991 (leadarticle).

(with Henry A. Giroux). Leon Golub's radical pessimism: Towards a pedagogy of representation. Exposure, Vol. 28, No. (1/2), 1991.

(with Rhonda Hammer). Rethinking the dialectic. Educational Theory, Vol. 41, No. 1, 1991.

Postmodernism, postcolonialism, and pedagogy: Introduction. Education and Society, (Australia), Vol. 9, No. 1, 1991.

Postcolonial pedagogy: Postcolonial desire and decolonized community. Education and Society, (Australia), Vol. 9, No. 2, 1991.

The emptiness of nothingness: Response to C. A. Bowers. Curriculum Inquiry, Vol. 21, No. 4, 1991.

外文（除英文外）出版物 2 篇

La Teoría de la Sociología Crítica y sus Implicaciones en el Pensamiento Educativo Educere (Mexico), 1991, Vol. 8, No. 3, (Spanish)

Rytuaine wymiary oporu – blaznowanie i symboliczna inwersja, Nieobecne Dyskursy, 1, 1991 Torun, Poland, 66 – 79. (Polish)

1992 年（44 岁）

学术著作 1 篇

McLaren, P. (1992). *Pedagogia Crítica y Postmodernidad*. Xalapa City, Mexico: Universidad Pedagogica Veracruzana y Secretaría de Educación.

参著篇章 4 篇

(with Henry A. Giroux). Leon Golub's radical pessimism: Towards a pedagogy of representation. In Henry A. Giroux, Border crossings. New York: Routledge, 1992. Reprint.

Critical pedagogy, postcolonial politics, and redemptive remembrance. Learner factors/teacher factors: issues in literacy research and instruction. Fortieth Yearbook: National Reading Conference, Chicago, IL, 1992. (invited address)

Education as a political issue. What's missing in the public conversation about education? In Joe Kincheloe and Shirley R. Steinberg (eds.), Thirteen questions: reforming education's conversation. New York and Berlin, Peter Lang Publishers, 1992.

Critical literacy and the postmodern turn: Cautions from the margins. In R. Beach, J. Green, M. Kamil, and T. Shanahan (eds.), Multidisciplinary perspectives on literacy research. Urbana, IL: National Conference on Research in English, 1992.

期刊论文 10 篇

Critical literacy and postcolonial praxis: A Freirian perspective. College Literature Double issue, 19: 3 (October 1992) /20: 1 (February 1993), pp. 7 – 27 (lead article). This issue was sole runnerup in Council of Editors of Learned Journals Best Special Issue Competition for 1993.

(with Henry Giroux) Critical pedagogy and rural education: A challenge from Poland. Peabody Journal of Education, Vol. 67, No. 4, (Summer 1990; published in 1992).

Eminent Scholar Conversation #30. Martha L. King Language and Literacy Center, The

Ohio State University, Columbus, Ohio, 1992. Published in Educational Foundations, Vol. 6, No. 4, 1992.

(with Henry Giroux) Writing from the margins: Geographies of identity, pedagogy, and power. Journal of Education, Vol. 174, No. 1, 1992 (lead article).

(with Rhonda Hammer). Media knowledges, warrior citizenry, and postmodern literacies. Journal of Urban and Cultural Studies, Vol. 2, No. 2, 1992. Also published in Journal of Curriculum Theorizing, Vol. 10, No. 2, 1992.

(with Rhonda Hammer). Spectacularizing subjectivity: Media knowledges and the new world order. Polygraph, Vol. 5, 1992.

Critical pedagogy, multiculturalism, and the politics of risk and resistance: A reponse to Kelly and Portelli. Journal of Education, Vol. 173, No. 3, 1991. (Published in 1992.)

Collisions with otherness. International Journal of Qualitative Studies in Education, Vol. 5, No. 1, 1992.

(with Shirley Steinberg). Critical multiculturalism and democratic schooling: An interview with Peter McLarenand Joe Kincheloe. International Journal of Educational Reform, Vol. 1, No. 4, 1992.

The Gulf War: News, entertainment or structuring of colonialist modes of subjectivity? Insights: The John Dewey Society for the Study of Education and Culture (Dec. 1992), Vol. 27, No. 2.

著作前言5篇

Preface. In James Sears (ed.), Sexuality and the curriculum. New York: Teachers College Press, 1992.

Preface (with Henry Giroux). In Annette Street, Inside Nursing. New York: SUNY Press, 1992.

(with Henry Giroux) Introduction. In Jesse Goodman, Elementary schooling for critical democracy. New York: SUNY Press, 1992.

(with Henry Giroux) Introduction. In James Schwoch, Mimi White, and Susan Reilly (eds.), Media knowledge. Albany, NY: State University of New York Press, 1992.

(with Henry Giroux) Introduction. In Bill Stanley, Curriculum for Utopia. New York: SUNY Press, 1992.

外文（除英文外）出版物7篇

Schooling as a Ritual Performance: Portuguese translation. Rituais Na Escoal: Em

Direção a una economia política de símbolos e gestos na educação. Petropolis: Vozes, 1992.

(with Rhonda Hammer) Le Paradoxe de L'Image: Connaissance Médiatique et Déclin de la Qualité de la Vie. Anthropologie et Sociétés, Vol. 16, No. 1, 1992 (lead article).

¿Nuevos Rumbos Para la Educación Critica? McLaren y la Pedagogia Posmoderna. Enrique Recio Avil y Vicente Carvera Alvarez, Colaboradores de Psiyque, entrevistan a Peter McLaren. Psiyque, Vol. 1, No. 2, 1992–1995.

Ritual e Ideología (Afterword to the Brazilian Edition of Schooling as a Ritual Performance). Brazil: Editora Vozes Ltda, 1992.

La Pedagogía Crítica, el multiculturalismo y La Política del Riesgo y de la Resistencia. Investigación Educativa, Universidad lberoamericana, Plantel Golfo – Centro, Puebla – Aflixco, Mexico, 1992.

Peter McLaren: La educación en los bordes del pensamiento moderno. Propuesta Educativa, Año 4, No. 7, Octubre de 1992. (Spanish)

Jezyk, struktura spoleczna i tworzenie podmiotowosci. Nieobecne Dyskursy, 2, Torun, Poland, 1992. (Polish)

1993年（45岁）

学术著作3部

McLaren, P. (1993). *Life in Schools. An Introduction to Critical Pedagogy in the Foundations of Education* (2nd ed.). New York, NY: Longman (Pearson PLC).

McLaren, P. (1993). *Schooling as A Ritual Performance: Toward A Political Economy of Educational Symbols and Gestures* (2nd ed.). London and New York: Routledge.

McLaren, P. (1993). *Hacia una Pedagogía Crítica de la Formación de la Identidad Posmoderna*. Paraná Entre Ríos, Argentina: Facultad de Ciencias de la Educación Universidad Nacional de Entre Ríos.

主编书籍2部

Lankshear, C., & McLaren, P. (Eds.) (1993). *Critical Literacy: Politics, Praxis, and the postmodern.* Albany, NY: SUNY Press.

Leonard, P., & McLaren, P. (Eds.) (1993). *Paulo Freire: A Critical Encounter.* New York, NY: Routledge.

参著篇章6篇

(with Colin Lankshear). Introduction. In Peter McLaren and Colin Lankshear (eds.),

Politics of liberation: Paths from Freire. London and New York: Routledge, 1993.

(with Colin Lankshear). Critical Literacy and the Postmodern Turn. In Colin Lankshear and Peter McLaren (eds.), Critical literacy: Politics, praxis, and the postmodern. Albany, NY: SUNY Press. 1993.

(with Tomaz Tadeu da Silva). Decentering pedagogy: Critical literacy, resistance, and the politics of memory. In Peter McLaren and P. Leonard (eds.), Paulo Freire: A critical encounter. London: Routledge, 1993.

(with Tomaz Tadeu da Silva). Knowledge under siege: The Brasilian debate. In P. McLaren and P. Leonard (eds.), Paulo Freire: A critical encounter. London: Routledge, 1993.

Border disputes: Multicultural narrative, critical pedagogy, and identity formation in postmodern America. In J. McLaughlin and William G. Tierney (eds.), Naming silenced lives. Routledge: New York, 1993.

Broken dreams, false promises, and the decline of public schooling. In William Dan Perdue (ed.), Systemic crisis: Problems in society, politics, and world order. New York: Harcourt Brace Javanovich, 1993. (Previously published in Journal of Education, January 1989.)

期刊论文 5 篇

Moral panic, schooling, and gay identity: Critical pedagogy and the politics of resistance. The High School Journal, Oct/Nov 1993, Dec/Jan 1994, White terror. Strategies, 7, 1993.

Essay Review: School Subjects and Curriculum Change by Ivor Goodson, International Journal of Qualitative Studies in Education, Vol. 6, No. 2, 1993.

Multiculturalism and the postmodern critique: Towards a pedagogy of resistance and transformation. Cultural Studies, Vol. 7, No. 1, January 1993.

Critical literacy and postcolonial praxis: A Freirian perspective. College Literature Double issue, 19: 3 (October 1992) /20: 1 (February 1993), (lead article). This issue was sole runnerup in Council of Editors of Learned Journals Best Special Issue Competition for 1993.

Decentering Violence, a U. S. Perspective, Orbit, March, Vol. 24, No. 1, 1993.

著作前言 1 篇

Foreword. In Ivor Goodson, School subjects and curriculum change Curriculum differentiation and cultural politics in the age of postmodernism: Revised edition, Falmer

Press, 1993.

访谈学者论文 3 篇

Interview with Alicia de Alba of Mexico. International Journal of Educational Reform, Vol. 2, No. 4, 1993.

Interview with Marcia Moraes of Brasil. International Journal of Educational Reform, Vol. 2, No. 3, 1993.

Interview with Adriana Puiggrós of Argentina. International Journal of Educational Reform, Vol. 2, No. 2, 1993.

外文（除英文外）出版物 7 篇

(with Joe Kincheloe) El Multiculturalismo Crítico y La Escuela Democrática: Una Entrevista con Peter McLaren y Joe Kincheloe. Revista Iniciativa: Educación Cultura y Sociedad, No. 2, May 1993.

(with Kelly Estrada) Un dialogo sobre multiculturalismo y cultura democraticia. Collection/Pedagogica/Universitaria. Enero – diciembre 1993. Universidad Veracruzana. (Reprint) (Spanish)

(with Henry A. Giroux) Teacher education and the politics of engagement. In Nathan Gover and Itai Zimran (eds.), Extraordinarily Re – experiencing the Ordinary. Jerusalem, Israel: David Yellin Teachers College, 1993. (Hebrew)

(with Henry A. Giroux) Introduction. In Nathan Gover and Itai Zimran (eds.), Extraordinarily Re – experiencing the Ordinary. Jerusalem, Israel: David Yellin, Teachers College, 1993. (Hebrew)

Las Colisiones con los otros: Teoría del "viajero," crítica post – colonial y la política como práctica etnográfica. La misión del etnógrafo comprometido. Perspectivas Docentes, No. 10, Enero – Abril, 1993. (Spanish)

Peter McLaren y La Pedagogia Critica. Interview with G. Angélica Valenzuela Ojeda. Diorama Educativo, Año 3, No. 5, Segunda época, 1993, Mexico. (Spanish)

(with Henry Giroux) Linguagem, escola e subjetividade: Elementos para um discurso pedagógico critico, Educaçao and Realidade, Vol. 18, No. 2, 1993. (Portuguese)

1994 年（46 岁）

学术著作 1 部

McLaren, P. (1994). *Pedagogía Crítica, Resistencia Cultural y la Producción Del deseo*. Buenos Aires, Argentina: Instituto para la Investigación Acción.

主编书籍 2 部

Giroux, H. A., & McLaren, P. (Eds.). (1994). *Between Borders: Pedagogy and the Politics of Cultural Studies*. New York, NY: Routledge.

McLaren, P. L., & Lanshear, C. (Eds.). (1994). *Politics of Liberation: Paths from Freire*. New York, NY: Routledge.

参著篇章 2 篇

(with Joe Kincheloe). Rethinking critical theory and qualitative research. In Norman K. Denzin and Yvonna S. Lincoln (eds.), Handbook of qualitative research. London and Thousand Oaks: Sage. 1st Edition, 1994; 2nd Edition, 2000; 3rd Edition, 2005.

Postmodernism and the death of politics: A Brazilian reprieve. In Peter McLaren and Colin Lankshear (eds.), Politics of liberation: Paths from Freire. London and New York: Routledge, 1994.

期刊论文 4 篇

Response to Marian Wright Edelman. Religious Education, Vol. 89, No. 4, 1994.

Critical pedagogy, political agency and the pragmatics of justice: The case of Lyotard. Educational Theory. Vol. 44, No. 3, summer 1994.

Moral panic, schooling, and gay identity: Critical pedagogy and the politics of resistance. The High School Journal, Oct/Nov 1993, Dec/Jan 1994.

Collisions with otherness: Multiculturalism, the politics of difference, and the ethnographer as nomad. New Coda to Schooling as a Ritual Performance. American Journal of Semiotics, Vol. 9, No. 2 - 3, 1994, (lead article).

书评论文 1 篇

Review of The Body, Schooling, and Culture by David Kirk. Australian Journal of Education, Vol. 38, No. 2, 1994.

著作前言 4 篇

(with Joe Kincheloe and Shirley Steinberg). In Donaldo Macedo, Literacies of power: What Americans are not allowed to know. Boulder, CO: Westview Press, 1994.

Preface. In Miguel Escobar (ed.), Paulo Freire on higher education: A dialogue with Paulo Freire. Alfredo Fernandez and Gilberto Guevara. Albany, New York: SUNY Press, 1994.

(with Henry Giroux) Introduction. In Moacir Gadotti, How to read Paulo Freire. SUNY

Press, 1994.

Foreword. In Kerry S. Walters (ed.), Rethinking reason: New perspectives in critical thinking. SUNY Press, 1994.

访谈学者论文 4 篇

Asian – American Feminism: A Dialogue with Lisa Chin. International Journal of Educational Reform, Vol. 3, No. 4, Oct. 1994.

Dialogue with Kris Gutierrez: Pedagogies of Dissent and Transformation: A Dialogue aboutPostmodernity, Social Context, and the Politics of Literacy. International Journal of Educational Reform, Vol. 3, No. 3, 1994.

Interview with Heinz Sünker of Germany, "Germany Today: History and Future" (or "Dilemmas, Dangers, and Hopes"). International Journal of Educational Reform, Vol. 3, No. 2, April 1994.

An exchange with Eugene Garcia. International Journal of Educational Reform, Vol. 3, No. 1, 1994.

外文（除英文外）出版物 3 篇

Life in Schools, 4th Edition, Spanish translation, La vida en las esuelas: Una introduccíon a la pedagogia crítica en los fundamentos de la educacíon. (Life in Schools, first edition). (Spanish) Mexico City: Siglo veintiuno editores, 1994.

Die Politik eines kritischen Multikulturalismus. Widersprüche, HEFT 51, August 1994. (German)

Edukacja jako system kulturowy. Nieobecne Dyskursy, 4, (pod redakcja Zbigniewa Kwiecinskiego) 1994. (Polish)

1995 年（47 岁）

学术著作 2 部

McLaren, P., Hammer, R., Sholle, D., & Reilly, S. (1995). *Rethinking Media Literacy: A Critical Pedagogy of Representation.* New York, NY: Peter Lang Publishing.

McLaren, P. (1995). *Critical Pedagogy and Predatory Culture: Oppositional Politics in A Postmodern Era.* New York, NY: Routledge.

主编书籍 4 部

McLaren, P. (Ed.). (1995). *Postmodernism, Post – Colonialism and Pedagogy.* Albert Park, Australia: James Nicholas Publishers.

Kanpol, B. & McLaren, P. (Eds.). (1995). *Critical Multiculturalism.* Westport, CT: Bergin and Garvey (Greenwood Publishing Group).

Sleeter, C. E., & McLaren, P. (Eds.). (1995). *Multicultural Education, Critical Pedagogy, and the Politics of Difference.* Albany, NY: SUNY Press.

McLaren, P. & Giarelli, J. M. (Eds.). (1995). *Critical Theory and Educational Research.* Albany, NY: SUNY Press.

参著篇章6篇

Critical pedagogy: Constructing an arch of social dreaming and a doorway to hope. In Canadian sociology of education. Toronto: Copp/Clark and Longman, Ltd., 1995. Reprint.

Critical Multiculturalism, Media Literacy, and the Politics of Representation. In Jean Frederickson (ed.), Reclaiming our voices: Bilingual education, critical pedagogy and praxis. Ontario, CA: California Association of Bilingual Education, 1995.

Moral panic, schooling, and gay identity: Critical pedagogy and the politics of resistance. In Gerald Unks (ed.), The gay teenager. New York: Routledge, 1995. Reprint. Published in Chinese, Location and Praxis of Emancipation: Perspective of Critical Pedagogy, Journal of Educational Research (Taiwan) 146, 2006.

(with Michael Peters). Critical pedagogy and the pragmatics of justice. In Michael Peters (ed.), Lyotard and education. Westport, CT: Bergin and Garvey Publishers, 1995. Reprint.

White terror and Oppositional Agency: Towards a Critical Multiculturalism. In David Theo Goldberg (ed.), Multiculturalism: A critical reader. London: Basil Blackwell, 1995. Reprint. (lead chapter)

White Terror and Oppositional Agency: Towards a Critical Multiculturalism. In Siebren Miedema, Gert Biesta, Ben Boog, Adri Amaling, Winn Wardecker, and Bas Levering (eds.), The politics of human science. Brussels: VUB University Press, 1995. Reprint.

期刊论文7篇

(with Jeff McSwan) Basil Bernstein's Sociology of Language: Comments on Alan R. Sadovnik's Knowledge and Pedagogy: The Sociology of Basil Bernstein (1995) and Paul Atkinson, Brian Davis and Sara Delamont's Discourse and Reproduction: Essays in Honor of Basil Bernstein (1995). Bilingual Research Journal, NABE, Fall, Vol. 21, No. 4, 1997.

(with Kris Gutierrez) Global politics and local antagonisms: Research and practice as dissent and possibility. Anuãrio de educacão 1995/ 1996. (Brasil).

Critical Pedagogy in the Age of Global Capitalism: Some Challenges for the Educational

Left. (The Claude A Eggerston Lecture.) The Australian Journal of Education, Vol. 39, No. 1, 1995, A version of this article appeared as Critical Pedagogy andthe Age of Global Capitalism: A Challenge for the Future, Pedagogia, Vol. 30, 1995 – 1996. (La Facultad de Education de la Universidad de Puerto Rico). (lead article)

The Educator as an Agent of History. Educational Theory (Afterwords section), Vol. 45, No. 2, 1995.

Predatory Culture and the Politics of the Popular. Cultural Studies Times. Routledge, New York, 1995.

Serial Killer Pedagogy. Taboo, Vol. 1, 1995, Reprint in Pedagogia em tempos de cultura predatoria. In Nize Maria Campos Pellanda and Luiz Ernesto Cabral Pellanda (orgs.) Psicanalise Hoje: Uma Revolucao do Olhar. Petropolis, Brasil: Editora Vozes, 1996.

Gangsta pedagogy and ghettocentricity: The hip – hop nation as counterpublic sphere. Suitcase, Vol. 1, No. 1, 2, 1995.

著作前言3篇

(with Henry Giroux) Preface. In Raymond Morrow and Carlos Torres, Social theory and education. New York: SUNY Press, 1995.

(with Henry Giroux) Introduction. In Stephen Haymes, Race, culture and the city: A pedagogy for black urban struggle. New York: SUNY Press, 1995.

Preface. In Moacir Gadotti, Pedagogy of praxis, SUNY Press, 1995.

访谈麦克拉伦论文2篇

An Interview with Peter McLaren. Comenius (The Netherlands), Vol. 15, 1995. (Interviewed by Gert Biesta and Siebren Miedema)

Revolution and Reality: An Interview with Peter McLaren. Education (University of Malta, Faculty of Education), Vol 5, No. 2. 1995. Interviewed by Carmel Borg, Peter Mayo and Ronald Sultana. Reprinted as book chapter in Curriculum: Toward New Identities. Edited by Bill Pinar.

访谈学者论文4篇

Pedagogy of praxis: A dialogue with Moacir Gadotti of Brasil. International Journal of Educational Reform, Vol. 4, No. 3, 1995.

A Dialogue with Concepcíon Valadez. International Journal of Educational Reform, Vol. 4, No. 3, 1995.

Radical Education in Brasil: A Dialogue with Movimento Boneco. International Journal of

Educational Reform, Vol. 4, No. 2, 1995.

Ecology and Reform: A Dialogue with Edgar Gonzalez. International Journal of Educational Reform, Vol. 4, No. 1, Jan, 1995.

外文（除英文外）出版物 5 篇

Schooling as a Ritual Performance: Spanish translation. La escuela como un performance ritual: Hacia una economía politica de los símbolos y gestos educativos. Mexico City: Siglo Veintiuno Editores, 1995.

El Escritor como educador: El educador como escritor, Communidad Educativa. No. 7, año 2, September – October, 1995. (Spanish).

(with Henry Giroux) Por una pedagogia Crítica da representação. In Tomaz Tadeu da Silva and Antonio Flavio Moreira, eds. Territórios Constestados. Petrópolis: Vozes, 1995. (Portuguese)

Estrutura da narrativa, Amnésia colonial e sujeitos decentrados: Rumo a una pedagogia crítica de formação de identidad pós – moderna, Educação. Ano XVIII, No 28 (1995). (Portuguese)

Peter McLaren: La educación en los bordes del pensamiento moderno. Communidad Educativa, No. 3, Año 2, Enero – Febrero, 1995.

1996年（48岁）

主编书籍 1 部

Giroux, H. A., Lankshear, C., McLaren, P., & Peters, M. (Eds.). (1996). *Counternarratives: Cultural Studies and Critical Pedagogies in Postmodern Spaces*. New York, NY: Routledge.

参著篇章 2 篇

(with Henry A. Giroux) Teacher education and the politics of engagement: The carefor democratic schooling, in Pepi Leistyna, Arlie Woodrum, Stephen A. Sherblom (eds.), Breaking free: The transformative power of critical pedagogy. Cambridge: Harvard Educational Review, 1996. Reprint.

Response to Chapter 18. In Joe Kincheloe, Shirley R. Steinberg, and Aaron Gresson III (eds.) Measured Lies: The Bell Curve Examined. New York: St. Martin's Press, 1996.

期刊论文 7 篇

La Lucha Continua: Freire, Boal, and the Challenge of History. Keynote address delivered at the 1996 Pedagogy of the Oppressed Conference, Omaha, Nebraska. In theme issue of Critical Pedagogy. Researcher: Northern Rocky Mountain Educational Research Association, Vol. 11, No. 2. December 1996.

(with Pat McDonough) Critical, postmodern studies of gay and lesbian lives in academia. Harvard Educational Review, Vol. 66, No. 2, (1996).

Freirean pedagogy and higher education: The challenge of postmodernism and the politics of race. Cultural Critique, No. 33, 1996.

Gangsta pedagogy and ghettocentricity: The hip - hop nation as counterpublic sphere. Socialist Review, Vol. 95, No. 2, 1996. (Expanded from Suitcase)

Serial Killer Pedagogy. Taboo, Vol. 1, 1995. Reprint in Pedagogia em tempos de cultura predatoria. In Nize Maria Campos Pellanda and Luiz Ernesto Cabral Pellanda (orgs.) Psicanalise Hoje: Uma Revolucao do Olhar. Petropolis, Brasil: Editora Vozes, 1996.

(with Patricia Dueñas) Dismantling Gabachismo in Contempory Capitalism. Razateca. November/December, 1996.

Las Maestras usan rituales para bendecir la buena conducta. El Financiero (Mexico City, Mexico), June 6, 1996. (Interview in Spanish)

著作前言1篇

Foreword. In Marcia Moraes, Bilingual education: A dialogue with the Bakhtin Circle. Albany, New York, State University of New York Press, 1996.

访谈学者论文5篇

Living the Border: An interview with Rudolfo Chávez Chávez. International Journal of Educational Reform, Vol. 5, No. 3, July 1996.

Interview with Herman Gárcia. International Journal of Educational Reform, Vol. 5, No. 3, July 1996.

La lucha continua en gringolandia: Interview with Carlos Tejeda, Juan Muñoz, Zeus Leonardo, Tara Yosso, Jill Pinkney - Pastrana, and Joaquin Ochoa. International Journal of Educational Reform, Vol. 5, No. 3, July 1996.

Interview with the Front Range Critical Theory Group. International Journal of Educational Reform, Vol. 5, No. 2, April 1996.

A New Metaphysics of Hope: An Interview with Barry Kanpol. International Journal of Educational Reform, Vol. 5, No. 1, January 1996.

学术百科全书词条 2 条

(with Zeus Leonardo) Paulo Freire. In Ellis Cashmore, (ed.), Dictionary of Race and Ethnic Relations, Fourth Edition. London and New York: Routledge, 1996.

(with Marc Pruyn) Indoctrination. In Philosophy of Education: An Encyclopedia. J. J. Chambliss (editor). New York: Garland Publishing, 1996.

外文（除英文外）出版物 4 篇

La postmodernidad y la muerte de la politica: Un indulto brasileño. In Alica da Alba (ed.), Postmodernidad y Educación. Mexico City: CESU, 1996, (Spanish)

Kritische erziehungswissenschaft in zeitalter der postmoderne—einige herausforderungen für die zukenft. In Werner Helsper, Heinz – Hermann Krüger and Hartmut Wenzel (eds.), Schule und Gesell Schaft in Umbruch. Deutsche Studien Verlag: Weinheim, 1996. (German)

Critical pedagogy and predatory culture. In Luiz E. Pellanda and Nize Pellanda (eds.), Psicanálise: A Revolução do Olhar, Petropolis: Vozes, 1996. (Portuguese)

Die Ausgepräte Gleichgültigkeit Gegenber dem Kummer und Leiden der jungen Generation. Neue Themen, (May) 1996. (German)

1997 年（49 岁）

学术著作 3 部

McLaren, P. (1997). *Life in Schools. An Introduction to Critical Pedagogy in the Foundations of Education* (3rd ed.). New York, NY: Longman (Pearson PLC).

McLaren, P. (1997). *Revolutionary Multiculturalism: Pedagogies of Dissent for the New Millennium.* Boulder, CO: Westview Press.

McLaren, P. (1997). *Multiculturalismo Critico.* São Paulo, Brasil: Cortez.

参著篇章 6 篇

(with Henry A. Giroux). Paulo Freire, postmodernism and the utopian imagination: A Blochian reading. In Jamie Owen Daniel and Tom Moylan (eds.), Not Yet: Reconsidering Ernst Bloch. London and New York: Verso Press, 1997.

(with Janet Morris). Mighty Morphon Power Rangers: The aesthetics of Phallo – Militaristic Justice. In Joe Kinchloe and Shirley Steinberg (eds.), Kinderculture. Boulder, CO: WestviewPress, 1997.

Freirean pedagogy: The challenge of postmodernism and the politics of race. In Paulo

Freire (ed.), Mentoring the mentor: A critical dialogue with Paulo Freire. New York: Peter Lang Publ., 1997.

The ethnographer as postmodern Flâneur: Critical reflexivity and post-hybridity as narrative engagement. In Yvonna Lincoln and William Tierney (eds.), Representation and the text: Reframing the narrative voice. Albany: State University of New York Press, 1997.

Critical Pedagogy and Predatory Culture. In R. Farnen, H. Sunker, D. Timmermann and I. U. Kolbe (eds.), Politics, sociology, and economics of education: Interdisciplinary philosophical and comparative perspectives, London: MacMillan Press, 1997. Reprint.

Multiculturalism and the Postmodern Critique: Towards a Pedagogy of Resistance and Transformation. In Phillip Brown, A. H. Halsey, Hugh Lauder, and Amy Stuart Wells (eds.), Education, Culture, Economy and Society. London: Oxford University Press 1997. Reprint.

期刊论文 8 篇

Review of Critical Ethnography in Educational Research: A Theoretical and Practical Guide by Phil Francis Carspecken. Teachers College Record, Vol. 99, No. 2, Winter 1997.

Paulo Freire's Legacy of Hope and Struggle. Theory, Culture and Society, Vol. 14, No. 4, November 1997.

Introduction ("Critical Pedagogy" Enquiry Space Editor) First Special Issue of Teaching Education. Vol. 9.1 1997. Expanded intro on website http://www.teaching education.com.

Revolutionary Praxis: Toward a Pedagogy of Resistance and Transformation. An essay review of The Social Construction of Urban Schooling: Situation the Crisis by Lou Miron. Educational Researcher. August/September, 1997.

(with Jeff McSwan) Basil Bernstein's Sociology of Language: Comments on Alan R. Sadovnik's Knowledge and Pedagogy: The Sociology of Basil Bernstein (1995) and Paul Atkinson, Brian Davis and Sara Delamont's Discourse and Reporduction: Essays in Honor of Basil Bernstein (1995). Bilingual Research Journal, NABE, Fall, Vol. 21, No. 4, 1997.

Decentering Whiteness. Multicultural Education, Vol. 5, No. 1, Fall, 1997. (lead article)

Paulo Freire Died May 2, 1997. International Journal of Educational Reform, Vol. 6, No. 3, July 1997.

Unthinking Whiteness, Rethinking Democracy: Or Farewell to the Blonde Beast. Educational Foundations, Vol. 11, No. 2, 1997. (lead article)

著作前言 3 篇

Forward. In Joe Kincheloe and Shirley Steinberg. Changing Multiculturalism. Buckingham and Philadephia: Open University Press, 1997.

(with Henry Giroux) Preface. In Adriana Hernandez, Pedagogy, democracy, and feminism. Albany, New York: State University of New York, 1997.

Preface. InTom Oldenski, Catholic education: Critical theory and practice in a liberation theology context. New York: Garland Publishers, 1997.

访谈学者论文 4 篇

Reclamando Historia, Reclamando Identidad: Education de Maestros y Maestras y la lucha para la liberaciaon. An Interview with Educational Activists Marta Baltodano and Gina Castillo. International Journal of Educational Reform. Vol 6, No. 3, July 1997.

(with Zeus Leonardo) Review of H. Bak, Multiculturalism and the Canon of American Culture; D. Thelen and F. Hoxie, Discovering America: Essays in Search for an Identity. In Journal of American Ethnic History, Vol. 16, No. 2, 1997.

AHistory of Tragedy; A Journey of Healing. (Interview with Michael Pavel) International Journal of Educational Reform, Vol. 6, No. 1, January 1997.

Academic Language and Chicana/o Activist Scholars: Balancing the Academy and the Communities One Hopes to Serve: An Interview with Dolores Delgado Bernal and Daniel Solorzano. International Journal of Educational Reform, Vol. 6, No. 2, /April 1997.

Dialogue with Puerto – Rican Scholar – Activist Lola Gordon – Mora. International Journal of Educational Reform, Vol. 6, No. 2, April 1997.

学术百科全书词条 1 条

(with Joe Kincheloe and Shirley Steinberg) Entries: Critical theory, cultural studies, difference. Dictionary of multicultural education. Oryx Press, 1997.

外文（除英文外）出版物 6 篇

Life in Schools, 4th Edition: Portuguese translation, A Vida nas escolas (Life in schools). Foreword by Leonardo Boff. Porto Alegre: Artes Medicas, 1997.

Pedagogia critica y cultura depredadora (Critical Pedagogy and Predatory Culture) (Spanish) Paidos. Barcelona, Buenos Aires, Mexico, 1997.

Entrevista a Peter McLaren. Despliegos/2 En Sociedad Y Cultura, Año 1 – 2 – Rosario, 1997.

El Legado deLucha y Esperanza de Paulo Freire. Aula Hoy, Año 3, No. 9, 1997.

Unthinking Whiteness, Rethinking Democracy: Critical Citizenry. In Chikashi Furukawa (ed.) Language Management for Multicultural Comunities: Individuals and Communites – – Living the Differences. Tokyo, Japan: The National Language Research Institute (1997). (Japanese)

Um Legado de Luta e de Esperanca. Pátio. Ano l No. 2, Agosto/Outoburo 1997. (Portuguese)

1998年（50岁）

主编书籍1部

McLaren, P. & Gadotti, M. (Eds.). (1998). *Paulo Freire: Poder, Desejo A Memórias da Libertação*. Porto Alegre, Brasil: Artes Médicas.

参著篇章7篇

Rethinking Whiteness. In Joe Kincheloe and Shirley Steinberg (eds.), White Reign. St. Martin's Press, 1998, Reprint.

Multiculturalism and the Postmodern Critique: Toward a Pedagogy of Resistance and Transformation. In Fred Schultz, ed., Sources: Notable Selections in Education (Second Edition). Guilford, Connecticut: Dushkin/McGraw – Hilll. Reprint. Also reprinted in Third Edition. 1998.

Education as a Political Issue. In H. Svi Shapiro and David E. Purpel, eds. Critical SocialIssues in American Education: Transformation in a Postmodern World. New Jersey, Lawrence Erlbaum Associates, Reprint. (second edition) 1998.

(with Zeus Leonardo) From Marxism to Terrorist Pedagogy: Jean Baudrillard's Chamber of Horrors. In Michael Peters (ed.), Naming the multiple: Poststructuralism and Education. Westport, Connecticut: Greenwood Press, 1998.

(with Kris Gutierrez) Global Politics and Local Antagonisms. In Dennis Carlson and Michael Apple (eds.), Power/Knowledge/Pedagogy: The Meaning of Democratic Education in Unsettling Times. Boulder, Colorado, Westview Press, Reprint. 1998.

(with Carlos Alberto Torres). Voicing from the Margins: The Politics and Passion of Pluralism in the Work of Maxine Greene. In William Ayers and Janet Miller (eds.), Maxine Greene. New York: Teachers College Press, 1998.

Response interview. In James Sears and James Carper (eds.), Curriculum, Religion, and Public Education: Conversations for an Enlarging Public Square. New York: Teachers

College Press, 1998.

期刊论文 10 篇

The Struggle for Social Justice: Some Brief Reflections on Multicultural Education in the United States. Ethnic and Multicultural Issues Round Table, Vol. xvi, No. 1, Fall, 1998.

Beyond Phallogocentrism: Critical Pedagogy and its Capital Sins – A Response to Donna LeCourt. Strategies: Journal of Theory, Culture and Politics, (Theory in Dialogue Special Issue), No. 11/12, Fall 1998.

(with Linda Crawford) A Critical Perspective on Culture in the Second Language Classroom. In Culture as the Core: Interdisciplinary Perspectives on Culture, Teaching, and Learning in the Second Language Curriculum. Edited by Dale L. Lange, Carol A. Klee, R. Michael Paige, and Yelena A. Yershova. The Center for Advanced Research on Language Acquisition Working Paper Series, #11, November, 1998. Also published in Culture as the Core: Perspectives on Culture in Second Language Learning. Greenwich Connecticut: Information Age Publishing, 2003.

(with Gustavo Fischman). Reclaiming Hope: Teacher Education and Social Justice in the Age of Globalization. Invited Article for Teacher Education Quarterly. Special 25th anniversary year (1998, Vol. 25, No. 4). Response to the editor, Alan Jones: "Ten Points of Debate in Teacher Education" (Fall, 1998).

Revolutionary Pedagogy in Post – Revolutionary Times: Rethinking the Political Economy of Critical Education. Educational Theory, Vol. 48, No. 4, 1998. (this is followed by five national and international responses to my article) Reprinted in Casopis za Kritiko Znanosti (XXXIX, 2001, 202 – 203) pages 23 – 53. (Slovenia). (lead article)

The Pedagogy of Che Guevara: Critical Pedagogy and Globalization Thirty Years After Che. Cultural Circles, Vol. 3, Summer 1998.

(with Gustavo Fischman, Silvia Serraand Estanislao Antelo) The Specters of Gramsci: Revolutionary Praxis and the Committed Intellectual. Journal of Thought, Fall 1998, Vol. 33, No. 3. Reprinted in Carmel Borg, Joseph Buttigieg, and Peter Mayo, Eds., Gramsci and Education. Lanham, Maryland, 2002.

(with Zeus Leonardo) Dead Poets Society: Deconstructing Surveillance Pedagogy. Studies in the Literary Imagination. (Special issue on "Cultural studies and the pedagogical imagination" edited by Robert Newman) Vol. XXXI, No. 1, Spring 1998.

(with Ricky Lee Allen) Review of Social Cartograpy: Mapping Ways of Seeing Social and Educational Change. edited by Rolland G. Paulson. Comparative Educational Review, Vol. 42, No. 2, May 1998.

Introduction (Critical Pedagogy´Enquiry Space Editor) Second Special Issue of Teaching Education. Vol. 9. 2 Winter/Spring 1998.

Testimony as Distinguished Panelist at Community Hearings for Roberto Clemente High School. In Community Hearings: Determining the Truth Behind the Clemente Story. Published by the Ad – Hoc Committee for Clemente Community Hearings. (Chicago, Illinois, November, 1998).

前言/后记 6 篇

Afterword. Ya Basta! In Yali Zou and Enrique T. Trueba (eds.) Ethnic Identity and Power: Cultural Contexts of Political Action in School and Society Albany, New York: State University of New York, 1998.

Foreword. In Mark Pruyn, Discourse Wars in Gotham – West: A Latino Immigrant Urban Tale of Resistance and Agency. Boulder, Colorado: Westview Press, 1998.

Preface. In Sherry Shapiro, Pedagogy and the Politics of the Body: A Critical Praxis. New York: Garland, 1998.

Series Editor Preface (with Shirley Steinberg and Joe Kincheloe). Teachers as Cultural Workers, by Paulo Freire. Boulder, Colorado: Westview Press, 1998.

Preface. In Antonia Darder, Guest Editor, A Special Occasional Paper in Memory of Paulo Freire. Reclaiming Our Voices. Teaching as an Act of Love: Reflections on Paulo Freire and His Contributions ot Our Lives and Our Work. Los Angeles: CABE. 1998.

Preface. In Linda Rogers, ed. Wish I Were: Felt Pathways to the Self. Madison, WI.: Atwood Press, 1998.

访谈学者论文 3 篇

"An Interview with Gene Provenzo" International Journal of Educational Reform. Vol 7, No 4, Oct 1998.

School Choice and the Struggle for Social Justice: An Interview with Amy Stuart Wells. International Journal of Educational Reform. Vol 7, No. 3, July 1998.

(with Aimee M. Carrillo – Rowe, Rebecca Clark and Philip Craft) "Storming the White House: Critical Interrogations of Whiteness", International Journal of Educational Reform. Vol 7, No. 1, January 1998.

外文（除英文外）出版物6篇

A luta contra a globalizacao. O Contemporaneo. Ano 11, No. 14, July, 1998 (Portuguese).

(with Zeus Leonardo and Ricky Lee Allen) Violencia Cool en el Espacio Y el Discurso Educativo. Cuaderno de Pedagogia Rosario. Ano II, No. 4, Noviembre 1998.

A Luta por Justiça Social: Breves Reflexões sobre o Ensino Multicultural nos Estados Unidos. Patio: Revista Pedagogica. Ano 2, No. 6, Agosto/Outubro 1998.

La Crisis Contemporánea De La Pedagogía Crítica. Bien: Revista Especializada en Ciencias Sociales y de la Educación. Vol. 1, No. 1, 1998.

Kritische Erziebungswissenschaft im Zeitalter der Globalisierung. In Heinz Sunker und Heinz – Hermann Kruger, eds., Kritische Erziehungswissenschaft am Neubeginn?! Germany: Suhrkamp, 1998.

Traumas do capital: Pedagogia, política e práxis nomercado global. In Luiz Heron Da Silva (ed.) A Escola Cidadã No Contexto Da Globalização. (pp. 81 – 98) Petropolis, RJ Brazil: Editora Vozes Ltda., 1998.

1999年（51岁）

学术著作3部

McLaren, P. (1999). *Schooling as A Ritual Performance: Toward A Political Economy of Educational Symbols and Gestures* (3rd ed.). Lanham, MD: Rowman & Littlefield Publishers.

McLaren, P. (1999). *Pedagogia, Poder e Identidad*. Rosario, Argentina: Homo Sapiens.

McLaren, P. (1999). *Utopias Provisorias: As Pedagogias Criticas num Cenario Pos – colonial*. Rio de Janeiro, Brasil: Editora Vozes.

主编书籍1部

Hill, D., McLaren, P., Cole, M., & Rikowski, G. (Eds.). (1999). *Postmodernism in Educational Theory*. London, UK: Tufnell Press..

参著篇章7篇

(with Ramin Farahmandpur). Critical Pedagogy, Postmodernism, and the Retreat from Class: Towards a Contraband Pedagogy. In Dave Hill, Peter McLaren, Mike Cole, and Glenn Ritkowski, eds. Postmodern Excess in Educational Theory: Education and the Politics of Human Resistance. England, Tufnell Press 1999.

(with Dave Hill, Mike Coleandand Glenn Ritkowski) Postmodernism Adieu: Towards a Politics of Human Resistance. In Dave Hill, Peter McLaren, Mike Cole, and Glenn Ritkowski, eds. Postmodernism in Educational Theory: Education and the Politics of Human Resistance. England, Tufnell Press, 1999.

The politics of multicultural research. In Carl Grant (ed.), Multicultural research: A reflective engagement with race, class, gender and, sexual orientation. London: Falmer Press, 1999.

Resisting Whiteness: Revolutionary Multiculturalism as Counterhegemonic Praxis. In David Slayden and Rita Kirk Whillock (eds.) Soundbite Culture: The Death of Discoursein a Wired World. London and Thousand Oaks: Sage, 1999.

Critical Pedagogy. In David Gabbard (ed.) Power Knowledge and the Politics of Educational Meaning. New York: Erlbaum, 1999.

Unthinking whiteness, rethinking democracy. In Christine Clark and James O'Donnell (eds.), Becoming and Unbecoming White: Owning and Disowning a Racial Identity. Greenwood Press. Reprint, slightly revised. 1999.

(with Rudy Torres) Racism and Multicultural Education: Rethinking 'Race' and 'Whiteness' in Late Capitalism. In Stephen May (ed.) Critical Multiculturalism: Rethinking multicultural and antiracist education. London: Falmer Press, 1999.

期刊论文 9 篇

(with Valerie Scatamburlo) Paulo Freire and the Pedagogy of Possibility. Democracy and Education. Vol 13, No. 1 (Spring, 1999).

(with Ramin Farahmandupur). Critical Multiculturalism and the Globalization of Capital: Some Implications for a Politics of Resistance. Journal of Curriculum Theorizing, Vol. 15, No. 4, Winter 1999.

The Pedagogy of Possibility: Reflecting Upon Paulo Freire's Politics of Education. Educational Researcher, Vol. 28, No. 2, 1999.

(with Ricky Lee Allen) Is democratic schooling possible in an ecology of accountability and outcomes? [A review of the books Redesigning American Education, by James S. Coleman, Barbara Schneider, Sephen Plank, Kathryn S. Schiller, Roger Shouse, Huayin Wang, and Seh-Ahn Lee and Reading, and Writing, and Justice: School Reform as if Democracy Matters, by James W. Fraser]. Contemporary Sociology, Vol. 28, No. 2, 1999.

(with Ramin Farahmandpur) Globalization and Contraband Pedagogy. Theoria June, No. 93, 1999.

"Contesting Capital: Critical Pedagogy and Globalism: A Response to Mike Apple." Current Issues in Comparative Education, Vol. 1, No. 2, April 30, 1999. www. tc. columbia. edu/cice

Che Guevara, Globalization and Leadership. International Journal of Leadership in Education, Vol. 2, No. 3, 1999.

A Response to Spencer Maxcy. International Journal of Leadership in Education, Vol. 2, No. 3, 1999.

(with Rick Allen and Zeus Leonardo) The Gift of Si (gh) ted Violence: Towards a Discursive Intervention into the Organization of Capitalism. Discourse: Theoretical Studies in Media and Culture Vol. 21, No. 2, 1999.

前言/后记 6 篇

Foreward. In Paula Allman, Revolutionary Social Transformation: Democratic Hopes, Political Possiblilites and Critical Education Westport, Connecticuct: Bergin and Gavey. 1999.

Preface. In Phil Francis Carspecken. Four Scenes for Posing the Question of Meaning and Other Explorations in Critical Philosophy and Critical Methodology. New York: Peter Lang Publishers, 1999.

Preface. Alternatives in Education: Critical Pedagogy for Disaffected Youth by Greg Goodman. New York. Peter Lang Publishers, 1999.

(with Glenn Ritkowski) Introduction. In Dave Hill, Peter McLaren, Mike Cole, and Glenn Ritkowski, eds. Postmodernism in Educational Theory: Education and the Politics of Human Resistance. England, Tufnell Press, 1999.

Introduction. Traumatizing Capital. Critical Education in the New Information Age by Manuel Castells, Ramon Flecha, Paulo Freire, Henry A. Giroux, Donaldo Macedo, and Paul Willis. New York: Rowman & Littlefield, 1999.

Afterword: Teachers Committed to the Struggle for Democracy: Cuesta lo que Cuesta. In J. Cynthia McDermott, editor, Beyond the Silence: Listening for Democracy. Portsmouth, N. H. : Heinemann, 1999.

访谈麦克拉伦论文 1 篇

"Peter McLaren: A Call for a Multicultural Revolution", Gustavo Fischman Interviews

Peter McLaren. Multicultural Education, Vol. 6, No. 4, Summer, 1999, Reprinted in Multicultural Education. Ninth Edition. McGraw – Hill. 2002. Also reprinted in In Notes & Abstracts in American International Education. No. 87, Spring, 1999.

访谈学者论文 4 篇

(with Peter Mayo) "Value Commitment, Social Change, and Personal Narrative", International Journal of Educational Reform, Vol. 8, No. 4, October 1999.

(with David Gabbard). "This Hard Land: DavidGabbard on the Path of Resistance", International Journal of Educational Reform, Vol. 8, No. 3, July 1999.

(with Jose Solis Jordan). "The Struggle for Liberation! La Lucha Continua! Jose Solis Jordan's Fight for Justice", International Journal of Educational Reform, Vol. 8, No. 2, April, 1999.

(with Jumara Novaes Sotto Maior and Cláudio Orlando Costa do Nascimento) "A Critical Pedagogy of the Streets: An Interview with Desafio of Salvador da Bahia, Brasil", International Journal of Educational Reform, Vol. 8, No. 1, January, 1999.

学术百科全书词条 1 条

An Encyclopedia of Cultural Theorists. Edward Arnold Publishers, London, England. Entries: Paulo Freire. 1999.

外文（除英文外）出版物 2 篇

Revolutionary Multiculturalsim: Spanish translation. Revolutionario multiculturalismo. Mexico City: Siglo Veintiuno Editores. 1999

(with Henry Giroux) O Pessimismo Radical de Leon Golub: rumo a uma Pedagogia Critical da Representacao. In Henry Giroux, Cruzando as Fronteiras do Discurso Educacional. Porto Alegre, Brasil: Artmed, 1999.

2000 年（52 岁）

学术著作 1 部

McLaren, P. (2000). *Che Guevara, Paulo Freire, and the Pedagogy of Revolution*. Lanham, MD: Rowman & Littlefield Publishers.

主编书籍 2 部

Steiner, S. S., Babruth, R., Krank, M., & McLaren, P. (Eds.). (2000). *Freireian Pedagogy, Praxis and Possibilities: Projects for the New Millennium*. New York, NY: Routledge.

Ovando, C. J. , & McLaren, P. (Eds.). (2000). *The Politics of Multiculturalism and Bilingual Education: Students and Teachers Caught in the Crossfire.* Columbus, OH: McGraw‐Hill.

参著篇章 14 篇

(with Ramin Farahmandpur) Reconsidering Marx in Post – Marxist Times: A Requiem for Postmodernism? Anuário de Edudação – Ano 2000: Reflexões para o novo milênio 2001.

Developing a Pedagogy of Whiteness in the Context of a Postcolonial Hybridity: White Identities in Global Context. In Nelson M. Rodriguez and Leila E. Villaverde, eds. , Dismantling White Privilege: Pedagogy, Politics, and Whiteness, New York: Peter Lang. 2000.

Critical Multiculturalism and Globalization: Transgressive Pedagogies in Gringolandia, Cueste Lo Que Cueste (with Peter McLaren). In C. Tejada, C. Martinez, & Z. Leonardo (Eds.), Charting New Terrains of Chicana (o) /Latina (o) Education. Creskill, NJ: Hampton Press, 2000.

Unthinking Whiteness: Rearticulating Diasporic Practice. In Peter Pericles Trifonas, Editor. Revolutionary Pedagogies: Cultural Politics, Instituting Education, and the Discourse of Theory. New York and London: Routledge/Falmer, (Reprint) 2000.

Pedagogia Revolucionaria em Tempos Pos – Revolucionaarios: Repensar a Economia Politica da Educacao Critica. In F. Imbernon A Educacao No Seculao XXI, Artmed Editora, (reprint) 2000.

(with Joe Kincheloe). Rethinking critical theory and qualitative research. In Norman K. Denzin and Yvonna S. Lincoln (eds.), Handbook of qualitative research. London and Thousand Oaks: Sage, 2000. Revised significantly from 1994 first edition. Reprinted in Yali Zou and Enrique Trueba, eds. , Ethnographies and Schools: Qualitative Approaches to the Study of Education. Boulder, Colorado: Rowman and Littlefield.

(with Enrique Trueba). Critical ethnography for the study of Immigrants. In Enrique Trueba and Lilia Bartolome (Eds) Immigrant Voices: In Search of Pedagogical Reform. Boulder, CO. : Rowman and Littlefield Publishers, 2000.

(with Zeus Leonardo and Ricky Lee Allen). Epistemologies of Whiteness. In Ram Mahalingam and Cameron McCarthy (Eds.), Multicultural Curriculum: New Directions for Social Theory, Practice, and Policy. New York and London: Routledge, 2000.

(with Rick Allen and Zeus Leonardo) Space, Violence and Pedagogy. In Stephanie Urso Spina (ed.) Smoke and MIrrors: The Hidden Context of Violence in Schools and

Society. Boulder, CO. : Rowman and Littlefield, 2000.

Gangsta Pedagogy. In Cameron McCarthy and Glen Hudak (eds.) Sound Identities: Pop Music, Youth and Education. New York: Peter Lang, Reprint. 2000.

Gangsta Pedagogy and Ghettoethnicity. In Karen McClafferty, Carlos Alberto Torres, and Theodore Mitchell (eds.) Challenges of Urban Education: Sociological Perspectives for the Next Century. Albany, NY: State University of New York Press, Reprint. 2000.

(with Zeus Leonardo and Xochitl Perez) Response to Guy Parcel. Settings for health promotion: Linking theory and practice. Blake Poland, Larry Green and Irving Rootman (eds.). Toronto, Canada: SAGE, 2000.

Can Critical Pedagogy Work in the Inner City? A Conversation with Peter McLaren. In Barry Kanpol and Fred Yeo (eds.), From Nihilism to Possibility: Transforming Inner – City Education. Hampton Press, 2000.

(with Juan S. Muñoz) Contesting Whiteness: Critical Perspectives on the Struggle for Social Justice. In Carlos Julio Ovando and Peter McLaren (eds). The Politics of Multiculturalism: Students and Teachers in the Crossfire. McGraw – Hill, 2000.

期刊论文 9 篇

(With Kellie Rollstad and Jeff MacSwan) Padagogik und Sprache. Sozialwissenschaftliche Literatur Rundschau11. 41 (2000). (reprint revised)

Corporate Citizenry and the Preferred Teacher. Discourse: Studies in the Cultural Politics of Education. Vol. 21, No. 2, 2000.

Rethinking the Political Economy of Critical Pedagogy in the Age of Globalization. Una Miranda Critica a la Educacion. Edited by Alicia Gurdian Fernandez. Editorial de la Universidad de Costa Rica, 2000.

Che Guevara, Paulo Freire, and the Politics of Hope. Cultural Studies/Critical Methodologies. Vol 1, No. 1 Feb., 2000.

(with Ramin Farahmandpur). "Reconsidering Marx in Post – Marxist Times: A Requiem for Postmodernism?" Educational Researcher, Vol. 29, No. 3 (April, 2000). Reprinted in Reflexoes Para o Tercerio Milenio: Anuario de Educacao 1999/2000, Directora Barbara Freitag.

(with Marta Baltodano). "The Future of Teacher Education and the Politics of Resistance", Teaching Education, Vol. 11, No. 1, April 2000.

(with Gustavo Fischman). "Schooling for Democracy: Toward a Critical Utopianism",

A special issue of Contemporary Sociology, Vol, 29, 2000.

(with Jill – Pinkney – Pastrana) "The Search for the Complicit Native", A special issue of the International Journal of Qualitative Studies in Education, Vol. 13, No. 2, 2000.

Unthinking Whiteness, Rethinking Democracy. Education Policy. Edited by James Marshall and Michael Peters. The International Library of Comparative Public Policy. An Elgar Reference Collection. Cheltenham, UK, Northampton, MA. Edward Elgar Publishing, Inc. , 2000. reprint.

著作前言 4 篇

Postfacio: La Pedagogia de la Possibilidad De Paulo Freire. Paulo Freire: Educador Para Una Nueva Civilizacion. Ediciones Universidad de la Frontera (Temuco, Chile) & Instituto Paulo Freire. 2000.

Preface. In Walter de Oliveira. "We are in the streets, because they are in the streets: The emergence of street social pedagogy in Brazil", Binghampton, NY: Haworth. Press, 2000.

Foreword. In Lourdes Diaz Soto (ed). The Politics of Early Childhood Education. New York: Peter Lang Publishers, 2000.

Introduction. Immigrant Voices: In Search of Pedagogical Reform, edited by Enrique Trueba andLilia Bartolome. Boulder, CO. : Rowman and Littlefield Publishers, 2000.

访谈学者论文 3 篇

(with Pepi Leistyna) "Presence of Mind: Education and the Politics of Deception", International Journal of Educational Reform. Vol. 9, No. 3, July 2000.

(with Emily Hicks) "Border Crossing with the Wrestler Bride: An Inteview with Performance Artist and Critical Educator Emily Hicks", International Journal of Educational Reform Vol. 9, No. 2, April 2000.

(with Sandy Marie Anglas Grande). "Critical Theory and American Indian Geographics of Identity, Pedagogy and Power", International Journal of Educational Reform, Vol. 9, No. 1, January 2000.

(电子) 新闻和日报文章 3 篇

Both candidates' education plans tout responsibility (with Ramin Farahmandpur). [Online] In Daily Bruin, October 26, 2000. Available at: http: //www. dailybruin. ucla. edu/db/articles. asp? ID = 1651.

Bush's 'tough love' proposal raises troubling ideas (with RaminFarahmandpur). [Online] In Daily Bruin, October 9, 2000. Available at: http://www.dailybruin.ucla.edu/db/articles.asp? ID =1357.

Corporate sponsorship threatens quality of education (withRamin Farahmandpur). [Online] In Daily Bruin, April 19, 2000. Available at: http://www.dailybruin.ucla.edu/db/issues/00/04.19/view.farahmandpur.html.

外文（除英文外）出版物1篇

Revolutionary Multiculturalsim: Portuguese translation. Multiculturalismo Revolucionario. Porto Alegre: Artes Medicas. 2000.

2001年（53岁）

学术著作4部

McLaren, P. & Giroux, H. A. (2001). *Kriittinen Pedagogiikka*. Tampere, Finland: Vastapaino.

Cole, M., Hill, D., McLaren, P., & Rikowski, G. (2001). *Red Chalk: On Schooling, Capitalism and Politics*. London, UK: The Institute for Education Policy Studies.

McLaren, P. (2001). *A Pedagogia da Utopia*. Santa Cruz do Sul, Brasil: Editora da Universidade de Santa Cruz do Sul.

McLaren, P. (2001). *La Pedagogia del Che Guevara*. San Luis Potosí, Mexico: Universidad Pedagogica Nacional.

参著篇章4篇

(with Ramin Farahmandpur) Slightly expanded version of The Globalization of Capitalism and the New Imperialism: Notes Towards a Revolutionary Critical Pedagogy. The Review of Education, Pedagogy & Cultural Studies, Vol. 23, No. 3 (2001).

(with Ramin Farahmandpur) Reconsidering Marx in Post – Marxist Times: A Requiem for Postmodernism? Anuário de Edudação – Ano 2000: Reflexões para o novo milênio 2001.

(with Aimee M. Carrillo – Rowe, Rebecca L. Clark, and Philip Craft). Rearticulating the Blizzard of Modernity: Whiteness asa Label for Western Cultural Politics. In Glenn M. Hudak and Paul Kihn, eds. Labelling: Pedagogy and Politics. New York and London: Falmer Press. 2001.

Freirean Praxis and the Politics of Pedagogy. In Michael Richards, Pradip N. Thomas and Zaharom Nain, eds., Communication and Development: the Freirean Connection. New Jersey: The Hampton Press, 2001.

期刊论文 10 篇

Wayward Multiculturalists: A Response to Gregor McLennan. Ethnicities, 2001, Vol. 1, No. 3 (December), With a final response by Gregor McLennan.

(with Glenn Rikowski) Pedagogy for Revolution Against Education for Capital: A Dialogue. Cultural Logic, October, 2001.

(with Ramin Farahmandpur) The Globalization of Capitalism and the New Imperialism: Notes Towards a Revolutionary Critical Pedagogy. The Review of Education, Pedagogy & Cultural Studies, Vol. 23, No. 3 (2001).

Mapping Capital's Life Forms: Marx, McMurtry, and the Money Sequence. (essay review). Interchange, Vol. 32, No. 3, 2001.

(with Noah de Lissovoy). Icon of Liberation. Educate! A Quarterly on Education & Development, Vol 1, issue 2. (Pakistan). 2001.

(with Jill Pinkney – Pastrana). Cuba, Yanquizacion, and the Cult of Elian Gonzales: A View from the 'Enlightened' States. International Journal of Qualitative Studies in Education, in press. A special issue on Cuba, co – edited by Denise Blum and Peter McLaren. Vol. 14, No. 2, March – April 2001.

(with Ramin Farahmandpur) Marx After Post – Marxism: Reclaiming Critical Pedagogy for the Left. Working Papers in Cultural Studies No. 25. Department of Comparative American Cultures. Washington State University. Pullman, Washington, 2001.

(With Ramin Farahmandpur). Class, Cultism, and Multiculturalism: A Notebook on Forging a Revolutionary Politics. Multicultural Education. Vol. 8, No. 3 (Spring, 2001), Reprinted in Multicultural Education, Ninth Edition. Edited by Fred Schultz. McGraw – Hill.

(With Ramin Farahmandpur) Socialist Dreaming and Socialist Imagination: Revolutionary Citizenship and a Pedagogy of Resistance. Educational Policy. Vol. 15, No. 3, July 2001.

(With Ramin Farahmandpur). Teaching against Globalization and the New Imperialism Towards a Revolutionary Pedagogy. Journal of Teacher Education, Vol. 52, No. 2, (March/April 2001), Reprinted in: In *Vzgoja & Izobrazevanja*. 4, 2007, (Slovenia)

前言/后记 4 篇

Foreword. Social Movements, Civil Society, and Radical Adult Education by John Holt. Westport, Connecticut: Bergin and Garvey, 2001.

Preface. Multi/Intercultural Conversations: A Reader Ed. Shirley R. Steinberg Peter Lang, New York, 2001.

Coda. Multi/Intercultural Conversations: A Reader Ed. Shirley R. Steinberg Peter Lang, New York, 2001.

Foreward. In Paula Allman. Critical Education Against Global Capitalism: Karl Marx and Revolutionary Critical Education. Westport, Connecticuct: Bergin and Garvey, 2001.

访谈麦克拉伦论文3篇

Muñoz, L. C. (Interviewer). McLaren, P. (Interviewee). (2001). The role of critical pedagogy in the globalization era and the aftermath of September 11, 2001: Interview with Peter McLaren. *Revista Electronica de Investigacion Educativa*, 3 (2), 1 – 19. Retrieved from http://redie.ens.uabc.mx/vol3no2/contenido – coral.html

The above interview was revised and extended as: Muñoz, L. C. (Interviewer). McLaren, P. (Interviewee). (2001, Winter). The role of critical pedagogy in the globalization era and the aftermath of September 11, 2001: Interview with Peter McLaren. *The School Field: International Journal of Theory and Research in Education*, 11 (5 – 6), 109 – 156.

The above interview was translated into Spanish as: Muñoz, L. C. (Interviewer). McLaren, P. (Interviewee). (2002). El papel de la pedagogía crítica en la era de la globalización y las secuelas del 11 de septiembre 2001. *Opciones Pedagogicas*, 25, 11 – 26.

The above interview was also published as: Muñoz, L. C. (Interviewer). McLaren, P. (Interviewee). (2002, Fall). The role of critical pedagogy in the globalization era and the aftermath of September 11, 2001: Interview with Peter McLaren. *Multicultural Education*, 10 (1), 7 – 17.

Pedagogy Against Capital. By Glenn Rikowski. In Hobgoblin: The Journal of Marxist Humanism (England), No. 4, Winter 2001 – 2002, pp. 31 – 38. (A shortened version was previously published in News & Letters Vol. 46, No. 4, May 2001).

"Rage and Hope: The Revolutionary Pedagogy of Peter McLaren." By Mitja Sardoc. Educational Philosophy and Theory. Vol. 33, No. 3 & 4, August & November 2001. Pp 411 – 439. Repeated in: Casopis za Kritiko Znanosti (XXXIX, 2001, 202 – 203) pages 11 – 21. (Slovenia) Herramienta (Argentina, in Spanish), http://www.herramienta.com.ar/article.php?sid=23. Filosofia da Educacao. (Brasil, in Portuguese) and http://filosofia.pro.br/textos/furia – esperanca.htm Curriculo sem Fronteiras (US and Portugal), http://www.curriculosemfronteiras.org.

访谈学者论文1篇

Special Edition of International Journal of Educational Reform dedicated to the work of

Peter McLaren. Interviews with Juha Suoranta, Roberto Flores, Greg Tanaka, Glenn Rikowski, Dave Hill, and Mike Cole, Vol. 10. No. 2/ Spring 2001.

（电子）新闻和日报文章 2 篇

Critical Literacy for Global Citizenship (with Ramin Farahmandpur). Center X Forum, Vol. 1 (2). Spring/Summer 2001.

Clouded election foreshadows wealth – biased presidency (with Ramin Farahmandpur). [Online] In Daily Bruin, January 10, 2001. Available at: http://www.dailybruin.ucla.edu/db/articles.asp? ID = 2355.

外文（除英文外）出版物 2 篇

Critica Pedagogica para o novo Milenio – Perdoando uma Politica Revolutionaria na Era da Globalizacao. Parte 1. Bolando Aula De Historia. Ano 4, No. 30, June/July 2001.

Critica Pedagogica para o novo Milenio – Perdoando uma Politica Revolutionaria na Era da Globalizacao. Parte 2. Bolando Aula De Historia. Ano 4, No. 31, August/September 2001.

2002 年（54 岁）

学术著作 2 部

McLaren, P. (2002). *Life in Schools. An Introduction to Critical Pedagogy in the Foundations of Education* (4th ed.). Boston, MA: Allyn & Bacon Publishers (Pearson PLC).

McLaren, P. &Farahmandpur, R. (2002). *Pedagogia Revolucionaria na Globalizacao*. Rio de Janeiro, Brasil: Deutsche Presse – Agentur.

主编书籍 1 部

Hill, D., McLaren, P., Cole, M., & Rikowski, G. (Eds.). (2002). *Marxism Against Postmodernism in Educational Theory*. Lanham, MD: Lexington Books, Rowman & Littlefield.

参著篇章 8 篇

(with Cindy Cruz). Queer Bodies and Configurations: Towards a Critical Pedagogy of the Body. Body Works: Pedagogy, Politics, and Social Change. Edited by Sherry Shapiro and Svi Shapiro. New York: Hampton Press. 2002.

(with Farahmandpur, R. Globalization) Class, and Multiculturalism: Fragments from a Red Notebook. In M. Singh (Ed.), Global Learning. Altona, VIC, AU: Common Ground Publishing Group. 2002.

Critical Pedagogy: A Look at the Major Concepts. (Reprint) In Antonia Darder at alia. , Editors, The Critical Pedagogy Reader, New York and London: Routlege/Falmer. 2002.

Revolutionary Pedagogy in Post – revolutionary Times: Rethinking the Political Economy of Critical Education. (Reprint) In Antonia Darder at alia. , Editors, The Critical Pedagogy Reader, New York and London: Routlege/Falmer. 2002.

(with Ramin Farahmandpur) Freire, Marx, and the New Imperialism: Toward a Revolutionary Praxis. In J. , J. Slater, Stephen Fain, Cesar Rossatto, 2002.

(with Ramin Farahmandpur) Breaking Signifying Chains: A Marxist Position on Postmodernism In Hill, McLaren, Cole & Rikowski (Eds.), Marxism Against Postmodernism in Educational Theory. Lexington Press. 2002.

(With Ramin Farahmandpur) Recentering Class: Wither Postmodernism? Towards a Contraband Pedagogy. In Hill, McLaren, Cole & Rikowski (Eds.), Marxism Against Postmodernism in Educational Theory, pp. Lexington Press. 2002.

Richard Rorty's Self – Help Liberalism: A Marxist Critique of America's Most Wanted Ironist (with Ramin Farahmandpur & Juha Suoranta). In M. Peters & P. Ghiraldelli, Jr. (Eds.), Richard Rorty: Education, Philosophy and Culture. Boulder, Colorado: Roman and Littlefield, 2002.

期刊论文 7 篇

Kritische Padagogik und der Ruckzug derLinken. Herausforderungen fur Eine Revolutionare Padagogik. Das Argument, 246. 44. Jahrgang. Heft 3, 2002, Translated into English at: http: //portland. indymedia. org/en/2003/01/39846. shtml

Responses to Lynne V. Cheney: From Peter McLaren, Taboo, Vol. 6, No. 1, Spring – Summer, 2002.

Global Media and the Making of a Garrison State. Movement for a Socialist Future (England), Vol. 10, No. 2 (2002).

Marxist Revolutionary Praxis: A Curriculum of Transgression. Journal of Curriculum Inquiry Into Curriculum and Instruction, Vol. 3, No. 3 (2002).

The Dialectics of Terrorism: A Marxist Response to September 11. (Part One: Remembering to Forget) Cultural Studies/Critical Methodologies, (Vol, 2, No. 2, May, 2002).

George Bush, Apocalypse Sometime Soon, and the American Imperium. Cultural Studies/Critical Methodologies, (Vol. 2, No. 3, August, 2002).

Critical Pedagogy in the Shadow of Terror. Educate! A Quarterly on Education and Development (Pakistan), issue 2, 2002.

著作前言1篇

Introduction. Defining and Designing Multiculturalism: One School System's Efforts by Pepi Leistyna. (ix – xvii) Albany: New York. State University of New York Press. 2002.

访谈麦克拉伦论文6篇

Moraes, M. (Interviewer). McLaren, P. (Interviewee). (2002). An interview with Peter McLaren. *Forum Critico da Educacao*, *1* (1), 67 – 82.

An expanded version of this interview was published as: Moraes, M. (Interviewer). McLaren, P. (Interviewee). (2003, April). The path of dissent: An interview with Peter McLaren. *Journal of Transformative Education*, *1* (2), 117 – 134.

Maldonado, I. J. & Sotelo, G. (Interviewers). McLaren, P. (Interviewee). (2002, July – August). En la educacion se pretende acabar con el multiculturalismo: McLaren. *Gaceta*: *Universidad Veracruzana*, (55 – 56), 68 – 69.

Álvarez, R. A. (Interviewer). McLaren, P. (Interviewee). (2002, July – August). Entrevista a Peter McLaren: Práctica revolucionaria en las entrañas de la bestia. *El Latino America*. Retrieved from http://www.stormpages.com/marting/entrevismc.htm.

Rizvi, M. (Interviewer). McLaren, P. (Interviewee). (2002). Educating for social justice and liberation: An interview with Peter McLaren. Retrieved fromzmag.org.

Rizvi, M. (Interviewer). McLaren, P. (Interviewee). (2002). Peter McLaren: An interview for educate! *Educate! A Quarterly on Education & Development*, *1* (2).

Popular Culture and Pedagogy: An Interview with Peter McLaren. By Dianne Smith. Journal of Curriculum Theorizing, Vol. 18, No. 2 (Summer, 2002).

学术百科全书词条2条

(with Noah de Lissovoy) Paulo Freire. In J. W. Guthrie (Ed.), Encyclopedia of Education (second edition). New York: Macmillan. 2002.

McLaren, P., & Datnow, A. Ethnography. In D. Levinson, A. Sadnovik, & P. Cookson, Jr. (Eds.), Education and Sociology: An Encyclopedia. Routledge Falmer Publishers, 2002.

外文（除英文外）出版物3篇

Paulo Freire: Un encontre Critic. (Paulo Freire: A Critical Encounter). Catalan Translation. Centre de Recursos i Educacio Continua Editions del CREC, Noguerra 10, 46800 Xativa. 2002.

Politiques d'Alliberament: Sendes de Freire. (Politics of Liberation: Paths from Freire). Catalan Translation. Centre de Recursos i Educacio Continua Editions del CREC, Noguerra 10, 46800 Xativa. 2002.

Critica Pedagogica para o novo Milenio – Perdoando uma Politica Revolutionaria na Era da Globalizacao. Parte 3. Bolando Aula De Historia. Ano 4, No. 34, April/May 2002.

2003年（55岁）

参著篇章7篇

A Pedagogy of Possibility. In Allan C. Ornstein, Linjda S. Behar – Horenstein, and Edward F. Pajak, editors. (pp. 26 – 35) Contemporary Issues in Curriculum, Vol. 3. Allyn & Bacon, 2003.

(with Ramin Farahmandpur). Critical Pedagogy and Marxism: Rethinking Revolutionary Praxis in Education. In D. Carlson & G. Dimitriadis (Eds), Promises to Keep: Cultural Studies, Democratic Education, and Public Life. 2003.

(with Ramin Farahmandpur). Critical Pedagogy at Ground Zero: Renewing the Educational Left After 9 – 11. In D. Gabbard and K. Saltman (Eds.), Education as Enforcement: The Militarization and Corporatization of Schools. New York and London: Routledge. 2003.

Critical Pedagogy in the Shadow of Terror: A Marxist Educator's Reflections from Ground Zero. In Heinz Sunker, Russel Farnen, and Gyorgy Szell, eds., Political Socialisation, Participation and Education. Berlin & New York: Peter Lang. Revised from previous articles. 2003.

(with Ramin Farahmandpur). Class, Cultism, and Multiculturalism: A Notebook on Forging a Revolutionary Multiculturalism. (Reprint) In F. Schultz (Ed.), Annual Editions: Multicultural Education 03/04, Tenth Edition. Guilford, CT: McGraw – Hill. 2003.

The Dialectics of Terrorism. In Carl Boggs, editor. Empire, War, and Terrorism: U.S. Militarism and the New World Order, New York and London: Routledge, pp. 149 – 189. See also revised version of article in The Dialectics of Terrorism: A Marxist Response to 9 – 11 in 9/11 in American Culture, edited by Norm Denzin and Yvonna Lincoln. Lanham and New York: Altamira Press. 2003.

(with Paula Allman and Glenn Rikowski) After the Box People: The labour – capital relation as class constitution – and its consequences for Marxist educational theory and human resistance. In John Freeman – Moir and Alan Scott, editor, Yesterday's Dreams: International and Critical Perspectives on Education and Social Class. Edited by Alan Scott. New Zealand: University of Canterbury Press, 2003.

期刊论文 11 篇

(with Valerie Scatamburlo – D'Annibale) Operation Human Freedom. The Hobgoblin: A Journal of Marxist Humanism (London, England), No. 5, 2003.

Pedagogia Critica en la Epoca de la Resignacion. Barbecho: Revista de Reflexion Socioeducativa. Diciembre – Abril de 2003, No. 2.

Slavoj Zizek's Naked Politics: Opting for the Impossible, A Secondary Elaboration, Journal of Advanced Composition Quarterly, Vol. 21, No. 3 (summer) 2003.

With a response by Slavoj Zizek. Reprinted in Michael Peters, Colin Lankshear, Mark Olssen (eds.) Futures of Critical Theory: Dreams of Difference. New York: Rowman and Littlefield, 2003.

(with Greg Martin). The "Big Lie" Machine Devouring America. Socialist Future Review, Summer, 2003.

(with De Lissovoy, N.). *Educational "Accountability" and the Violence of Capital: A Marxian Reading.* Journal of Education Policy, 18 (2), 2003, pp. 131 – 143. Reprinted in Portuguese in Educacao Unisinos (Revista do Programa de Pos – Graducao em Educacao da Universidade do Vale do Rio dos Sinos, No. 11, Vol. 6, Julho/Dezembro, 2002).

Critical Pedagogy in the Age of Neoliberal Globalization: Notes fromHistory's Underside. Democracy and Nature, Vol. 9, No. 1, 2003.

(with Nathalia Jaramillo). Critical Pedagogy as Organizational Praxis: Challenging the Demise of Civil Society in a Time of Permanent War. Educational Foundations, Vol. 16, No. 4, Fall, 2002, (but published in Summer 2003).

(with Valerie Scatamburlo – D'Annibale) Class Dismissed? Historical Materialism and the Politics of Difference. Educational Philosophy and Theory, 2003, Reprinted as Adios a la clase? El materialismo historico y la politica de la 'diferencia', in Herramienta, Vol. 20, ano VII.

(with Valerie Scatamburlo – D'Annibale) The Strategic Centrality of Class in the Politics of Race and 'Difference' Cultural Studies/Critical Methodologies, Vol. 3. No. 2 (2003)

The Dialectics of Terrorism: A Marxist Response to September 11. (Part Two: Unveiling the Past, Evading the Present) Cultural Studies/Critical Methodologies (Vol. 3, No. 1, February, 2003).

访谈麦克拉伦论文 3 篇

Pozo, M. (Interviewer). McLaren, P. (Interviewee). (2003). Toward a critical revolutionary pedagogy – an interview with Peter McLaren. *St. John's University Humanities Review*, 2 (1), 1 – 26.

The above interview was also published as: Pozo, M. (Interviewer). McLaren, P. (Interviewee). (2003, December 8). Toward a critical revolutionary pedagogy: An interview with Peter McLaren. *Dissident Voice*. Retrieved from http://www.dissidentvoice.org/Articles9/Pozo_McLaren – Interview.htm.

McClelland, K. (Interviewer). McLaren, P. (Interviewee). (2003, Winter). Traveling the road of most resistance: Peter McLaren's pedagogy of dissent. *Professing Education*, 1.

McClelland, K. (Interviewer). McLaren, P. (Interviewee). (2003, Fall). Traveling the road of most resistance: Peter McLaren's pedagogy of dissent. *Professing Education*, 2.

The two interviews above were also published as: McClelland, K. (Interviewer). McLaren, P. (Interviewee). (2003). Traveling the road of most resistance: Peter McLaren's pedagogy of dissent. *Correspondence*, 3. Indian Institute of Marxist Studies (Delhi Chapter).

学术百科全书词条 1 条

(with Noah de Lissovoy) Paulo Freire. In J. W. Guthrie (Ed.), Encyclopedia of Education, German Translation: (with Noah de Lissovoy) Paulo Freire. Klassiker der Padagogik (Classic Pedagogues). Volume Two, Von John Dewey bis Paulo Freire, Munchen: Verlag C. H. Beck. 2003.

外文（除英文外）出版物 1 篇

Life in Schools, 4th Edition: Chinese translation (Taiwan) Chu Liu Book Co., 2003.

2004 年（56 岁）

学术著作 1 部

McLaren, P., & Farahmandpur, R. (2004). *Teaching Against Global Capitalism and the New Imperialism: A Critical Pedagogy*. Lanham, MD: Rowman & Littlefield Publishers.

主编书籍 1 部

McLaren, P. (Ed.). (2004). *Che Guevara, Paulo Freire dan Politik Harapan: Tin-*

jauan Kritis Pendidikan. Indonesia: Diglossia Publishers.

参著篇章 1 篇

(with Nathalia Jaramillo). Critical Pedagogy in a Time of Permanent War. In Jeffrey R. Di Leo and Walter R. Jacobs (eds.). If Classrooms Matter: Progressive Visions of Educational Environments. New York and London: Routledge. 2004.

期刊论文 5 篇

(with Donna Houston). Education and Environmental Crisis: Ecosocialist Critical Pedagogies in Theory and Praxis. Educational Studies, Vol. 36, No. 1, August 2004.

(with Greg Martin). The Legend of the Bush Gang: Imperialism, War and Propaganda, Cultural Studies/Critical Methodologies, Vol. 4, No. 3, 2004. This is an expanded verson of "Orbiting Fascism" published in the newsletter, New Correspondence, Vol. 1, No. 1 (New Delhi, India).

(with Gregory Martin, Ramin Farahmandpur and Nathalia Jaramillo). Teaching in and against the Empire: Critical Pedagogy as Revolutionary Praxis. Teacher Education Quarterly, Vol. 31, No. 3 (winter, 2004).

(with Nathalia Jaramillo). A Moveable Fascism: Fear and Loathing in the Empire of Sand. Cultural Studies/Critical Methodologies, Vol. 4, No. 2 (May, 2004).

(with Valerie Scatamburlo – D'Annibale, Nathalia Jaramillo and Juha Suoranta). "No Carnival Here: Oppressed Youth and Class Relations in *City of God*", for a special issue of Workplace (February, 2004) guest edited by Pepi Leistyna on the theme of Youth as a Category Through Which Class is Lived. The special issue is scheduled also to appear in book form. http://www.cust.educ.ubc.ca/workplace/issue6p1/mclaren.html.

著作前言 3 篇

Foreword. Performance Theories in Education: Power, Pedagogy and the Politics of Identity. Edited by Bryant Keith Alexander, Gary Anderson, and Bernardo Gallegos. (xv – xix) Lawrence Erlbaum Associated, Inc. 2004.

Preface. Karen Cadiero – Kaplan, The Literacy Curriculum & Bilingual Education: A Critical Examination. (ix – xii) New York: Peter Lang Publishers. 2004.

Preface. Greg Goodman and Karen Carey. Critical Multicultural Conversations. Peter Lang Publishers, (xi – xiv) Cresskill, New Jersey, Hampton Press. 2004.

外文（除英文外）出版物 1 篇

(with Nathalia Jaramillo) Los Cruzados Guerreros de Dios: Cristianidad, Globaliacion y

Falsos Profetas del Imperialismo, Opciones Pedagogicas, numeros 29 y 30, 2004.

2005年（57岁）

学术著作3部

McLaren, P. (2005). *Capitalists and Conquerors: A Critical Pedagogy Against Empire*. Lanham, MD: Rowman & Littlefield Publishers.

McLaren, P. (2005). *Red Seminars: Radical Excursions into Educational Theory, Cultural Politics, and Pedagogy*. Cresskill, NJ: Hampton Press.

McLaren, P. &Farahmandpur, R. (2005). *Teaching Against Global Capitalism and the New Imperialism: A Critical Pedagogy*. Lanham, MD: Rowman & Littlefield Publishers.

主编书籍1部

Fischman, G., Sunker, H., Lankshear, C., & McLaren, P. (Eds.). (2005). *Critical Theories, Radical Pedagogies, and Global Conflicts*. Boulder, CO: Rowman & Littlefield.

参著篇章8篇

(with Nathalia Jaramillo) God's Cowboy Warrior: Christianity, Globalization, and the False Prophets of Imperialism. In Pratyush Chandra, Anuradha Ghosh, and Ravi Kumar, eds., The Politics of Imperialism and Counterstrategies. New Delhi: India. A shortened version of this chapter appeared in Arena (Australia). An expanded version of this chapter is found in in Peter McLaren, Capitalists and Conquerors: Critical Pedagogy Against Empire. Lanham, Maryland: Rowman and Littlefield, 2005.

(with Joe Kincheloe). Rethinking critical theory and qualitative research. In Norman K. Denzin and Yvonna S. Lincoln (eds.), Handbook of qualitative research. London and Thousand Oaks: Sage. 1st Edition, 1994; 2nd Edition, 2000; 3rd Edition, 2005.

(with Nathalia Jaramillo) In Patricia F. Goldblatt and Deirdre Smith, editors. Cases for Teacher Development: Preparing for the Classroom. "Case Commentary". Thousand Oaks: SAGE publications, 2005.

(with Nathalia Jaramillo) Alternative Globalizations: Critical Globalization Studies. In Critical Globalization Studies, edited by William I. Robinson. New York: Routledge, 2005.

(with Valerie Scatamburlo-D'Annibale) Paul Willis, Class Consciousness, and Critical Pedagogy: Toward a Socialist Future. In Learning to Labor in New Times. Edited by Nancy Dolby and Greg Dimitriadis (with the assistance of Paul Willis). New York: Routledg/Falmer, 2005.

Critical Pedagogy and Class Struggle in the Age of Neoliberal Globalzation: Notes from History's Underside. Previously published in Democracy and Nature. In Peter Trifonas, editor, Communities of Difference: Language, Culture, Media. Palgrave/St. Martins Press. 2005.

(with De Lissovoy, N.) Towards A Contemporary Philosophy of Praxis. In Gray – Rosendale, L., & Gray – Rosendale, S. (Eds.), Radical Relevance. Albany, NY: State University of New York Press. 2005.

(with Jaramillo, N.) Neoliberal Citizenship and Federal Education Policy: A Critical Analysis of the No Child Left Behind Act in co – edited book by O'Donnell, J., Pruyn, M., & Chavez, R. Information Age Publishing, Inc. 2005.

期刊论文 5 篇

Munoz, J., Ordonez – Jasis, R., Young, P., & McLaren, P. (2005). The hidden curriculum of domestication: Targeting faculty of promise. *Urban Review*, *Vol. 36*, *No. 3*.

(*with Gustavo Fischman*) *Rethinking Critical Pedagogy and the Gramscian and Freirean Legacies: From Organic to Committed Intellectuals*. Cultural Studies/Critical Methodologies. Vol. 5, No. 4, 2005.

Fire and Dust. International Journal of Progressive Education, Vol. 1, No. 3, 2005.

Critical Pedagogy Reloaded: Dispatches from Las Entranas de la Bestia. Cultural Studies/Critical Methodologies, Vol. 5, No. 2, August, 2005, .

(with Donna Houston). The Nature of Political Amnesia: Response to C. A. Bowers. Educational Studies, Vol. 37, No. 2, April, 2005.

关于麦克拉伦的著作 1 部

Pruyn, M., & Charles, L. M. H. (Eds.). (2005). *De la Pedagogía Crítica A La Pedagogía de la Revolución. Ensayos Para Comprender A Peter McLaren.* New York, NY: Peter Lang Publications.

访谈麦克拉伦论文 1 篇

Sardoc, M. (Interviewer). McLaren, P. (Interviewee). (2005, February). Ira y esperanza: La pedagogía revolucionaria de Peter McLaren. *Docencia*, *12*, 74 – 82.

外文（除英文外）出版物 2 篇

Life in Schools, 4th Edition: Spanish translation, La vida en las esuelas: Una introduccíon a la pedagogia crítica en los fundamentos de la educacíon. (Life in Schools, first edition). (Spanish) Mexico City: Siglo veintiuno editores, Fourth edition, 2005

Teaching Peter McLaren: Paths of Dissent, edited by Marc Pruyn and Luis Huerta – Charles,

Peter Lang Publishers, 2005, is being translated into Chinese and Spanish (Siglo XX1).

2006年（58岁）

学术著作1部

McLaren, P. (2006). *Life in Schools. An Introduction to Critical Pedagogy in the Foundations of Education* (5th ed.). Upper Saddle River, NJ: Pearson PLC.

主编书籍1部

McLaren, P. (Ed.). (2006). *Rage and Hope: Interviews with Peter McLaren on War, Imperialism, and Critical Pedagogy.* New York, NY: Peter Lang Publishing.

参著篇章3篇

(with Ramin Farahmandpur) Who Will Educate the Educators? Critical Pedagogy in the Age of Globalization. in Arif Dirlik, editor, *Pedagogies of the Global: Knowledge in the Human Interest.* Boulder, Colorado: Paradigm Publishers, 2006.

(with Noah De Lissovoy) Ghosts in the Procedure. In Karyn Cooper and Robert White (eds). The Practical Critical Educator: Critical Inquiry and Educational Practice. Springer, The Netherlands. 2006.

Global Culture of Terror: A Marxist Riposte. In Olli-Pekka Moisio and Juha Suoranta, eds. Education and the Spirit of Time: Historical, Global and Critical Reflections. Rotterdam, Sense Publishers. 2006.

期刊论文4篇

(with Nathalia Jaramillo). Introduction to the Special Edition of Ethnicities, edited by Peter McLaren and Nathalia Jaramillo, Vol. 6, No. 3, 2006.

(with Ramin Farahmandpur) The Pedagogy of Oppression: A Brief Look at 'No Child Left Behind'. Monthly Review, Vol. 58, No. 3, July August, 2006.

(with Nathalia E. Jaramillo) Critical Pedagogy and Latina/o Education, Cultural Studies/Critical Methodologies, Vol. 6, No. 1, 2006, in a special edition on critical pedaogogy guest edited by Antonia Darder and Lou Miron.

Let Them Blister Paint: Response to Rebecca Martusewicz. Educational Studies, Vol. 39, No. 1, 2006.

著作前言5篇

Preface: Marxism and Communication Studies: The Point is to Change It (Media and Culture). Lee Artz, Steve Macek, and Dana Cloud, editors. New York: Peter Lang Pubishers, 2006.

Preface: Fashion a Bulwark Against Barbarism. Education, Equality and Human Rights: Issues of Gender, 'Race', Sexuality, Disability and Social Class. 2nd edition. Edited by Mike Cole. London and New York: Routledge. 2006

Preface: Teachers as Cultural Workers (the expanded paperback 2nd edition) by Paulo Freire. Boulder, Colorado: Westview Press, 2006.

Preface: The Power of the "Personal". Literacies of power: What Americans are not allowed to know, Expanded 2nd Edition by Donaldo Macedo. Boulder, CO: Westview Press, 2006.

Preface. Learning and Social Difference by Carmel Borg and Peter Mayo. Boulder, Colorado: Paradigm Publishers, 2006.

访谈麦克拉伦论文3篇

Fassbinder, S. D. (Interviewer). McLaren, P. (Interviewee). (2006). The "dirty thirty's": Peter McLaren reflects on the crisis of academic freedom. *Monthly Review Zine*. Retrieved from http://mrzine.monthlyreview.org/fassbinder060406.html.

Shaughnessy, M. F. (Interviewer). M. F. (Interviewer). McLaren, P. (Interviewee). (2006, October). Understanding Peter McLaren in the age of global capitalism and the new imperialism. *The International Journal of Progressive Education*, Vol. 2, No. 3.

Shaughnessy, M. F. (Interviewer). McLaren, P. (Interviewee). (2006). An interview with Peter McLaren: Comments on the state of the world – 2005. *International Journal of Progressive Education*, 2(3). Retrieved from http://www.inased.org/v2n3/shaughnessy.pdf

外文（除英文外）出版物1篇

(with Glenn Rikowski, Mike Cole and Dave Hill). Red Chalk. Published in Turkish by Kalkedon Press, 2006.

2007年（59岁）

学术著作2部

McLaren, P. (2007). *Pedagogia Critica: Contra o Imperio*. Mangualde, Portugal: Edicones, Pedago, LDA.

Jaramillo, N. & McLaren, P. (2007). *Pedagogy and Praxis in the Age of Empire: Toward A New Humanism*. Rotterdam, Netherlands: Sense Publishers.

主编书籍 1 部

McLaren, P. , & Kincheloe, J. L. （Eds. ）. （2007）. *Critical Pedagogy*：*Where Are We Now*?, 299. New York, NY：Peter Lang Publishing.

参著篇章 3 篇

（with Nathalia Jaramillo）. The Politics of Erasure. *The Praeger Handbook of Latino Education in the U. S.* （Vol. 2）Edited by Lourdes Diaz Soto. Westport Connecticut and London：Praeger, 2007.

Revolutionary Peacemaking：Using a Critical Pedagogy Approach for Peacemaking with "Terrorists", Dr. Steven Best, Dr. Peter McLaren and Anthony J. Nocella, II Journal for Critical Education Policy Studies, Vol. 5, No. 2（November 2007）. Reprinted in One Paradigm, Many Worlds：Approches to Conflict Resolution across the Disciplines. Edited by Mitch Rosenwald（2008）. Cambridge Scholars Press：Newcastle, England.

The Future of the Past：Reflections on the Present State of Empire and Pedagogy, in Peter McLaren and Joe Kincheloe, eds. , *Critical Pedagogy*：*Where Are We Now*?, New York：Peter Lang Publishers, 2007.

期刊论文 3 篇

（with Crawford and Jaramillo）. "Os Politios da Cultura Juvential e o Educacao Multicultural"（The Politics of Youth Culture and Multicultural Education）. Patio, Vol. 3, Issue 2, 2007, Educacao Infantil, Artmed Ed. S. A. Porto Alegre, RS, Brazil.

（with Nathalia Jaramillo）. Katrina and the Banshee's Wail：The Racialization of Class Exploitation. Cultural Studies/Critical Methodologies. Vol. 7, No. 2, 2007, pp. 202 – 221. A shortened version of this was reprinted as a chapter in Schooling and the Politics of Disaster, edited by Kenneth J. Saltman. New York and London：Routlege, 2007.

（with Rhonda Hammer）. Media Knowledges, Warrior Citizenry, and Postmodern Literacies. In *Media Literacy*：*A Reader*. Edited by Donaldo Macedo and Shirley Steinberg. New York：Peter Lang Publishers, 2007. reprinted.

著作前言 2 篇

Preface. "Immigrant Workers Justice in the Anglosphere". In Latinos in theWest：The Student Movement and Academic Labor in Los Angeles by Carlos Mora. Lanham, Maryland and New York：Rowman and Littlefield Publishers, 2007.

Foreword. The Future of the Past：Foreword to The Marxism of Che Guevara by Michael Lowy. Lanham, Maryland：Rowman and Littlefield, 2007.

关于麦克拉伦的著作 1 部

Pruyn, M., & Charles, L. M. H. (Eds.). (2007). *Teaching Peter McLaren: Paths of Dissent*. New York, NY: Peter Lang Publications.

访谈麦克拉伦论文 6 篇

McLaren, P. (Interviewee). (2007, May). *Black Angel* (Greece).

McLaren, P. (Interviewee). (2007, December 6). Paulo Freire é o mais importante educador crítico lido nos EUA. *Revista do Instituto Humanitas Unisinos*, Brasil. (IHU On – Line).

McLaren, P. (Interviewee). (2007, August 10). Entrevista com Peter McLaren: Por um socialismo based em criterios politicos e eticos. (Interview with Peter McLaren: For a socialism based on political and ethical criteria). *Revista do Instituto Humanities Unisinos*, Brasil. (IHU On – Line).

McLaren, P. (Interviewee). (2007, June 11). Paulo Freire é o mais importante educador crítico lido nos EUA. *Revista do Instituto Humanitas Unisinos*, Brasil. (IHU On – Line).

Cohen, S. (Interviewer). McLaren, P. & Jaramillo, N. (Interviewee). (2007, Fall). An interview with Peter McLaren and Nathalia Jaramillo. *The Humanities Review*, 6 (1), 75 – 100. Retrieved from http://facpub.stjohns.edu/~ganterg/sjureview/vol6 – 1/07McLaren – Jaramillo.pdf.

McLaren, P. (Interviewee). (2007, April). Ladies and Gentleman by Peter McLaren (Greece). Reproduced in *Black Angel*. Retrieved from http://mavrosaggelos.blogspot.com/2007/05/peter – mc – laren.html.

学术百科全书词条 2 条

(with Crawford) "Radicalidade na Obra de Paulo Freire", In: Dicionário Paulo Freire. Eds. Streck, D., et al.

(with Crawford) "Revolução na Obra de Paulo Freire", In: Dicionário Paulo Freire. Eds. Streck, D., et al.

外文（除英文外）出版物 1 篇

Life in Schools, 4th Edition: Russian translation, 2007.

2008 年（60 岁）

参著篇章 3 篇

(with Nathalia Jaramillo). Rethinking Critical Pedagogy: Socialismo Nepantla and the

Specter of Che. In the *Handbook of Critical and Indigenous Methodologies*, Norman K. Denzin, Yvonna S. Lincoln and Linda Tuhiwai Smith, Editors. Thousand Oaks, California, and London, England: SAGE Publications.

Decolonizing Democratic Education: Marxian Ruminations. In *Decolonizing Democratic Education: Trans – disciplinary Dialogues*. Edited by Ali A. Abdi and George Richardson. Tapei and Rotterdam: Sense Publications, 2008.

The Struggle for Critical Teacher Education: Critical Pedagogy for Teacher Educators. Published in Conference Proceedings, International Conference on Teacher Education, Transformative Society and Teacher Education Reform. Northeast Normal University, Changchun China. 2008.

期刊论文 4 篇

Pedagogia Publica en el vientre de la Bestia. Proceedings of the Instituto de Pedagogia Popular. Lima, Peru. August, (2009). Revised version of Antipode, Vol. 42, edition 3, 2008.

(with Nathalia Jaramillo). A book review of *Homegirls: Language and Cultural Practice among Latina Youth Gangs*. By Norma Mendoza – Denton. Malden, Mass.: Blackwell, 2008.

This Fist Called My Heart: Public Pedagogy in the Belly of the Beast, Antipode, Vol. 40, Issue 3, 2008.

(with Nathalia Jaramillo). No neo – marxista, no post – marxista, no marxiana: en defensa de la critical cultural marxista. RevistaOpciones Pedagogicas. (Bogota, Colombia), Numero 38, Ano 2008.

书评论文 1 篇

(with Nathalia Jaramillo). A book review of *Homegirls. Language and Cultural Practice among Latina Youth Gangs*. By Norma Mendoza - Denton. Malden, MA: Blackwell Publishing, 2008. pp. ix + 339. In the *American Journal of Sociology. AJS* Vol. 115, No. 2 (September 2009).

著作前言 3 篇

Foreword. "Capitalism's Bestiary: Rebuilding Urban Education". In Bradley Porfilio and Curry Malott (Eds.) The Destructive Path of Neoliberalism: An International Examination of Urban Education. Rotterdam, New York and Taipei: Sense Publishers, 2008.

Foreword. Marxism and Educational Theory: Origins and Issues by Mike Cole. London and New York: Routledge, 2008.

Foreword. The Education of Ignorance by Christos Katsikas and Costas Therianos. Gutenberg, Athens, 2008.

访谈麦克拉伦论文 2 篇

McLaren, P. (Interviewee). (2008, July). Professores devem ser os "novos agentes da esperançca." *A Página da Eucaçao*, 180.

McMurry, A., McGuirk, K. (Interviewers) &McLaren, P. (Interviewee). (2008). Department of English Language and Literature at the University of Waterloo, Canada. Condensed version retrieved from https: //uwaterloo. ca/english/sites/ca. english/files/uploads/files/2008NEWSLETTER_ final – 1_ 007. pdf.

学术百科全书词条 3 条

(with Ryoo, JJ, Crawford, J. and Moreno, D.). 2008 "Critical Pedagogy" In: *Encyclopedia of Curriculum Studies*. Ed. Kridel. Sage Publications, NY.

(with Ryoo, JJ, Crawford, J. and Moreno, D.). 2008 "Critical Praxis" In: *Encyclopedia of Curriculum Studies*. Ed. Kridel. Sage Publications, NY.

(with Ryoo, JJ, Crawford, J. and Moreno, D.). 2008 "Paulo Freire" *Encyclopedia of Political Theory*. Ed. Craig. Sage Publications, NY.

外文（除英文外）出版物 1 篇

Che Guevara, Paulo Freire, and the Pedagogy of Revolution. Published in Turkish by Kalkedon Press, 2008, and published in Korean, 2009, and Italian, 2009 and Finnish 2009.

2009 年（61 岁）

主编书籍 2 部

Sandlin, J. A., & McLaren, P. (Eds.). (2009). *Critical Pedagogies of Consumption: Living and Learning in the Shadow of the "Shopocalypse"*. New York, NY: Routledge.

Macrine, S., McLaren, P., & Hill, D. (Eds.). (2009). *Revolutionizing Pedagogy: Education for Social Justice Within and Beyond Global Neo – Liberalism*. London, UK: Palgrave Macmillan.

参著篇章 5 篇

(with Jenifer Crawford, Nana Gyamfi). Unplaguing the Stomach: Curing the University of California Admissions Policy with an Ethic of Communal Justice and Care. Edited by H. Svi Shapiro. Education and Hope in Troubled Times. New York and London: Routledge.

A Possible Praxis. In Mark Abenroth, editor, Rebel Literacy: Cuba's National Literacy Campaign and Critical Global Scholarship. Litwin Books: Duluth Minnesota.

(with Suoranta, J.). Socialist Pedagogy. In Hill, D. (ed.). Contesting Neoliberal Education. New York & London: Routledge.

(with Nathalia Jaramillo). Borderlines: bell hooks and the Pedagogy of Revolutionary Change. In *Critical Perspectives on bell hooks*, edited by Maria del Guadalupe Davidson and George Yancy. London and New York: Routledge.

(with Scatamburlo – D'Annibale and Valerie). The Reign of Capital: A Pedagogy and Praxis of Class Struggle. The Routledge *International Handbook of Critical Education.* Edited by Michael Apple, Wayne Au, and Luis Armando Gandin. New York and London: Routledge.

期刊论文 7 篇

(with Smith, M. and Ryoo, J. J.). A revolutionary critical pedagogy manifesto for the twenty – first century. In Zajda, J. (Ed.), Education and Society, Vol. 27, No. 3, 2009.

Guided by a Red Star: The Cuban Literacy Campaign and the Challenge of History. Journal of Critical Education Policy Studies. Vol. 7, No. 2, 2009. (November). http://www.jceps.com/?pageID=article&articleID=161.

The Return of the Transformative Intellectual. Left Curve. No. 33, 2009.

(with Lin, Zhou) Revolutionary Critical Pedagogy: The Antidote for Teacher Education Programs. Journal of Northeast Normal University (Philosophy and Social Sciences) No. 2, Summer 2009.

Pedagogia Publica en el vientre de la Bestia. Proceedings of the Instituto de Pedagogia Popular. Lima, Peru. August, (2009). Revised version of Antipode, Vol. 42, edition 3, 2008.

(with Jean Ryoo). Assessment in American schools. Pátio – Ensino Médio, 1 (2), 2009.

(with Jean Ryoo, Jen Crawford and Dianna Moreno). Critical Spiritual Pedagogy: Reclaiming humanity through a pedagogy of integrity, community, and love. Power and Education. Vol. 1, No. 1, 2009.

书评论文 1 篇

Book review in the American Journal of Sociology. Vol. 115, No. 2, September 2009.

前言/后记 6 篇

Foreword. "E. San Juan: The Return of the Transformative Intellectual" in Critique and

Social Transformation: Lessons from Antonio Gramsci, Mikhail Bakhtin and Raymond Williams by E. San Juan. London: Edwin Mellen Press, 2009.

Afterword. Kelsh, D., Hill, D., and Macrine, S. (eds.) Class in Education: Knowledge, Pedagogy, Subjectivity. New York: Routledge, 2009.

Preface. Hill, D. and Robertson, L. Helavaara (eds.) Equality in the Primary School: Promoting good practice across the curriculum. London: Continuum, 2009.

Afterword. Peter McLaren, Education and the Struggle for Liberation: Revolution as Education. Edited by Mustafa Eryaman. New Jersey: Hampton Press, 2009.

Foreword. In Contesting Neoliberal Education: Public Resistance and Collective Advance. Edited by Dave Hill. London and New York: Routlege, 2009.

Foreword. Breaching the Colonial Contract: Anti-Colonialism in the US and Canada. Series: Explorations of Educational Purpose. Kempf, Arlo (Ed.) New York: Springer Publishing Company, Vol. 8. 2009.

关于麦克拉伦的著作1部

Eryaman, M. (Ed.). (2009). *Peter McLaren, education, and the struggle for liberation*. New York, NY: Hampton Press.

访谈麦克拉伦论文3篇

Leban, S. (Interviewer). McLaren, P. (Interviewee). (2009). Revolutionary critical pedagogy: The struggle against the oppression of neoliberalism: A conversation with Peter McLaren, part I. *Reartikulacija*, 5. (Internet Journal, Slovenia).

Leban, S. (Interviewer). McLaren, P. (Interviewee). (2009). Revolutionary critical pedagogy: The struggle against the oppression of neoliberalism: A conversation with Peter McLaren, part II. *Reartikulacija*, 6. (Internet Journal, Slovenia).

The two interviews above were also published as: McLaren, Peter. (2011). Critical pedagogy as revolutionary practice. In Jones, P. E. (Ed.). *Marxism and Education: Reviewing the Dialogue, Pedagogy, and Culture* (216 – 234). New York, NY: Palgrave/Macmillan.

Kumar, R. (Interviewer) & McLaren, P. (Interviewee). (2009). Being, becoming and breaking-free: Peter McLaren and the pedagogy of liberation. *Radical Notes*.

The above interview was later published as: McLaren, P. (2012). Being, becoming and breaking free: Peter McLaren and the pedagogy of liberation. In Kumar, R. (Ed.), *Education and the Reproduction of Capital: Neoliberal Knowledge and Counterstrategies*. (209 –

239). New York, NY: Macmillan.

学术百科全书词条 1 条

(with Crawford, J.). "Paulo Freire", In *Chicago Companion to the Child*, Ed. Laur, M. August. University of Chicago Press, Chicago, IL. p. 380.

外文（除英文外）出版物 4 篇

Che Guevara, Paulo Freire, and the Pedagogy of Revolution. Published in Turkish by Kalkedon Press, 2008, and published in Korean, 2009, and Italian, 2009 and Finnish 2009.

(withNathalia Jaramillo). Pedagogy and Praxis in the Age of Empire (2009). Published in Turkish by Kalkedon Press. Published in Spanish by Editora Popular, and currently being translated into Portuguese and Greek.

Critical Pedagogy: Where Are We Now? Peter McLaren and Joe Kincheloe, editors. (Peter Lang Publications, New York). Published in Spanish in Barcelona, Spain by GRAO. (2009).

Polskie Reminiscencje wobec wyzwania rytualu w szkole. In Zbigiew Kwiencinski and Monika Jaworska – Witkowska, editors Ku Integralnosci Edukacji I Humanistyki. 2009. pp. 833 – 842). Wydawnictowo Adam Marszalek, publishers. Torun: Poland. （Polish）

2010年（62岁）

主编书籍 2 部

Nocella, A., Best, S., & McLaren, P. (Eds.). (2010). *Academic Repression: Reflections from the Academic – Industrial Complex*. Oakland, CA: A K Press.

Martin, G., Houston, D., McLaren, P., & Suoranta, J. (Eds.). (2010). *The Havoc of Capitalism: Publics, Pedagogies and Environmental Crisis*. Rotterdam, The Netherlands: Sense Publishers.

参著篇章 7 篇

(with Scatamburlo – D´Annibale and Valerie). (2010). Contesting the New "Young Hegelians": Interrogating Capitalism in a World of "Difference", In Peter Trifonas, ed. Worlds of Difference: Rethinking the Ethics of Global Education for the 21st Century. Boulder and London: Paradigm Publishers.

(with Ryoo, J. J.). (2010). Aloha for Sale: A class analysis of Hawai'i. In D. Chapman (Ed.), Examining Social Theory. New York: Peter Lang Publishers.

(with Scatamburlo – D'Annibale and Valerie). (2010). Classifying Race: The Compassionate Racism of the Right and Why Class Still Matters. In Zeus Leonardo, editor. Handbook of Cultural Politics and Education. Rotterdam and Tapei: Sense Publications.

This Fist Called My Heart: Public Pedagogy in the Belly of the Beast. In Jennifer A. Sandlin, Brian Schultz, and Jake Burdick, eds. Handbook of Public Pedagogy: Education and Learning Beyond Schooling. London and New York: Routledge. [An expanded version of McLaren, Peter. (2008). This Fist Called My Heart: Public Pedagogy in the Belly of the Beast, Antipode, Vol. 40, issue 3.

(with Ryoo, J.). (2010). Seeking Democracy in American Schools: Countering Epistemic Violence Through Revolutionary Critical Pedagogy. In R. Hoosain and F. Salili, (eds.), Democracy and Multicultural Education. N. J.: Information Age Publishing.

Educating Against Imperialism: Critical Pedagogy, Social Justice, and the Struggle for Peace. Voices for a Culture of Peace, Vol. 1. Compendium of the SGI – USA Culture of Peace Distinguished Speaker Series, Santa Monica, California: Culture of Peace Press, Soka Gakkai International – USA.

(with Scatamburlo – D'Annibale and Valerie). (2010). Class – ifying Race: The Compassionate Racism of the Right and Why Class Still Matters. In Zeus Leonardo, editor. Handbook of Cultural Politics and Education. Rotterdam and Tapei: Sense Publications.

期刊论文 7 篇

Rehearsing Disaster's Rehearsal: The Election and It's Aftermath in Obamerica. Cultural Studies/Critical Methodologies, Cultural Studies < = > Critical Methodologies. Vol. 9 No. 6, December 2010.

(with Jaramillo and Nathalia). Not Neo – Marxist, Not Post – Marxist, Not Marxian: Some Notes on Critical Pedagogy and Marxist Thought. Cultural Studies/Critical Methodologies, Vol. 10, No. 3, June, 2010.

(with Ryoo, J. J.). Revolucionando a educação multicultural. Revista da FAEEBA – Educação e Contemporaneidade, Salvador, Vol. 19, No. 34, 2010.

Revolutionary Critical Pedagogy. Interactions: UCLA Journal of Education and Information Studies. No. 7, 2010.

Memories of Natural – Born World Shaker. Cultural Studies /Critical Methodologies, Vol. 10, No. 5, October 2010.

(with Jean J. Ryoo). Revolucionando a educacao multicultural. Educacao e Movimentos

Sociais. Vol. 19, No. 34, Jul/Dez 2010.

(with Ryoo, J. J.). Case commentary: Bridging the gap. In G. L. Porter & D. Smith (Eds.), Case studies in inclusive education. (2010). Ontario College of Teachers and Canadian Assoc. for Community Living, Toronto, Ontario.

前言/后记 5 篇

Afterword. "Public pedagogy and the challenge of historical time" in Handbook of Public Pedagogy: Education and Learning Beyond Schooling. Edited by Jennifer A. Sandlin, Brian Schultz, Steven "Jake" Burdick, Routledge. 2010.

Preface. Crimes of Empire: The History and Politics of an Outlaw Nation by Carl Boggs. London: Pluto Press, 2010.

Foreword. In Valerie Hill‐Jackson and Chance Lewis, eds. *Transforming Teacher Education: What Went Wrong With Teacher Training and How we can Fix It*. Stylus Publishing. 2010.

Afterword. A Fado For Freire. Memories of Paulo. Edited by Tom Wilson, Peter Park and Anaida Colon‐Muniz. Sense Publishers: Tapei and Rotterdam, 2010.

Foreword. The Crimes of Empire: Rogue Superpower and World Domination. By Carl Boggs. London and New York: Pluto Press, 2010.

访谈麦克拉伦论文 1 篇

Macrine, S., Hill, D., & McLaren, P. (Eds.) (2010). *Revolutionizing Pedagogy: Education for Social Justice within and Beyond Global Neoliberalism*. New York, NY: Palgrave Macmillian.

学术百科全书词条 1 条

(withRyoo, J. J.). (2010). Critical theory. In: P. Peterson, E. Baker, & B. McGaw (Eds.), International Encyclopedia of Education (Vol. 6), . Oxford: Elsevier.

外文（除英文外）出版物 1 篇

(with Nathalia Jaramillo) Нінеомарксистський, ні постмарксистський, ні марксовий, ні автономістський марксизм: рефлексія на революційну (марксистську) критичну педагогіку / Пітер Макларен, Наталія Харамійо // Філософія освіти: Наук. часопис. ‐ 2010. ‐ № 1‐2 (9) / Ін‐т вищо ї освіти НАПН Укра ї ни, Нац. пед. ун‐т ім. М. П. Драгоманова, Укр. академія політ. наук. ‐ К.: Вид‐во НПУ імені М. П. Драгоманова, 2010. ‐ 320 с. ‐ С. 22‐35. (Russian)

2011 年（63 岁）

主编书籍 1 部

Best, S. , Kahn, R. , Nocella, A. J. , & McLaren, P. （Eds. ）. （2011）. *The Global Industrial Complex: Systems of Domination.* Lanham, MD: Lexington Books, Rowman & Littlefield.

参著篇章 7 篇

Is There Anyone Out There...? In Paul R. Carr and Brad J. Porfilio, eds. , The Phenomenon of Obama and the Agenda for Education: Can Hope Audaciously Trump Neoliberalism? Charlotte, N. C. : Information Age Publishing, Inc.

（withSuoranta, Juha and Jaramillo, Nathalia）. （2011）. Becoming a Critical Citizen: A Marxist – Humanist Critique. In Alexander, Hanan, Pinson, Halleli, and Yonah, Yossi, eds. , Citizenship, Education, and Social Conflict: Israeli Political Education in a Global Perspective. London and New York: Routledge.

Critical Pedagogy in Stark Opposition to Western Neoliberalism and the Corporatization of Schools: A Conversation with Peter McLaren. In Pierre Orelus, editor, Rethinking Race, Class, Language, and Gender: A Dialogue with Noam Chomsky and Other Leading Scholars. Lanham, Boulder, Plymouth （UK） and Toronto: Rowman and Littlefield Publishers.

Class Struggle Unchained: Higher Education and the Crisis of Capitalism. International Conference on Higher Education Management – 2011. Taiwan, 12. 23. This consists of material reprinted from other publications.

（withKincheloe, Joe and Steinberg, Shirley R）. （2011）. In Denzin, Norm and Lincoln, Yvonna, eds. The Sage Handbook of Qualitative Research, Vol. 4. Thousand Oaks, California, and London, SAGE Publications, Inc. （Substantially rewritten from previous volumes）.

Paulo Freire: Defending His Heritage to Remake the Earth. In James D. Kirlyo, ed. Paulo Freire: The Man from Recife. New York and Oxford: Peter Lang Publishers.

Critical Pedagogy as Revolutionary Practice. In Peter E. Jones, ed. Marxism and Education: Reviewing the Dialogue, Pedagogy, and Culture. New York and Basingstoke, Hampshire.

期刊论文 3 篇

The Death Rattle of the American Mind. Cultural Studies/Critical Methodologies. Vol. 11, No. 4, 2011.

(with Jaramillo, N. E. and Lázaro, F.). A critical pedagogy of recuperation. Policy Futures in Education, 9 (6), 2011.

Radical Negativity: Music Education for Social Justice. Action, Criticism & Theory for Music Education. Vol. 10, No. 1, August 2011.

著作前言3篇

Preface: Revolutionary Critical Pedagogy Against the Resurgence of Confederate Ideology. In Pierre Orelus, editor, Rethinking Race, Class, Language, and Gender: A Dialogue with Noam Chomsky and Other Leading Scholars. (2011) Lanham, Boulder, Plymouth (UK) and Toronto: Rowman and Littlefield Publishers.

Foreword. In Freedom Fighters: Struggles Instituting the Study of Black History in K – 12 Education by Abul Pitre. Cognella: San Diego, 2011.

Preface: Towards a Decolonizing Epistemology. Erik Malewski and Nathalia Jaramillo (eds). *Epistemologies of Ignorance in Education*. Charlotte, North Carolina: Information Age Publishers. 2011.

访谈麦克拉伦论文3篇

Education as class warfare. Socialist Web Zine. The Socialist, 4. Retrieved from http://socialistwebzine.blogspot.com/2011/09/education – as – class – warfare – interview.html.

Пітер Макларен. (2011). Революционная критическая педагогика XXI СТ. Відповілі на запитання Іріні Предьорскьо Ї. *Філософія Оосвіті: Наукчасопіс*, 9 (1 – 2): 56 – 67.

Predborska, I. (Interviewer) & McLaren, P. (Interviewee). (2011). Revolutionary critical pedagogy in the 21st century. Philosophy of Education: A Research Journal, 9 (1 – 2): 56 – 67. [Ukrainian translation, 2011]

学术百科全书词条2条

(withRyoo, JJ). (2011). Entry. Casebook for Teacher Education. Montreal, Canada: Laval University Press.

(withRyoo, JJ). (2011). Multiculturalism. Definition for the Dicionário sobre Trabalho, Profissão e Condição DocenteI. Belo Horizonte, Brazil: Federal University of Minas Gerais School of Education Research Group on Educational Policy and Teachers' Work & the Secretary of Basic Education of the Ministry of Education and Culture of Brazil.

外文（除英文外）出版物1篇

In Pep Aparicio Guadas, ed., El Poder de Educar y de Educarnos: Transformar la practica docente desde una perspectiva critical. Pedagogia Critica revolutcionaria de las epocas oscuras. 2011. Editions de CREC. Xativa, Spain.

2012年（64岁）

学术著作1部

McLaren, P. (2012). *La Pedagogia Critica Revolucionaria: El Socialismo y los Desafios Actuales*. Buenos Aires, Argentina: Herramienta Ediciones.

参著篇章3篇

(withHouston, D., Martin, G.). (2012), In the Market for Reconciliation? In Reconciliation and Pedagogy. Edited by Pal Ahluwalia et alia. New York, Routledge.

Class Struggle Unchained. In Pierre Orelus and Curry Malott, eds. Radical Voices for Democratic Schooling: Exposing Neoliberal Inequalities. London and New York: Palgrave Macmillan.

(withJean J. Ryoo). (2012). Revolutionary Critical Pedagogy Against Capitalist Multicultural Education. Handel Kashope Wright, Michael Singh and Richard Race (Eds.) Precarious International Multicultural Education: Hegemony, Dissent and Rising Alternatives. Rotterdam, Boston and Taipei: Sense Publishers.

期刊论文5篇

Objection Sustained: revolutionary pedagogical praxis as an occupying force, Policy Futures in Education, Vol. 10, No. 4, 2012.

(with Gutierrez, Alberto). To Be or Not to Be a Snitch or a Whistle bower: Years of Silence at Penn State. Cultural studies/Critical Methodologies, Vol. 12, No. 4, 2012.

Revolutionary Critical Pedagogy for a Socialist Society: A Manifesto. The Capilano Review. Vol. 3, No. 13, 2012.

(with Jonathan Grady, Rigoberto Marquez). A Critique of Neo – Liberalism with Fierceness: Queer Youth of Color Creating Dialogues of Resistance for a special issue entitled, Sexualities and Genders in an Age of Neoliberalism, Journal of Homosexuality 59: 982 – 1004. 2012. Guest Edited by, John P. Elia, Ph. D. & Gust A. Yep, Ph. D. McLaren, Peter.

Remembering a Loving Warrior Ilan Gur – Ze'ev 1955 – 2012. Educational Philosophy and Theory, Vol. 44, No. 2, 2012.

前言/后记 3 篇

Foreword. McLaren, P. & Jaramillo, N. (2012). Dialectical thinking: Towards a critical tourism Studies.

Afterword. Best, S., Kahn, R., Nocella, A. and McLaren, P., eds. Systems of Domination: The Global Industrial Complex. Lanham, Maryland: Lexington Books, 2012.

Preface. Education, Equality and Human Rights: Issues of gender, 'race', sexuality, disability and social class, edited by Mike Cole. Third Edition. London and New York: Routledge, 2012.

2013 年（65 岁）

参著篇章 1 篇

Revolutionary critical pedagogy for a socialist society: A manifesto. In Reitz, C. (Ed.). *Crisis of Commonwealth: Marcuse, Marx, McLaren*, Lanham, MD: Lexington Books, Rowman & Littlefield.

期刊论文 4 篇

(withCole, M.) Searching for the Future in the Streets of Caracas. Cultural Studies Critical Methodologies, Vol. 13, No. 6.

Farewell tothe Man in the Red Beret, Enter the Man in the White Silk Mitre: 'there is a crack in everything, that's how the light gets in', Policy Futures in Education, 11 (4), 2013.

Seeds of resistance: Towards a revolutionary critical ecopedagogy. Socialist Studies, 9 (1), 84 – 108.

A Critical Patriotism for Urban Schooling: A Call for a Pedagogy Against Fear and Denial and For Democracy. Texas Education Review, 2013, Vol. 1. As retrieved from: http://txedrev. org/wp – content/uploads/2013/11/McLaren_ A – Critical – Patriotism – for – Urban – Schooling_ TxEdRev. pdf

关于麦克拉伦的著作 1 部

Reitz, C. (Ed.). (2013). *Crisis of Commonwealth: Marcuse, Marx, McLaren*. Lanham, MD: Lexington Books, Rowman & Littlefield.

访谈麦克拉伦论文 3 篇

Tristan, J. M. B. (Interviewer) & McLaren, P. (Interviewee). (2013). Critical pedagogy against capitalist schooling: Towards a socialist alternative. An interview with Peter

McLaren. *Global Education Magazine*. Retrieved from http：//www. globaleducationmagazine. com/tag/peter – mclaren/.

Education as class warfare：An interview with scholar/author Peter McLaren. *Praxis Educativa*, 17 (2), 91 – 101. Retrieved from http：//ojs. fchst. unlpam. edu. ar/ojs/index. php/praxis/article/viewFile/603/722.

Richardson, S. (Interviewer) & McLaren, P. (Interviewee). (2013, June 13). Latin waves interviews author/educator Dr. Peter McLaren. *NCRA Program Exchange*, *Latin Waves*, 256. Audio retrieved from http：//previous. ncra. ca/exchange/dspProgramDetail. cfm? programID = 137779.

2014 年（66 岁）

学术著作 1 部

McLaren, P. (2014). *Life in Schools. An Introduction to Critical Pedagogy in the Foundations of Education* (6th ed.). Herndon, VA：Paradigm Publishers.

参著篇章 2 篇

Eine marxistische Epistel an die transnationale kapitalische Klasse. In Erler, I. , etc. (Eds.). *Wenn Weiterbildung die Antwort Ist*, *Was War Die Frage*? Austria：Studien Verlag Innsbruck.

(withRodriguez, A.). (2014). Human rights, states' rights, and linguistic apartheid. In Orelus, P. (Ed) *Affirming Language Diversity in Schools and Society*：*Beyond Linguistic Apartheid*, London and New York：Routledge.

期刊论文 12 篇

Contemporary youthresistance culture and the class struggle. *Critical Arts*：*A South – North Journal of Cultural and Media Studies*, Vol. 28, No. 1.

America in ruins as Belgrade dreams：Challenging the capitalist road to fascism through critical pedagogy and critical patriotism. *Pedagogija*, 2.

Education agonistes：An epistle to the transnational capitalist class. *Policy Futures in Education*, Vol. 12, No. 4.

(withMonzó, L. D.). (2014). Critical pedagogy and the decolonial option：Challenges to the inevitability of capitalism. *Policy Futures in Education*, Vol. 12, No. 4.

(with Jandrić, P). (2014). Critical revolutionary pedagogy is made by walking – in a world where many worlds coexist. *Policy Futures in Education*, Vol. 12, No. 6.

Comrade Jesus: An Epistolic Manifesto. Knowledge Cultures. Vol. 2, No. 6, 2014.

(with Monzó, L. D. and Rodriguez, A.). Distribución de armas a comunidades prescindibles. Baño de sangre en México, imperialismo estadounidense y capital transnacional: por una pedagogía crítica revolucionaria. In Tiempos violentos Barbarie y decadencia civilizatoria. Buenos Aires, Argentina: Ediciones Herramientas, 2014.

(with Monzó, L. D.). Critical pedagogy and the decolonial option: Challenges to the inevitability of capitalism. Policy Futures in Education, Vol. 12, No. 4, 2014.

Reflections on Love and Revolution, International Journal of Critical Pedagogy, Vol. 5 No. 1, 2014.

(with Mike Cole). Austerity/Immiseration Capitalism. What Can We Learn from Venezuelan Socialism? In Truthout, Wednesday June 11, 2014. As retrieved from: http://truth-out.org/news/item/24264-austerity-immiseration-capitalism-what-can-we-learn-from-venezuelan-socialism. Also reprinted in Venezuelan Analysis, June 14, 2014. Also reprinted in Iberamericano Social, 2014. As retrieved from: http://iberoamericasocial.com/austerityimmiseration-capitalism-can-learn-venezuelan-socialism/.

(with Monzó, L. D.). Toward a red theory of love, sexuality, and the family. Iberoamérica Social: revista-red de estudios sociales (III), 2014. Retrieved http://iberoamericasocial.com/toward-a-red-theory-of-love-sexuality-and-the-family.

(with Monzó, L. D.). Red love: Toward racial, economic and social justice. Truthout, Dec. 18, 2014. Retrieved http://www.truth-out.org/opinion/item/28072-red-love-toward-racial-economic-and-social-justice.

前言/后记 4 篇

Endword: Michael Peters: Gentle polymath and commanding intellectual. In Lazaroiu, G. (Ed.), *Liber Amicorum: A Philosophical Conversation Among Friends*, New York: Addleton Academic Publishers.

Foreword. In Orelus, P. W. & Chomsky, N. (Eds.), *On Language, Democracy, and Social Justice*, Peter Lang International Academic Publisher.

Foreword. In Freire, P., *Pedagogy of the Oppressed* (Chinese Edition), East China Normal University Press.

Foreword. In Frey, L. R. & Palmer, D. L. (Eds.), *Teaching Communication Activism: Communication Education for Social Justice*. New York: Hampton Press.

访谈麦克拉伦论文1篇

Jandrić, P. (Interviewer) & McLaren, P. (Interviewee). (2014). Critical revolutionary pedagogy is made by walking: In a world where many worlds coexist. *Policy Futures in Education*, Vol. 12, No. 6.

2015年（67岁）

学术著作2部

McLaren, P. (2015). *Pedagogy of Insurrection: From Resurrection to Revolution*. New York, NY: Peter Lang Publishers.

McLaren, P. (2015). *Camarada Jesus*. Buenos Aires, Argentina: Herramienta (in press).

参著篇章7篇

(with Monzó, L. D.). (2015) The future is Marx: Bringing back class and changing the world – A moral imperative. In M. Y. Remain & B. Bruce (Eds.), *International Handbook of Progressive Education*. PEGEM.

Reflections on Paulo Freire, Critical Pedagogy, and the Current Crisis of Capitalism. In Michael Peters and Tina Besley, eds. *Paulo Freire: The Global Legacy*. New York: Peter Lang Publishers. 2015.

Self and social formation and the political project of teaching: Some reflections. In Porfilio, B. J. & Ford, D. R. (Eds.). *Leaders in Critical Pedagogy: Narratives for Understanding and Solidarity*, Rotterdam: Sense Publishers.

(with Jandrić, P.). (2015). The critical challenge of networked learning: using information technologies in the service of humanity. In Jandrić, P. & Boras, D. (Eds.), *Critical Learning in Digital Networks*, New York: Springer.

(with Monzó, L. D.). (2015). Marked for labor: Latina bodies and transnational capital – A critical pedagogy approach. For C. R. Monroe, (Ed.), *Race and colorism in education*. New York: Routledge.

(with Monzó, L. D.). (2015). Critical pedagogy: Past, present, and future. In M. Y. Eryaman & B. Bruce (Eds.), *International Handbook of Progressive Education*. PEGEM.

Red Bones: Toward a Pedagogy of Common Struggle: Response 2. In Grande, S. *Red Pedagogy: Native American Social and Political Thought* (Tenth Anniversary Edition), (99

—108). Lanham·Boulder·New York·London：Rowman & Littlefield.

期刊论文 3 篇

(with Monzó, L. D.). (2015). Pedagogy of possibility：Socialism on the way to "deep democracy." *Anthropology & Education Quarterly*, Vol. 46, No. 4.

(with Monzó, L. D.). (2015). Women and violence in the age of migration. *Iberoamérica Social：revista – red de estudios sociales*, June 10. Retrieved http：//iberoamericasocial. com/women – and – violence – in – the – age – of – migration/.

Ondialectics and human decency：Education in the dock. *Open Review of Educational Research*, Vol. 2, No. 1, DOI：10. 1080/23265507. 2014. 986187.

著作前言 5 篇

Foreword. In Loughead T. *Critical University：Moving Higher Education Forward*, Lanham：Lexington Books.

Preface. In Berryman, M., Nevin, A., SooHoo, S., & Ford, T. (Eds.). *Relational and Responsive Inclusion：Contexts for Becoming and Belonging*. NY：Peter Lang.

Foreword. Being and becoming Communist：Toward a revolutionary critical pedagogy of becoming. In Malott, C. S. & Ford D. R., *Marx, Capital, and Education：Towards a Critical Pedagogy of Becoming*, NY：Peter Lang.

Preface：Revolutionary Critical Pedagogy and the Commonwealth Counter – Offensive. In Charles Reitz (Ed.), *Crisis and commonwealth：Marx, Marcuse, McLaren*. Lanham：Lexington Books.

Foreword. In Normore, A. H. & Esposito, K. (Eds.), *Inclusive Practices and Social Justice Leadership for Special Populations in Urban Settings：A Moral Imperative*, Information Age Publishing Inc.

访谈麦克拉伦论文 6 篇

McLaren, P. (Interviewee) & Jose Maria Barroso Tristan (Interviewer). (2015). Pedagogia critica Vs educazione capitalista. Verso un' alternativa socialista [translation of the interview (Critical pedagogyagainst capitalist schooling：Towards a socialist alternative) published in *Global Education Magazine*]. In Gisella Vismara, *Educare Allo Sguardo 3：Esperienza, Arte, Educazione nel Tempo Dell' "Oggettivita"*. Milano：BRERA Accademia di Belle Arti.

Yu, W. (Interviewer) & McLaren, P. (Interviewee). (2015, June). Critical pedagogy and the struggle for social justice：Interview with Peter McLaren. *Studies in Foreign Education*（外国教育研究）, Vol. 42, No. 6.

Ford, D. R. (Interviewer) & McLaren, P. (Interviewee). (2015, June 16). Revolutionary critical pedagogy and the struggle against capital today: An interview with Peter McLaren. The Hampton Institute: A Working - Class Think Tank. Retrieved from http://www.hamptoninstitution.org/peter-mclaren-interview.html#.Vb6_AZNViko.

Davis, C. (Interviewer) & McLaren, P. (Interviewee). (2015, March 8). An interview with arevolutionary, professor Peter McLaren. *Huffington Post*. Retrieved from http://www.huffingtonpost.com/creston-davis/an-interview-with-a-revol_b_6825766.html.

Fassbinder, S. D. (Interviewer) & McLaren, P. (Interviewee). (2015, February). Interview with Peter McLaren: His job, his visit to Turkey and popular struggles in progress. Buenos Aires, Argentina: *Tool Magazine*.

Cummings, J. (Interviewer) & McLaren, P. (Interviewee). (2015). The abode of educational production: An interview with Peter McLaren. *Alternate Routes: A Journal of Critical Social Research*, 26.

外文（除英文外）出版物 1 篇

McLaren, P. (2015). *Life in Schools: An Introduction to Critical Pedagogy in the Foundations of Education* (6th Ed.). (Dziemianowicz - Bak, A., Dzierzgowski, J., Starnawski, M., & Naukowe, W., Trans.). Wroclaw, Poland: Scientific Publishing House.

2016 年（68 岁）

主编书籍 1 部

SooHoo, S. & McLaren, P. (Eds.) (2016). Radical Imagine - nation (Journal). Chapman University & Peter Lang Publications.

参著篇章 2 篇

(with Monzó, L. D.). (2016). Reclaiming Che! A pedagogy of love and revolution toward a socialist alternative. In Ness, I. & Maty Bâ, S. (Eds.). *Palgrave Encyclopedia of Imperialism and Anti - Imperialism*. Houndmills, Basingstoke, Hampshire, UK: Palgrave Macmillan.

Critical pedagogy and class struggle in the age of neoliberal terror. In Kumar R. (Ed.). *Neoliberalism, Critical Pedagogy and Education*. London: Routledge.

期刊论文 2 篇

(with Monzó, L. D.). (2016). Challenging the violence and invisibility against women of Color – A Marxist imperative. *Iberoamérica Social：Revista – red de Estudios Sociales.*

(with Monzó, L. D. and Rodriguez, A.). Deploying guns to expendable communities：Bloodshed in Mexico, US imperialism and transnational capital – A call for revolutionary critical pedagogy. Cultural Studies/Critical Methodologies, 2016.

前言/后记3篇

Forword：Philosophy and pedagogy of insurrection. In C. Reitz, *Philosophy & Critical Pedagogy：Insurrection & Commonwealth*, (xiii – xvi). NY：Peter Lang.

(with SooHoo, S.). (2016). Afterword. In Colon – Muniz, A. & Lavandez, M. (Eds.) *Latino Civil Rights in Education*, NY：Paradigm Publishers.

Foreword. Questos da Educacao. Marcia Moraes, Editor. *Rio De Janeiro*, Brazil. Ventura.

关于麦克拉伦的著作1部

Pruyn, M. & Huerta – Charles, L. (Eds.). (2016). *This Fist Called My Heart：The Peter McLaren Reader.* Charlotte, NC：Information Age Publishers.

访谈学者论文1篇

"She Led by Transgression"：Margaret Randall on Cuban Feminist Haydée Santamaría. *Truthout.* Retrieved from http：//www. truth – out. org/news/item/37238 – she – led – by – transgression – margaret – randall – on – cuban – feminist – haydee – santamaria.

（电子）新闻和日报文章2篇

(with SooHoo, S.). (August, 2016) Critical Pedagogy in China？Really？Chapman University Blog. Retrieved from：https：//blogs. chapman. edu/ces/2016/08/12/critical – pedagogy – in – china – really/.

En Dialogo con Peter McLaren：Pedagogias criticas para nuevos horizontes emancipadores. Revista Hariek. pp. 12 – 21. Retrieved from：http：//iberoamericasocial. com/pedagogias – criticas – nuevos – horizontes – emancipadores/.

2017年（69岁）

参著篇章2篇

(with Jandric, P.). (2017). Peter McLaren's Liberation Theology：Karl Marx meets Jesus Christ. In J. S. Brooks & A. Normore (Eds.). *Leadership Lessons：Great Thinkers on Equity, Justice and Education.* New York：Teachers College Press.

(withMonzo, L.). (2017). Marked for Labor：Latina Bodies and Transnational Capital—A Marxist Feminist Critical Pedagogy. In Carla R. Monroe. *Race and Colorism in Education*. London and New York: Routledge.

期刊论文 1 篇

(withHartlep, N. D., Hensley, B. O., Wells, K. E., Brewer, T. J., Ball, D.). (2017). Homophily in Higher Education: Historicizing the AERA Member – to – Fellow Pipeline Using Theories of Social Reproduction and Social Networks. *Policy Futures in Education*, *0* (0), 1 – 25.

著作前言 3 篇

Foreword. In E. Wayne Ross. *Rethinking Social Studies: Critical Pedagogy in Pursuit of Dangerous Citizenship*. Charlotte, North Carolina: Information Age Publishers.

Preface. In Joel Kovel, *The Lost Traveller's Dream: A Memoir*. New York: Autonomedia.

(with Monzó. L. D.). (2017). Preface – Unleashed: Whiteness as Predatory Culture. In T. Kennedy, J. Middleton, K. Rattcliffe, (Eds.). *Rhetorics of Whiteness: Postracial Hauntings in Popular Culture, Social Media, and Education*. Carbondale: Southern University Illinois Press.

关于麦克拉伦的著作 1 部

Pruyn, M., Huerta – Charles, L. & Malott, C. (Eds.). *Tracks to Infinity: The Peter McLaren reader*. (will be published Fall, 2017). Collected Essays by Peter McLaren. Charlotte, North Carolina: Information Age Publishers.

访谈麦克拉伦论文 1 篇

McLaren, P. (interviewee) & Jandric, P. (interviewer) (forthcoming). (advanced online preview, April 2017). From liberation to salvation: Revolutionary critical pedagogy meets liberation theology. Special Issue: Pedagogies of Insurrection. Policy Futures in Education.

(电子) 新闻和日报文章 1 篇

Chapman blog: What Unites Us? (March 15, 2017) https://blogs.chapman.edu/magazine/2017/03/15/what – unites – us.

2018 年 (70 岁)

主编书籍 1 部

McLaren, P. & SooHoo, S. (Eds.) (2018). The Radical Imagination: Public Pedagogy and Praxis (Book). New York: Peter Lang Publishers.

参著篇章 3 篇

Dare We Build a New Socialist Order? A Challenge to Educators of America in the Coming Trump Era. In Peter McLaren and Suzanne SooHoo, The Radical Imagine – Nation. New York: Peter Lang Publishers. (Vastly expanded from Truthout Op – Ed.)

Teaching and the Never Ending Story: Some Reflections On My Reflections. In Andrew Kemp, Dignity of the Calling. Information Age Publishers.

(withKincheloe, J. L., Steinberg, R. and Monzó, L. D.). (2018). Critical Pedagogy and Qualitative Research: Advancing the Bricolage. Revised from the original. The Sage Handbook of Qualitative Research. 5th Edition. Edited by Norman K. Denzin and Yvonna S. Lincoln. Sage: Los Angeles and Singapore.

期刊论文 6 篇

(with Jandric, P.). (2018). Paulo Freire and Liberation Theology: The Christian Consciousness of Critical Pedagogy. Vierteljahrsschrift für wissenschaftliche Pädagogik, (94), 246 – 264. Vierteljahrsschrift für wissenschaftliche Pädagogik is one of Germany's premier journals of education founded in 1925, and focused on humanities and cultural studies.

(with Jandric, P.). (2018). Karl Marx and Liberation Theology: Dialectical Materialism and Christianity in, Against, and Beyond Contemporary Capitalism. Triple C: Communication, Capitalism and Critique. Journal for a Global Sustainable Information Society, 16 (2).

(with Scatamburlo – D'Annibale, V. and Monzó, L.). (2018). The Complexity of Spivak's Project: A Marxist Interpretation. A special issue of Qualitative Research Journal—Revisiting "Can the Subaltern Speak?": 30 Years Later. Qualitative Research Journal, 18 (2), doi: 10.1108/QRJ – D – 17 – 00052.

(with Scatamburlo – D'Annibale, V. and Brown, B.). (2018). Marx and the Philosophy of Praxis. International Handbook of Philosophy of Education. 549 – 567.

(with Chang, B.). (2018). Emerging issues of teaching and social justice in Greater China: Neoliberalism and critical pedagogy in Hong Kong. Policy Futures in Education. 1 – 23.

Reflections on 1968. Chapman Magazine, 42 (2). 5. Expanded version at: https://blogs.chapman.edu/magazine/2018/07/10/memories – of – 1968 – an – historic – year – of – upheaval – stirs – reflection/.

前言/后记 3 篇

Afterword: The Defenestration of Democracy. In Marc Spooner and James McNich, (Eds.) Dissident Knowledge in Higher Education. Regina, Saskatchewan, Canada: The University of Regina Press.

Afterword. In Simon Boxley, Schooling and Value. London: Institute for Education and Policy Studies.

Foreword: The wretched state (Chapter length). In Mike Cole (Ed), Education, Equalityand Human Rights: Issues of gender, race, sexuality, disability and social class (4th editon). London: Routledge.

访谈麦克拉伦论文 5 篇

(with Jandrić, P.). (November, 2018). Interview: Paulo Freire y la Teología de la Liberación: La consciencia cristiana de la pedagogía crítica (Ⅰ). http://contrahegemoniaweb. com. ar/paulo – freire – y – la – teologia – de – la – liberacion – la – consciencia – cristiana – de – la – pedagogia – critica.

(with Jandrić, P.). (December, 2018). Interview: Paulo Freire y la Teología de la Liberación: La consciencia cristiana de la pedagogía crítica (Ⅱ). http://contrahegemoniaweb. com. ar/paulo – freire – y – la – teologia – de – la – liberacion – la – consciencia – cristiana – de – la – pedagogia – critica – ii.

(with Ruano, J. C.). (2018). Entrevista Peter McLaren "La Educacioćn Crítica debe transformar el mundo" (Interview with Peter McLaren: "Critical education must transform the world") Revista Científica RUNAE, 1: 15 – 31. https://www. academia. edu/35924872/interview_ with_ peter_ mclaren_ critical_ Education_ must_ transform_ the_ World_ .

Interview (pp. 207 – 210). In Paulo Freire. *Pedagogy of the Oppressed: 50th Anniversary Edition.* London: Bloomsbury Publishers.

Pablo Cortés – González interviews Peter McLaren: Pedagogía crítica y decolonial en tiempos de Trump: Entrevista a Peter McLaren. Devenir: Revista de estudios culturales y regionales (Devenir: Magazine of cultural and regional studies), (32). https://digitalcommons. chapman. edu/education_ articles/202.

（电子）新闻和日报文章 1 篇

McLaren Podcast (2018) The How, The Why: 194 – Peter McLaren Retrieved from: http://1888. center/the – how – the – why – 194 – peter – mclaren.

2019 年（71 岁）

学术著作 1 部

McLaren, P. & Wilson, M. (2019). Breaking Free: The Life and Times of Peter

McLaren, Radical Educator. New York: Myers Education Books.

参著篇章 4 篇

(with Monzo, L.). (2019). Growing the Revolutionary Intellectual, Creating the Counter – Public Sphere. In Patricia Leavy, editor. Oxford Handbook for Methods for Public Scholarship. Oxford: Oxford University Press.

(withVega, V.). (2019). Reclaiming the revolutionary power of critical pedagogy. In Peters, M. & Misaszek, G. (eds.). Encyclopedia of Teacher Education: Teaching critical pedagogy. Switzerland, AG: Springer Nature.

McLaren, P. (2019) Unconscious: Revolutionary Critical Pedagogy and the Macro-structural Unconscious, in Derek Ford (ed.) Keywords in Radical Philosophy and Education: Common Concepts for Contemporary Movements, 426 – 476. Brill | Sense. DOI: https://doi.org/10.1163/9789004400467_030 (This chapter was originally published as McLaren, P. (2016). Revolutionary critical pedagogy: Staking a claim against the macro-structural unconscious. Critical Education, 7 (8), 1 – 42. Reprinted here with permission.) https://brill.com/view/book/edcoll/9789004400467/BP000038.xml.

Peter McLaren (2019). Foreword. Maisuria, A., & Helmes, S. Life for the Academic in the Neoliberal University. (1). Abingdon, Oxon: Taylor & Francis (Routledge).

期刊论文 6 篇

(withLevin, J. and Seale, S.). (2019). Race, Identity and Superheroes. The International Journal of Critical Media Literacy, 1 – 19. doi: 10.1163/25900110 – 00101001.

Reclaiming the Present or a Return to the Ash Heap of the Future? Postdigital Science and Education, 1 (1), 10 – 13. https://doi.org/10.1007/s42438 – 018 – 0015 – 6.

McLaren, P. (2019). God and Governance: Reflections on Living in the Belly of the Beast. *Postdigit Sci Educ* 1, 311 – 334. https://doi.org/10.1007/s42438 – 019 – 00050 – 1.

McLaren, P. (2019). Teaching against the grain: A conversation between the editors of the Griffith Journal of Law & Human Dignity and Peter McLaren on the importance of critical pedagogy in law school. Griffith Journal of Law & Human Dignity, 7 (1). Retrieved from https://griffithlawjournal.org/index.php/gjlhd/article/view/1173.

McLaren, P. (2019). Open letter: To Mr. Elliott Abrams (U.S. Venezuelan envoy). International Journal of Fear Studies, 1 (2), 38 – 41. http://hdl.handle.net/1880/111142.

McLaren, P. (October 10, 2019). "Carta abierta: a Eliott Abrams (enviado de los Estados Unidos a Venezuela)" in Iberoamerica social. https://iberoamericasocial.com/carta-abierta-a-eliott-abrams-enviado-de-los-estados-unidos-a-venezuela.

2020 年（72 岁）

学术著作 3 部

Peter McLaren and Petar Jandrić (2020). Postdigital Dialogues on Critical Pedagogy, Liberation Theology and Information Technology. London and New York: Bloomsbury Press.

Peter McLaren (2020). Tracks to Infinity, The Long Road to Justice: The Peter McLaren Reader, Volume II (edited by Marc Pruyn, Curry Malott, and Luis Huerta-Charles). Information Age Publishing.

Peter McLaren (2020). He Walks Among Us: Christian Fascism Ushering in the End of Times. New York: DIO Press.

期刊论文 22 篇

McLaren, P. (2020). Technologizing the Divine. *Postdigit Sci Educ* 2, 254–264. https://doi.org/10.1007/s42438-019-00071-w.

McLaren, P. (2020). Networked Religion: Metaphysical Redemption or Eternal Regret? *Postdigit Sci Educ*. https://doi.org/10.1007/s42438-020-00112-9.

McLaren, P., Jandrić, P. (2020). The Fellowship of the Crooked Cross: Trump's Evangelical Hounds of Hell. *Postdigit Sci Educ* 2, 302–329. https://doi.org/10.1007/s42438-019-00074-7.

McLaren, P. (2020). Religious Nationalism and the Coronavirus Pandemic: Soul-Sucking Evangelicals and Branch Covidians Make America Sick Again Postdigital Science and Education 2 (10): 1–22. https://doi.org/10.1007/s42438-020-00122-7.

McLaren, P. (2020). Peter McLaren's Response to 'The Armageddon Club' by Michael Peters, *Educational Philosophy and Theory*, 52. (an editorial) https://doi.org/10.1080/00131857.2019.1676497.

McLaren, P. (2020). Are those whiffs of fascism that I smell? Living behind the Orange Curtain. *Educational Philosophy and Theory*, 52, 1011–1015. https://doi.org/10.1080/00131857.2019.1672854.

Peter McLaren (December 31, 2019). Reflections on Critical Pedagogy in America Latina: La Lucha Continua. Iberoamerica Social.

https://iberoamericasocial.com/reflections-on-critical-pedagogy-in-america-latina-la-lucha-continua/.

McLaren, P. (Feb 11, 2020). "Resisting fascist mobilization: Some reflections on critical pedagogy, liberation theology and the need for revolutionary socialist change" in Educational Philosophy and Theory, https://doi.org/10.1080/00131857.2020.1716450.

Peter McLaren, Michael A. Peters, and Petar Jandrić (31 Mar 2020). Viral modernity? Epidemics, Infodemics, and the 'Bioinformational' Paradigm. Educational Philosophy and Theory. https://doi.org/10.1080/00131857.2020.1744226.

Peter McLaren, Michael A. Peters, and Petar Jandrić (13 Apr 2020), "A Viral Theory of Post Truth". Educational Philosophy and Theory. https://doi.org/10.1080/00131857.2020.1750090.

McLaren, P., Yan, W. & Jandrić, P. (2020). Reflections I and II: Reflections from Education and the Arts in the COVID-19 Era. *Communiars. Revista de Imagen, Artes y Educacion Crítica y Social*, 4, 10-13. Retrieved from: https://institucional.us.es/communiars/numero-4-especial-de-communiars/?fbclid=IwAR0SbimDz1CiK1mQggfTrbn7YTQp8GhjmRBmdtes7jvl2wvn8NRI_5BiklE.

McLaren, P. & Wang, Y. (2020). 批判教育学面临的挑战及其可能的未来 [The Challenges to and Possible Future for Critical Pedagogy]. 教育研究 *Educational Research*, 4, 16-25. (This article was reprinted in 2020 by *Education Digest*, 3, 13-16. Education Digest is operated by Renmin University of China.)

Peter Mclaren (2019). The future of critical pedagogy. Educational Philosophy and Theory, 52 (12): 1243-1248. DOI: 10.1080/00131857.2019.1686963 (The article was reprinted in a new Turkish journal, *Rethinking Critical Pedagogy*.)

Peter McLaren and the EPAT collective (25 Jun 2020). Reimagining the new pedagogical possibilities for universities post-Covid-19. Educational Philosophy and Theory. https://doi.org/10.1080/00131857.2020.1777655.

Peter McLaren (07 Jul 2020). Pandemic Abandonment, Panoramic Displays and Fascist Propaganda: The Month the Earth Stood Still. Educational Philosophy and Theory. https://doi.org/10.1080/00131857.2020.1781787.

Reader, J., Jandrić, P., Peters, M. A. et al. (2020). Enchantment-Disenchantment-Re-Enchantment: Postdigital Relationships between Science, Philosophy, and Religion. *Postdigit Sci Educ*. https://doi.org/10.1007/s42438-020-00133-4.

McLaren P. , Monzó L. D. (2020) Guevara, Ernesto 'Che' (1928 – 1967). In: Ness I. , Cope Z. (eds) The Palgrave Encyclopedia of Imperialism and Anti – Imperialism. Palgrave Macmillan, Cham. https://doi.org/10.1007/978-3-319-91206-6_299-1.

(December 2020) An Interview with Peter McLaren entitled "Radical and hopeful discussions about times of brutal conservatism – paths of struggle and transformation in the light of Paulo Freire" was published in Portuguese, Spanish and English in the journal *Praxis Educativa*.

https://revistas2.uepg.br/index.php/praxiseducativa/article/view/17204, https://doi.org/10.5212/PraxEduc.v.16.17204.010.

(October 2020) Peter McLaren published an article, "Four questions out of a hundred years of study on Dewey's 'Child – Centered' theory in China," with his Chapman visiting scholar, Hongjun Zou, in the Chinese education journal *Education Science*.

Zou, H. J. & McLaren, P. (2020). Four questions out of a hundred years of study on Dewey's 'Child – Centered' theory in China. *Education Science*, (5). 51 – 58. (Mandarin)

(October 2020) Peter McLaren and Petar Jandric published the article, "Critical intellectuals in postdigital times" in *Policy Futures in Education* (see attached)

Jandrić, P. , & McLaren, P. (2020). Critical intellectuals in postdigital times. *Policy Futures in Education*. https://doi.org/10.1177/1478210320964372.

参著篇章 6 篇

Peter McLaren and Petar Jandric (2020). The Postdigital Challenge of Paulo Freire's Prophetic Church in James Kirylo (ed.) *Reinventing Pedagogy of the Oppressed: Contemporary Critical Perspectives*. London and New York: Bloomsbury Press.

Peter McLaren (2020). Critical Revolutionary Pedagogy's Relevance for Today in Sheila L. Macrine (ed.) *Critical Pedagogy in Uncertain Times: Hope and Possibilities* (2nd ed.). Palgrave Macmillan.

McLaren P. , Monzó L. D. (2020). Guevara, Ernesto 'Che' (1928 – 1967). In: Ness I. , Cope Z. (eds) The Palgrave Encyclopedia of Imperialism and Anti – Imperialism. Palgrave Macmillan, Cham. https://doi.org/10.1007/978-3-319-91206-6_299-1.

Peter McLaren (2020). Foreword. In Carl Boggs. (2020). Facing Catastrophe: Food, Politics and the Ecological Crisis. Toronto and Chicago: Political Animal Press.

(December 2020) Peter McLaren published the chapter "Revolutionary Pedagogy" in the book *Critical Reflections on the Language of Neoliberalism in Education: Dangerous Words and Discourses of Possibility*, edited by Spyros Themelis.

Kincheloe, J., & McLaren, P. (2020). Interviews with joe kincheloe and peter mclaren. In S. R. Steinberg, & B. Down*The SAGE handbook of critical pedagogies* (Vol. 3, pp. 368 -379). SAGE Publications Ltd, https://www.doi.org/10.4135/9781526486455.n41.

（电子）新闻和日报文章 9 篇

Interviewed by The Panther: Q&A with Peter McLaren: discussing the Democratic presidential nominees. (Feb 24, 2020; Written By Louisa Marshall).

https://www.thepanthernewspaper.org/news/qampa-with-peter-mclaren-democratic-presidential-nominees? rq = Q%26amp%3BA%20with%20Peter%20McLaren%3A%20Discussing%20the%20Democratic%20Presidential%20Nominees.

McLaren, P. & Wang, Y. (April 13, 2020). US needs to move away from its blame-China trajectory. China Daily. Retrieved from: http://global.chinadaily.com.cn/a/202004/13/WS5e941a99a3105d50a3d15d91.html.

Peter McLaren was interviewed in the Latin American magazine, Otras Voces en Educación. (May 9, 2020) http://otrasvoceseneducacion.org/archivos/346751.

Peter McLaren's interview published in Otra Voces en Educación was reprinted in Iberoamérica Social.

(November 2020) Peter McLaren wasinterviewed by Mia Funk for the series The Creative Process.

(November 2020) Peter McLaren published a memorial tribute to the late Dr. Sergio Quiroz Miranda, Director General of Instituto McLaren de Pedagogia Critica, in the magazine, *Communistas Hoy*.

(October 2020) Peter McLaren published "The Imp of the Perverse" in *Major Threat: Punk Rock Academia*. https://www.punkrockacademia.com/issues.html

https://drive.google.com/file/d/16eY-2-4j1HOP97mEqgNCmODYVdtj3sAI/view.

(September 2020) Peter McLaren published "A Letter to the Branch Covidians" in*Major Threat: Punk Rock Academia*. https://www.punkrockacademia.com/issues.html.

https://drive.google.com/file/d/1kWRZa8MSc2Z-88hOdgqeFfCKGwXfBslb/view.

Peter McLaren (2020). Donald Trump's Traveling Vaudeville Presidency: Dying for Trump and the Attack of the Branch Covidians (inaugural column). Pesa Agora (Australia).

2021 年（73 岁）

学术著作 1 部

Peter McLaren (2021). Critical Pedagogy Manifesto: Teachers of the World Unite. New York: DIO Press.

期刊论文 16 篇

(May 2021) Peter McLaren published a review of the podcast series, "Learning Marx in the Podcast Era: A Review of Reading 'Capital' with Comrades", in the Hampton Institute online journal.

(May 2021) Peter McLaren published "Ocultismo, Trumpismo y lucho por el socialism" [Occultism, Trumpism and the Fight for Socialism] in the journal *VientoSur*.

(April 2021) Peter McLaren was interviewed in the *Journal of Higher Education Policy and Leadership Studies*. The interview is titled, "The Perilous Road to Justice".

McLaren P. The Perilous Road to Justice: An Interview with Prof. Peter McLaren. johepal. 2021; 2 (1): 145 – 156.

(April 2021) Peter McLaren published a two – act play entitled "The Day They Brought Ol' Liberty Down: The Reality of the Threat" in the journal *Postdigital Science and Education*.

(January 2021) Peter McLaren published the article "Camarada Freire" [Comrade Freire] in the journal *Revista Ideacao*.

Zou, H. J. & McLaren, P. (2021). Digital Age and Educational Reform: Research Background, Progress and Limitations. *Journal of Tianjun Normal University*, 22 (1). 7 – 12. (Mandarin)

(December 2021) Peter McLaren published an article on Paulo Freire in the journal, *Perfiles Educativos* [Educational Profiles].

(December 2021) Peter McLaren coauthored the article, "Public intellectuals in the age of viral modernity: An EPAT collective writing project", in *Educational Philosophy and Theory*. https://www.tandfonline.com/doi/full/10.1080/00131857.2021.2010543.

(December 2021) Peter McLaren and Petar Jandric published the article "Postdigitale Pädagogik der Befreiung" [A Postdigital Pedagogy of Liberation] in *Vierteljahrsschrift für Wissenschaftliche Pädagogik* [Quarterly Journal for Science Education].

(November, 2021) Peter McLaren and Petar Jandrić published the article "From

Learning Loss to Learning Opportunity" in the journal *Educational Philosophy and Theory*. https：//www. tandfonline. com/doi/full/10. 1080/00131857. 2021. 2010544? scroll = top&needAccess = true.

(November, 2021) Peter McLaren published the article "A cien años de la muerte de Paulo Freire, un educador" [One hundred years after the death of Paulo Freire, an educator] in *Herramienta*：*Revista de Debate y Critica Marxista* [Tool：Marxist Debate and Criticism Magazine].

(October, 2021) Peter McLaren was interviewed in the journal *Curriculo Sem Fronteiras* [Curriculum without Borders]: "Pedagogia Crítica e Resistência: contributos do pensamento de Paulo Freire em tempos de colapsos da democracia-entrevista com Peter McLaren" [Critical Pedagogy and Resistance: Contributions from Paulo Freire's Thought in Times of Collapse of Democracy-Interview with Peter McLaren].

(September, 2021) Peter McLaren published the article "Paulo Freire's ideas are just as important today as ever" in *Jacobin Magazine* to celebrate Paulo Freire's birth 100 years ago. https：//jacobinmag. com/2021/09/paulo – freires – ideas – are – just – as – powerful – today – as – ever.

(September, 2021) Peter McLaren published the article "Paulo Freire at 100" in the *Tribune* to celebrate Paulo Freire's birth 100 years ago. https：//tribunemag. co. uk/2021/09/paulo – freire – at – 100? fbclid = IwAR2vtCGIzu5KJVuxWuPukB_bbTU8FrNwVQKWkg DL-NJs6glm7_GBskvFY7p4.

(September, 2021) An interview (interviewer：George Yancy) with Peter McLaren entitled, "Paulo Freire: Critical Education in a World in Need of Repair", was published in the journal *Tikkun*：*The Prophetic Jewish, Interfaith & Secular Voice to Heal and Transform the World*. https：//www. tikkun. org/paulo – freire – critical – education – in – a – world – in – need – of – repair/.

参著篇章 5 篇

(June 2021) Peter McLaren published theintroduction for a special issue on Liberation Theology and Adult Education in the *Dialogues in Social Justice*：*An Adult Education Journal* (Vol. 6 No. 1) https：//journals. uncc. edu/dsj/article/view/1291.

(march 2021) Peter McLaren and Petar Jandric published a chapter, "Scallywag Pedagogy," in the book *The Epistemology of Deceit in a Postdigital Era*：*Dupery by Design*, edited by Alison MacKenzie, Jennifer Rose, and Ibrar Bhatt.

(December 2021) Peter McLaren and Luis Huerta Charles wrote the introduction to the book *Pase a calentar: Una invitación guambiana para ser parte del corazón de la casa* [Come in to warm up (your food): A Guambian Invitation to be Part of the Heart of the House] by anthropologist Adriana Isabel Orjuela Martínez, published by la Universidad Nacional de Colombia. The book is an investigation carried out in the Misak Reservoir (Guambiano) la María, Piendamó, Cauca, Colombia between 2014 and 2018. The objective was to analyze the ways in which indigenous policies are built and learned in *nakchak*, by understanding the words of women, to contribute to the strengthening of the community with the knowledge developed in everyday life. http://congreso.uch.edu.pe/shircon/programa.

(November, 2021) Peter McLaren published a chapter in the book *100 Voces (y una carta) para Paulo Freire* [100 Voices (and a Letter) to Paulo Freire], edited by Nicolás Arata and published in Colombia by CLACSO, the Latin American Council of Social Sciences. https://otrasvoceseneducacion.org/archivos/388620.

(October, 2021) Peter McLaren published a chapter, "Paulo Freire: A Homen Atemporal: Reflexoes Sobre Verdade e Sentido" [Paulo Freire: The Timeless Man: Reflections on Truth and Sense] in a collection of essays, Testamento da Presença de Paulo Freire o Educador do Brasil [Testament to the Presence of Paulo Freire, the Educator from Brazil], edited by Nita Freire (widow of Paulo Freire).

(电子) 新闻和日报文章 2 篇

(July 2021) Peter McLaren published "Una Carta al Gobernador Ron DeSantis, United States" [A Letter to Governor Ron DeSantis, United States] on the site Otras Voces en Educación [Other Voices in Education] https://www.otrasvoceseneducacion.org/archivos/381875

(December 2021) Peter McLaren published an article, "Towards a Good Faith Diplomatic Politics", in *China Daily*, published by the Publicity Department of the Chinese Communist Party.

2022 年（74 岁）

期刊论文 3 篇

(March 2022) Peter McLaren published an expanded version of his essay, The Invasion of Ukraine, in Otras Voces en Educación (3/20) https://otrasvoceseneducacion.org/archivos/392741

(January 2022) Peter McLaren was interviewed in *Revista Enfoques Educacionale*, a Chilean education journal: "Entrevista con Peter McLaren: Discusiones Radicales y Esperanzadoras en Tiempos de Conservadurismo Brutal-Caminos de Lucha y Transformacion" [Interview with Peter McLaren: Radical and Hopeful Discussions About Times of Brutal Conservatism—Paths of Fight and Transformation in the Light of Paulo Freire].

(January 2022) Ryan Allen and Peter McLaren published the article "Protecting the University as a Physical Place in the Age of Postdigitization" in the journal *Postdigital Science and Education*. https://link.springer.com/article/10.1007/s42438-021-00276-y.

（电子）新闻和日报文章 5 篇

(March 2022) Peter McLaren had an article published titled: The Invasion of Ukraine in Pesa Agora. https://pesaagora.com/ideas/the-invasion-of-ukraine.

(February 2022) Peter McLaren published a review of *Paulo Freire: A Philosophical Biography* in the *Book Review Symposium*: Walter Omar Kohan (2021) *Paulo Freire: A Philosophical Biography* [Translated by Jason Wozniak and Samuel D. Rocha]. Bloomsbury Academic Publishing. ISBN 978-1-3501-9598-1. Published in the Journal of Critical Educational Policy Studies, volume 19, no 3, 2022, part of The Institute for Education Policy Studies (IEPS). The free, online version is published in association with the Kapodistrian and National University of Athens (Greece).

(February 2022) Peter McLaren published "The Olympics Is Not a Place to Play Politics" in China Daily.

(January 2022) Peter McLaren and Lilia Monzó published the entry "Guevara, Ernesto 'Che' (1928–1967)" and Peter McLaren published the entry "Liberation Theology" in the *Encyclopedia of Marxism and Education*.

(February 2022) Peter McLaren published "Divided We Fall" in Counterpunch, February 4: www.counterpunch.org/2022/02/04/divided-we-fall-2.

后　　记

这本书是我博士论文修改完善后的成果。此书出版要特别感谢中国社会科学出版社的支持；感谢2022年度吉林省教育科学规划重点项目（ZD22167）"麦克拉伦批判教育学思想研究"的支持；感谢长春师范大学出版基金的大力支持！

博士毕业已经三年多了，但是回顾博士学习的历程仍是历历在目。有太多的感谢、感动和感慨！

一　致我的研究对象与他的爱人、朋友们

人的成长过程中，往往经历许多次的角色转换，生活空间、身边的师长朋友经常有着浓厚的时间属性。2014年博士生春季复试完我便结识了著名的美国批判教育学的奠基者之一彼得·麦克拉伦（Peter McLaren）教授和他的妻子王雁，当时的我怎么也不会想到，这对好CP会在我未来的生命中扮演着如此重要的角色。此时回想，如果在八年前的那个春天，我知道这次相遇会让我收获这么多的惊喜与感动，那时的我一定会双手合十，感谢这奇妙的缘分，感谢这注定的友谊。

因为麦克拉伦教授被东北师大聘为特聘教授每年为研究生授课的缘故，每年春季我都有机会与他和王雁在东北师大相聚一个月，聆听他的批判教育学课程并承担一部分翻译工作。开始时对批判教育学没有太多认知，随着时间推移，友谊加深，对他的批判教育学思想也逐步从了解到理解再到欣赏。在2015年开题时在于伟导师的鼓励下决定研究麦克拉伦教授的批判教育学思想，开始了对他的批判教育学的研究之旅。这种

研究对象是最熟悉的朋友的感觉无比奇妙，我知道我一定能够解构他的思想体系，还原其演进过程，并跟进他跳跃的变迁节奏。

2015 年我的导师于伟先生牵头组织了第一届批判教育学国际研讨会，在我的母校东北师大召开。最重量级的参加者便是我论文的研究主角——麦克拉伦教授。会议期间我又熟识了苏西教授（Suzi）、莉莉娅（Lilia）教授和阿内达（Anaida）教授这些美国批判教育学学者们，她们也是麦克拉伦教授的同事和好友。时间绝对是个奇妙的东西，七年的时间她们已经变成了我非常要好的师长和朋友，在美国访学期间她们对我在学术上的指导和生活上的照顾让我永远难忘。

我的车上有一张 CD，很长时间都未换过，每天开车的时候都会听一会儿。这张 CD 是麦克拉伦教授赠予我的，是他从新西兰淘到的土著人的音乐，风格独特，超级好听。第一次听这张 CD 是在麦克拉伦教授的家里，我一下子就被它迷住了，问他能否借我听听，他毫不犹豫的直接送给我了，并且给我讲了这张 CD 的由来和音乐风格。除了这张 CD，我收藏的珍贵物件里有各种麦克拉伦教授在世界各地淘到的宝贝，如智利的茶罐、袖扣、日本的音乐首饰盒、墨西哥的手工艺品等等。每次看着心目中的大师像孩子献宝一样与我分享他的各种珍藏，我都感动不已。

在美国访学的 13 个月里，几乎每天都能与麦克拉伦教授和王雁见面，除了在批判教育学上的指导，麦克拉伦教授给我讲了很多他的人生故事以及他对一些音乐、电影、文学作品、政治事件的理解，毫无保留地带领我走进他的思想和心灵世界。王雁的英文名字是 Angie，真是人如其名，她就像是落入人间的美丽天使，时常挂在脸上的真诚笑容和有力的拥抱总是给人温暖、感动和力量。如果用几个词来描述我对她的印象，那就是独立、坚强、善良、果敢、知性、美丽。几年来，我们早已成为了无话不说的亲密朋友。在我迷茫的时候，在我低落的时候她的言语、她的陪伴、她的帮助总是能让我豁然开朗。她不迷恋物质、不陷入世俗。她的身上总有一种自信的光芒让她走到哪里都非常受欢迎。我很幸运能够认识她并且与之为友！

虽然我与麦克拉伦教授私交甚好，但是这并未对我研究的客观性增加一点点的压力，在书里我做到了尽量客观评价他的思想，偶尔也会有些我认为公允的"黑评价",因为我知道麦克拉伦教授一直具有博大的胸襟与开放的精神,他不但不会因为我对他的批判而对我有任何不满,反而会表扬我有批判精神和独立思考能力。与大师为友、与大师的朋友为友实在是荣幸至极。

我这本书的主要内容是基于我的博士论文,博士论文始于2015年第一届批判教育学国际研讨会并将在2019年的第三届研讨会之后结束,冥冥中应该也是一种奇妙的学术缘分,有因果,有始终。虽然读博历程结束了,但是年会将届届持续,我的研究也将随着麦克拉伦教授的不断前进而持续深入。

二 致我最敬爱的导师于伟先生与我的师长、朋友们

能够师从于伟先生是我一生中最幸运的事,没有之一。先生雅量高致,儒雅大气,为人、治学的良好口碑业内无人不知。先生对自己的学生永远都是关爱有加、无微不至,必要时又嘘寒问暖、慷慨相助。先生酷爱读书并藏书无数,经常将心爱之书赠予我们这些弟子,承载着对学问和精神的延续,所受者往往有种接受衣钵传承的使命感,恨不得立刻读完、记住、消化掉,然后再去送给有需要的人。从我研究批判教育学开始,先生送给我的相关著作怕是不少于几十本,对于他的藏书和相关资料先生从来都是让我们随便借阅。每次他自己逛书店或在网上淘书时都会想着帮助我们挑选一些对我们有用的书。这些让人惊喜的礼物给疲惫前行的我带来的不仅仅是收获新知识的喜悦,更是呵护我前行的精神暖流。这些书是研究思想成型的关键所在,伴随着大量的文献阅读我的论文一步步完成。

先生只要是不出差,无论事务性工作有多么繁忙,他每周末都会抽出一天时间领着我们研讨,通过这种方式掌握到每个学生的动态,继而因人施教,不厌其烦。本书的选题、写作、修改自始至终都是在我的导师于伟先生的精心指导和引领下进行的。在整个写作过程中,每当遇到难解的困惑时先生都能创造性的激活我的研究思路,给我适当的引导和启发。可以说,这本专著倾注了先生的心血也承载着先生的期望。先生对于学术上不自信又有点愚钝的我一直以鼓励、启发为主,鼓励我往高

级别的期刊投稿、鼓励我申请国家留学基金委的项目，从来没有严厉地批评指责或者过度施压。在先生的指导和影响下我对读书和做研究越来越热衷，乐此不疲，最终能按照自己的节奏完成博士学业。师恩无以为报，只能铭记在心，亦步亦趋，心慕手追，希望自己也能成为一名好的导师。

特借本书对东北师大各位给予我谆谆教诲与无私帮助的师长们：柳海民教授、杨兆山教授、周霖教授、石艳教授、马卓老师、李长维老师等；对不断鼓励我、为我提供研究资料和指导的台湾屏东大学的简成熙教授；对师门中给予我帮助和支持的兄弟姐妹们：韩爽、许适琳、吴春薇、孙颖、关景圆、杨晶、高晓文、周丽丽、张敬威、白倩、杨落娃、尹璐、李春颖等；对我工作了近20年的长春师范大学给予我支持和帮助的领导同事朋友们：赵骥民教授、迟海波教授、姜维公教授、侯广庆教授、邹德文教授、张淑贤教授、李慧娟教授、孙中华教授、蔡杰、刘海洋、鲍悦、朱琳麒、梁磊、梁维、谢丽、高科、朱坚等，对多年来一直支持我、爱我的我最爱的朋友们：Mom Lois、杨艳丽、焦爱丽、王春艳、李磊，说一声最衷心的感谢！与你们相识的缘分，与你们相处的快乐，与你们一起走过的岁月对我来说都是人生最美好的馈赠！感谢一路有你们的支持和陪伴！时间继续前行，只要与你们结伴，路边已无所谓荆棘或是鲜花，唯愿能跟上大家的脚步。

三　致我最亲爱的妹妹

我的妹妹比我小一岁。由于我从小是被"藏"在乡下奶奶家的"黑户"，我和妹妹从我9岁的时候回城才开始生活在一起。从头几年的矛盾冲突不断到从初中开始的互相爱护、互相心疼，期间妹妹做的努力比我要多许多。她比我更宽容、更愿意妥协，才让性格非常倔强的我慢慢与她的关系从僵持到缓和再到亲密。多年来我亲爱的妹妹一直都是我重要的心理支撑，我们一直共同面对生活中的风雨和艰辛。我知道，无论何时，无论发生什么，妹妹都会在站我身边支持我。如果说读博士之前我对妹妹的照顾更多一点的话，读博士之后，妹妹更像是我的姐姐，我忙得基本顾不上她了。这么多年来是她一直在关心我、鼓励我、帮我分担生活的重担，尤其是在她又得照顾襁褓中的婴儿，又得拼命工作的同时还总在担心我的生活、学习，竭尽全力地为我提供各种支持，每每想到此，心中便十分有愧。妹妹总说我是她的榜样，怕我把她落得太远而一直在追赶我的脚步，其实她更是我的榜样：她总是保持着一颗纯净的心，不被世俗所左右；她做事极其认真负责，不计较得失；她常怀有感恩的心，对所得到的一切都心存敬畏与感激。

四 致自己

五年读博的各种艰辛让我曾无数次的想象等到我完成论文写后记时的心情，会不会慨极而泣。真的到了那个时刻的确感慨万千，但是没有泪水，有的是对那段旅程的敬畏和感谢，让我一再突破自己以为的极限，磨砺心魄，更加坚韧。

读博的前三年身体曾一度亮起了红灯，由于长期伏案工作学习，缺乏运动，患上了腰间盘突出和颈椎病，严重的时候腰疼得不能做幅度最小的弯曲、颈椎病导致的眩晕使我不能正常生活，天旋地转到怀疑人生。那个时候感觉自己是在用生命读博士，经常性去质疑自己当初的读博选择是否值得。我成了医院康复科的常客，每年至少报到两次，一次持续一个月，但是按摩、理疗都是治标不治本，在医生的建议下我开始有规律的身体锻炼。开始时是在健身房自己做基础的运动训练，在最后一年的论文写作冲刺阶段，我选择了每周健身3—5次，一次一个半小时的高效自由搏击运动。全方位锻炼身体的自由搏击帮我治愈了腰颈的不适，剧烈运动产生的多巴胺也帮我缓解了精神压力，增加了更多的自信，让我如期完成了艰难的论文写作。读书与运动真的缺一不可。在此特别感谢吉大一院二部康复科的张鉴栩主任和我的自由搏击教练马朔先生给予我的帮助！

"人生就是一场旅行，不在乎目的地，在乎的是沿途的风景以及看风景的心情"，这句话在漫长的博士学业中让我收获良多。读博如同修行，最开始只是为了拿到学位而克服着身体上和生理上的各种挑战艰难行走，并未有许多快乐可言。到了后期，随着先生的指引和研究的深入，渐渐从学习中感悟到收获的快乐。每次读完一本专著或是完成和麦克拉伦教授的一次沟通，都像拾到一颗珍珠，当自己用逻辑的线把一颗颗珍珠慢慢串成项链的时候，压抑的心情得以释放，不再畏研究如虎，颇有一种明悟在心头。虽然清楚地知道这种所谓的突破瓶颈也只是一个阶段性的成果，但心态上发生了巨大的改变，又变成了那个学海拾贝的顽童，要在海边搭建属于自己的小小城堡。

于是最后一年最紧张的论文冲刺反而成为最快乐的时光，自由搏击让身体重回巅峰，论文的小小城堡框架日渐成型，挚友的耐心陪伴消弭掉负面情绪，心态上又能做到不忘初心去探索去思考，这上述的一切让攻读博士的收官之战信心十足、斗志昂扬。过程中反省与收获甚至超过了学位本身，它可以支撑我在未来的时光里不再畏首畏尾、故步自封，可以用看风景的美丽心情继续谱写隽永的旋律，奏响属于自己的Solo，沐浴阳光、拥有爱。

虽然读博历程已经结束，我的研究却还在继续。教育者仅仅关注课堂是狭隘的、悲哀的，麦克拉伦超越了很多教育界人士对于教育理想实现方式的想象。他努力从坐而论道的理论家成为起而行的实践家，姑且不论其成功与否，但他致力于教育学的研究与实践活动之精神，值得教师和教育工作者学习借鉴。梦想的实现是必须通过行动得以落实的。这也正是革命性的批判教育学的最终精神之所在。

麦克拉伦教授一直在不断地致力于通过自身的理论、文章和行动揭露资本主义的真相、揭露各种不平等和不公正现象，仍然每天在用马克思主义人道主义的、辩证的批判视角去分析和解读教育与社会，仍然不断地与我分享他作为研究者的故事，尽显作为研究者，对那些被边缘化和被压迫者的（少数族裔、女性等）声音和故事的尊重，启发我作为研究者，不能为了研究而研究，而应该是通过自己的研究，思考如何能促进一个更好的世界，如何在苍凉的世界中寻找希望。

魏凤云

2022年7月28日于长春